THIEF OF THIEVES

CREATED BY ROBERT KIRKMAN

ROBERT KIRKMAN
STORY

NICK SPENCER
WRITER

SHAWN MARTINBROUGH
ARTIST

FELIX SERRANO
COLORIST

RUS WOOTON
LETTERER

SINA GRACE
EDITOR

SHAWN MARTINBROUGH
FELIX SERRANO
COVER

THIEF OF THIEVES, VOL. 1: "I QUIT."
ISBN: 978-1-60706-592-0
PRINTED IN U.S.A.
First Printing

Published by Image Comics, Inc. Office of publication: 2134 Allston Way, 2nd Floor, Berkeley, California 94704. Image and its logos are ® and © 2012 Image Comics Inc. All rights reserved. Originally published in single magazine form as THIEF OF THIEVES #1-7. THIEF OF THIEVES and all character likenesses are ™ and © 2012, Robert Kirkman, LLC. All rights reserved. All names, characters, events and locales in this publication are entirely fictional. Any resemblance to actual persons (living or dead), events or places, without satiric intent, is coincidental. No part of this publication may be reproduced or transmitted, in any form or by any means (except for short excerpts for review purposes) without the express written permission of the copyright holder.

For information regarding the CPSIA on this printed material call: 203-595-3636 and provide reference # RICH - 449729.

IMAGE COMICS, INC.
Robert Kirkman - chief operating officer
Erik Larsen - chief financial officer
Todd McFarlane - president
Marc Silvestri - chief executive officer
Jim Valentino - vice-president

Eric Stephenson - publisher
Todd Martinez - sales & licensing coordinator
Jennifer de Guzman - pr & marketing director
Branwyn Bigglestone - accounts manager
Emily Miller - administrative assistant
Jamie Parreno - marketing assistant
Sarah deLaine - events coordinator
Kevin Yuen - digital rights coordinator
Tyler Shainline - production manager
Drew Gill - art director
Jonathan Chan - design director
Monica Garcia - production artist
Vincent Kukua - production artist
Jana Cook - production artist
www.imagecomics.com

For SKYBOUND ENTERTAINMENT

Robert Kirkman - CEO
J.J. Didde - President
Sean Mackiewicz - Editorial Director
Shawn Kirkham - Director of Business Development
Tim Daniel - Digital Content Manager
Chad Manion - Assistant to Mr. Kirkman
Sydney Pennington - Assistant to Mr. Grace
Feldman Public Relations LA - Public Relations

For international rights inquiries,
please contact: foreign@skybound.com

WWW.SKYBOUND.COM

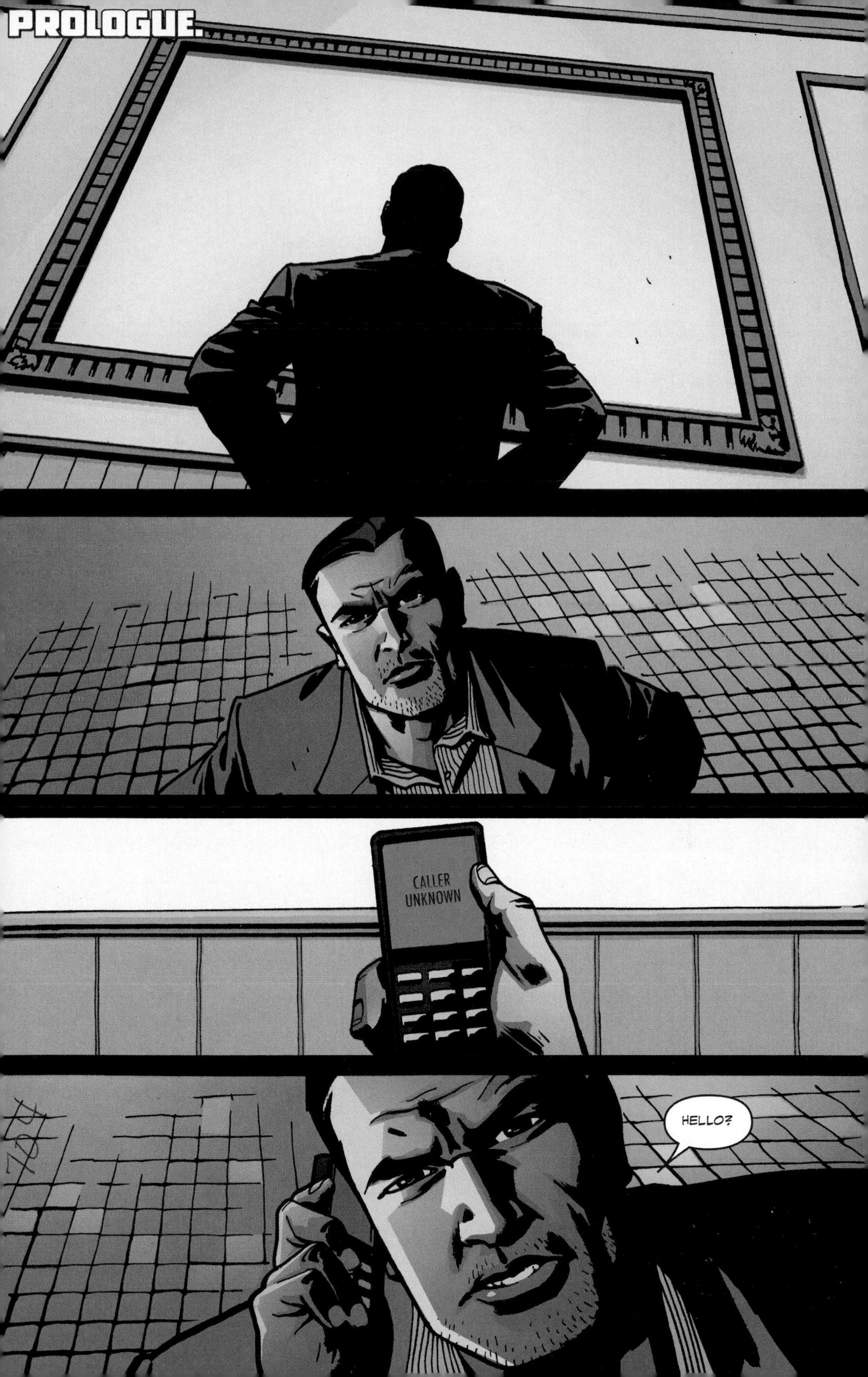
PROLOGUE.
CALLER UNKNOWN
HELLO?

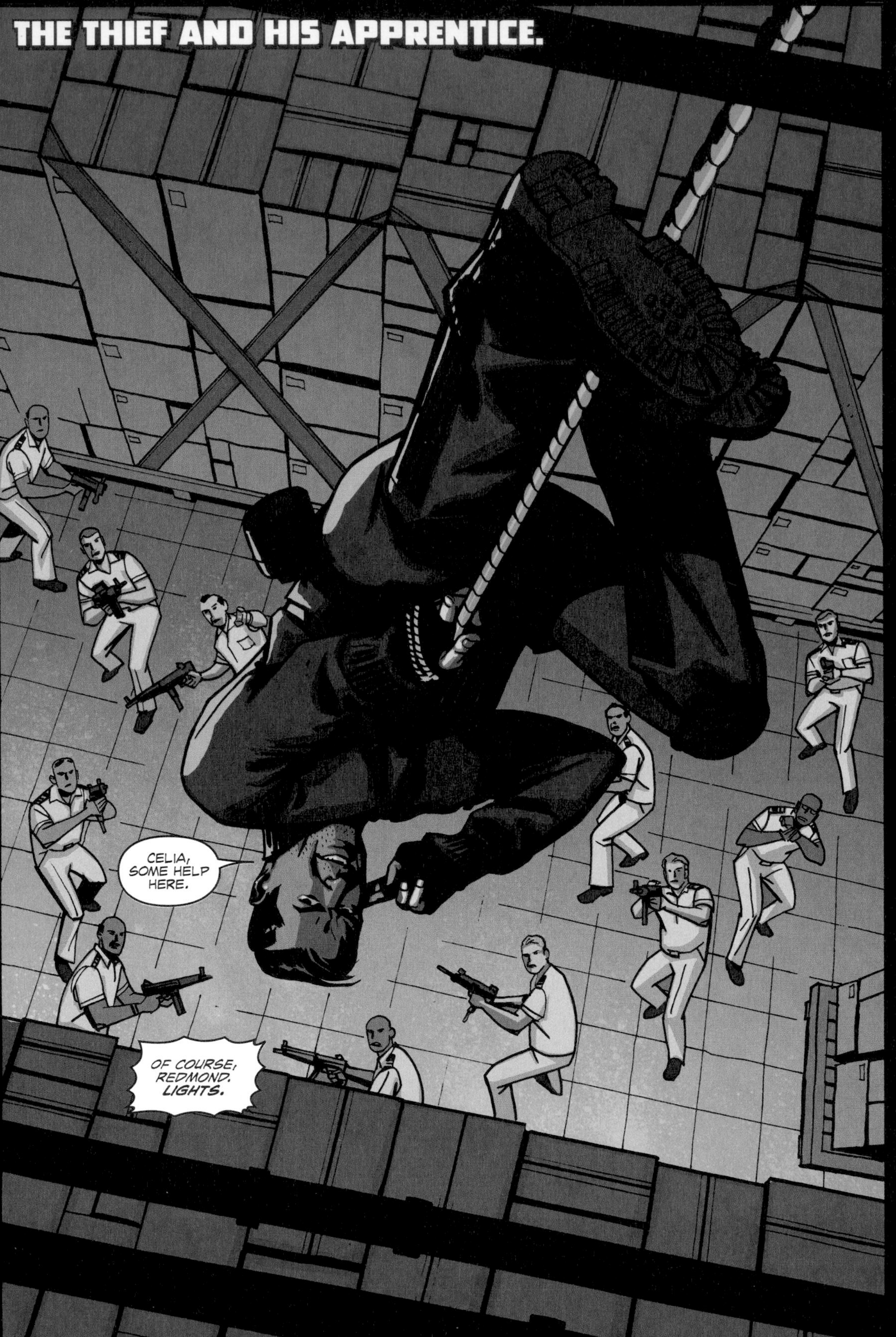
THE THIEF AND HIS APPRENTICE.
CELIA, SOME HELP HERE.
OF COURSE, REDMOND. LIGHTS.

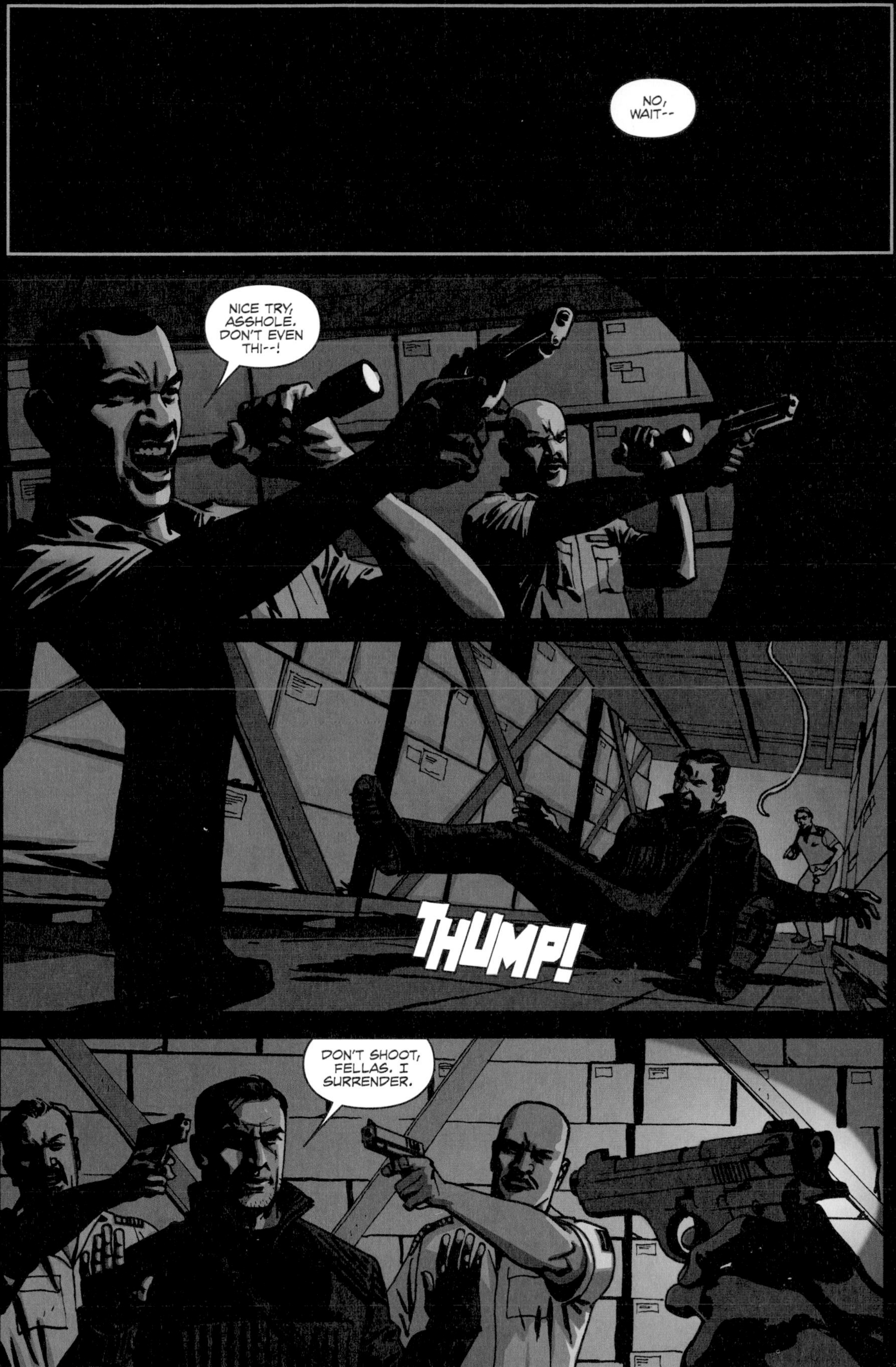
NO, WAIT--
NICE TRY, ASSHOLE. DON'T EVEN THI--!
THUMP!
DON'T SHOOT, FELLAS. I SURRENDER.

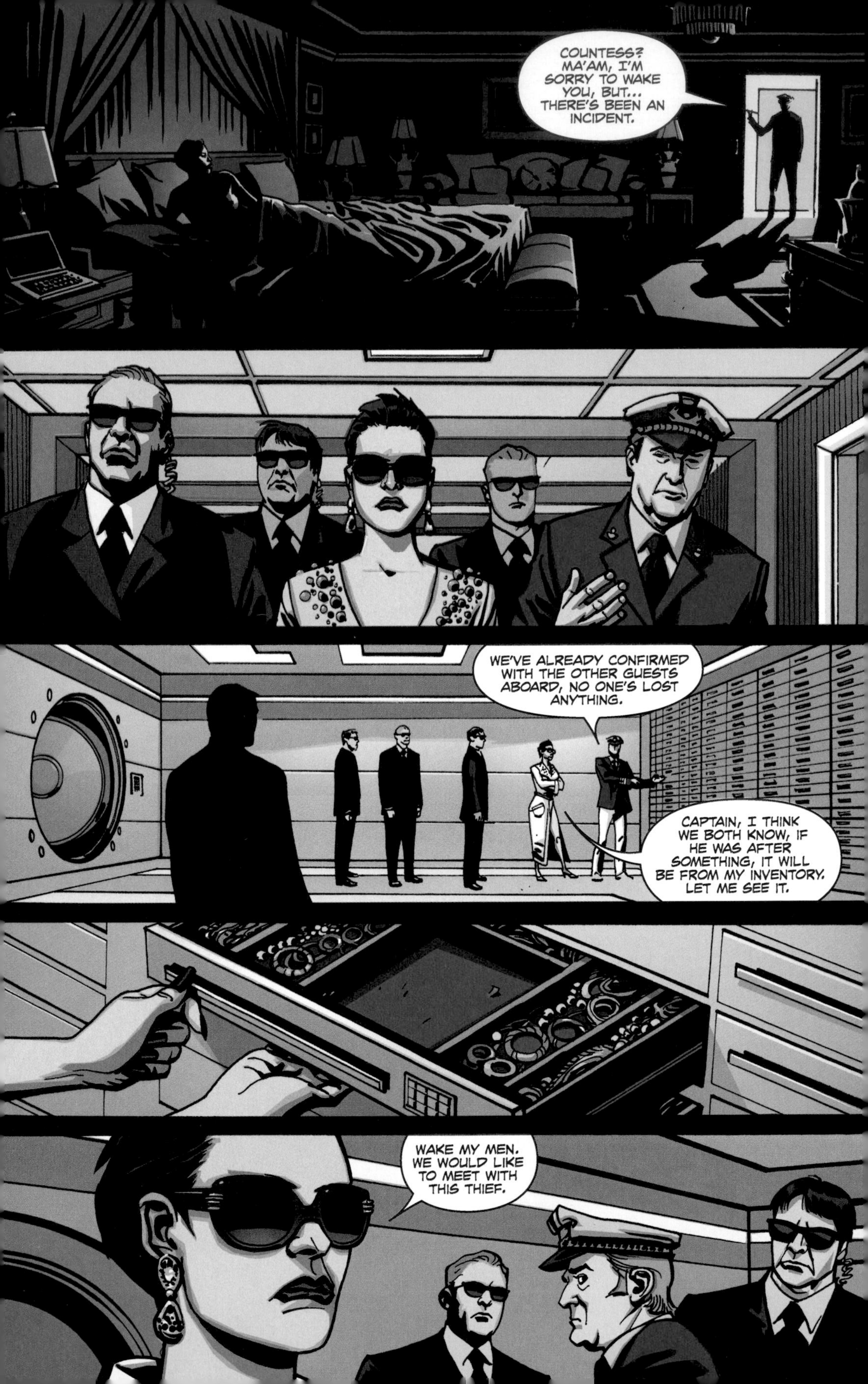
COUNTESS? MA'AM, I'M SORRY TO WAKE YOU, BUT... THERE'S BEEN AN INCIDENT.
WE'VE ALREADY CONFIRMED WITH THE OTHER GUESTS ABOARD, NO ONE'S LOST ANYTHING.
CAPTAIN, I THINK WE BOTH KNOW, IF HE WAS AFTER SOMETHING, IT WILL BE FROM MY INVENTORY. LET ME SEE IT.
WAKE MY MEN. WE WOULD LIKE TO MEET WITH THIS THIEF.

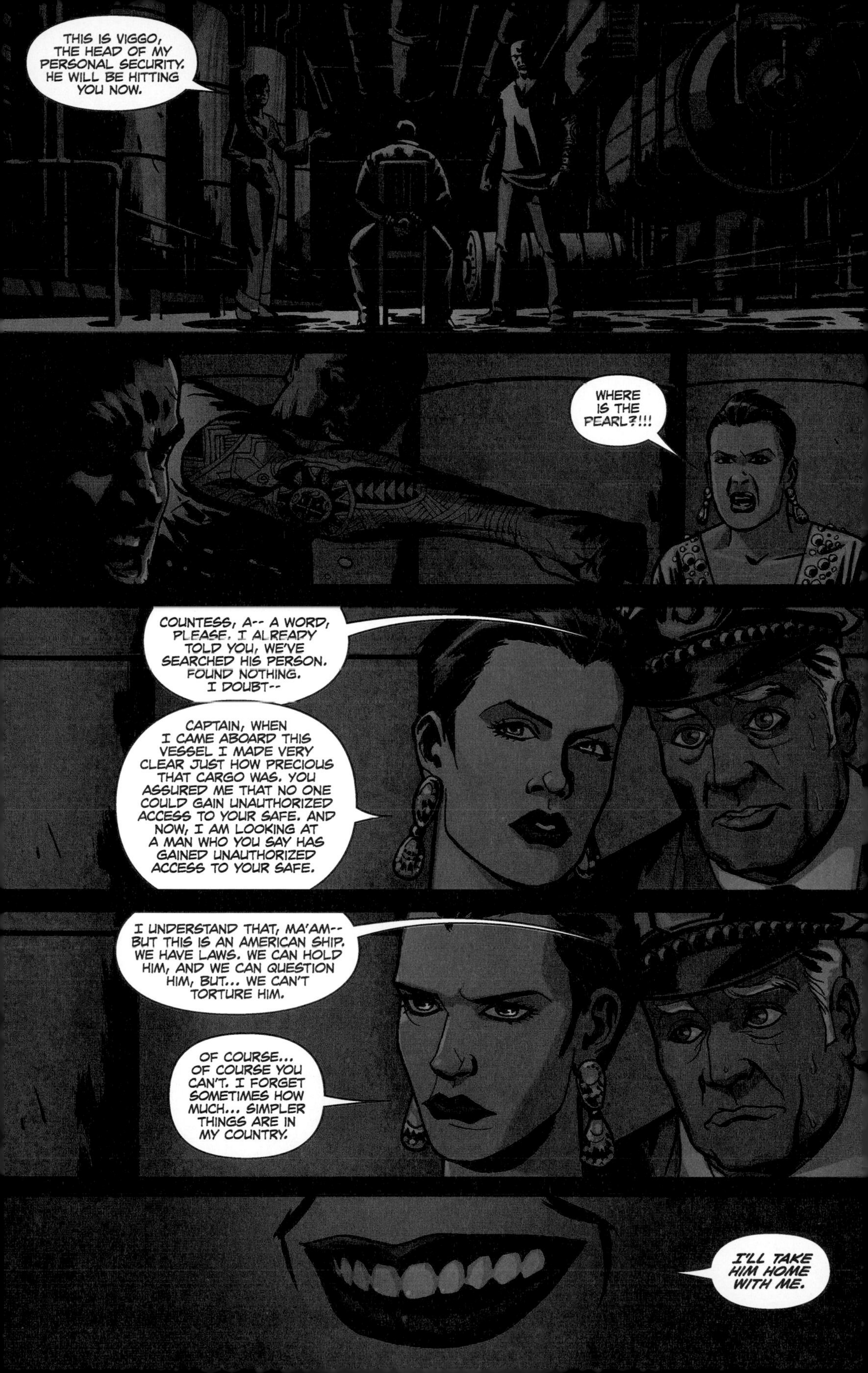
THIS IS VIGGO, THE HEAD OF MY PERSONAL SECURITY. HE WILL BE HITTING YOU NOW.
WHERE IS THE PEARL?!!!
COUNTESS, A-- A WORD, PLEASE. I ALREADY TOLD YOU, WE'VE SEARCHED HIS PERSON. FOUND NOTHING. I DOUBT--
CAPTAIN, WHEN I CAME ABOARD THIS VESSEL I MADE VERY CLEAR JUST HOW PRECIOUS THAT CARGO WAS. YOU ASSURED ME THAT NO ONE COULD GAIN UNAUTHORIZED ACCESS TO YOUR SAFE. AND NOW, I AM LOOKING AT A MAN WHO YOU SAY HAS GAINED UNAUTHORIZED ACCESS TO YOUR SAFE.
I UNDERSTAND THAT, MA'AM-- BUT THIS IS AN AMERICAN SHIP. WE HAVE LAWS. WE CAN HOLD HIM, AND WE CAN QUESTION HIM, BUT... WE CAN'T TORTURE HIM.
OF COURSE... OF COURSE YOU CAN'T. I FORGET SOMETIMES HOW MUCH... SIMPLER THINGS ARE IN MY COUNTRY.
I'LL TAKE HIM HOME WITH ME.

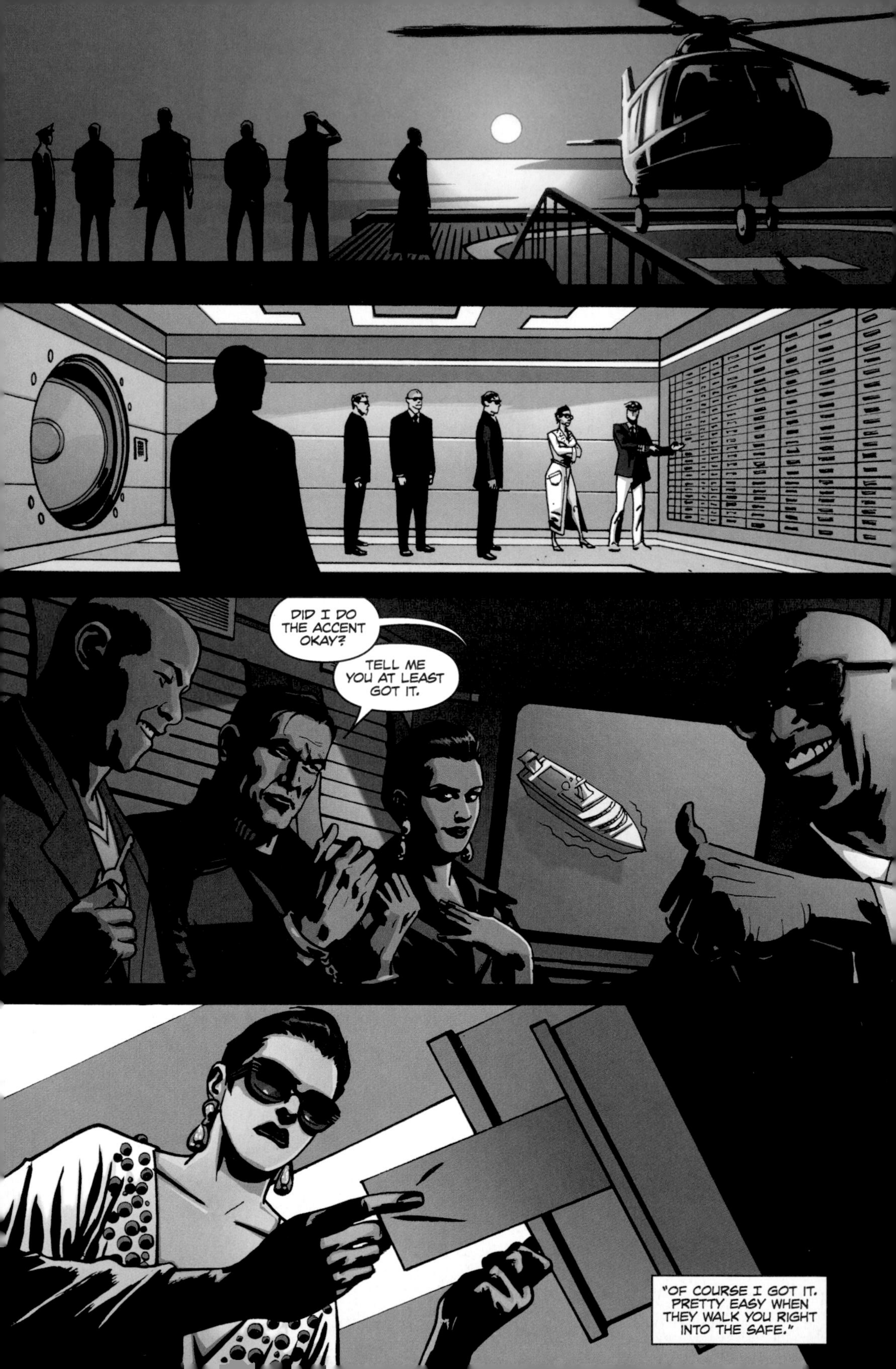
DID I DO THE ACCENT OKAY?
TELL ME YOU AT LEAST GOT IT.
"OF COURSE I GOT IT. PRETTY EASY WHEN THEY WALK YOU RIGHT INTO THE SAFE."

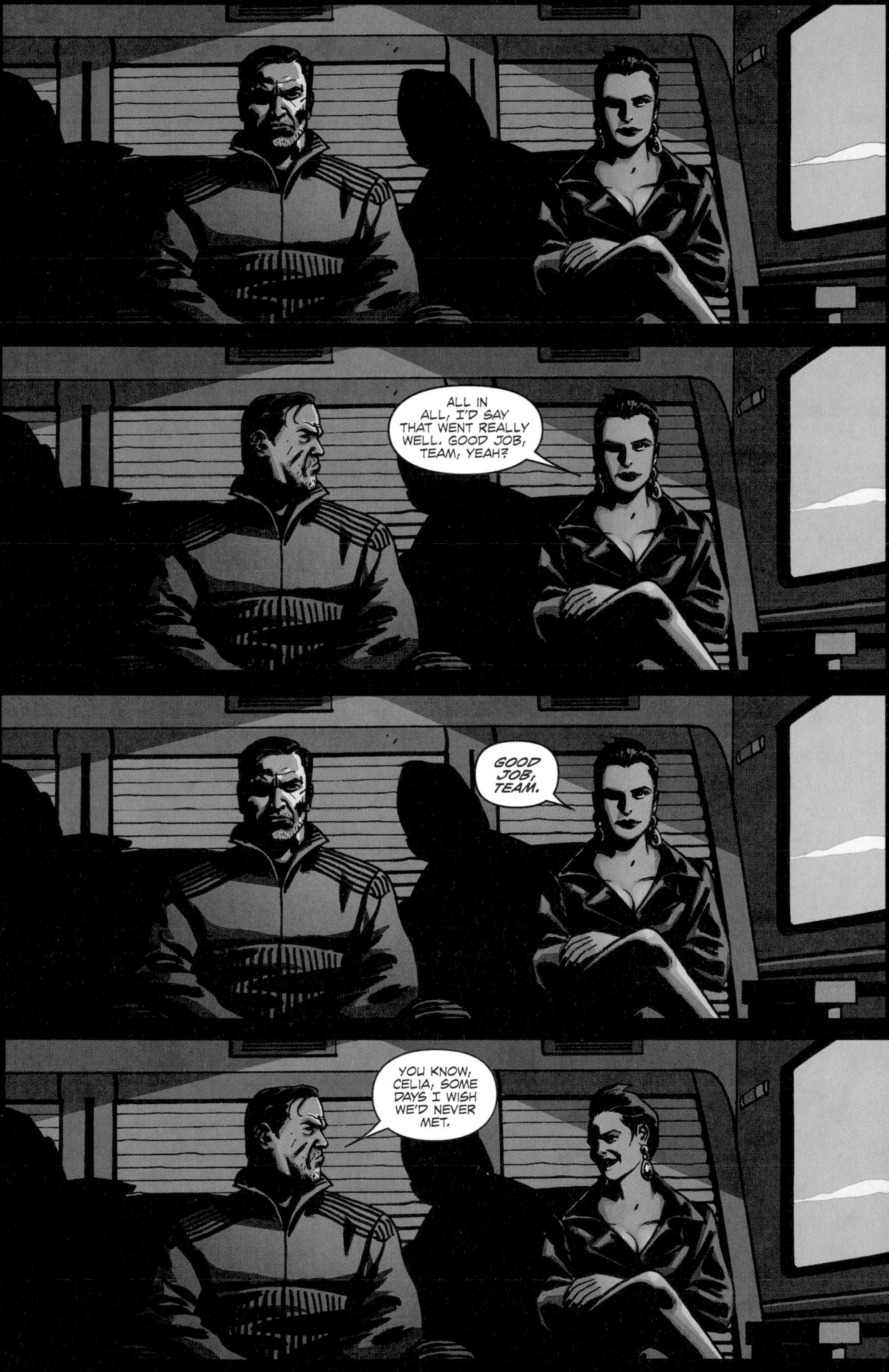
ALL IN ALL, I'D SAY THAT WENT REALLY WELL. GOOD JOB, TEAM, YEAH?
GOOD JOB, TEAM.
YOU KNOW, CELIA, SOME DAYS I WISH WE'D NEVER MET.

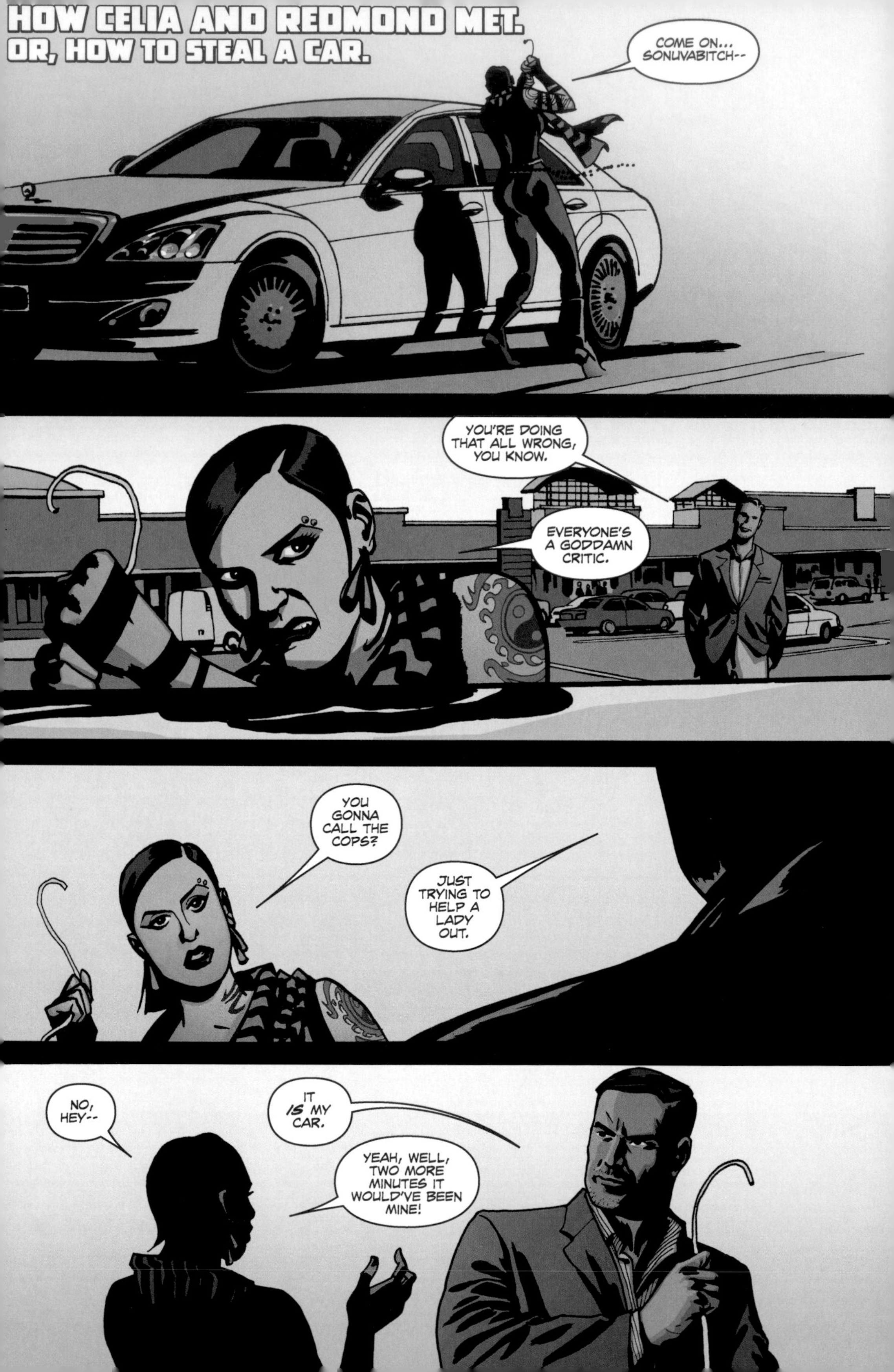
HOW CELIA AND REDMOND MET.
OR, HOW TO STEAL A CAR.
COME ON... SONUVABITCH--
YOU'RE DOING THAT ALL WRONG, YOU KNOW.
EVERYONE'S A GODDAMN CRITIC.
YOU GONNA CALL THE COPS?
JUST TRYING TO HELP A LADY OUT.
NO, HEY--
IT *IS* MY CAR.
YEAH, WELL, TWO MORE MINUTES IT WOULD'VE BEEN MINE!

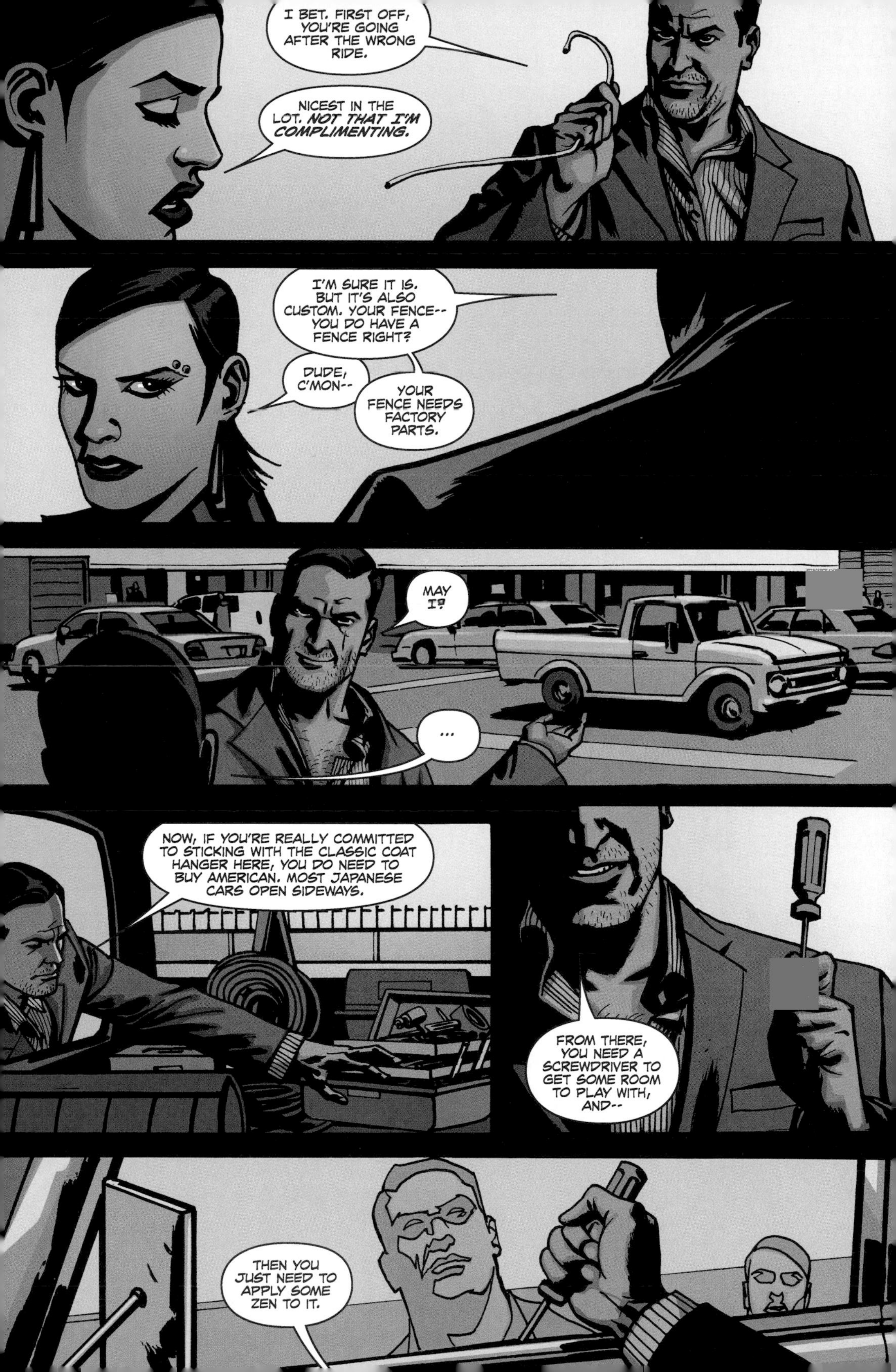
I BET. FIRST OFF, YOU'RE GOING AFTER THE WRONG RIDE.
NICEST IN THE LOT. *NOT THAT I'M COMPLIMENTING.*
I'M SURE IT IS. BUT IT'S ALSO CUSTOM. YOUR FENCE-- YOU DO HAVE A FENCE RIGHT?
DUDE, C'MON--
YOUR FENCE NEEDS FACTORY PARTS.
MAY I?
...
NOW, IF YOU'RE REALLY COMMITTED TO STICKING WITH THE CLASSIC COAT HANGER HERE, YOU DO NEED TO BUY AMERICAN. MOST JAPANESE CARS OPEN SIDEWAYS.
FROM THERE, YOU NEED A SCREWDRIVER TO GET SOME ROOM TO PLAY WITH, AND--
THEN YOU JUST NEED TO APPLY SOME ZEN TO IT.

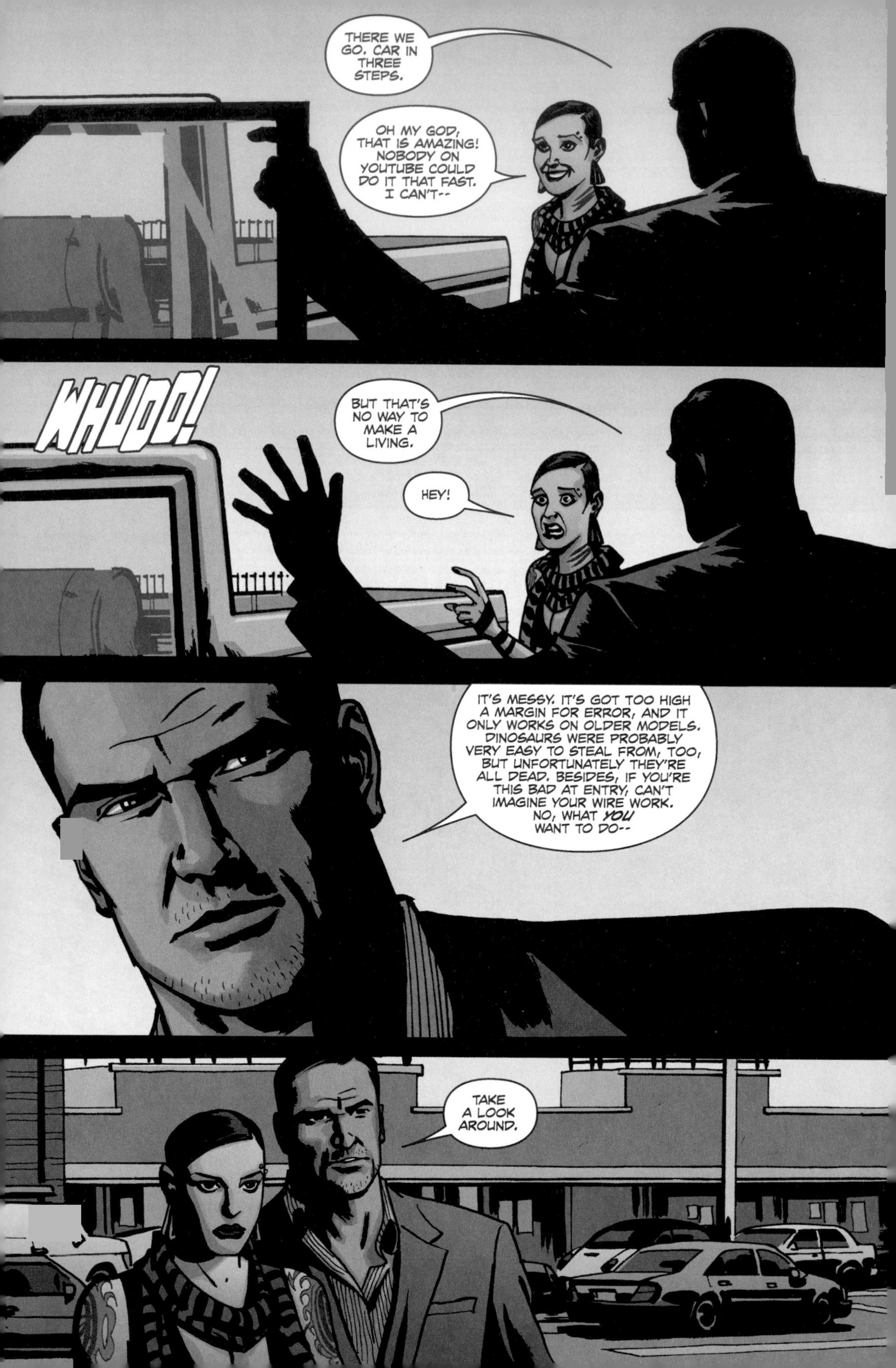
THERE WE GO. CAR IN THREE STEPS.
OH MY GOD, THAT IS AMAZING! NOBODY ON YOUTUBE COULD DO IT THAT FAST. I CAN'T--
WHUDD!
BUT THAT'S NO WAY TO MAKE A LIVING.
HEY!
IT'S MESSY. IT'S GOT TOO HIGH A MARGIN FOR ERROR, AND IT ONLY WORKS ON OLDER MODELS. DINOSAURS WERE PROBABLY VERY EASY TO STEAL FROM, TOO, BUT UNFORTUNATELY THEY'RE ALL DEAD. BESIDES, IF YOU'RE THIS BAD AT ENTRY, CAN'T IMAGINE YOUR WIRE WORK. NO, WHAT *YOU* WANT TO DO--
TAKE A LOOK AROUND.

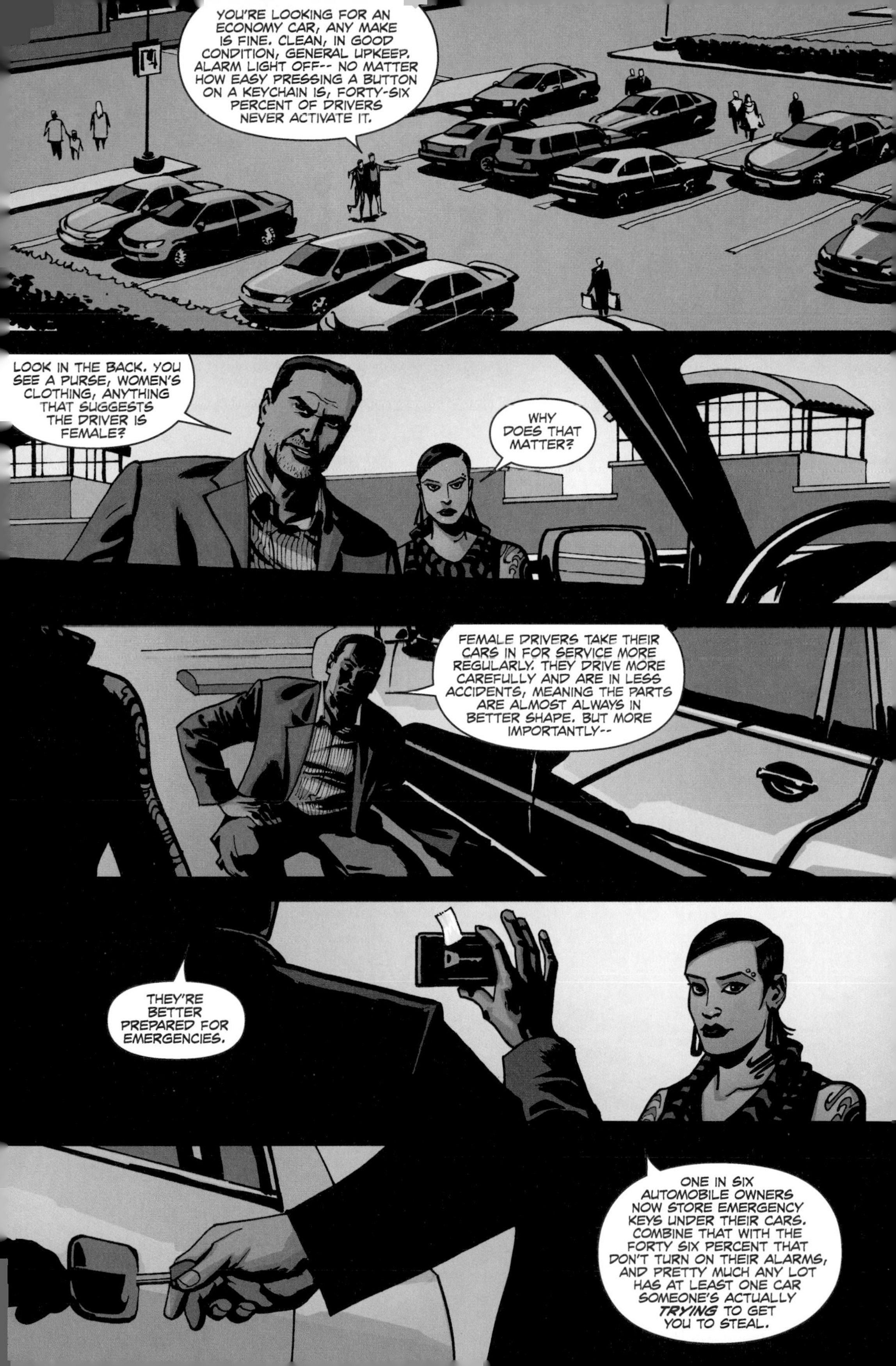
YOU'RE LOOKING FOR AN ECONOMY CAR, ANY MAKE IS FINE. CLEAN, IN GOOD CONDITION, GENERAL UPKEEP. ALARM LIGHT OFF-- NO MATTER HOW EASY PRESSING A BUTTON ON A KEYCHAIN IS, FORTY-SIX PERCENT OF DRIVERS NEVER ACTIVATE IT.
LOOK IN THE BACK. YOU SEE A PURSE, WOMEN'S CLOTHING, ANYTHING THAT SUGGESTS THE DRIVER IS FEMALE?
WHY DOES THAT MATTER?
FEMALE DRIVERS TAKE THEIR CARS IN FOR SERVICE MORE REGULARLY. THEY DRIVE MORE CAREFULLY AND ARE IN LESS ACCIDENTS, MEANING THE PARTS ARE ALMOST ALWAYS IN BETTER SHAPE. BUT MORE IMPORTANTLY--
THEY'RE BETTER PREPARED FOR EMERGENCIES.
ONE IN SIX AUTOMOBILE OWNERS NOW STORE EMERGENCY KEYS UNDER THEIR CARS. COMBINE THAT WITH THE FORTY SIX PERCENT THAT DON'T TURN ON THEIR ALARMS, AND PRETTY MUCH ANY LOT HAS AT LEAST ONE CAR SOMEONE'S ACTUALLY *TRYING* TO GET YOU TO STEAL.

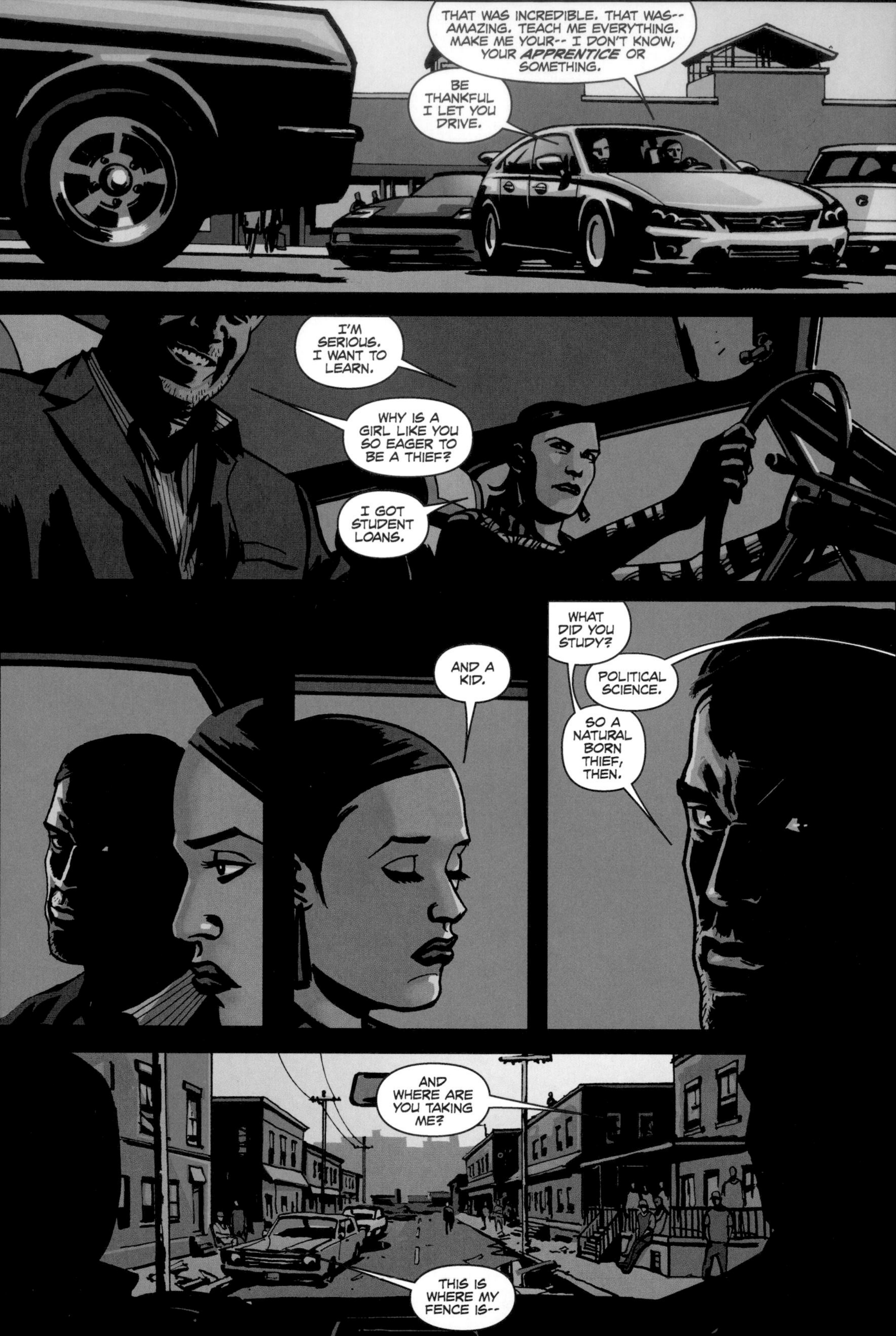
THAT WAS INCREDIBLE. THAT WAS-- AMAZING. TEACH ME EVERYTHING. MAKE ME YOUR-- I DON'T KNOW, YOUR APPRENTICE OR SOMETHING.
BE THANKFUL I LET YOU DRIVE.
I'M SERIOUS. I WANT TO LEARN.
WHY IS A GIRL LIKE YOU SO EAGER TO BE A THIEF?
I GOT STUDENT LOANS.
AND A KID.
WHAT DID YOU STUDY?
POLITICAL SCIENCE.
SO A NATURAL BORN THIEF, THEN.
AND WHERE ARE YOU TAKING ME?
THIS IS WHERE MY FENCE IS--

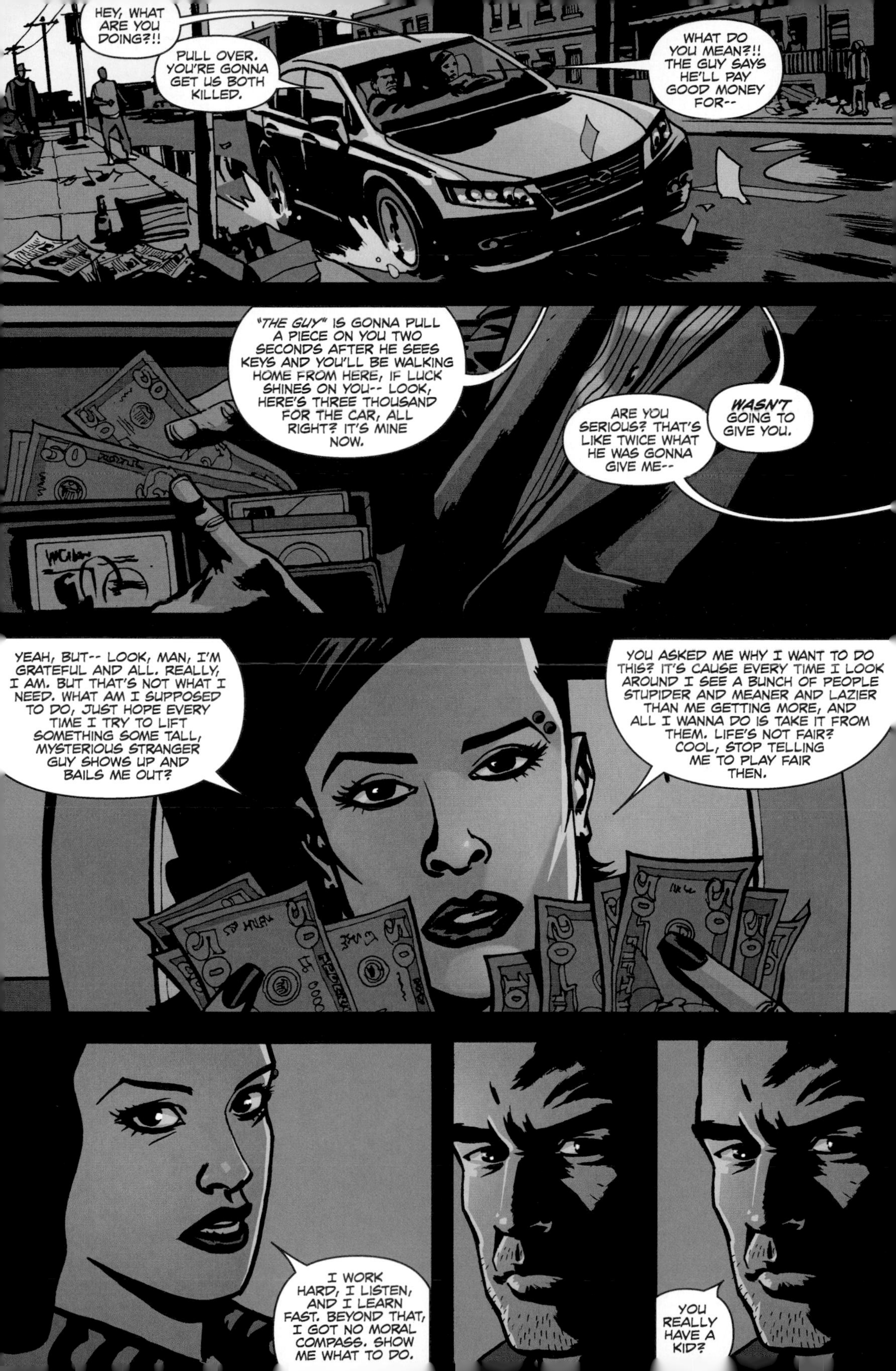
HEY, WHAT ARE YOU DOING?!!
PULL OVER. YOU'RE GONNA GET US BOTH KILLED.
WHAT DO YOU MEAN?!! THE GUY SAYS HE'LL PAY GOOD MONEY FOR--
"THE GUY" IS GONNA PULL A PIECE ON YOU TWO SECONDS AFTER HE SEES KEYS AND YOU'LL BE WALKING HOME FROM HERE, IF LUCK SHINES ON YOU-- LOOK, HERE'S THREE THOUSAND FOR THE CAR, ALL RIGHT? IT'S MINE NOW.
ARE YOU SERIOUS? THAT'S LIKE TWICE WHAT HE WAS GONNA GIVE ME--
WASN'T GOING TO GIVE YOU.
YEAH, BUT-- LOOK, MAN, I'M GRATEFUL AND ALL. REALLY, I AM. BUT THAT'S NOT WHAT I NEED. WHAT AM I SUPPOSED TO DO, JUST HOPE EVERY TIME I TRY TO LIFT SOMETHING SOME TALL, MYSTERIOUS STRANGER GUY SHOWS UP AND BAILS ME OUT?
YOU ASKED ME WHY I WANT TO DO THIS? IT'S CAUSE EVERY TIME I LOOK AROUND I SEE A BUNCH OF PEOPLE STUPIDER AND MEANER AND LAZIER THAN ME GETTING MORE, AND ALL I WANNA DO IS TAKE IT FROM THEM. LIFE'S NOT FAIR? COOL, STOP TELLING ME TO PLAY FAIR THEN.
I WORK HARD, I LISTEN, AND I LEARN FAST. BEYOND THAT, I GOT NO MORAL COMPASS. SHOW ME WHAT TO DO.
YOU REALLY HAVE A KID?

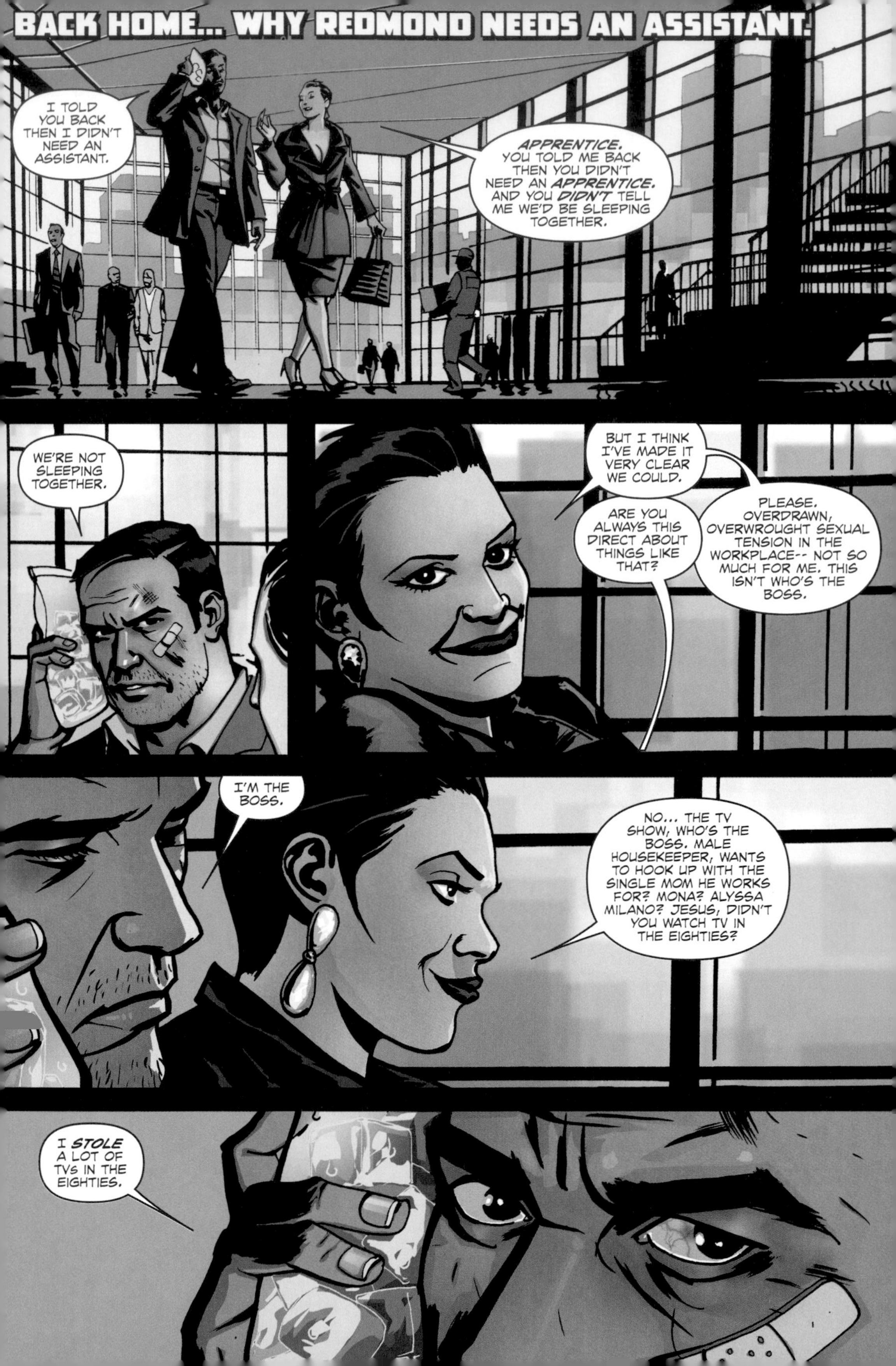
BACK HOME... WHY REDMOND NEEDS AN ASSISTANT.
I TOLD YOU BACK THEN I DIDN'T NEED AN ASSISTANT.
APPRENTICE. YOU TOLD ME BACK THEN YOU DIDN'T NEED AN *APPRENTICE.* AND YOU *DIDN'T* TELL ME WE'D BE SLEEPING TOGETHER.
WE'RE NOT SLEEPING TOGETHER.
BUT I THINK I'VE MADE IT VERY CLEAR WE COULD.
ARE YOU ALWAYS THIS DIRECT ABOUT THINGS LIKE THAT?
PLEASE. OVERDRAWN, OVERWROUGHT SEXUAL TENSION IN THE WORKPLACE-- NOT SO MUCH FOR ME. THIS ISN'T WHO'S THE BOSS.
I'M THE BOSS.
NO... THE TV SHOW, WHO'S THE BOSS. MALE HOUSEKEEPER, WANTS TO HOOK UP WITH THE SINGLE MOM HE WORKS FOR? MONA? ALYSSA MILANO? JESUS, DIDN'T YOU WATCH TV IN THE EIGHTIES?
I *STOLE* A LOT OF TVs IN THE EIGHTIES.

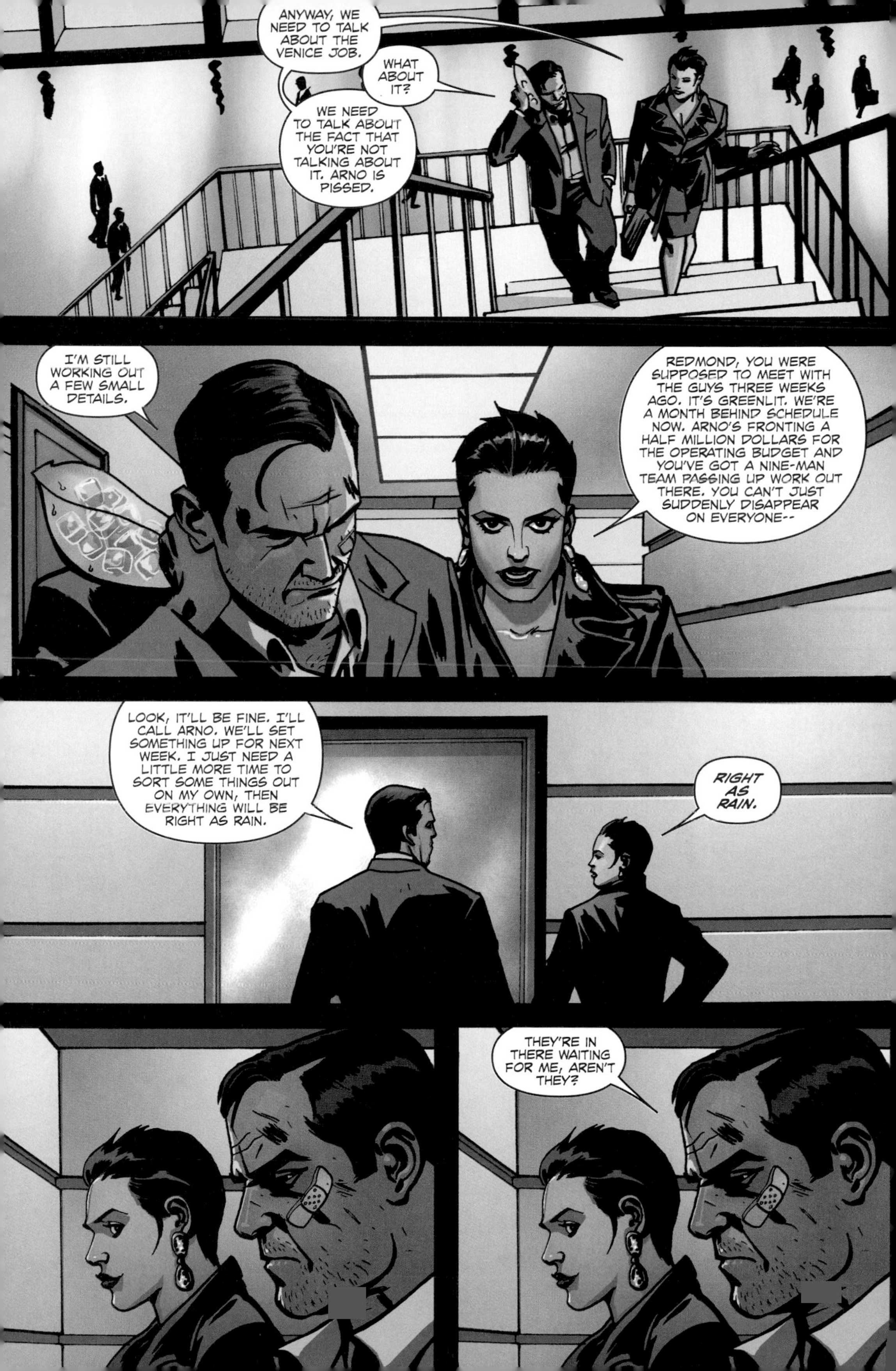
ANYWAY, WE NEED TO TALK ABOUT THE VENICE JOB.
WHAT ABOUT IT?
WE NEED TO TALK ABOUT THE FACT THAT YOU'RE NOT TALKING ABOUT IT. ARNO IS PISSED.
I'M STILL WORKING OUT A FEW SMALL DETAILS.
REDMOND, YOU WERE SUPPOSED TO MEET WITH THE GUYS THREE WEEKS AGO. IT'S GREENLIT. WE'RE A MONTH BEHIND SCHEDULE NOW. ARNO'S FRONTING A HALF MILLION DOLLARS FOR THE OPERATING BUDGET AND YOU'VE GOT A NINE-MAN TEAM PASSING UP WORK OUT THERE. YOU CAN'T JUST SUDDENLY DISAPPEAR ON EVERYONE--
LOOK, IT'LL BE FINE. I'LL CALL ARNO. WE'LL SET SOMETHING UP FOR NEXT WEEK. I JUST NEED A LITTLE MORE TIME TO SORT SOME THINGS OUT ON MY OWN, THEN EVERYTHING WILL BE RIGHT AS RAIN.
RIGHT AS RAIN.
THEY'RE IN THERE WAITING FOR ME, AREN'T THEY?

THE UNEXPECTED MEETING.
OR, AN UNCOMFORTABLE MOMENT.

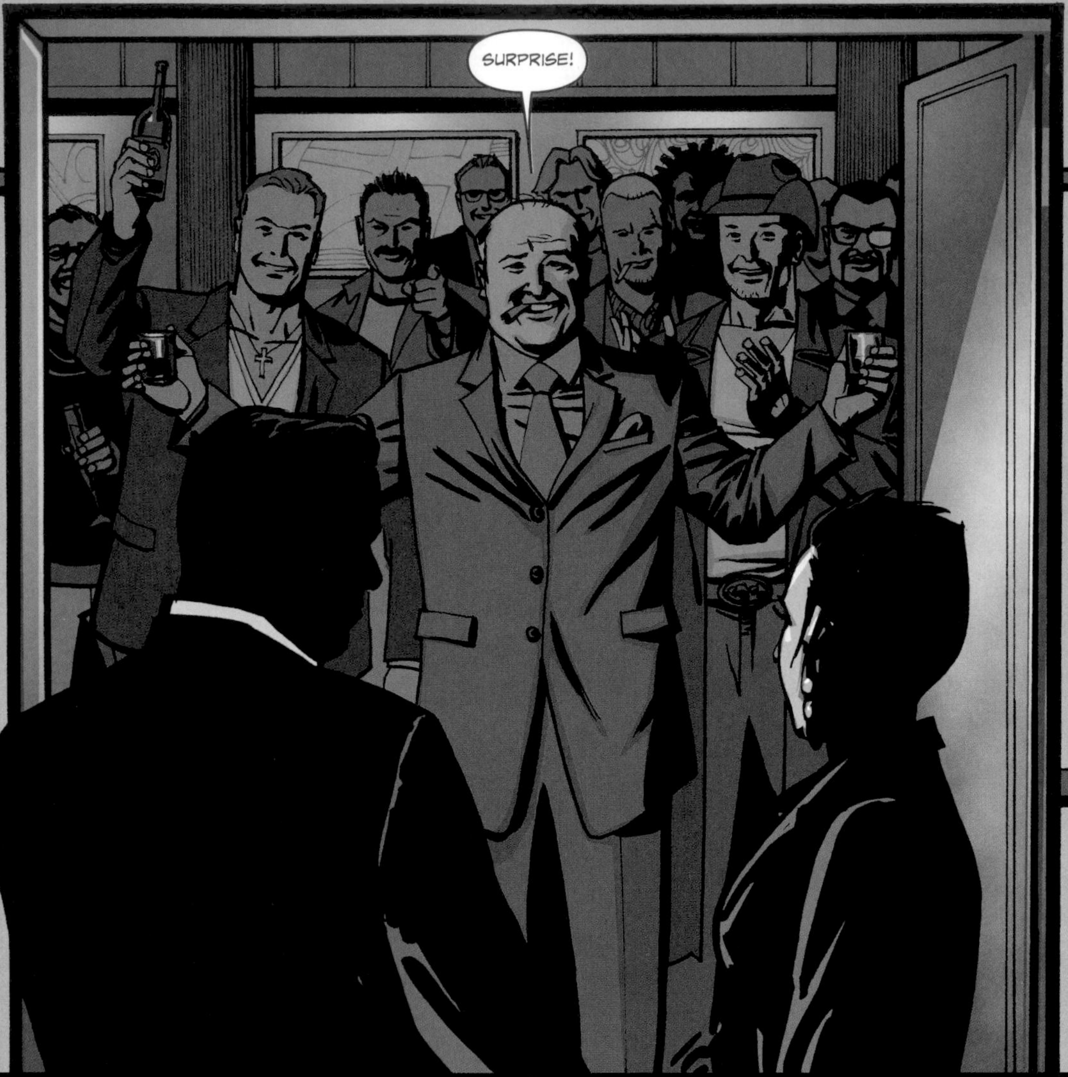
SURPRISE!

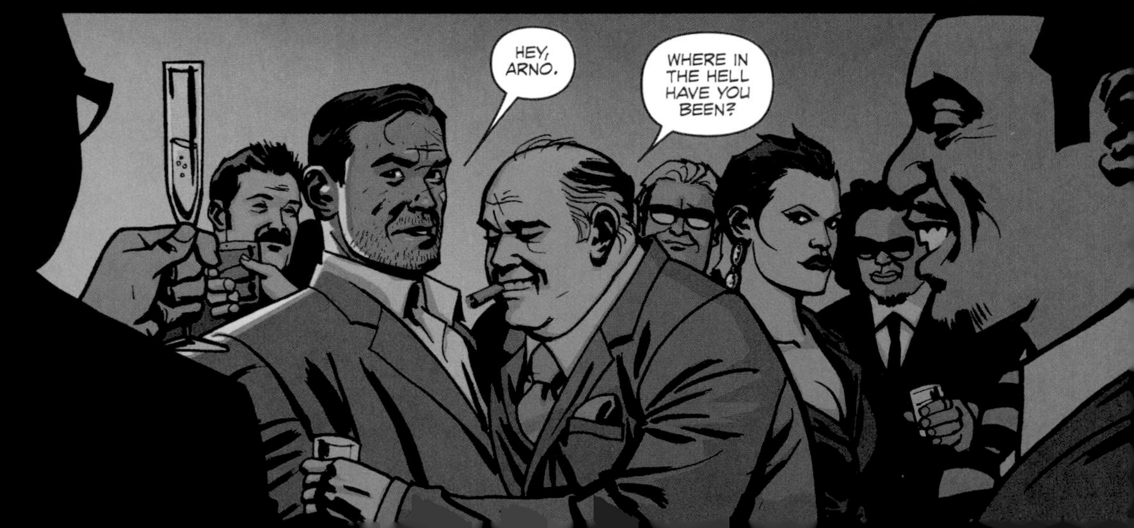
HEY, ARNO.
WHERE IN THE HELL HAVE YOU BEEN?

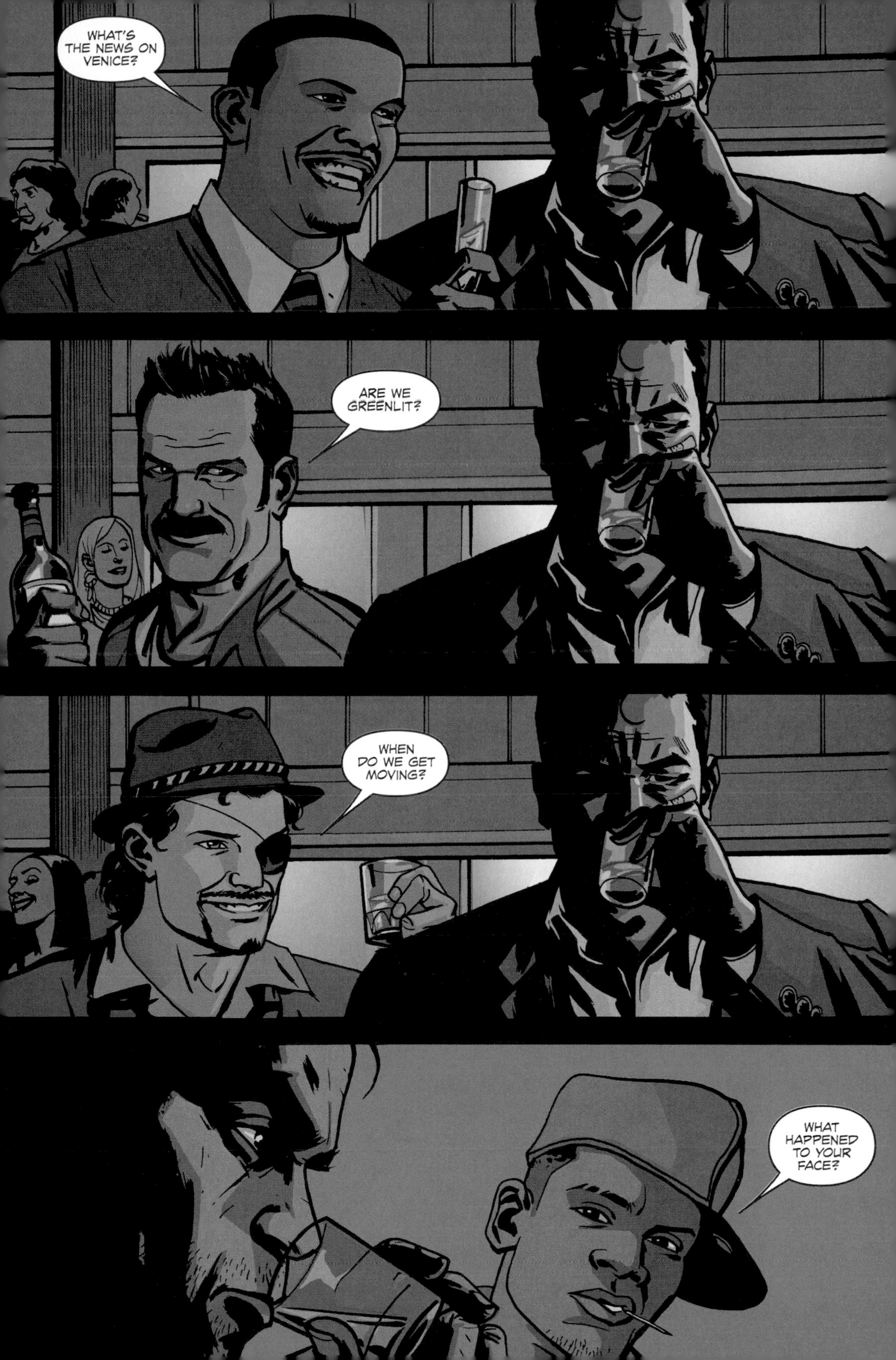
WHAT'S THE NEWS ON VENICE?
ARE WE GREENLIT?
WHEN DO WE GET MOVING?
WHAT HAPPENED TO YOUR FACE?

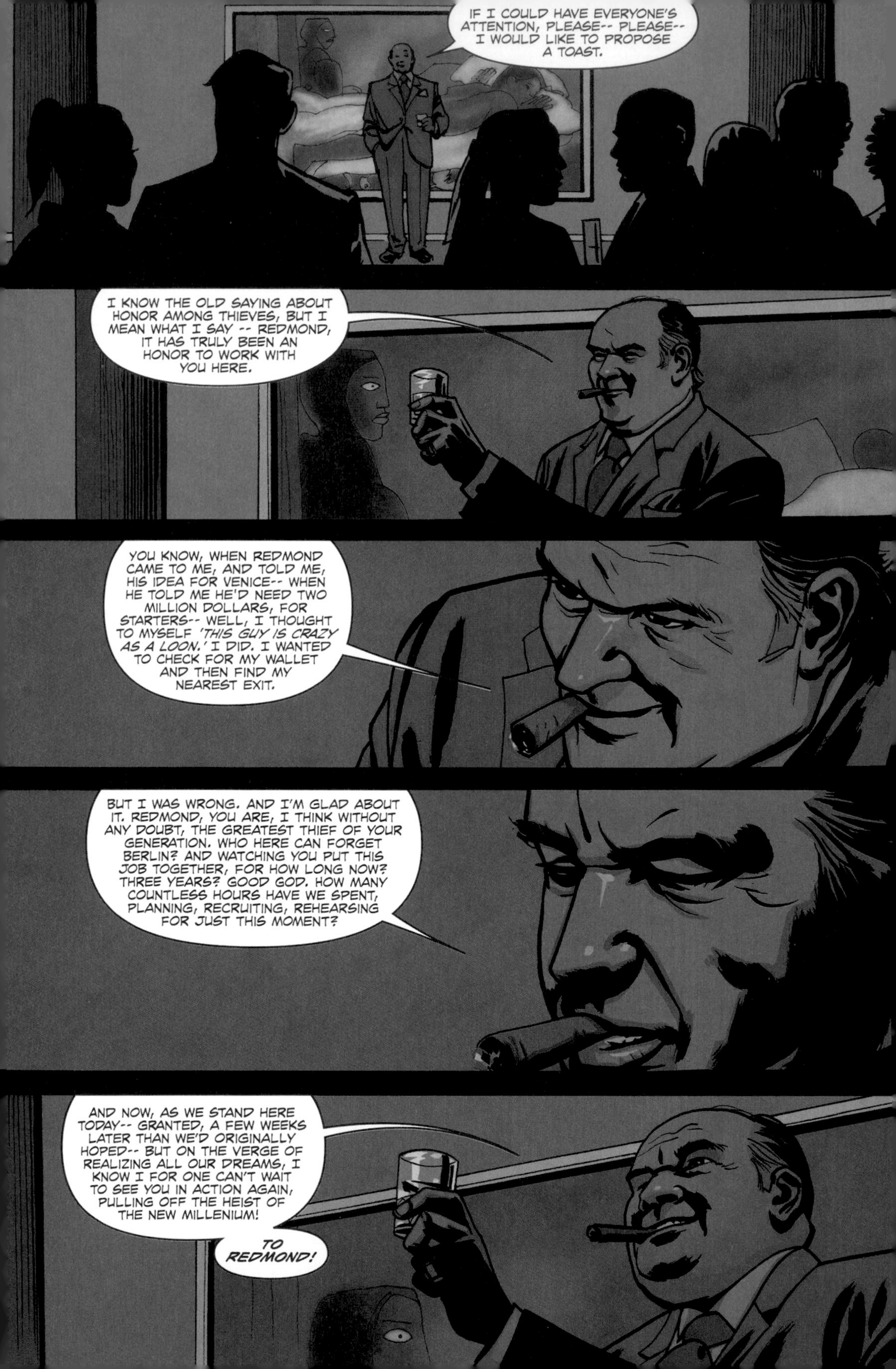
IF I COULD HAVE EVERYONE'S ATTENTION, PLEASE-- PLEASE-- I WOULD LIKE TO PROPOSE A TOAST.
I KNOW THE OLD SAYING ABOUT HONOR AMONG THIEVES, BUT I MEAN WHAT I SAY -- REDMOND, IT HAS TRULY BEEN AN HONOR TO WORK WITH YOU HERE.
YOU KNOW, WHEN REDMOND CAME TO ME, AND TOLD ME, HIS IDEA FOR VENICE-- WHEN HE TOLD ME HE'D NEED TWO MILLION DOLLARS, FOR STARTERS-- WELL, I THOUGHT TO MYSELF *'THIS GUY IS CRAZY AS A LOON.'* I DID. I WANTED TO CHECK FOR MY WALLET AND THEN FIND MY NEAREST EXIT.
BUT I WAS WRONG. AND I'M GLAD ABOUT IT. REDMOND, YOU ARE, I THINK WITHOUT ANY DOUBT, THE GREATEST THIEF OF YOUR GENERATION. WHO HERE CAN FORGET BERLIN? AND WATCHING YOU PUT THIS JOB TOGETHER, FOR HOW LONG NOW? THREE YEARS? GOOD GOD. HOW MANY COUNTLESS HOURS HAVE WE SPENT, PLANNING, RECRUITING, REHEARSING FOR JUST THIS MOMENT?
AND NOW, AS WE STAND HERE TODAY-- GRANTED, A FEW WEEKS LATER THAN WE'D ORIGINALLY HOPED-- BUT ON THE VERGE OF REALIZING ALL OUR DREAMS, I KNOW I FOR ONE CAN'T WAIT TO SEE YOU IN ACTION AGAIN, PULLING OFF THE HEIST OF THE NEW MILLENIUM!
TO REDMOND!

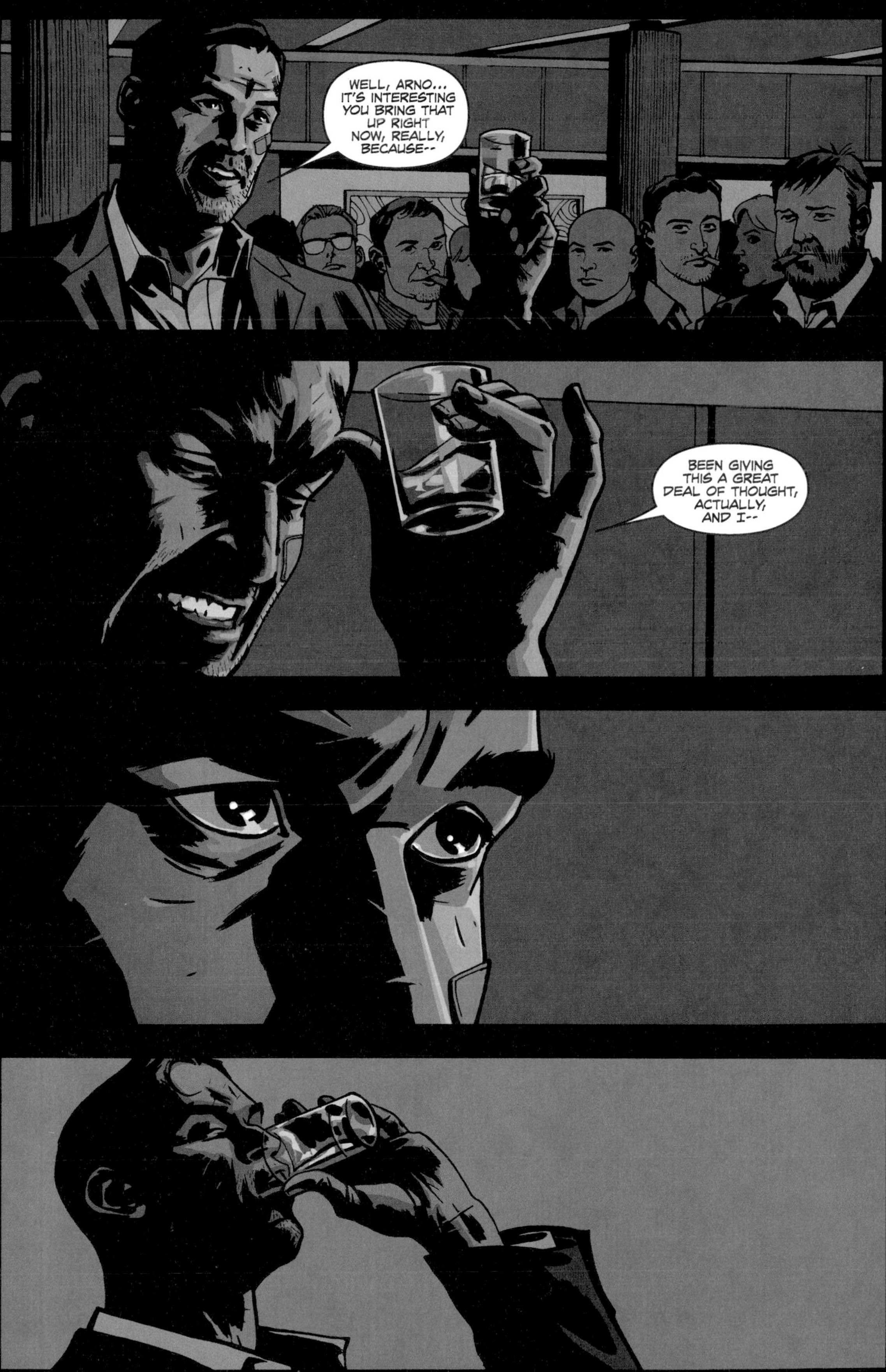
WELL, ARNO... IT'S INTERESTING YOU BRING THAT UP RIGHT NOW, REALLY, BECAUSE--
BEEN GIVING THIS A GREAT DEAL OF THOUGHT, ACTUALLY, AND I--

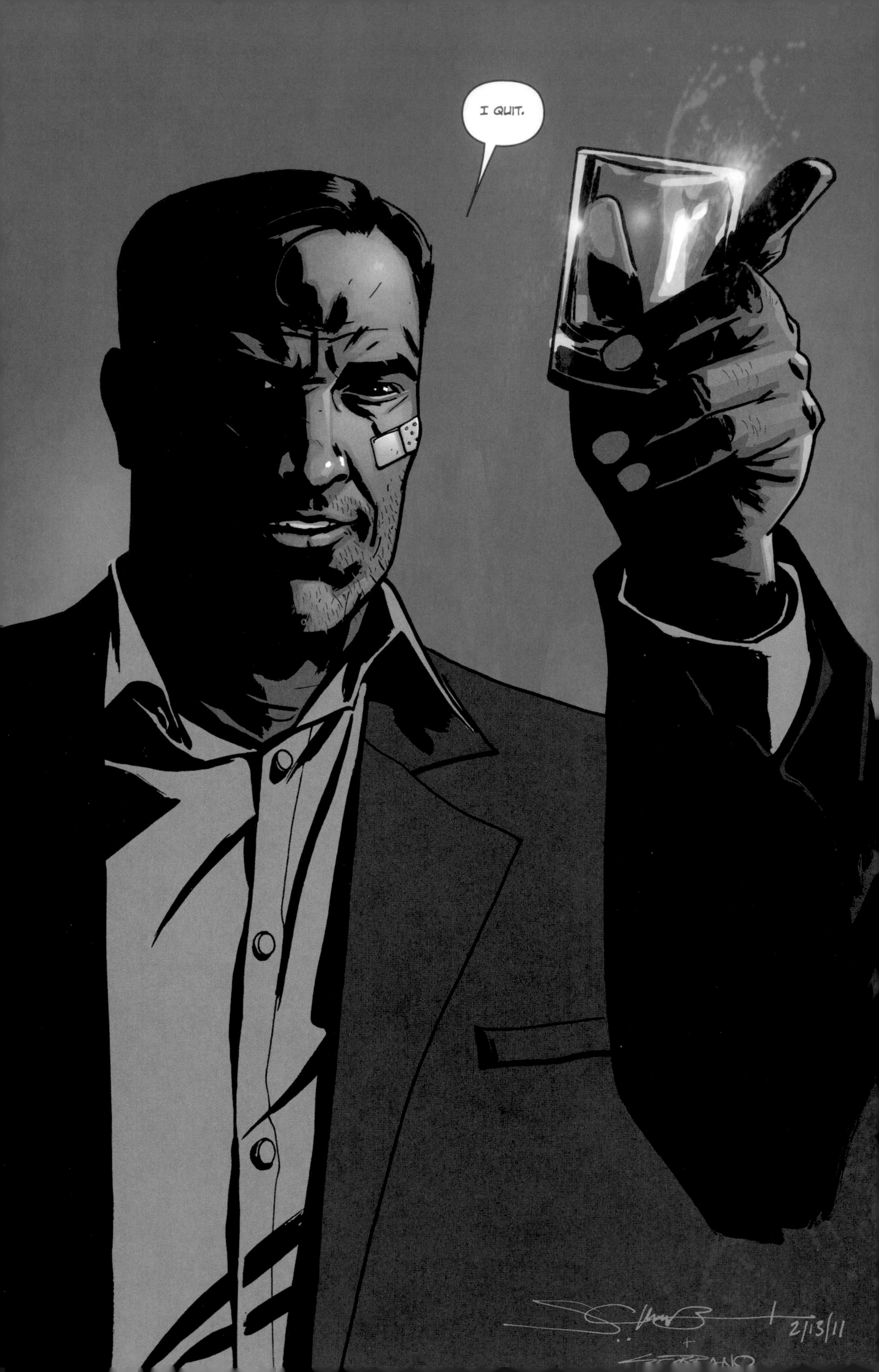
I QUIT.

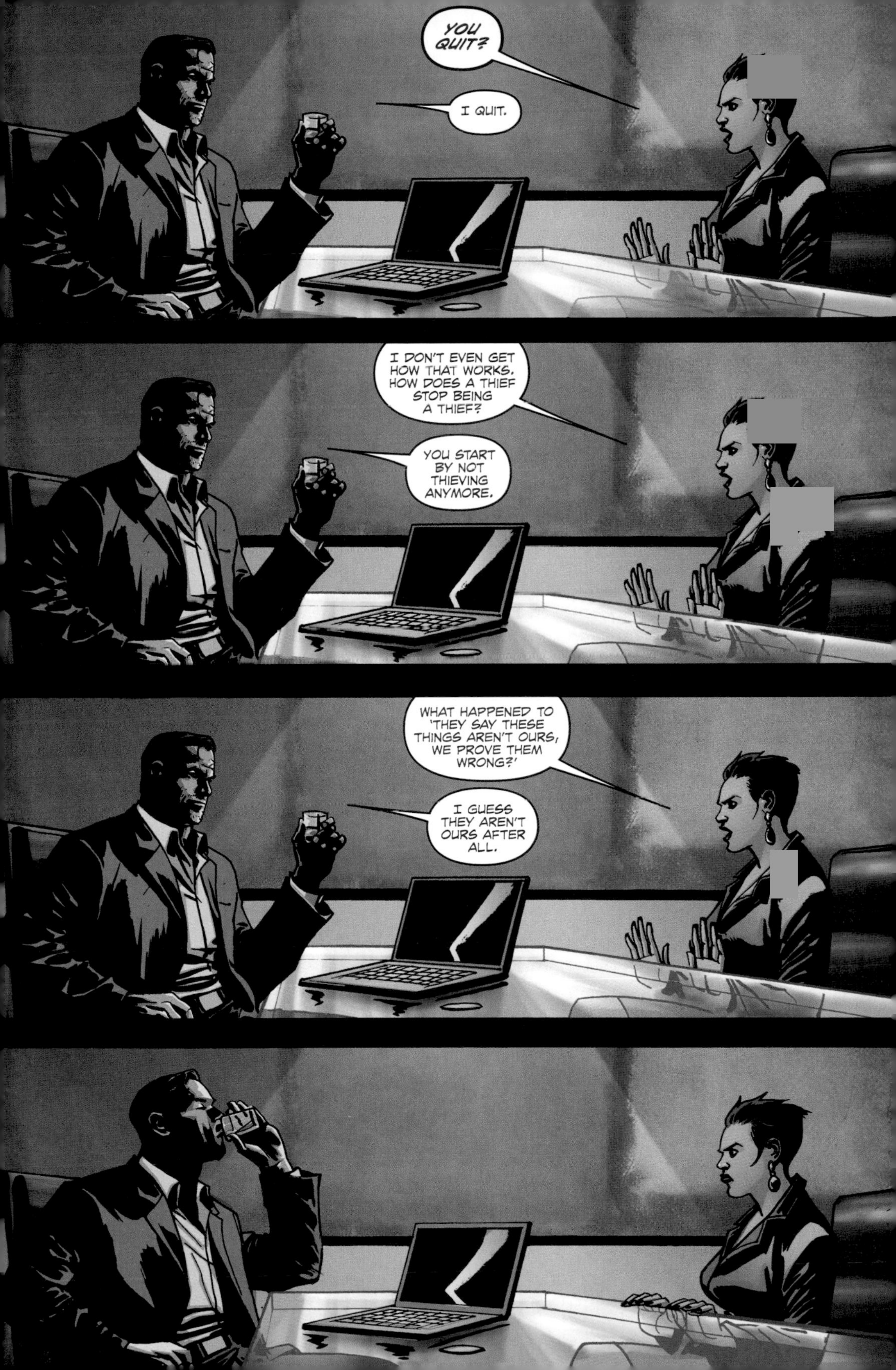
YOU QUIT?
I QUIT.
I DON'T EVEN GET HOW THAT WORKS. HOW DOES A THIEF STOP BEING A THIEF?
YOU START BY NOT THIEVING ANYMORE.
WHAT HAPPENED TO 'THEY SAY THESE THINGS AREN'T OURS, WE PROVE THEM WRONG?'
I GUESS THEY AREN'T OURS AFTER ALL.

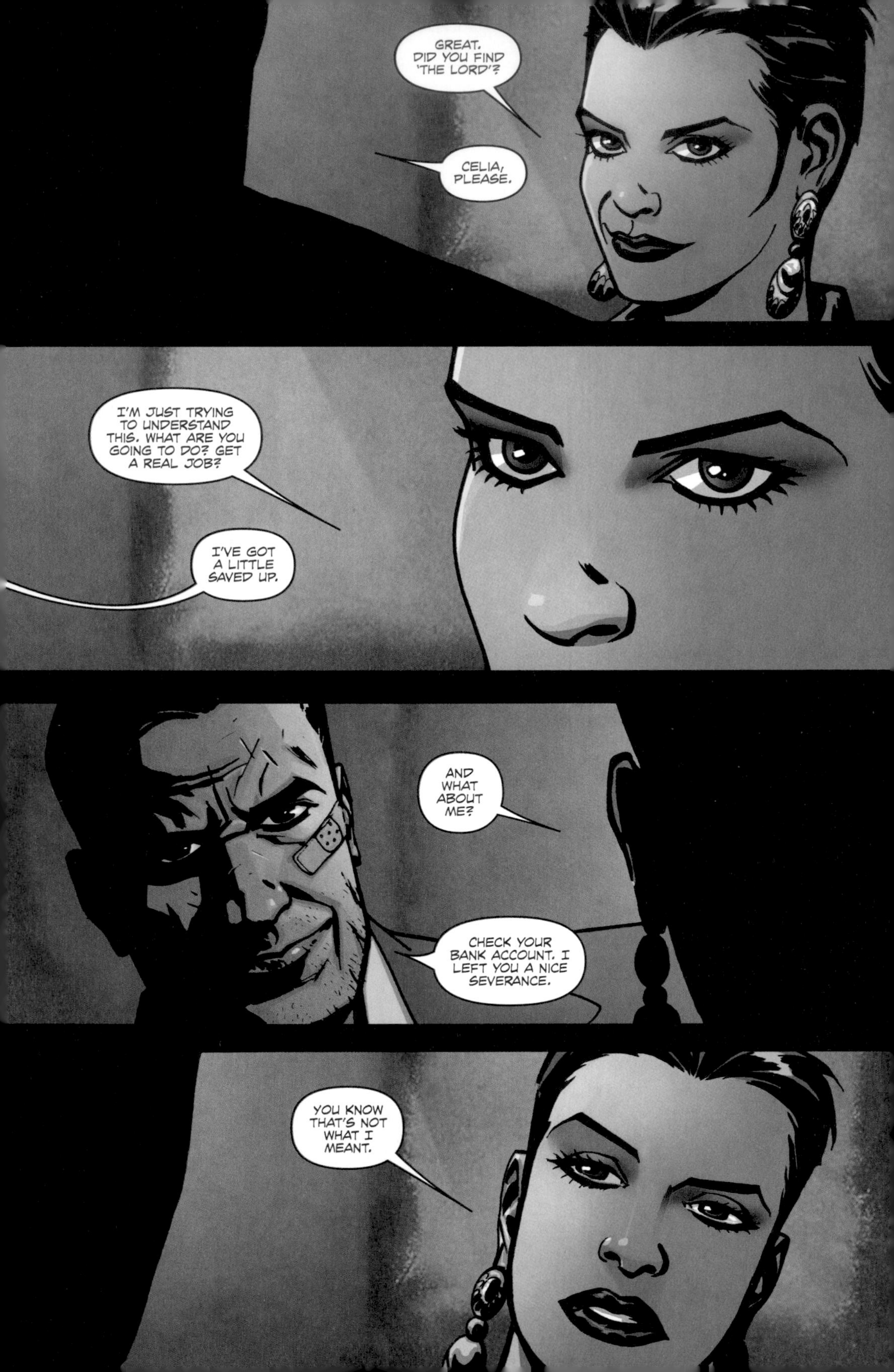
GREAT. DID YOU FIND 'THE LORD'?
CELIA, PLEASE.
I'M JUST TRYING TO UNDERSTAND THIS. WHAT ARE YOU GOING TO DO? GET A REAL JOB?
I'VE GOT A LITTLE SAVED UP.
AND WHAT ABOUT ME?
CHECK YOUR BANK ACCOUNT. I LEFT YOU A NICE SEVERANCE.
YOU KNOW THAT'S NOT WHAT I MEANT.

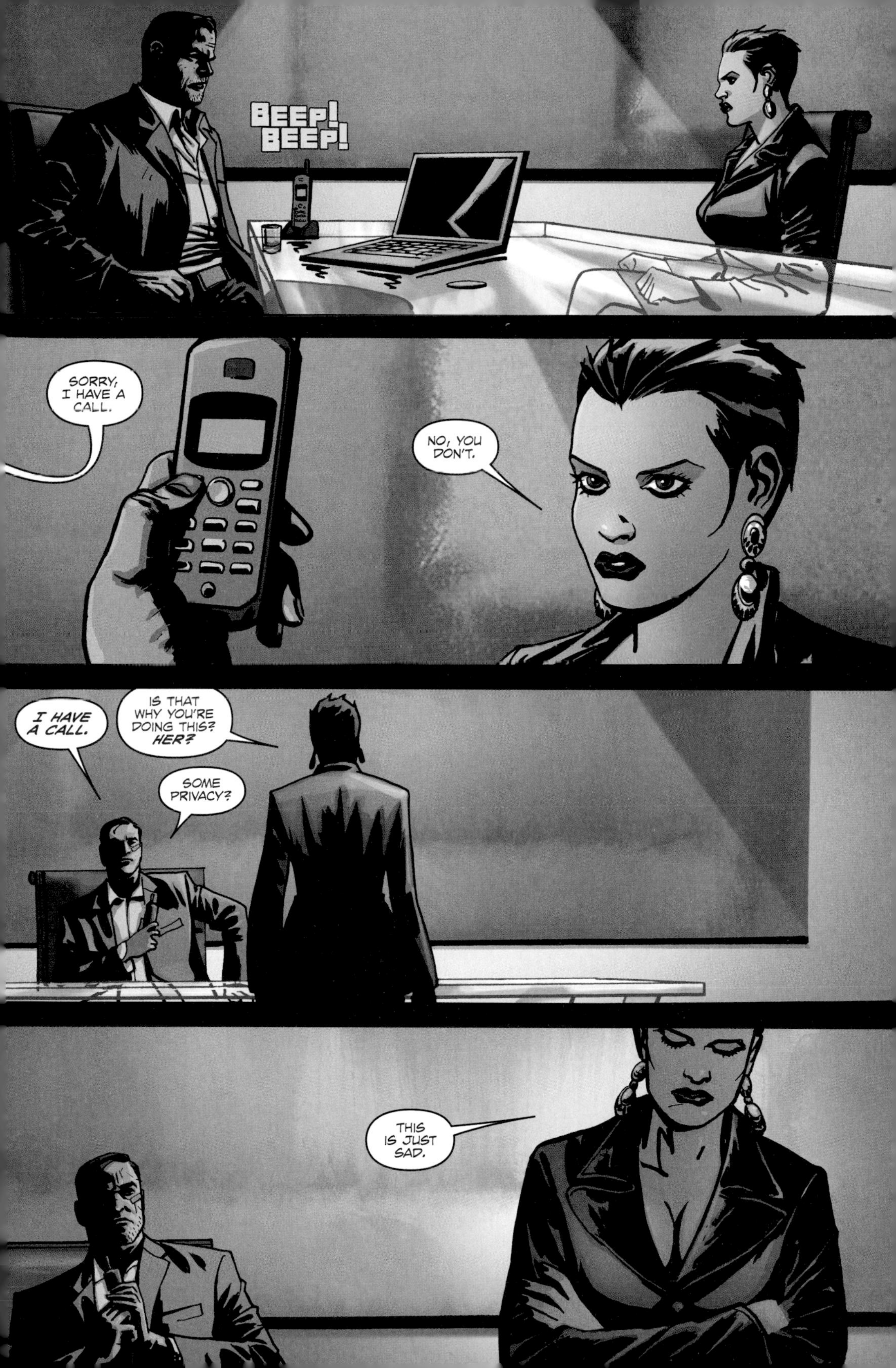
BEEP! BEEP!
SORRY, I HAVE A CALL.
NO, YOU DON'T.
I HAVE A CALL.
IS THAT WHY YOU'RE DOING THIS? HER?
SOME PRIVACY?
THIS IS JUST SAD.

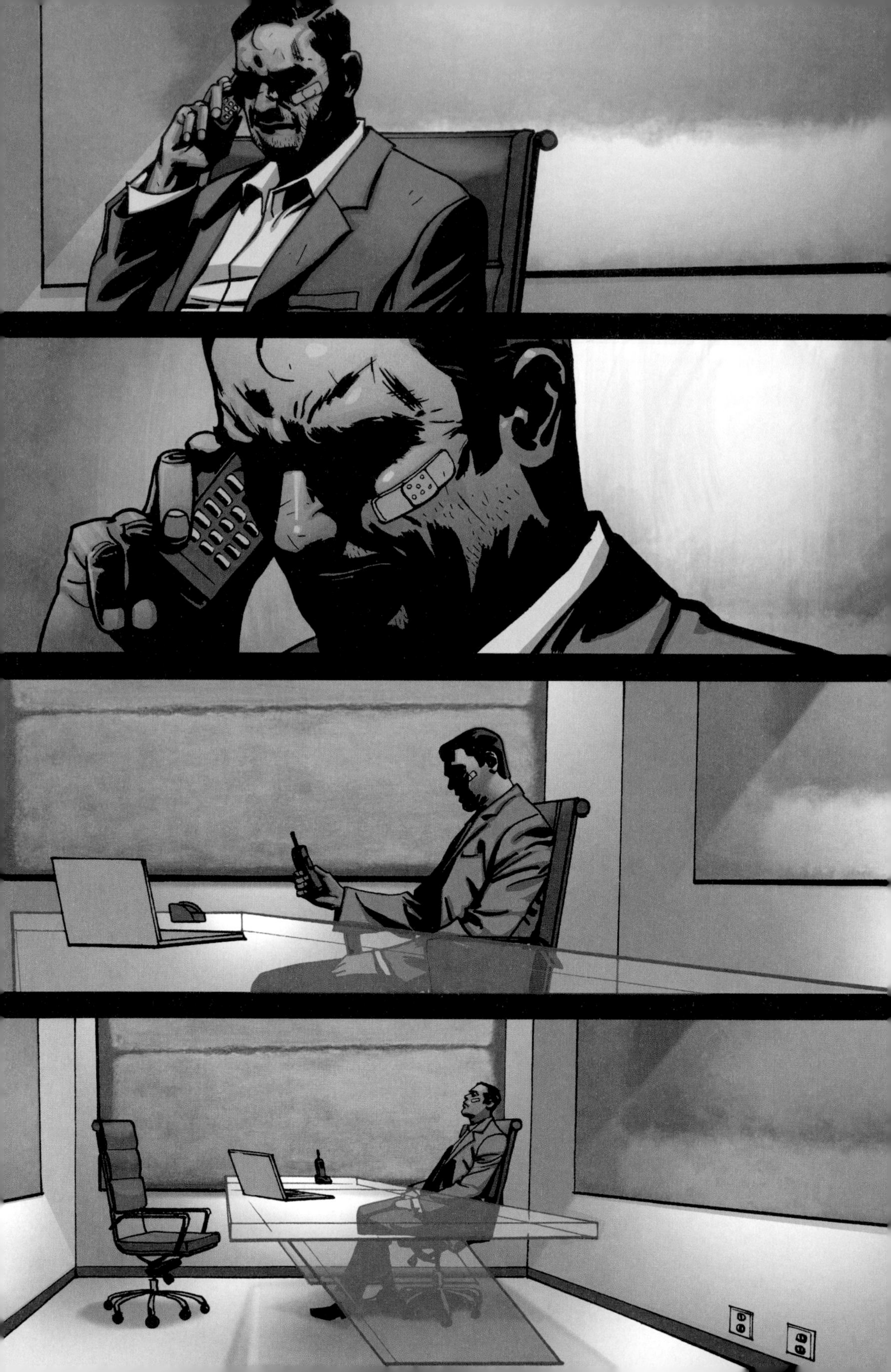

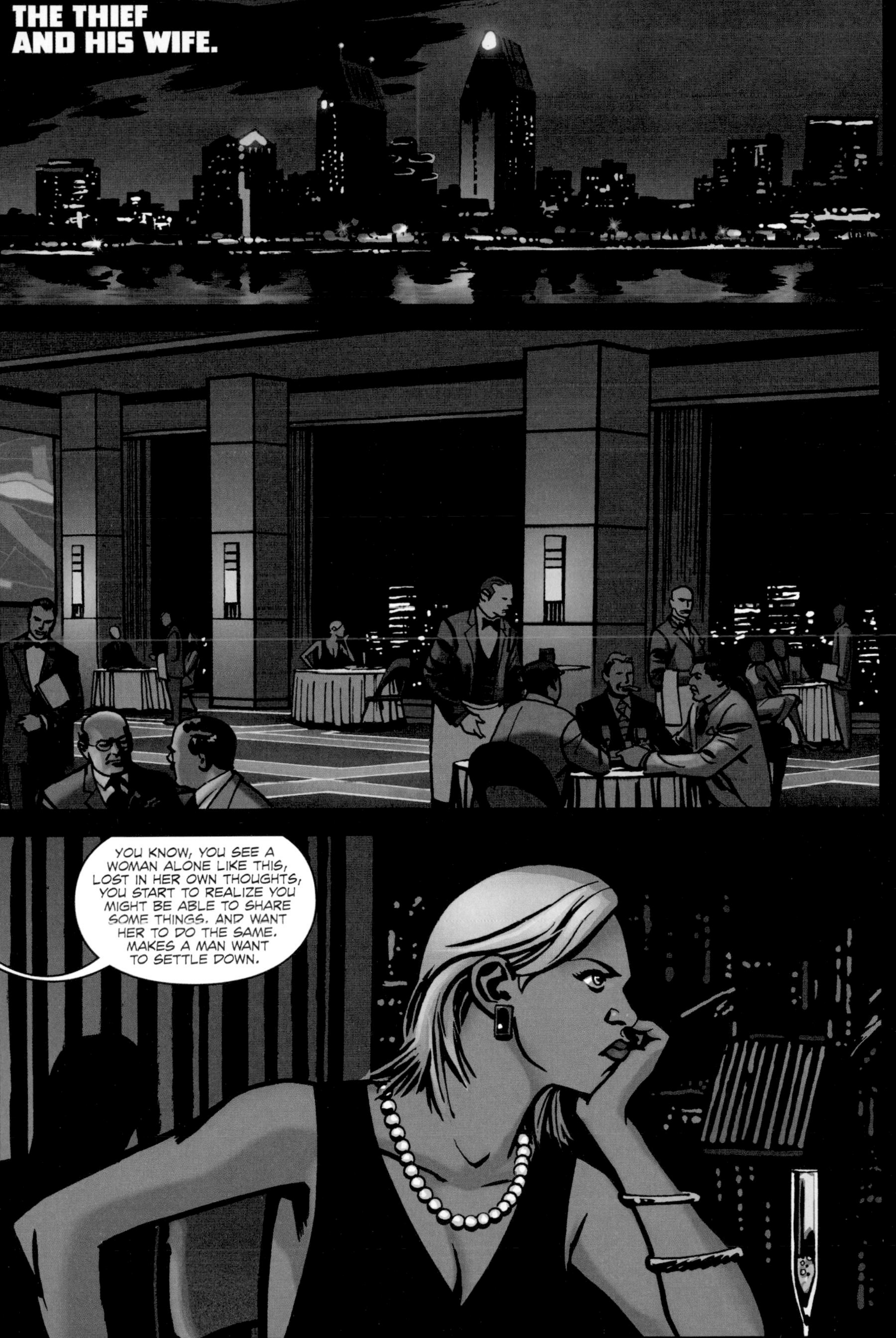
THE THIEF AND HIS WIFE.
YOU KNOW, YOU SEE A WOMAN ALONE LIKE THIS, LOST IN HER OWN THOUGHTS, YOU START TO REALIZE YOU MIGHT BE ABLE TO SHARE SOME THINGS. AND WANT HER TO DO THE SAME. MAKES A MAN WANT TO SETTLE DOWN.

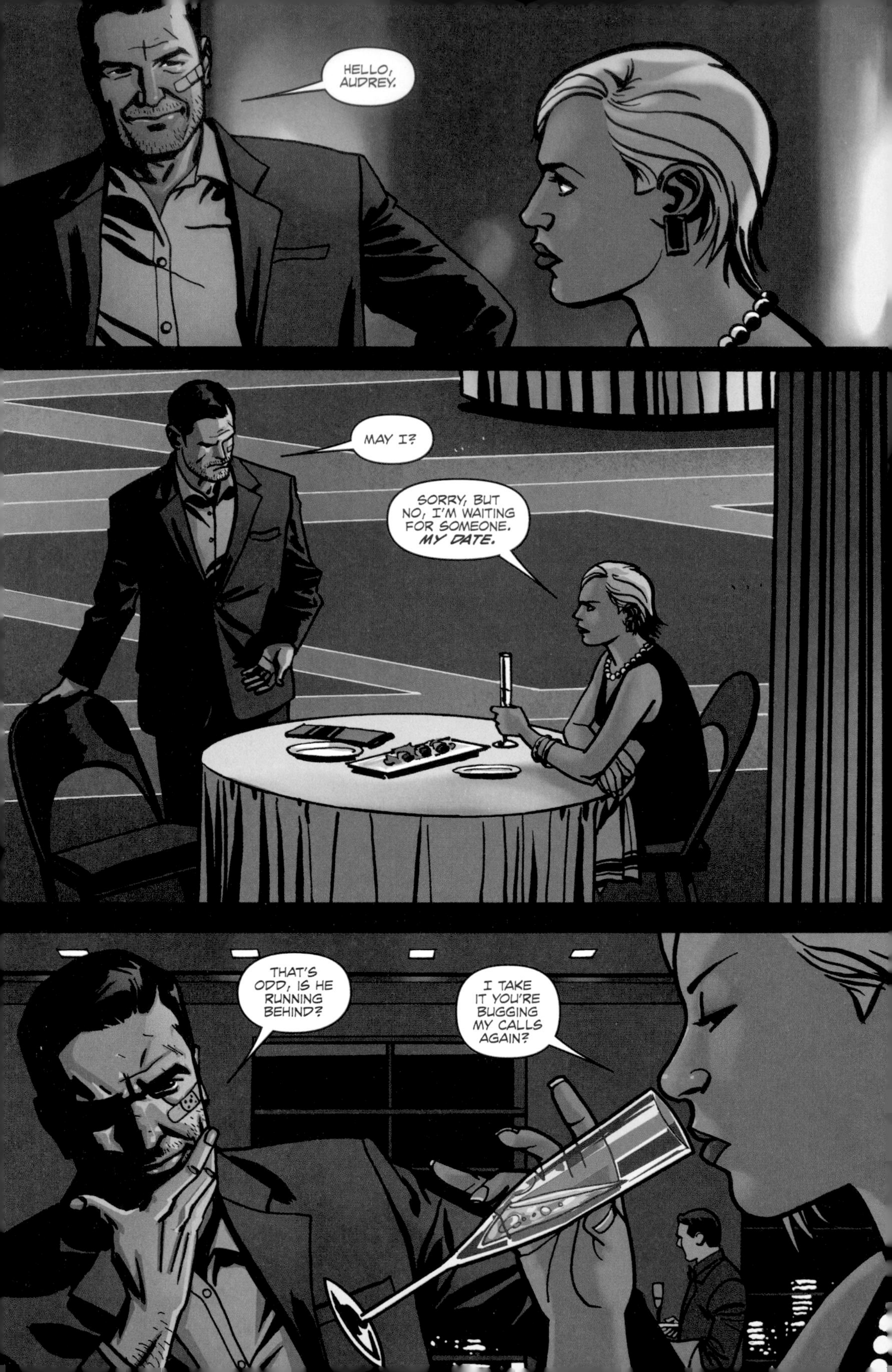
HELLO, AUDREY.
MAY I?
SORRY, BUT NO, I'M WAITING FOR SOMEONE. *MY DATE.*
THAT'S ODD, IS HE RUNNING BEHIND?
I TAKE IT YOU'RE BUGGING MY CALLS AGAIN?

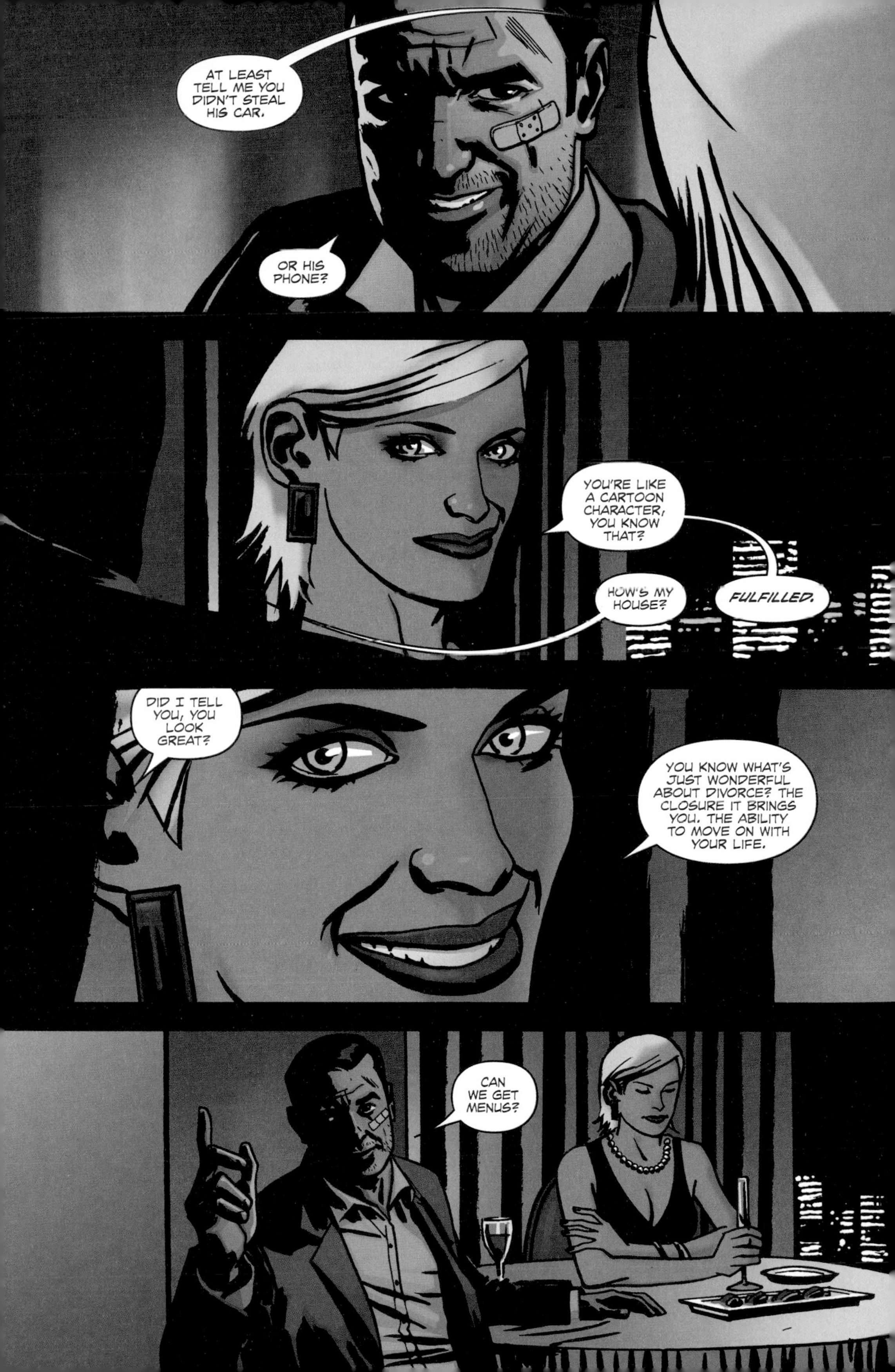
AT LEAST TELL ME YOU DIDN'T STEAL HIS CAR.
OR HIS PHONE?
YOU'RE LIKE A CARTOON CHARACTER, YOU KNOW THAT?
FULFILLED.
HOW'S MY HOUSE?
DID I TELL YOU, YOU LOOK GREAT?
YOU KNOW WHAT'S JUST WONDERFUL ABOUT DIVORCE? THE CLOSURE IT BRINGS YOU. THE ABILITY TO MOVE ON WITH YOUR LIFE.
CAN WE GET MENUS?

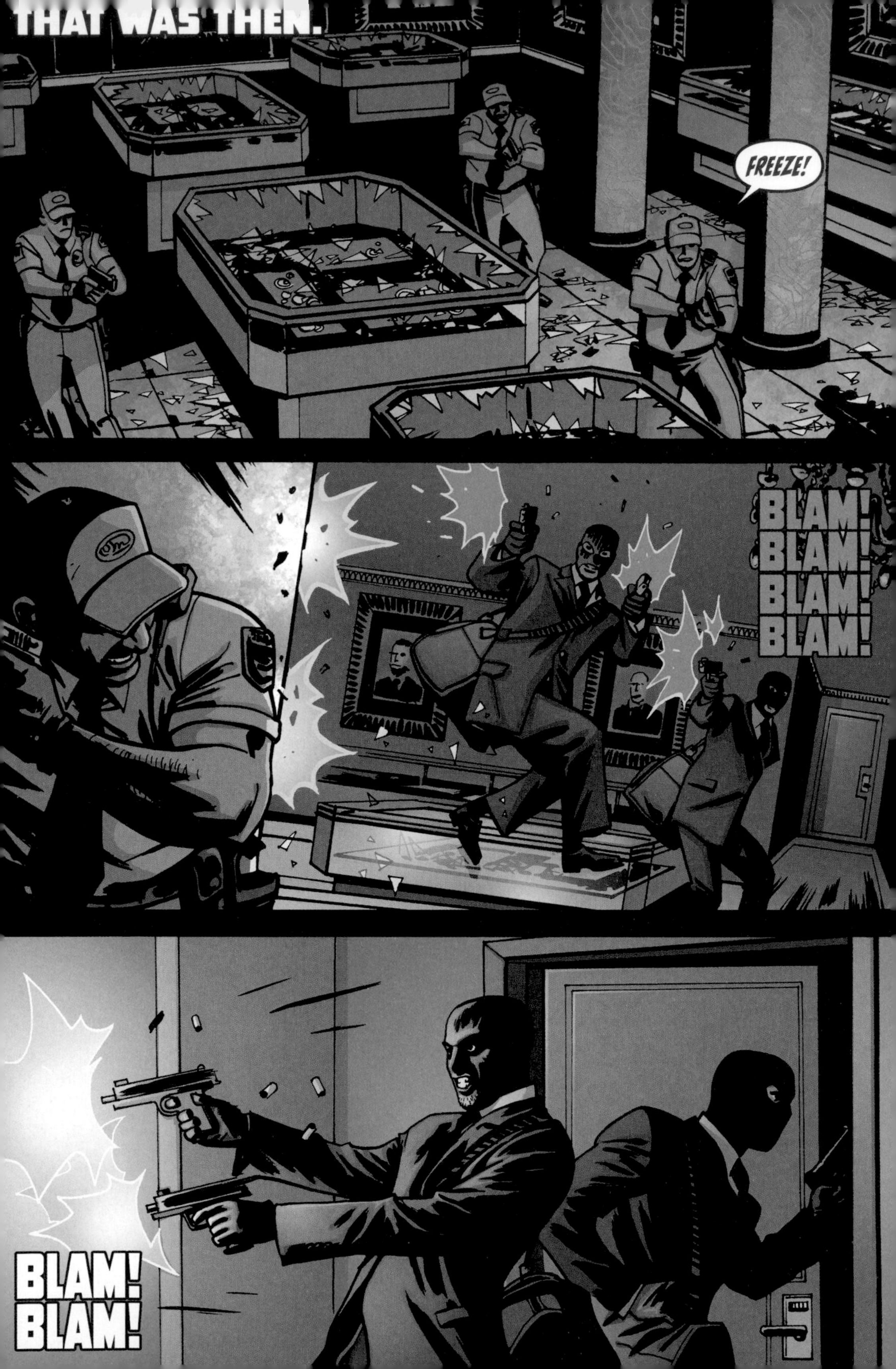
THAT WAS THEN.
FREEZE!
BLAM! BLAM! BLAM! BLAM!
BLAM! BLAM!

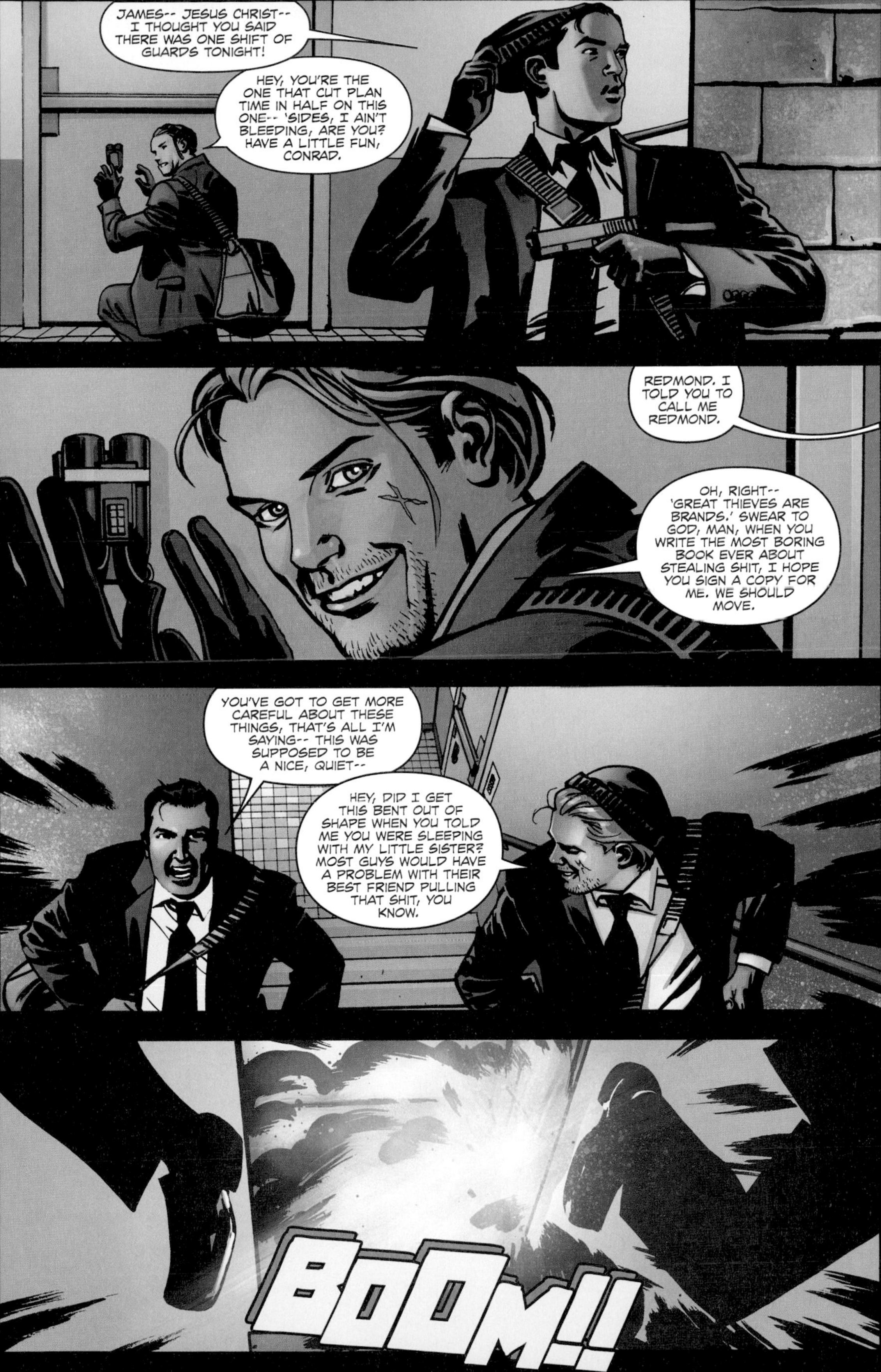
JAMES-- JESUS CHRIST-- I THOUGHT YOU SAID THERE WAS ONE SHIFT OF GUARDS TONIGHT!
HEY, YOU'RE THE ONE THAT CUT PLAN TIME IN HALF ON THIS ONE-- 'SIDES, I AIN'T BLEEDING, ARE YOU? HAVE A LITTLE FUN, CONRAD.
REDMOND. I TOLD YOU TO CALL ME REDMOND.
OH, RIGHT-- 'GREAT THIEVES ARE BRANDS.' SWEAR TO GOD, MAN, WHEN YOU WRITE THE MOST BORING BOOK EVER ABOUT STEALING SHIT, I HOPE YOU SIGN A COPY FOR ME. WE SHOULD MOVE.
YOU'VE GOT TO GET MORE CAREFUL ABOUT THESE THINGS, THAT'S ALL I'M SAYING-- THIS WAS SUPPOSED TO BE A NICE, QUIET--
HEY, DID I GET THIS BENT OUT OF SHAPE WHEN YOU TOLD ME YOU WERE SLEEPING WITH MY LITTLE SISTER? MOST GUYS WOULD HAVE A PROBLEM WITH THEIR BEST FRIEND PULLING THAT SHIT, YOU KNOW.
BOOM!!

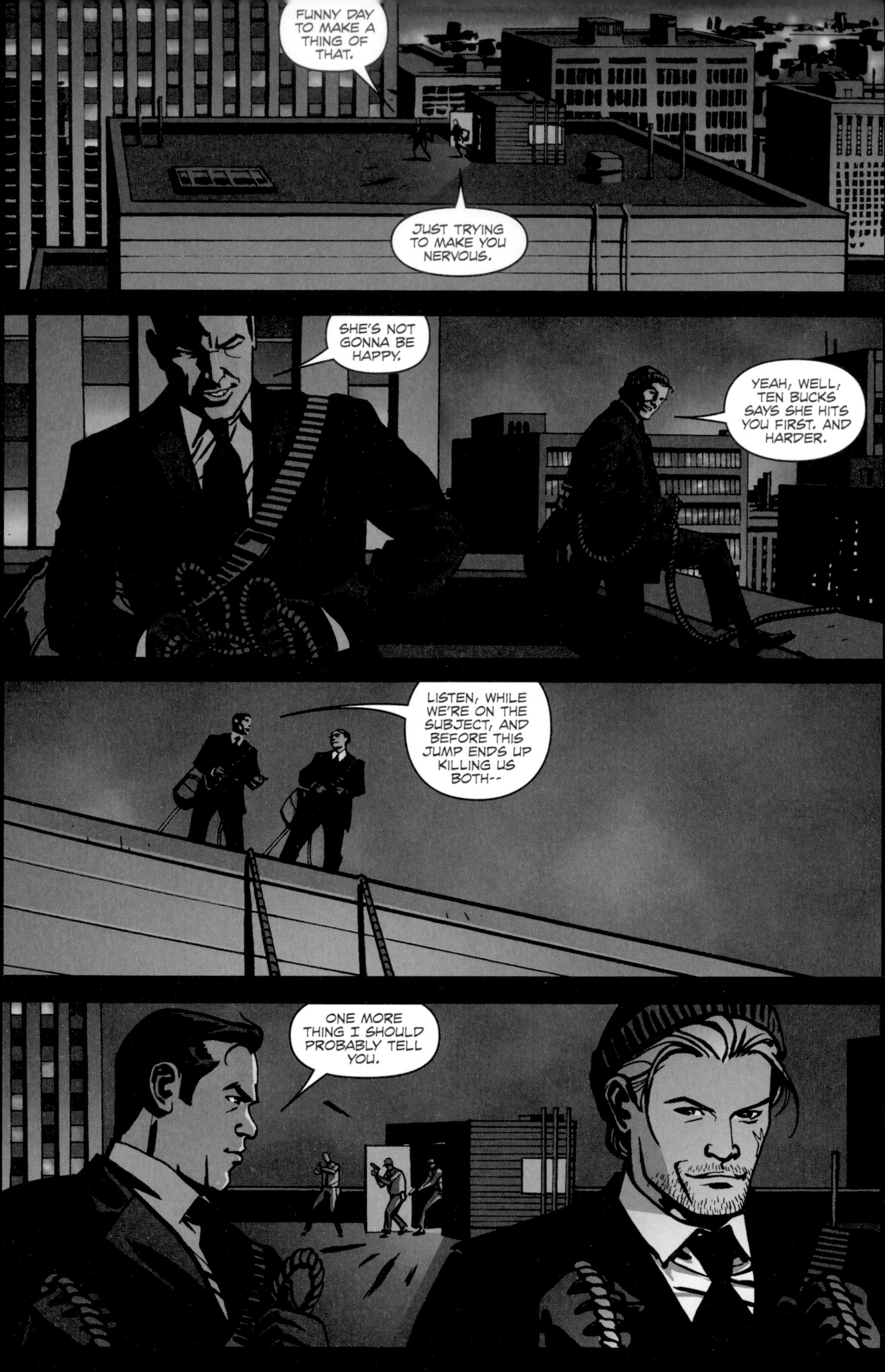
FUNNY DAY TO MAKE A THING OF THAT.
JUST TRYING TO MAKE YOU NERVOUS.
SHE'S NOT GONNA BE HAPPY.
YEAH, WELL, TEN BUCKS SAYS SHE HITS YOU FIRST. AND HARDER.
LISTEN, WHILE WE'RE ON THE SUBJECT, AND BEFORE THIS JUMP ENDS UP KILLING US BOTH--
ONE MORE THING I SHOULD PROBABLY TELL YOU.

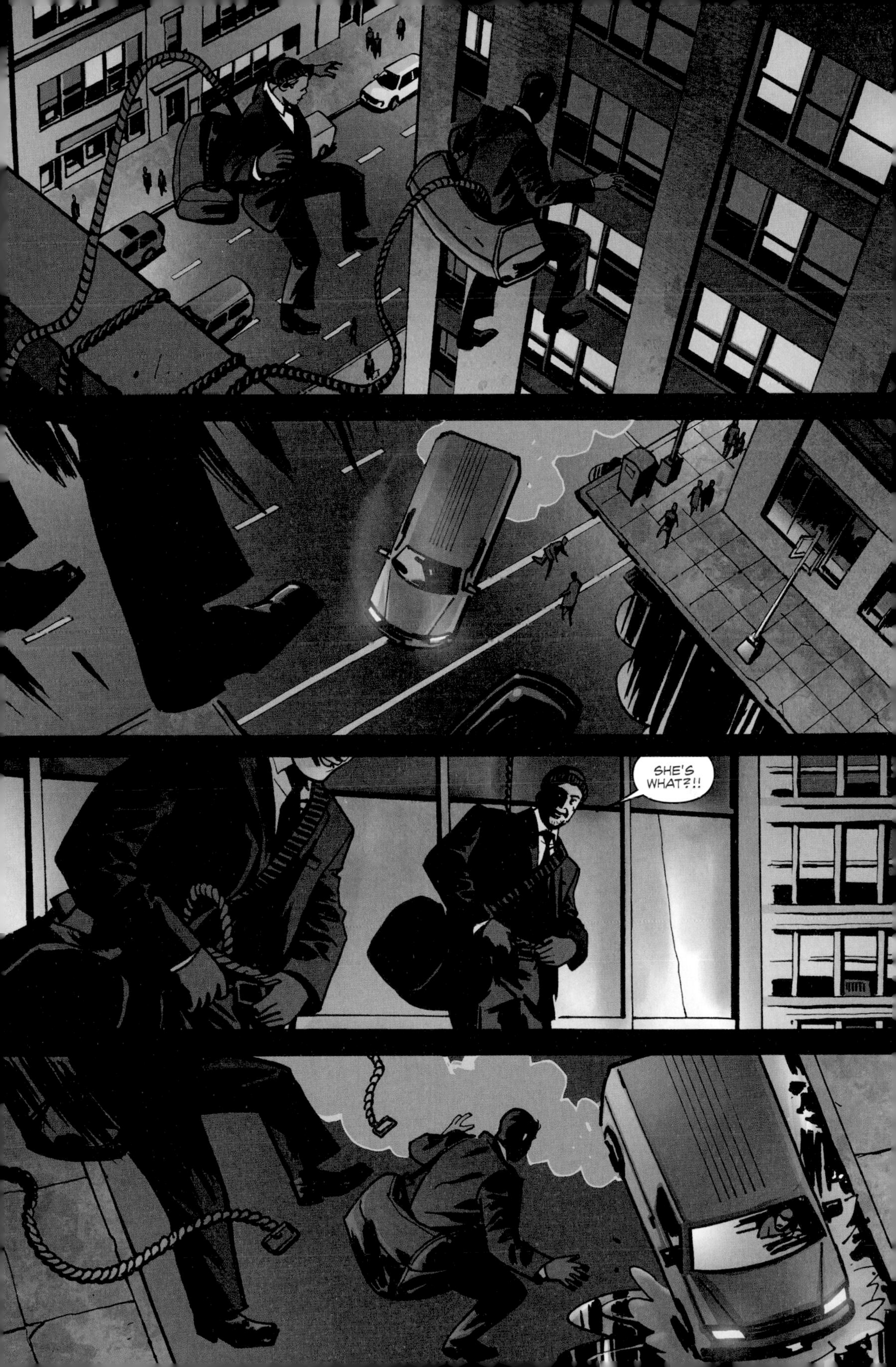
SHE'S WHAT?!!

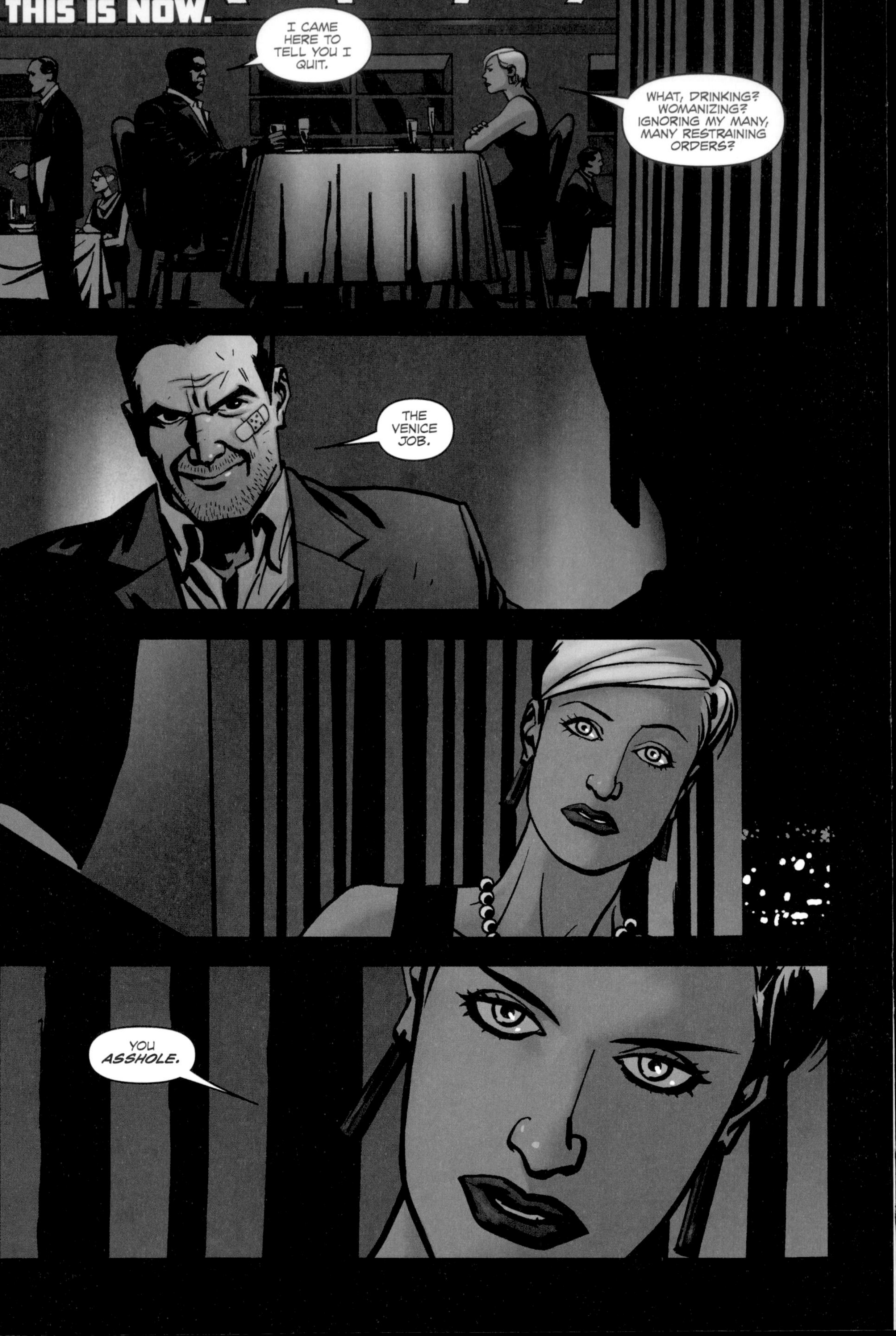
THIS IS NOW.
I CAME HERE TO TELL YOU I QUIT.
WHAT, DRINKING? WOMANIZING? IGNORING MY MANY, MANY RESTRAINING ORDERS?
THE VENICE JOB.
YOU ASSHOLE.

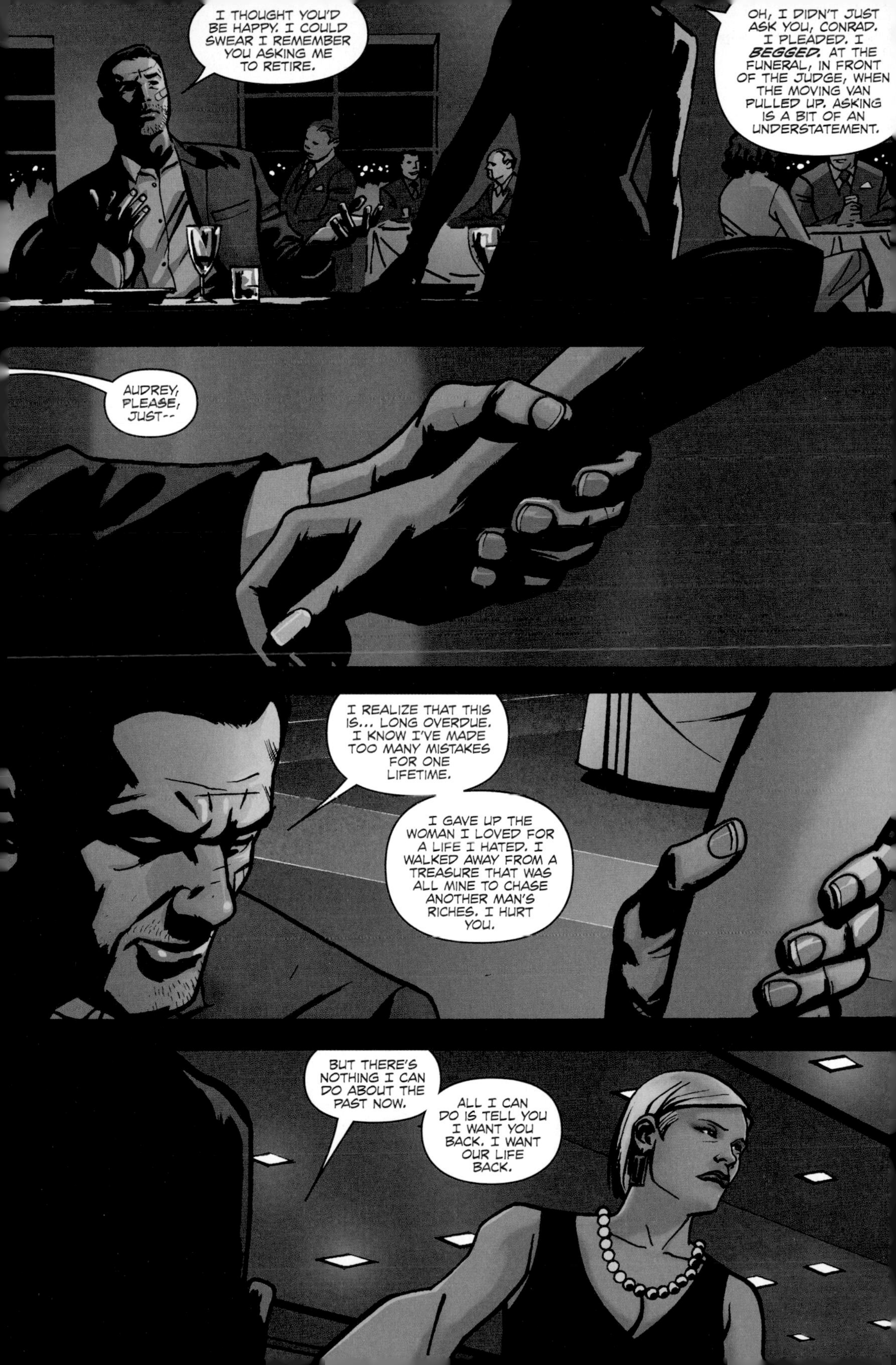
I THOUGHT YOU'D BE HAPPY. I COULD SWEAR I REMEMBER YOU ASKING ME TO RETIRE.
OH, I DIDN'T JUST ASK YOU, CONRAD. I PLEADED. I *BEGGED*. AT THE FUNERAL, IN FRONT OF THE JUDGE, WHEN THE MOVING VAN PULLED UP. ASKING IS A BIT OF AN UNDERSTATEMENT.
AUDREY, PLEASE, JUST--
I REALIZE THAT THIS IS... LONG OVERDUE. I KNOW I'VE MADE TOO MANY MISTAKES FOR ONE LIFETIME.
I GAVE UP THE WOMAN I LOVED FOR A LIFE I HATED. I WALKED AWAY FROM A TREASURE THAT WAS ALL MINE TO CHASE ANOTHER MAN'S RICHES. I HURT YOU.
BUT THERE'S NOTHING I CAN DO ABOUT THE PAST NOW.
ALL I CAN DO IS TELL YOU I WANT YOU BACK. I WANT OUR LIFE BACK.

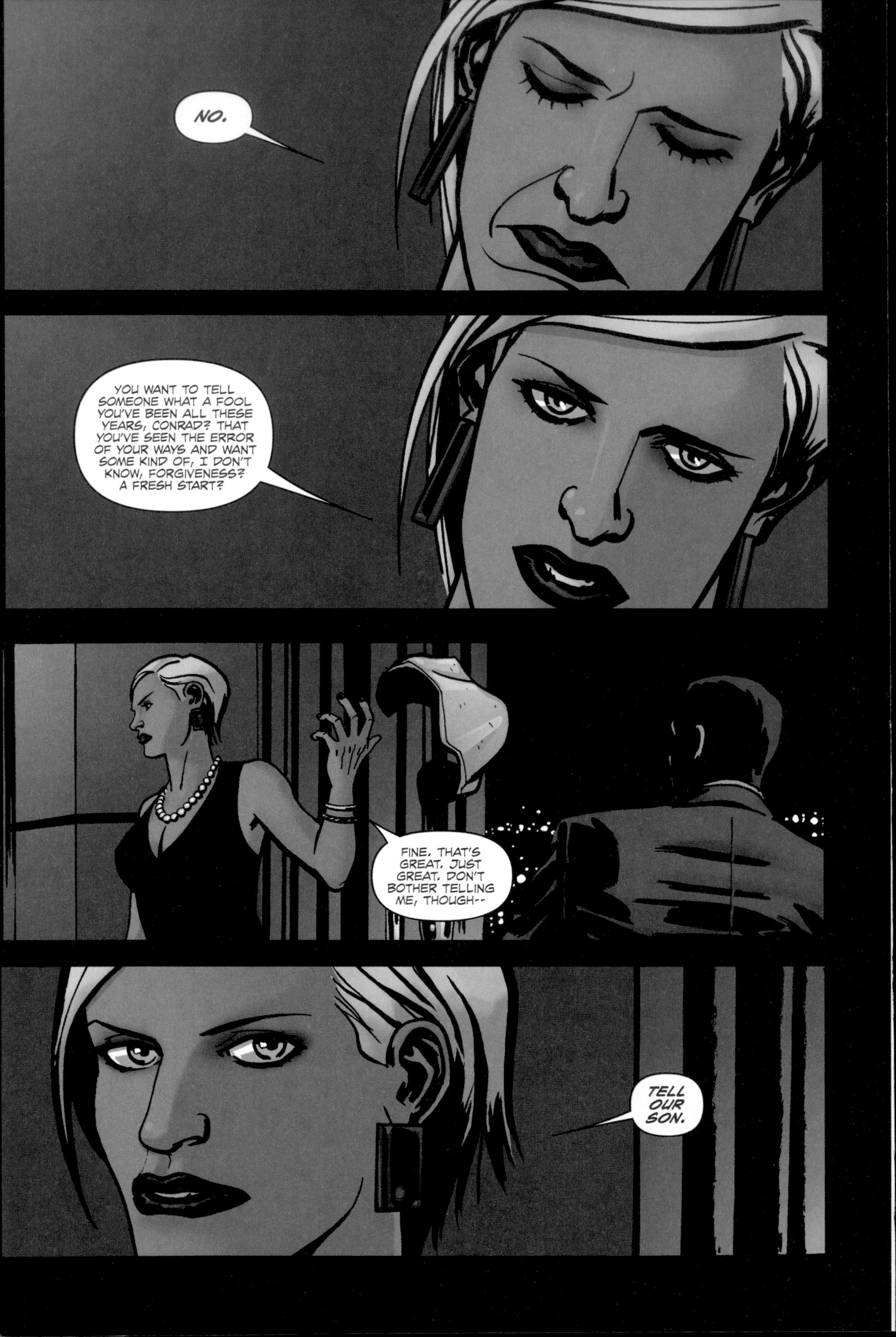
NO.
YOU WANT TO TELL SOMEONE WHAT A FOOL YOU'VE BEEN ALL THESE YEARS, CONRAD? THAT YOU'VE SEEN THE ERROR OF YOUR WAYS AND WANT SOME KIND OF, I DON'T KNOW, FORGIVENESS? A FRESH START?
FINE. THAT'S GREAT. JUST GREAT. DON'T BOTHER TELLING ME, THOUGH--
TELL OUR SON.

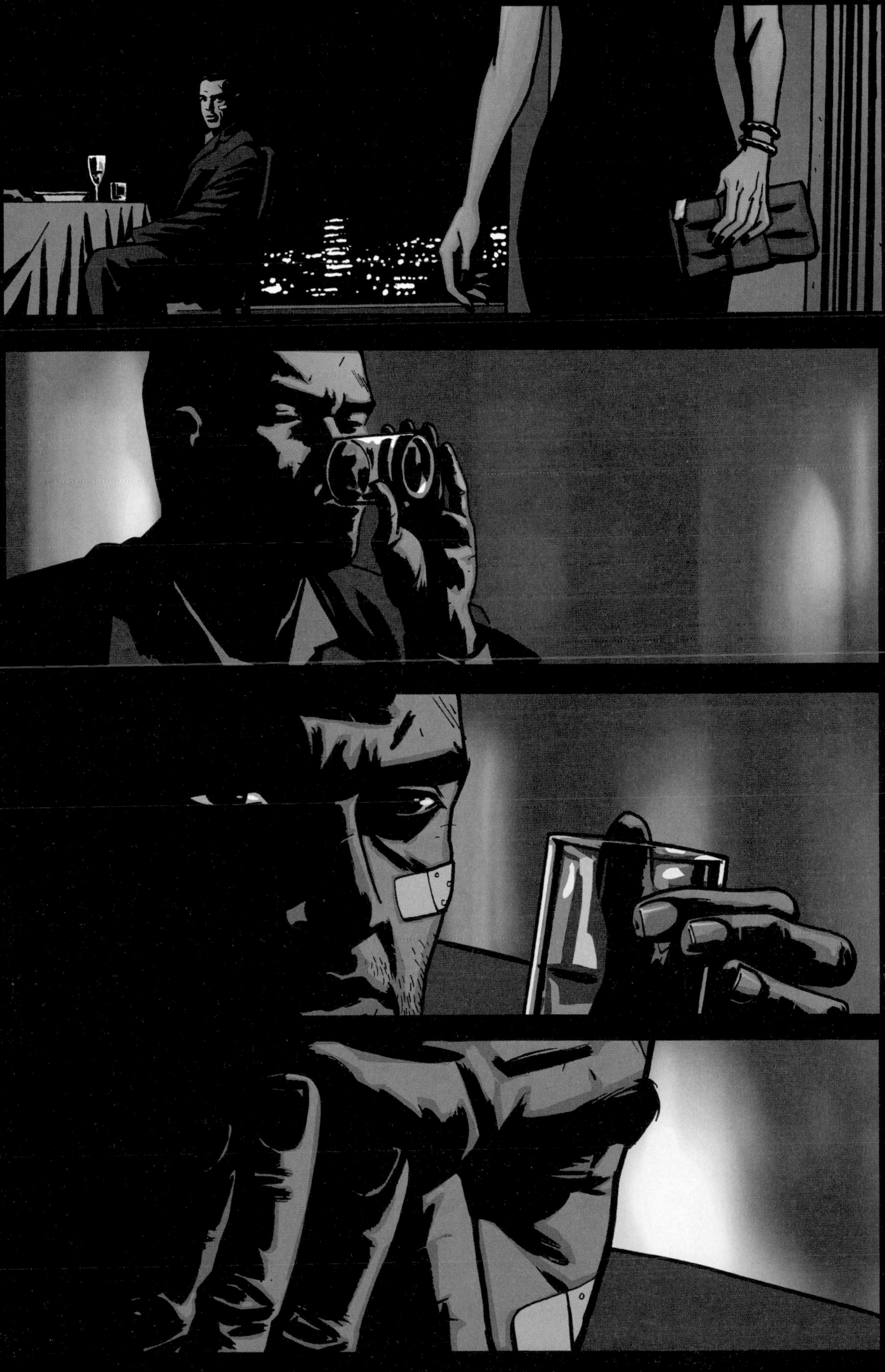

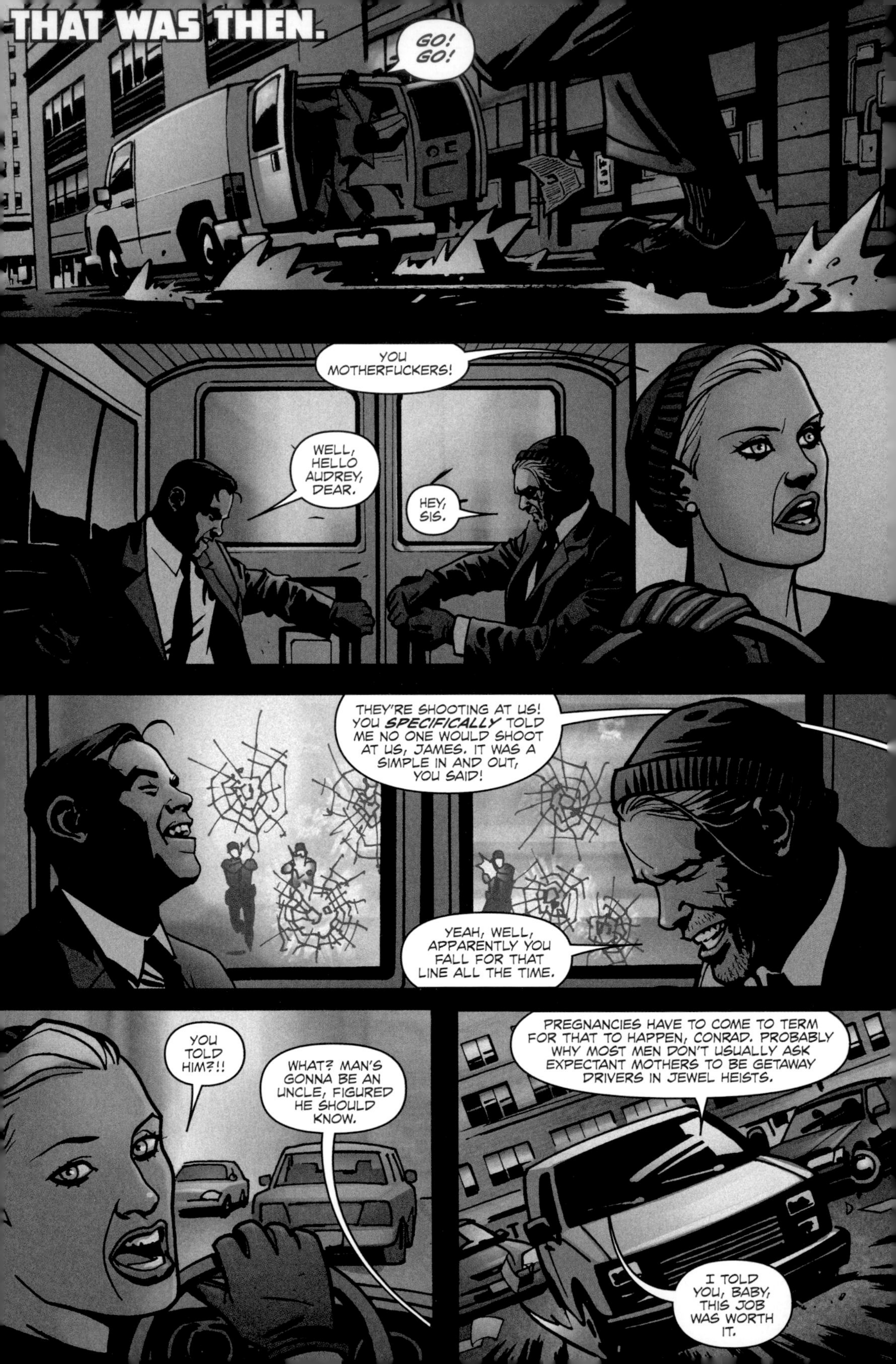
THAT WAS THEN.
GO! GO!
YOU MOTHERFUCKERS!
WELL, HELLO AUDREY, DEAR.
HEY, SIS.
THEY'RE SHOOTING AT US! YOU SPECIFICALLY TOLD ME NO ONE WOULD SHOOT AT US, JAMES. IT WAS A SIMPLE IN AND OUT, YOU SAID!
YEAH, WELL, APPARENTLY YOU FALL FOR THAT LINE ALL THE TIME.
YOU TOLD HIM?!!
WHAT? MAN'S GONNA BE AN UNCLE, FIGURED HE SHOULD KNOW.
PREGNANCIES HAVE TO COME TO TERM FOR THAT TO HAPPEN, CONRAD. PROBABLY WHY MOST MEN DON'T USUALLY ASK EXPECTANT MOTHERS TO BE GETAWAY DRIVERS IN JEWEL HEISTS.
I TOLD YOU, BABY, THIS JOB WAS WORTH IT.

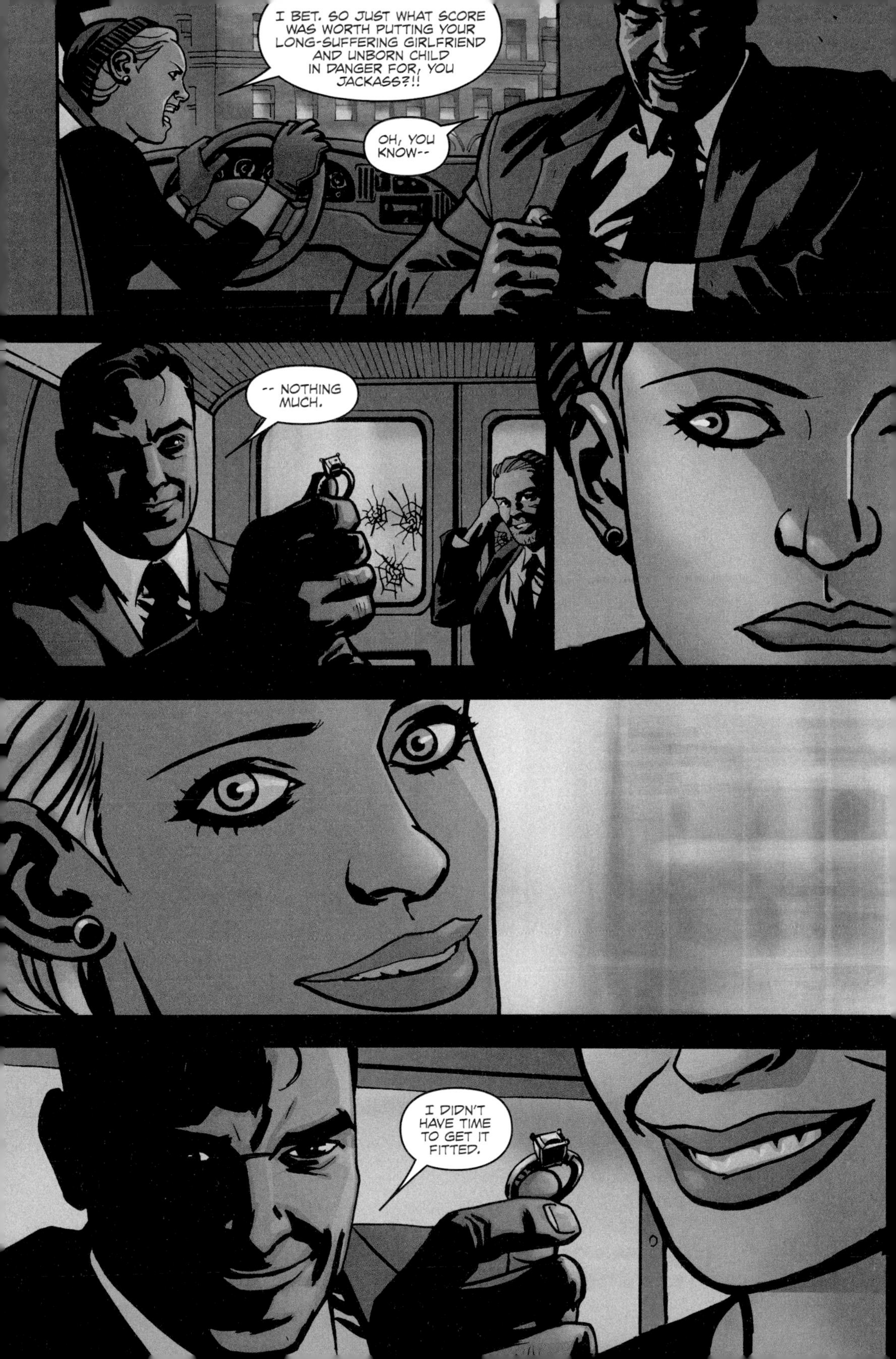
I BET. SO JUST WHAT SCORE WAS WORTH PUTTING YOUR LONG-SUFFERING GIRLFRIEND AND UNBORN CHILD IN DANGER FOR, YOU JACKASS?!!
OH, YOU KNOW--
-- NOTHING MUCH.
I DIDN'T HAVE TIME TO GET IT FITTED.

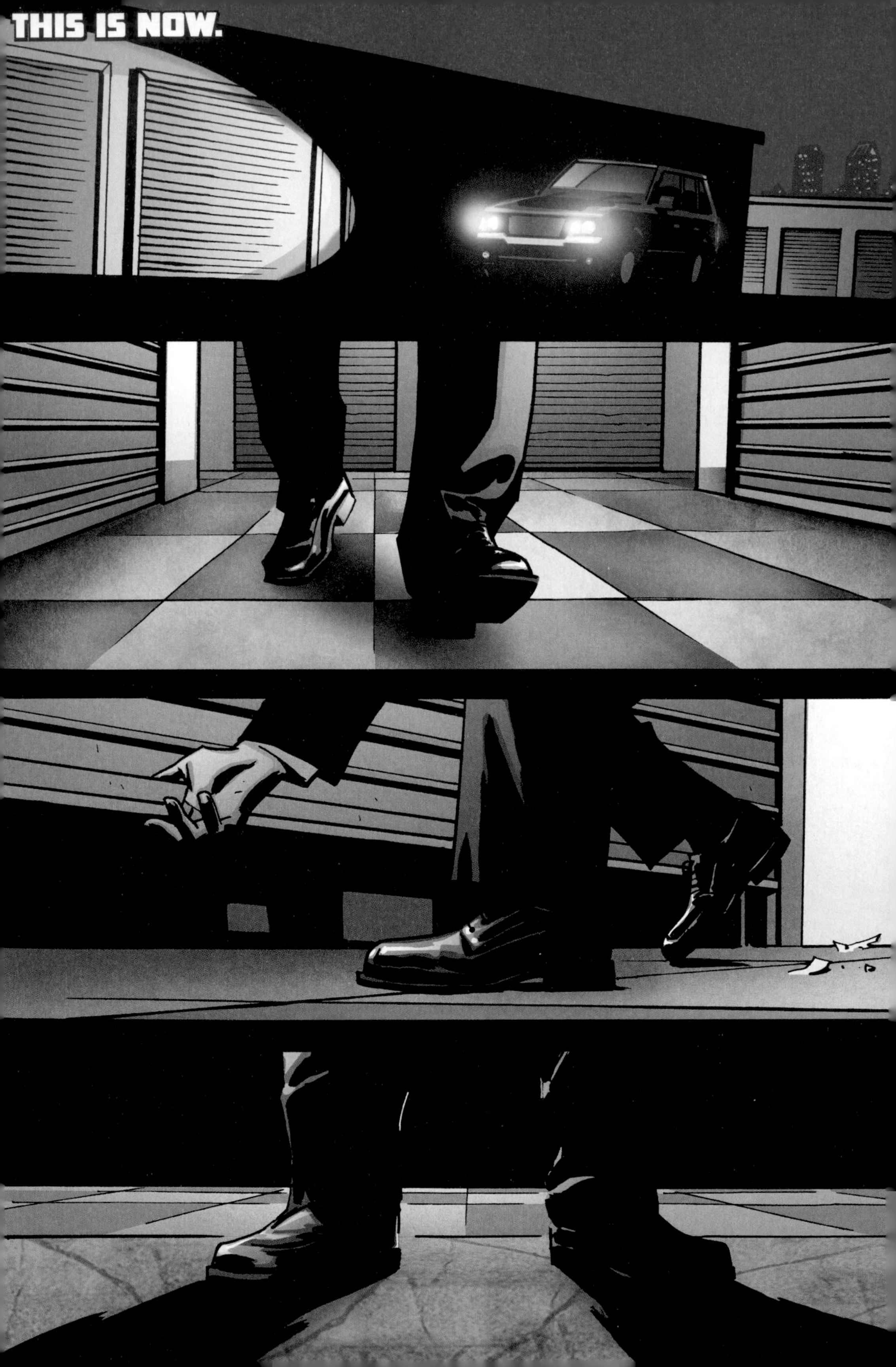
THIS IS NOW.

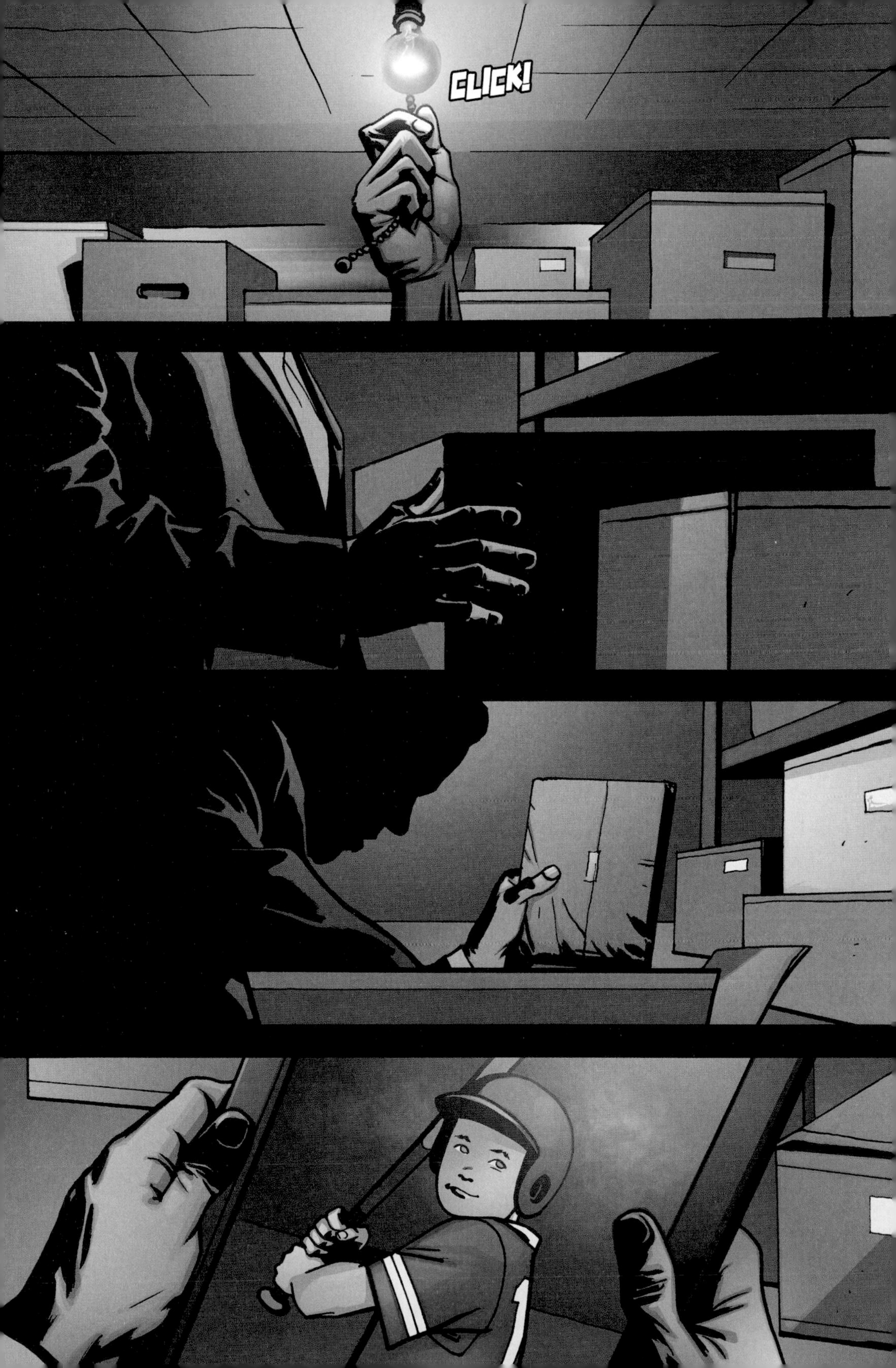
CLICK!

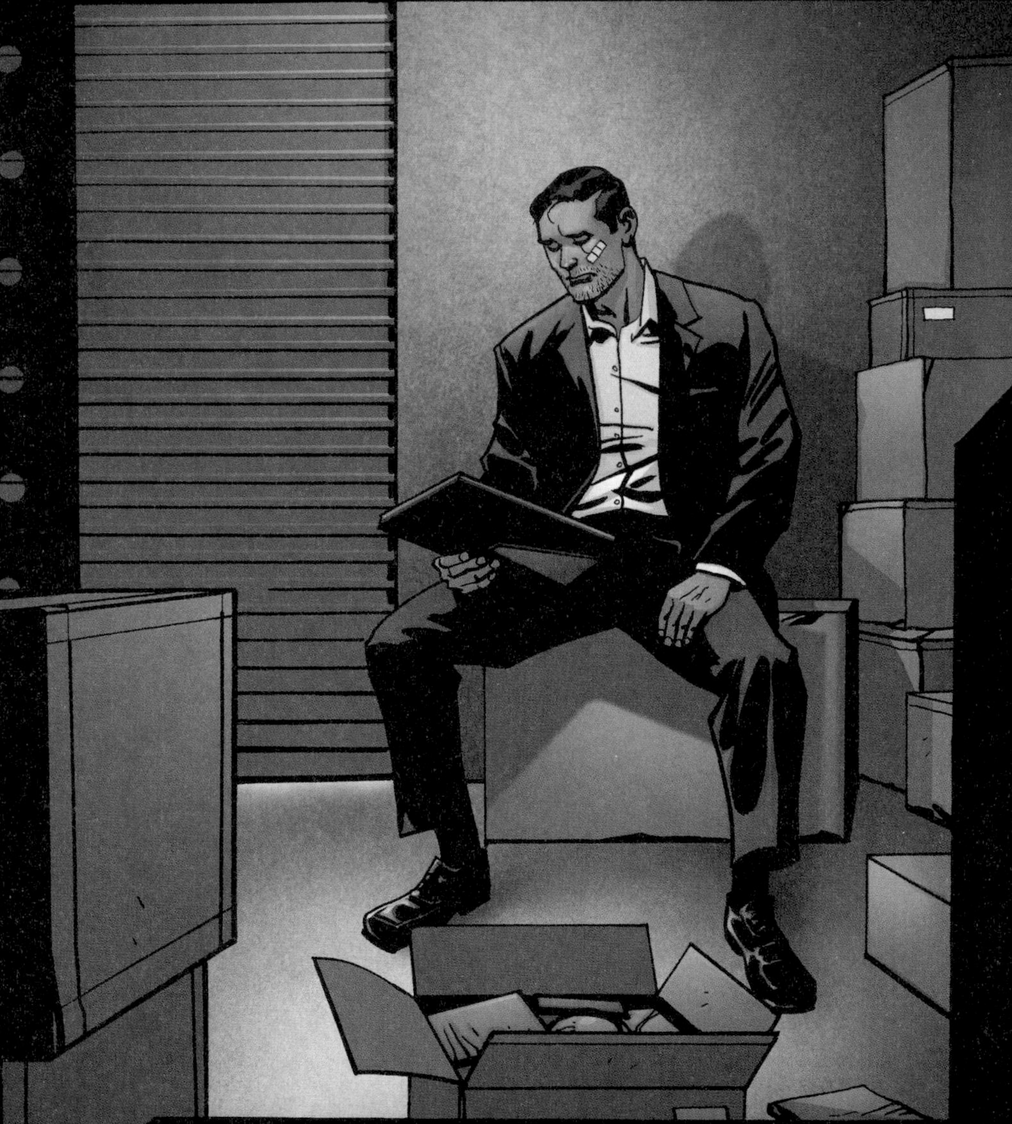

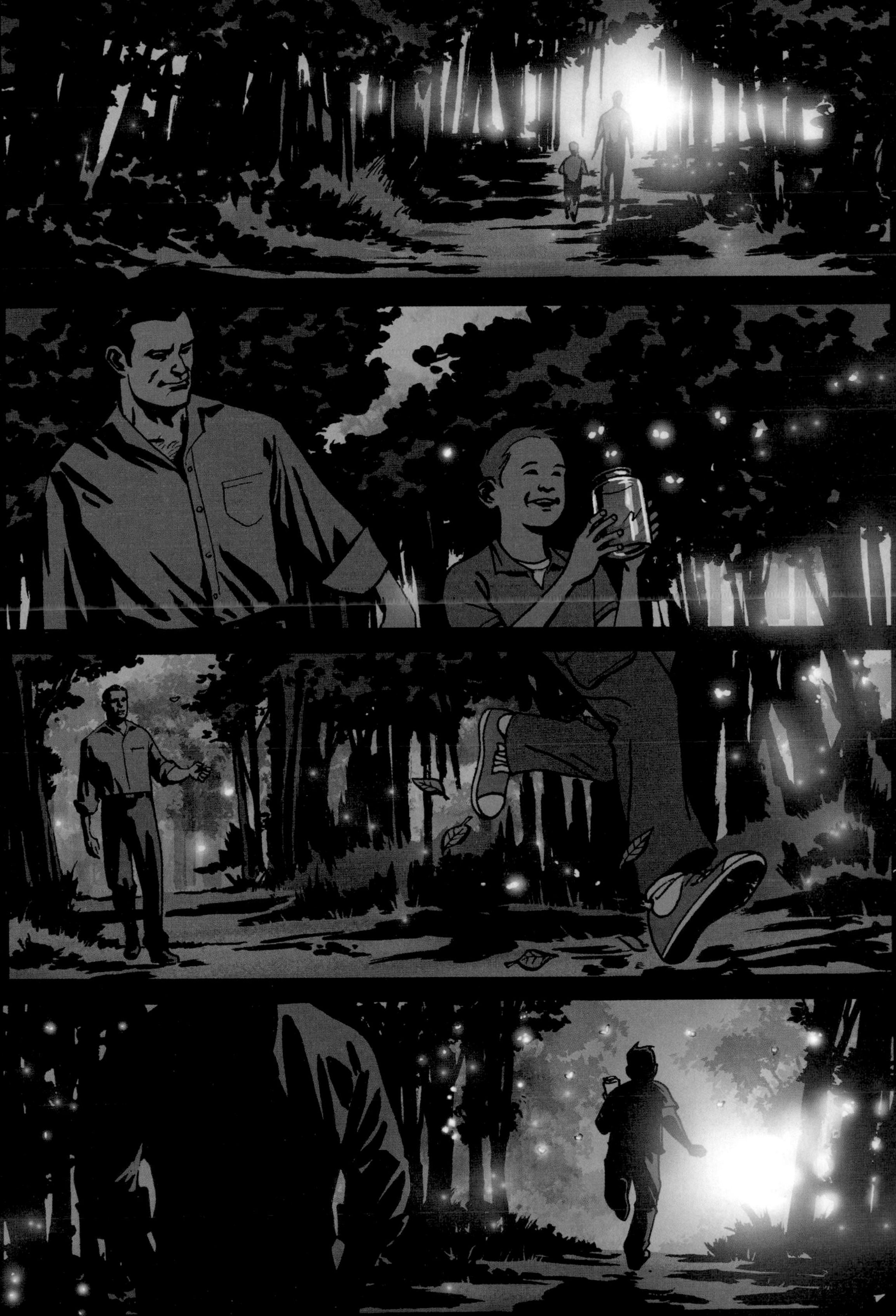

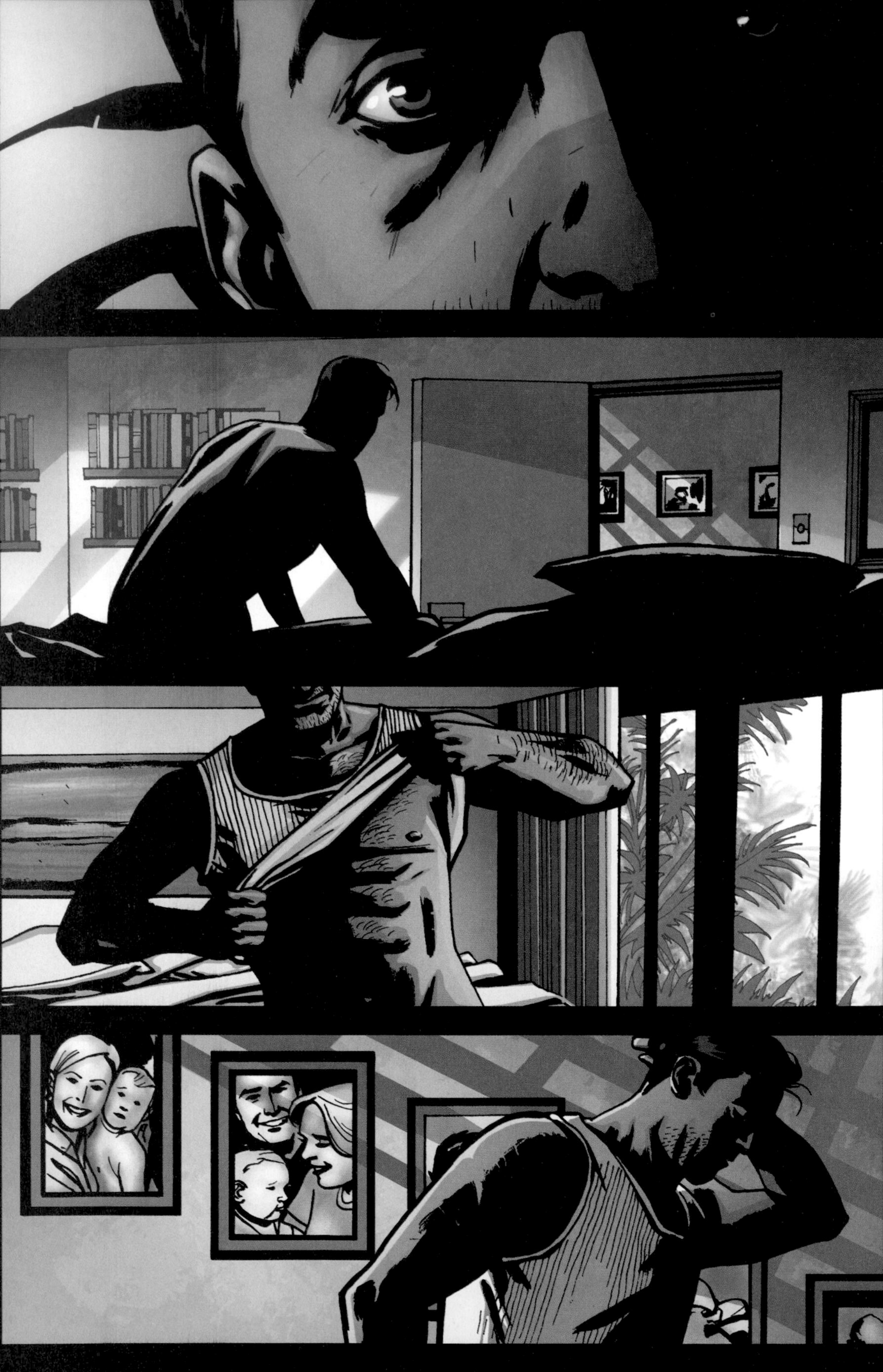

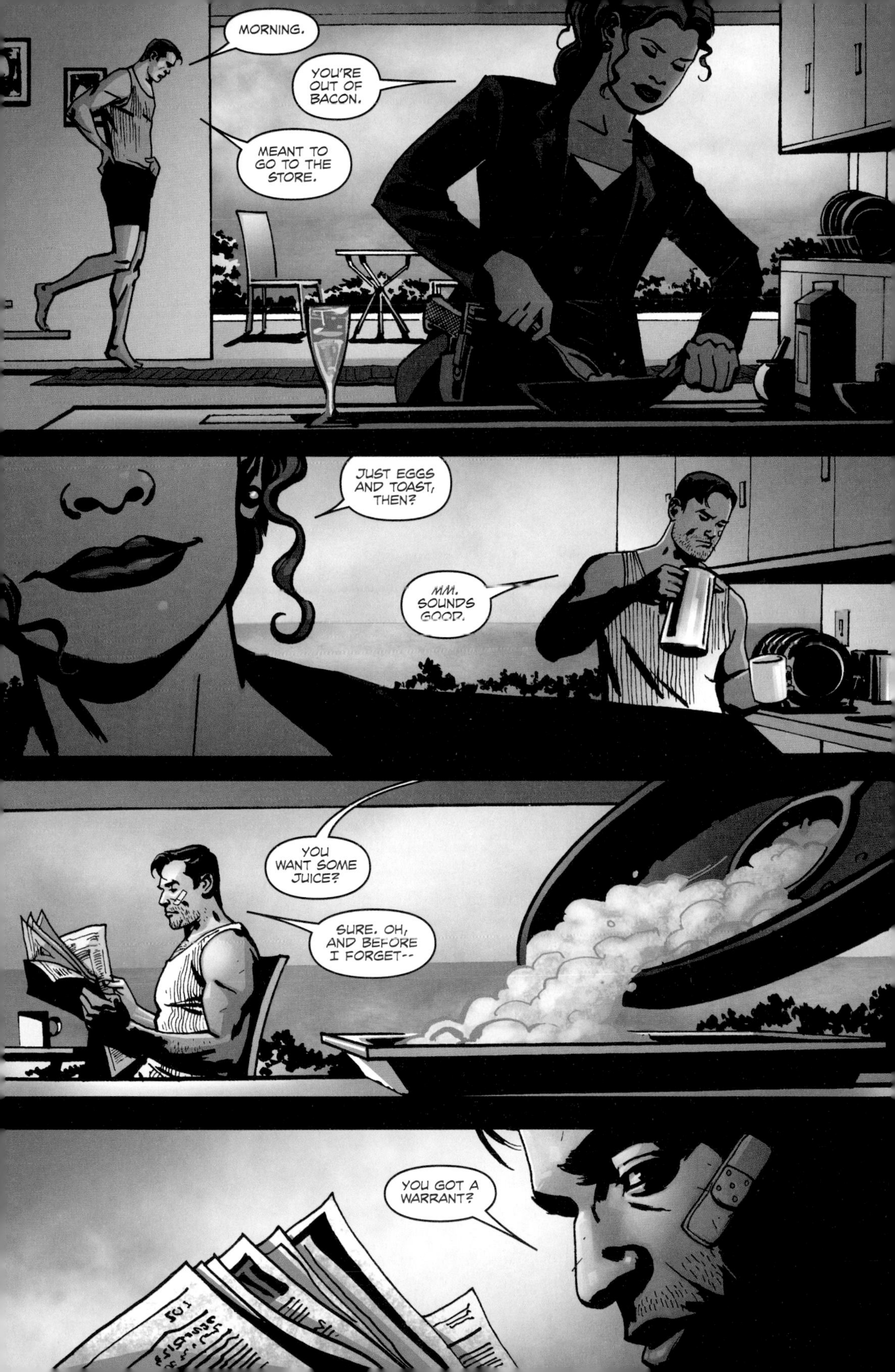
MORNING.
YOU'RE OUT OF BACON.
MEANT TO GO TO THE STORE.
JUST EGGS AND TOAST, THEN?
MM. SOUNDS GOOD.
YOU WANT SOME JUICE?
SURE. OH, AND BEFORE I FORGET--
YOU GOT A WARRANT?

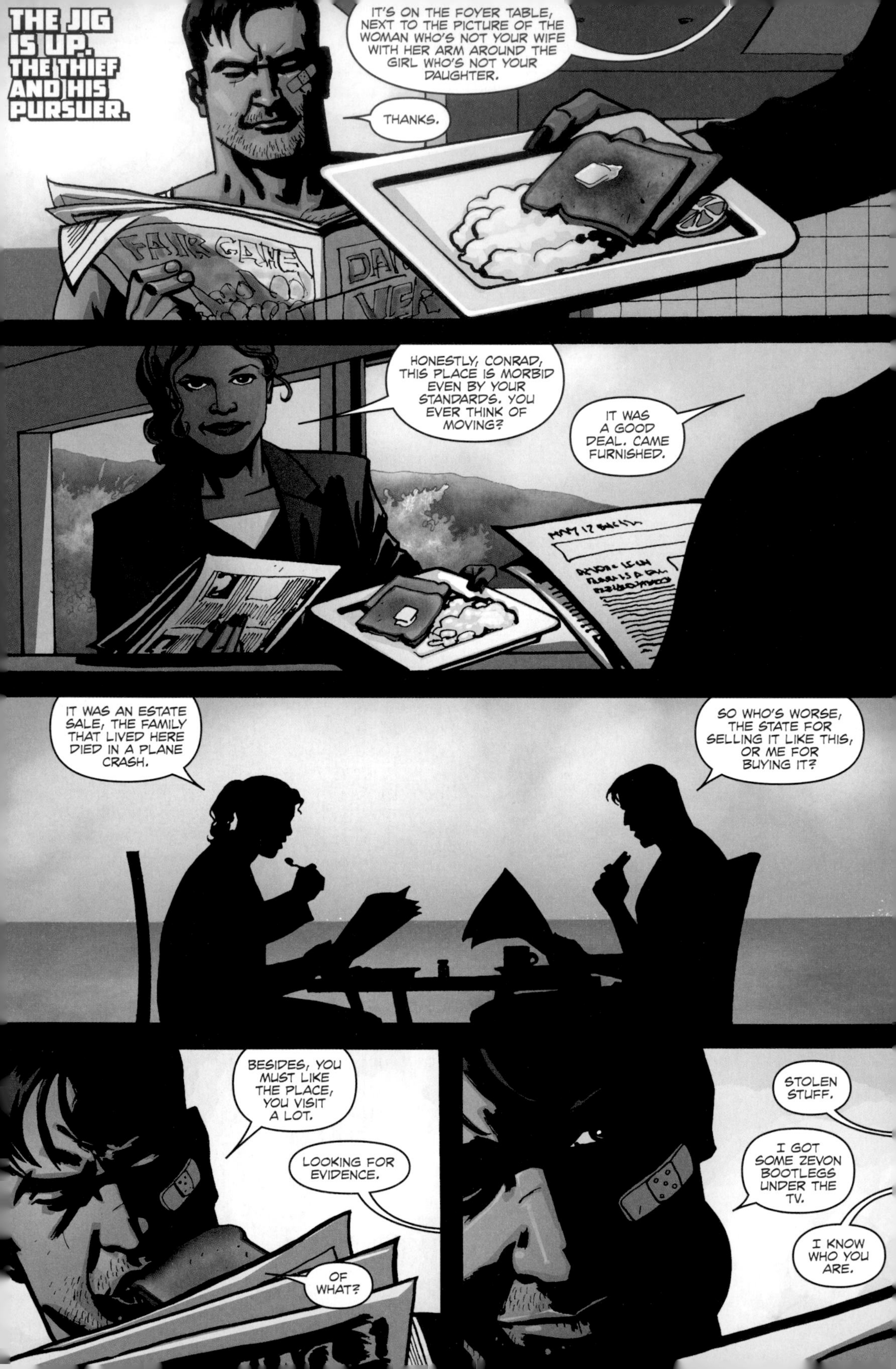
THE JIG IS UP. THE THIEF AND HIS PURSUER.
IT'S ON THE FOYER TABLE, NEXT TO THE PICTURE OF THE WOMAN WHO'S NOT YOUR WIFE WITH HER ARM AROUND THE GIRL WHO'S NOT YOUR DAUGHTER.
THANKS.
HONESTLY, CONRAD, THIS PLACE IS MORBID EVEN BY YOUR STANDARDS. YOU EVER THINK OF MOVING?
IT WAS A GOOD DEAL. CAME FURNISHED.
IT WAS AN ESTATE SALE, THE FAMILY THAT LIVED HERE DIED IN A PLANE CRASH.
SO WHO'S WORSE, THE STATE FOR SELLING IT LIKE THIS, OR ME FOR BUYING IT?
BESIDES, YOU MUST LIKE THE PLACE, YOU VISIT A LOT.
LOOKING FOR EVIDENCE.
OF WHAT?
STOLEN STUFF.
I GOT SOME ZEVON BOOTLEGS UNDER THE TV.
I KNOW WHO YOU ARE.

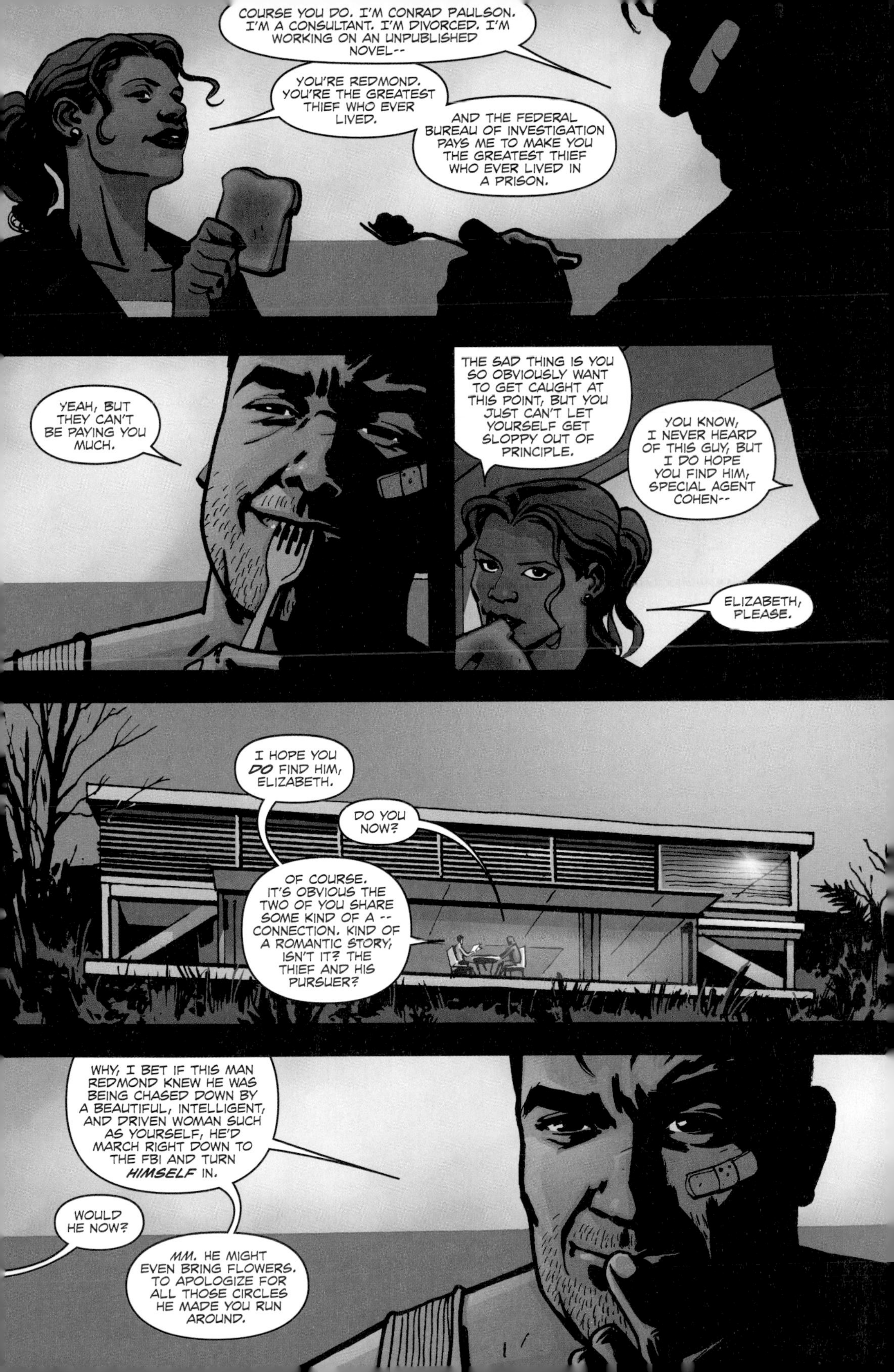
COURSE YOU DO. I'M CONRAD PAULSON. I'M A CONSULTANT. I'M DIVORCED. I'M WORKING ON AN UNPUBLISHED NOVEL--
YOU'RE REDMOND. YOU'RE THE GREATEST THIEF WHO EVER LIVED.
AND THE FEDERAL BUREAU OF INVESTIGATION PAYS ME TO MAKE YOU THE GREATEST THIEF WHO EVER LIVED IN A PRISON.
YEAH, BUT THEY CAN'T BE PAYING YOU MUCH.
THE SAD THING IS YOU SO OBVIOUSLY WANT TO GET CAUGHT AT THIS POINT, BUT YOU JUST CAN'T LET YOURSELF GET SLOPPY OUT OF PRINCIPLE.
YOU KNOW, I NEVER HEARD OF THIS GUY, BUT I DO HOPE YOU FIND HIM, SPECIAL AGENT COHEN--
ELIZABETH, PLEASE.
I HOPE YOU *DO* FIND HIM, ELIZABETH.
DO YOU NOW?
OF COURSE. IT'S OBVIOUS THE TWO OF YOU SHARE SOME KIND OF A -- CONNECTION. KIND OF A ROMANTIC STORY, ISN'T IT? THE THIEF AND HIS PURSUER?
WHY, I BET IF THIS MAN REDMOND KNEW HE WAS BEING CHASED DOWN BY A BEAUTIFUL, INTELLIGENT, AND DRIVEN WOMAN SUCH AS YOURSELF, HE'D MARCH RIGHT DOWN TO THE FBI AND TURN *HIMSELF* IN.
WOULD HE NOW?
MM. HE MIGHT EVEN BRING FLOWERS. TO APOLOGIZE FOR ALL THOSE CIRCLES HE MADE YOU RUN AROUND.

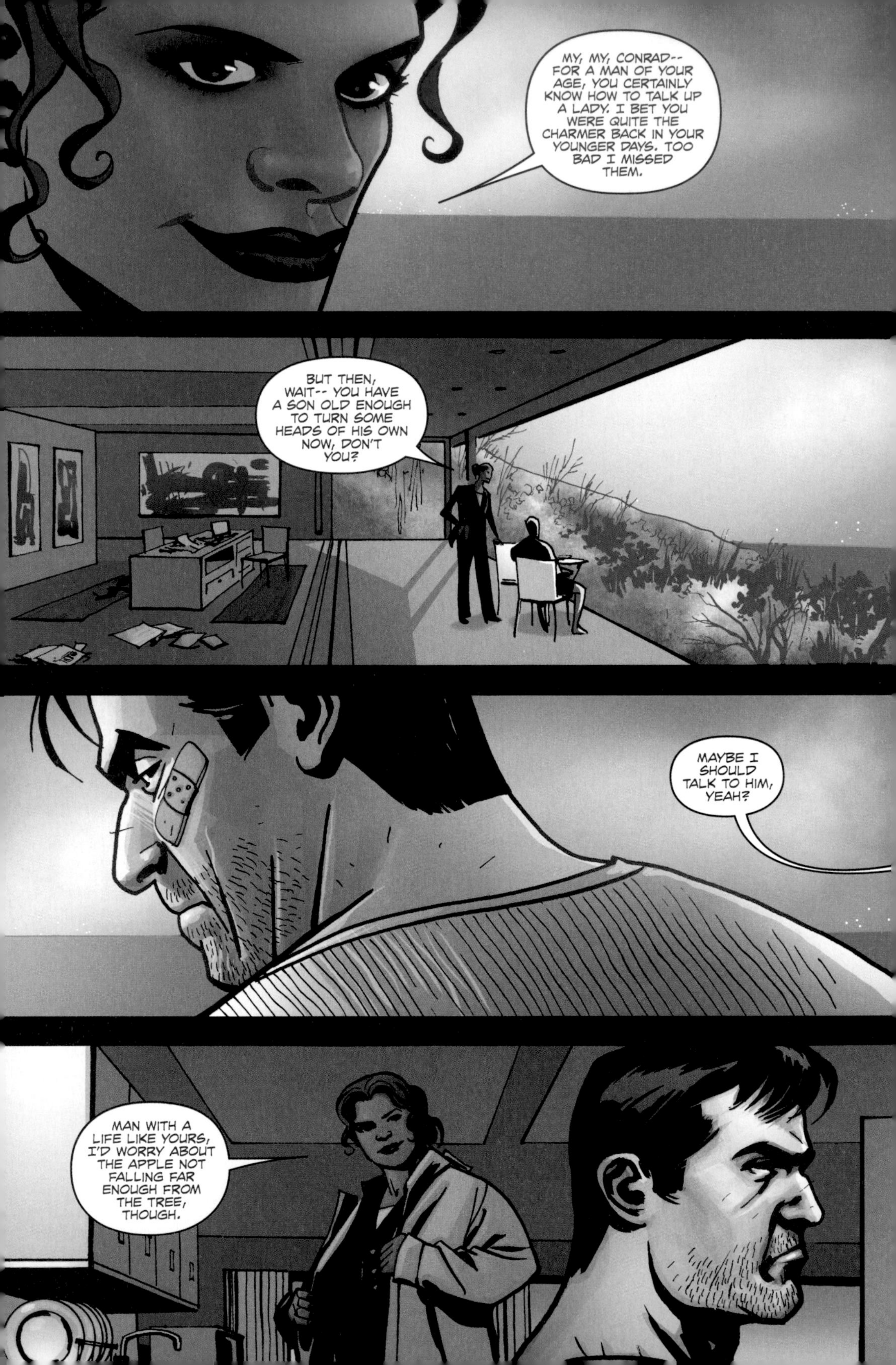
MY, MY, CONRAD-- FOR A MAN OF YOUR AGE, YOU CERTAINLY KNOW HOW TO TALK UP A LADY. I BET YOU WERE QUITE THE CHARMER BACK IN YOUR YOUNGER DAYS. TOO BAD I MISSED THEM.
BUT THEN, WAIT-- YOU HAVE A SON OLD ENOUGH TO TURN SOME HEADS OF HIS OWN NOW, DON'T YOU?
MAYBE I SHOULD TALK TO HIM, YEAH?
MAN WITH A LIFE LIKE YOURS, I'D WORRY ABOUT THE APPLE NOT FALLING FAR ENOUGH FROM THE TREE, THOUGH.

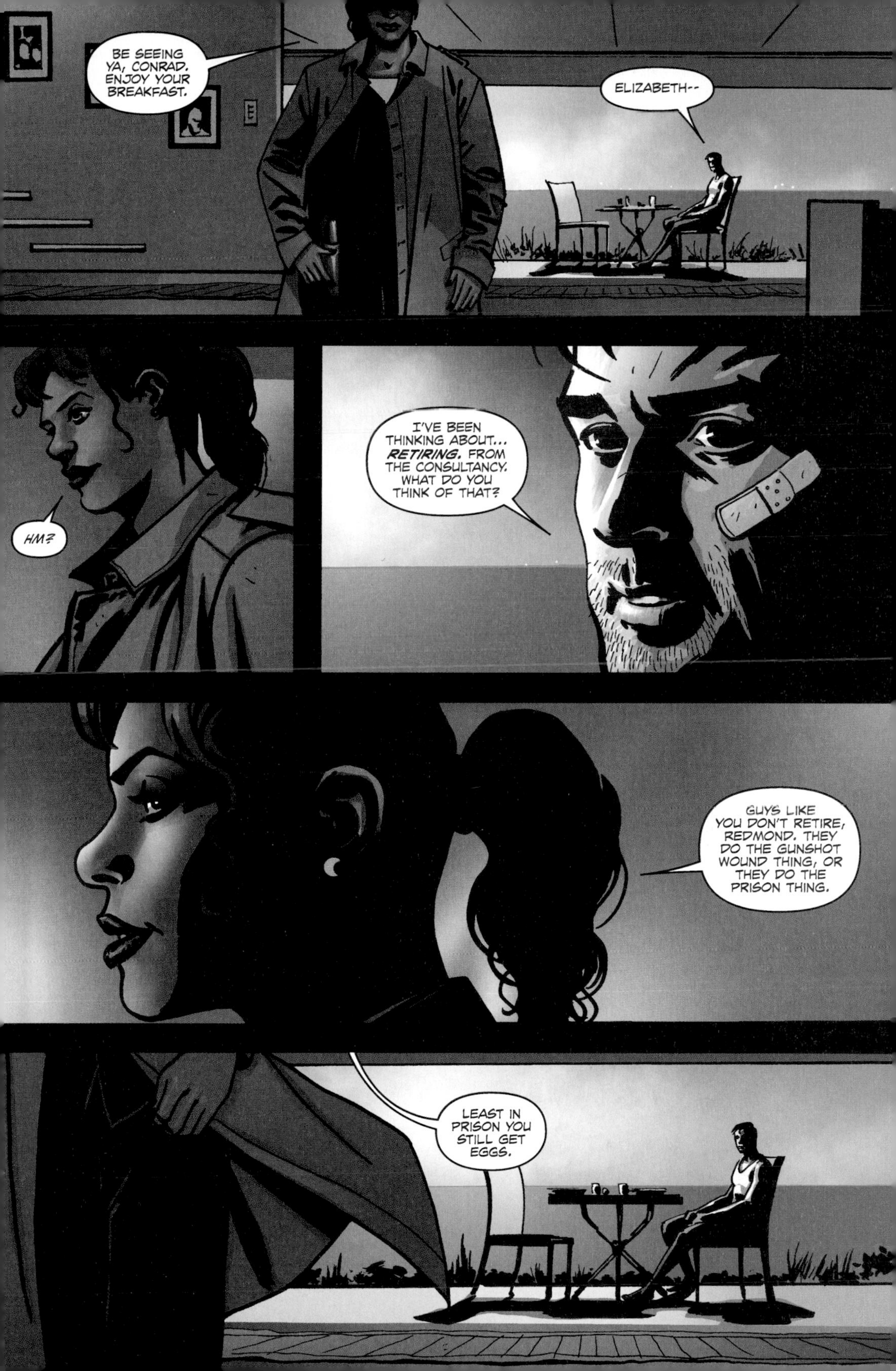
BE SEEING YA, CONRAD. ENJOY YOUR BREAKFAST.
ELIZABETH--
HM?
I'VE BEEN THINKING ABOUT... RETIRING. FROM THE CONSULTANCY. WHAT DO YOU THINK OF THAT?
GUYS LIKE YOU DON'T RETIRE, REDMOND. THEY DO THE GUNSHOT WOUND THING, OR THEY DO THE PRISON THING.
LEAST IN PRISON YOU STILL GET EGGS.

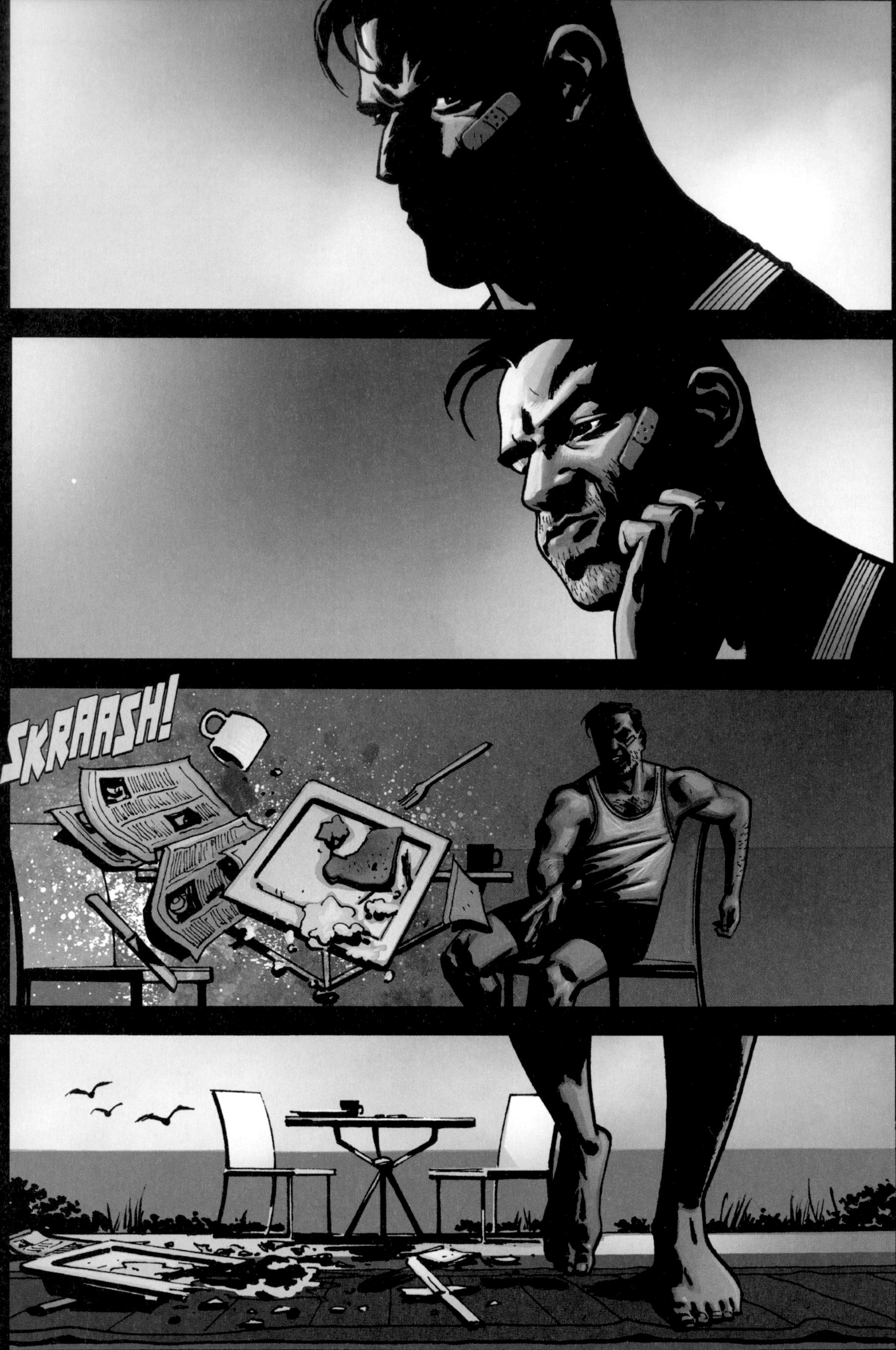
SKRAASH!

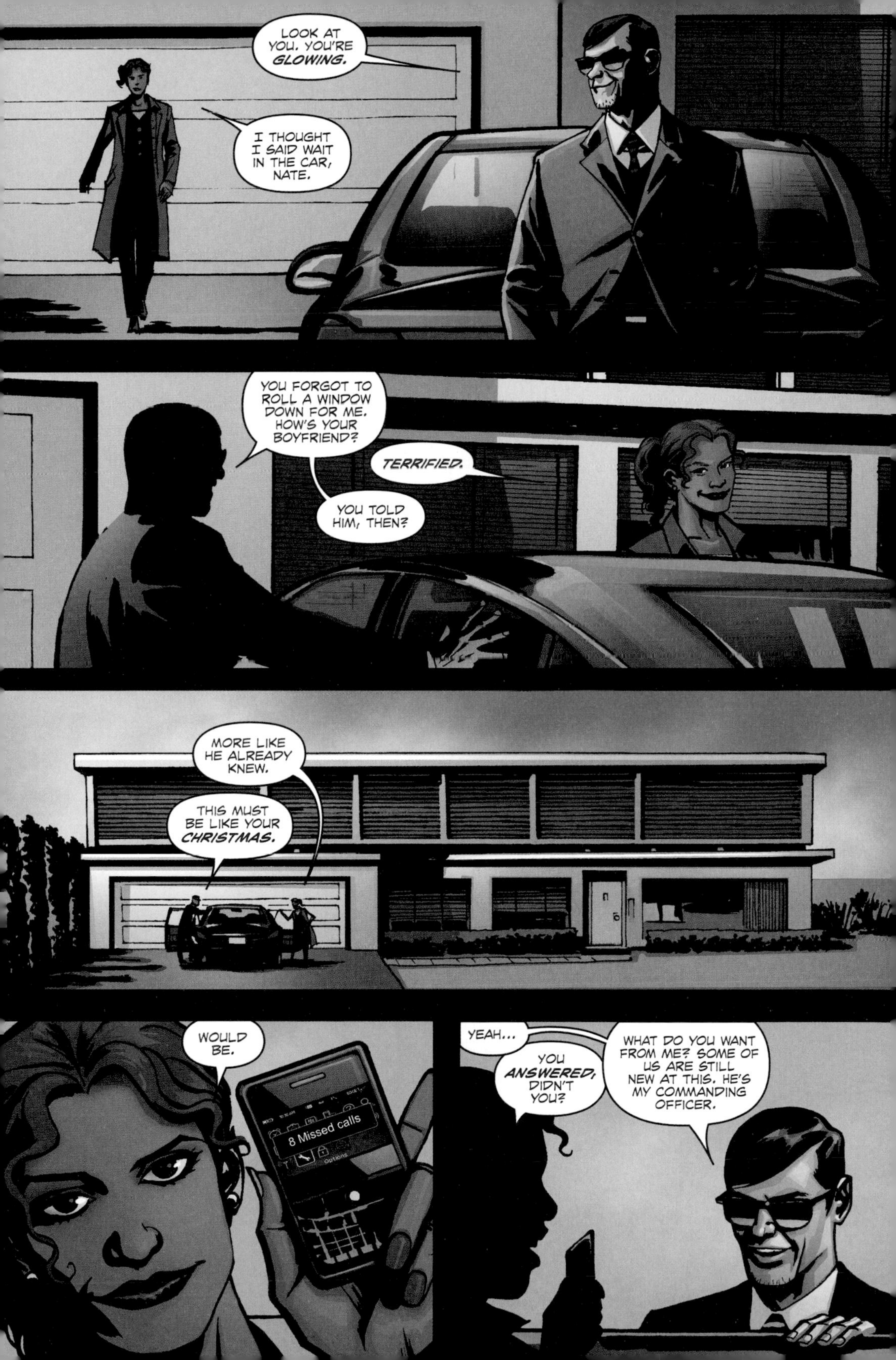
LOOK AT YOU. YOU'RE *GLOWING.*
I THOUGHT I SAID WAIT IN THE CAR, NATE.
YOU FORGOT TO ROLL A WINDOW DOWN FOR ME. HOW'S YOUR BOYFRIEND?
TERRIFIED.
YOU TOLD HIM, THEN?
MORE LIKE HE ALREADY KNEW.
THIS MUST BE LIKE YOUR *CHRISTMAS.*
WOULD BE.
8 Missed calls
Options
YEAH...
YOU *ANSWERED,* DIDN'T YOU?
WHAT DO YOU WANT FROM ME? SOME OF US ARE STILL NEW AT THIS. HE'S MY COMMANDING OFFICER.

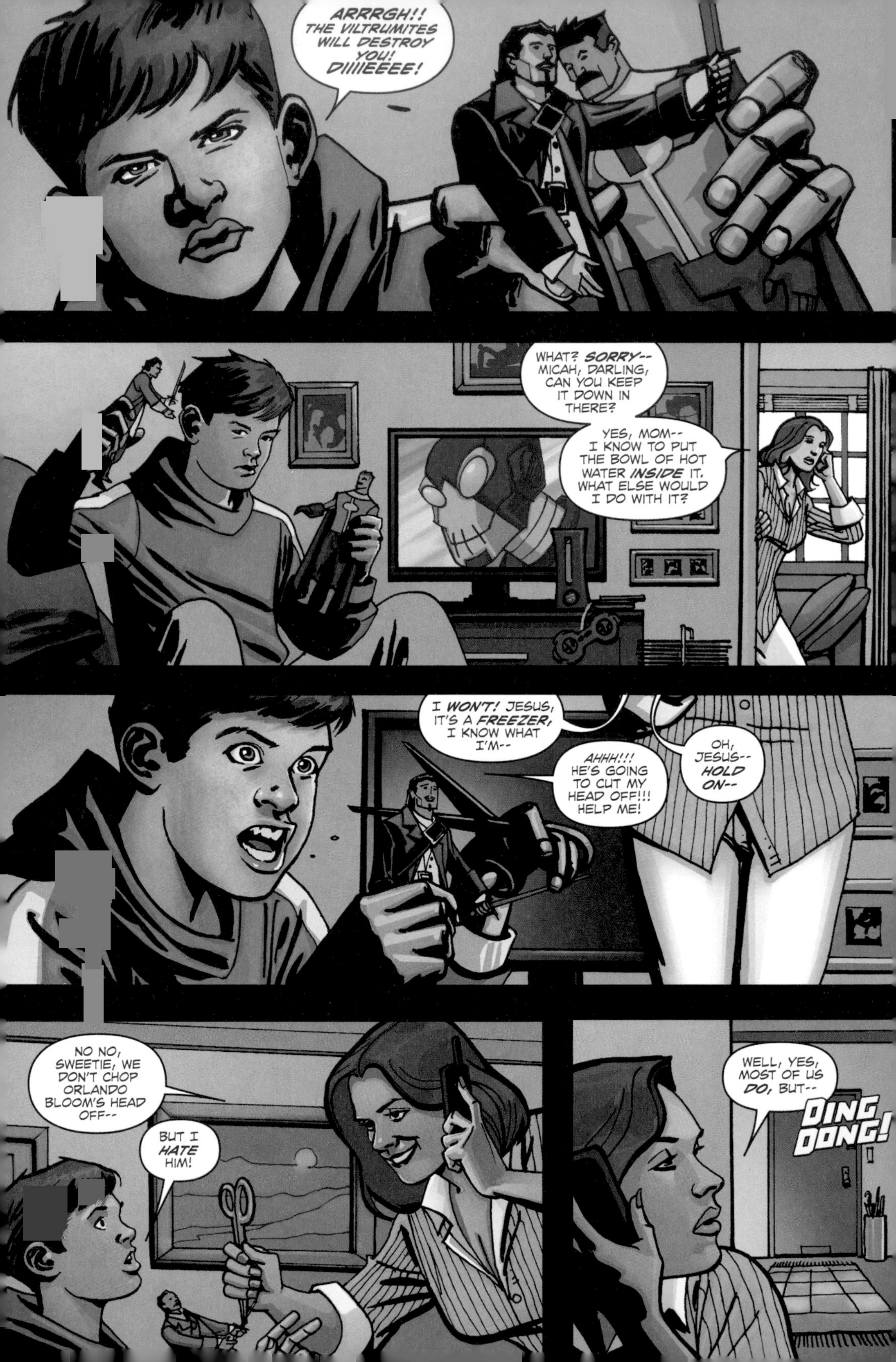
ARRRGH!! THE VILTRUMITES WILL DESTROY YOU! DIIIIEEEE!
WHAT? SORRY-- MICAH, DARLING, CAN YOU KEEP IT DOWN IN THERE?
YES, MOM-- I KNOW TO PUT THE BOWL OF HOT WATER INSIDE IT. WHAT ELSE WOULD I DO WITH IT?
I WON'T! JESUS, IT'S A FREEZER, I KNOW WHAT I'M--
AHHH!!! HE'S GOING TO CUT MY HEAD OFF!!! HELP ME!
OH, JESUS-- HOLD ON--
NO NO, SWEETIE, WE DON'T CHOP ORLANDO BLOOM'S HEAD OFF--
BUT I HATE HIM!
WELL, YES, MOST OF US DO, BUT--
DING DONG!

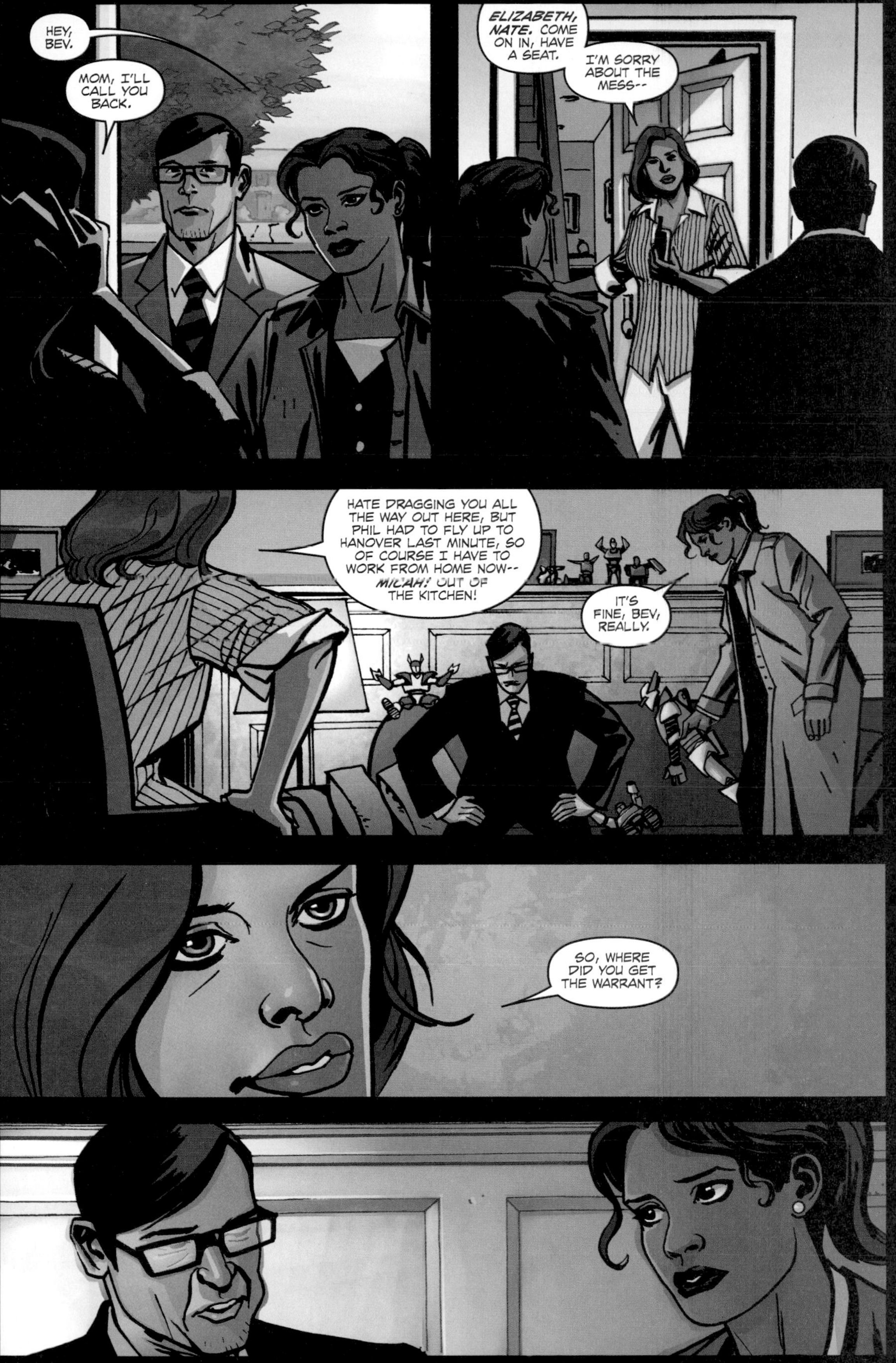
HEY, BEV.
MOM, I'LL CALL YOU BACK.
ELIZABETH, NATE. COME ON IN, HAVE A SEAT.
I'M SORRY ABOUT THE MESS--
HATE DRAGGING YOU ALL THE WAY OUT HERE, BUT PHIL HAD TO FLY UP TO HANOVER LAST MINUTE, SO OF COURSE I HAVE TO WORK FROM HOME NOW-- MICAH! OUT OF THE KITCHEN!
IT'S FINE, BEV, REALLY.
SO, WHERE DID YOU GET THE WARRANT?

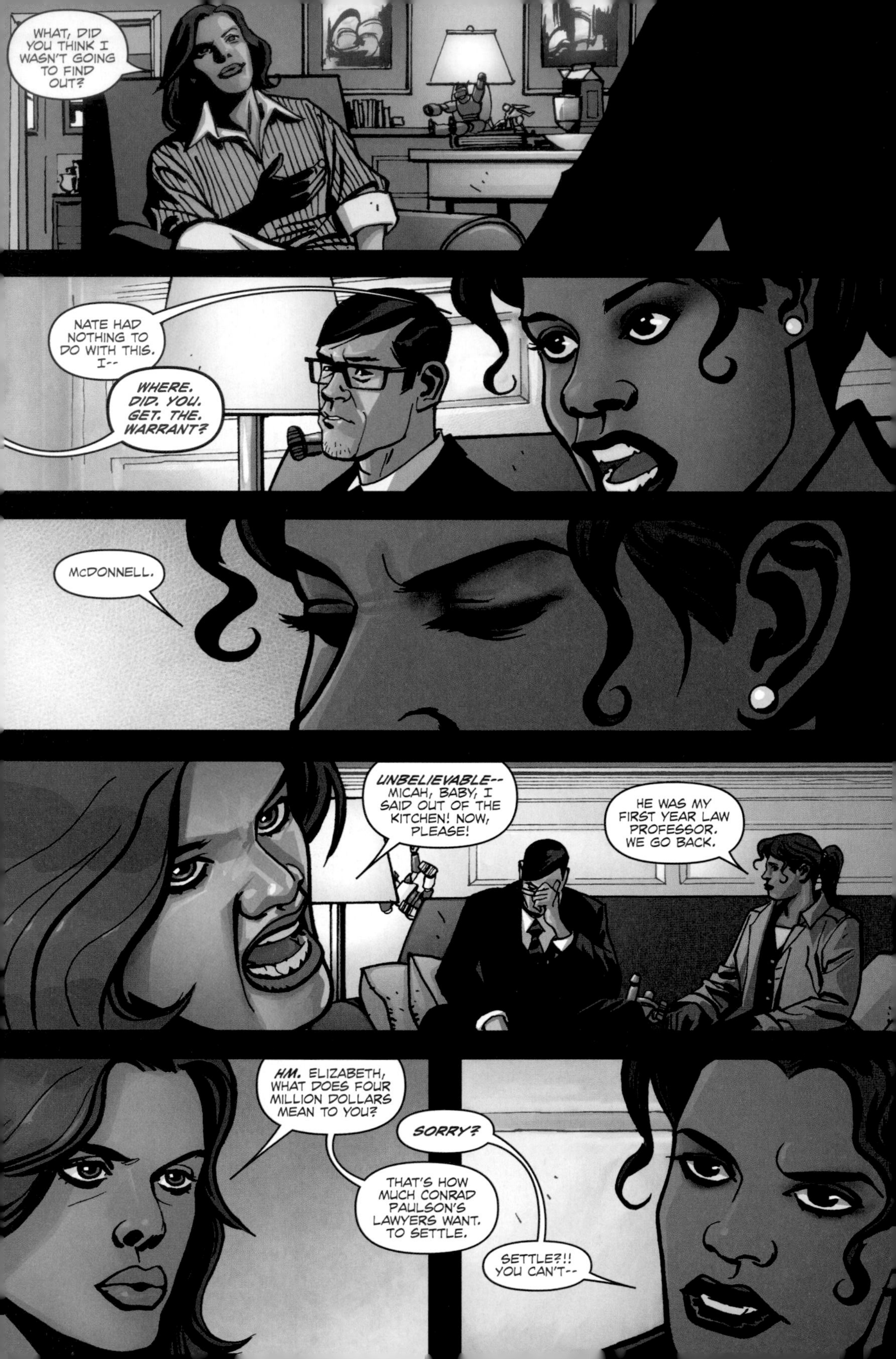
WHAT, DID YOU THINK I WASN'T GOING TO FIND OUT?
NATE HAD NOTHING TO DO WITH THIS. I--
WHERE. DID. YOU. GET. THE. WARRANT?
McDONNELL.
UNBELIEVABLE-- MICAH, BABY, I SAID OUT OF THE KITCHEN! NOW, PLEASE!
HE WAS MY FIRST YEAR LAW PROFESSOR. WE GO BACK.
HM. ELIZABETH, WHAT DOES FOUR MILLION DOLLARS MEAN TO YOU?
SORRY?
THAT'S HOW MUCH CONRAD PAULSON'S LAWYERS WANT. TO SETTLE.
SETTLE?!! YOU CAN'T--

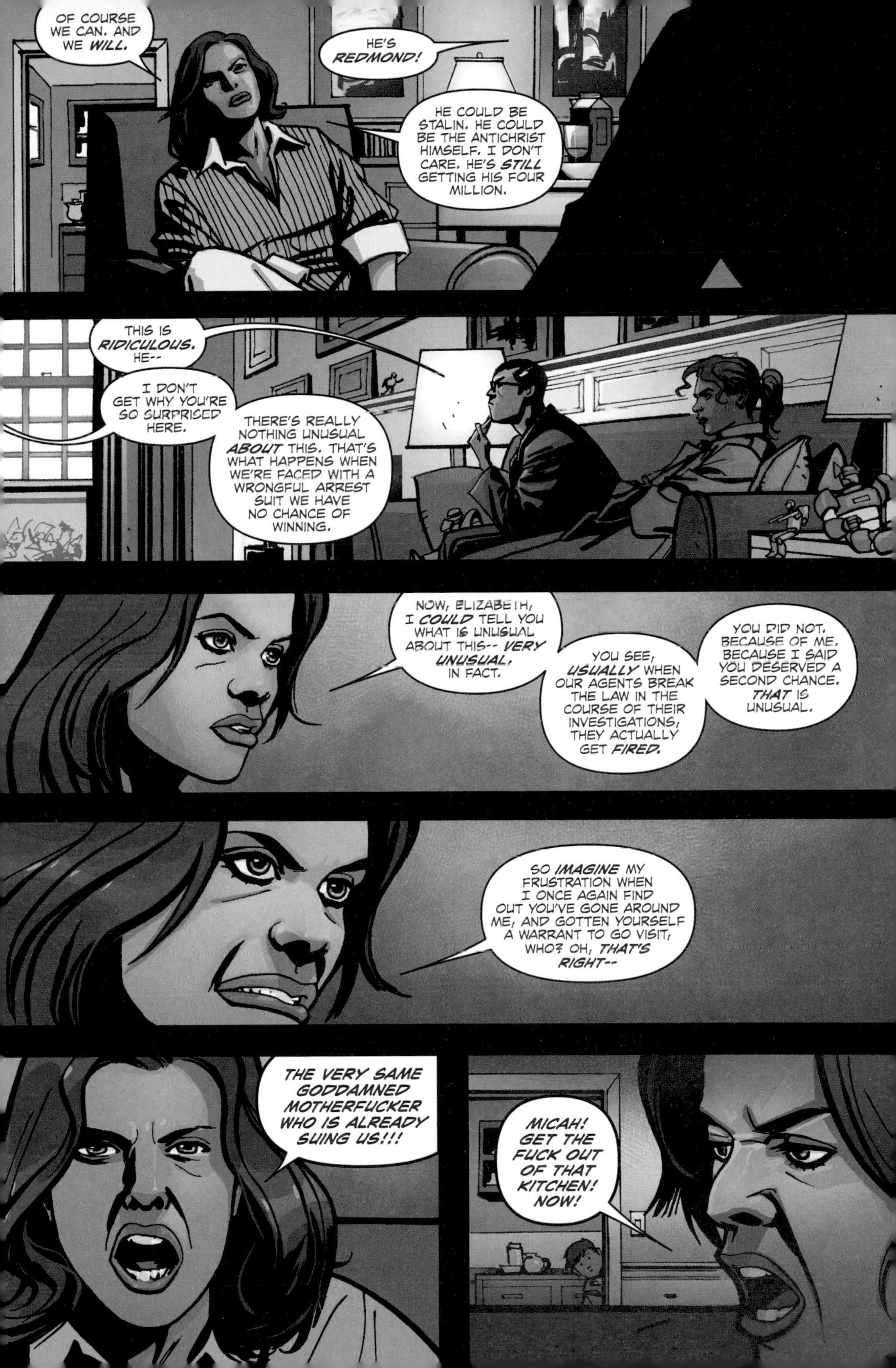

OF COURSE WE CAN. AND WE WILL.
HE'S REDMOND!
HE COULD BE STALIN. HE COULD BE THE ANTICHRIST HIMSELF. I DON'T CARE. HE'S STILL GETTING HIS FOUR MILLION.
THIS IS RIDICULOUS. HE--
I DON'T GET WHY YOU'RE SO SURPRISED HERE.
THERE'S REALLY NOTHING UNUSUAL ABOUT THIS. THAT'S WHAT HAPPENS WHEN WE'RE FACED WITH A WRONGFUL ARREST SUIT WE HAVE NO CHANCE OF WINNING.
NOW, ELIZABETH, I COULD TELL YOU WHAT IS UNUSUAL ABOUT THIS-- VERY UNUSUAL, IN FACT.
YOU SEE, USUALLY WHEN OUR AGENTS BREAK THE LAW IN THE COURSE OF THEIR INVESTIGATIONS, THEY ACTUALLY GET FIRED.
YOU DID NOT. BECAUSE OF ME. BECAUSE I SAID YOU DESERVED A SECOND CHANCE. THAT IS UNUSUAL.
SO IMAGINE MY FRUSTRATION WHEN I ONCE AGAIN FIND OUT YOU'VE GONE AROUND ME, AND GOTTEN YOURSELF A WARRANT TO GO VISIT, WHO? OH, THAT'S RIGHT--
THE VERY SAME GODDAMNED MOTHERFUCKER WHO IS ALREADY SUING US!!!
MICAH! GET THE FUCK OUT OF THAT KITCHEN! NOW!

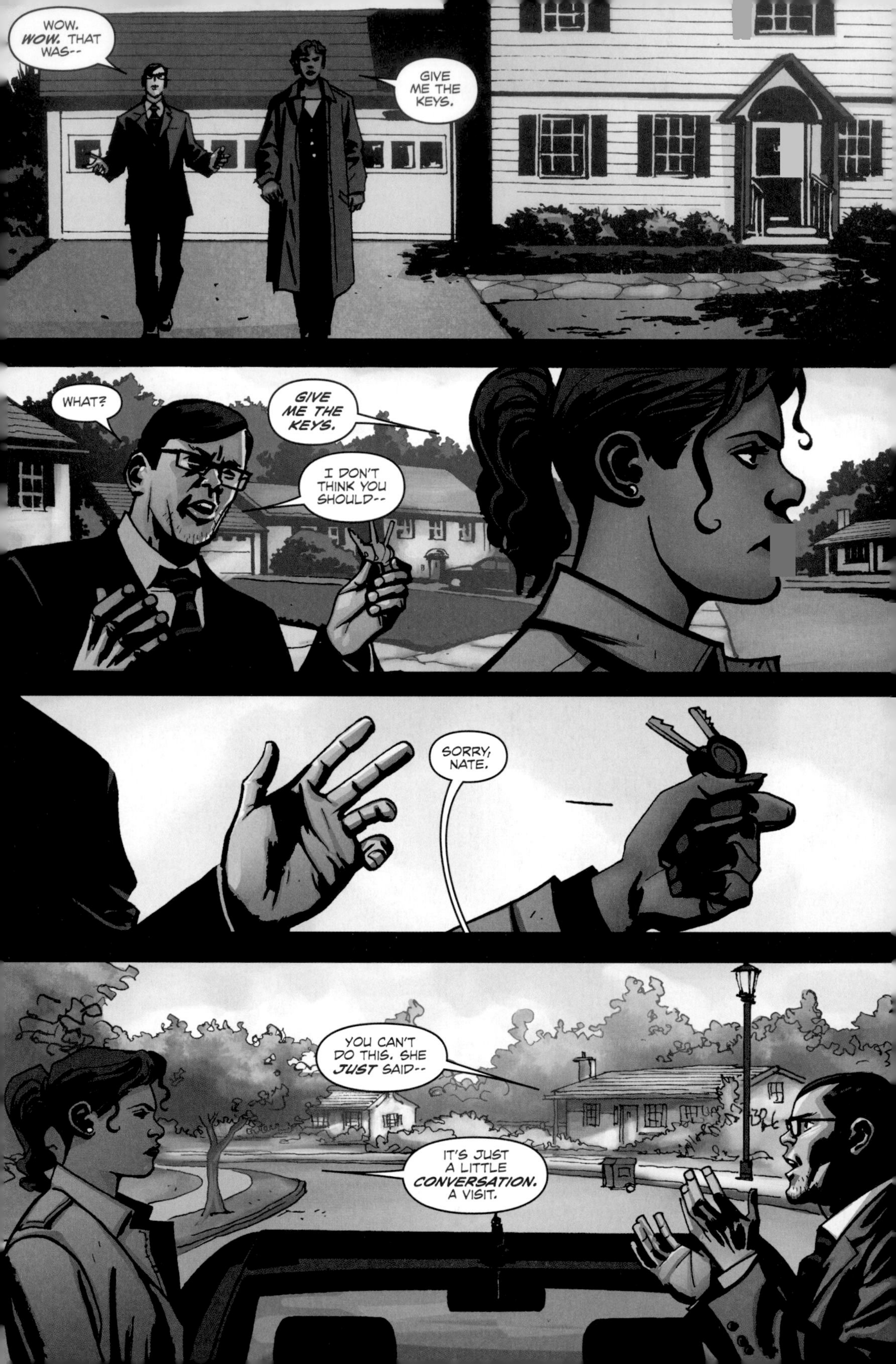
WOW. *WOW.* THAT WAS--
GIVE ME THE KEYS.
WHAT?
GIVE ME THE KEYS.
I DON'T THINK YOU SHOULD--
SORRY, NATE.
YOU CAN'T DO THIS. SHE *JUST* SAID--
IT'S JUST A LITTLE *CONVERSATION.* A VISIT.

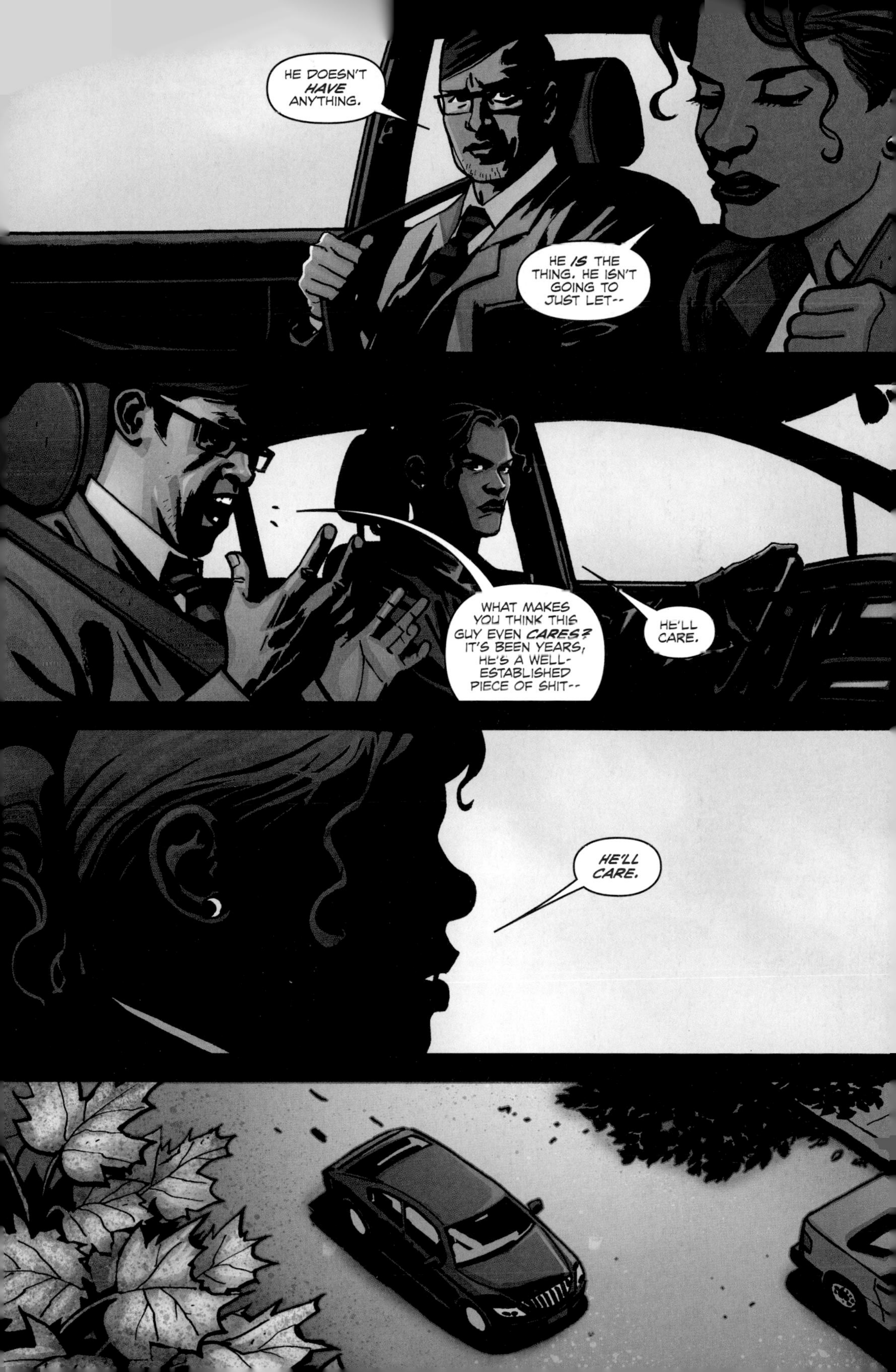
HE DOESN'T *HAVE* ANYTHING.
HE *IS* THE THING. HE ISN'T GOING TO JUST LET--
WHAT MAKES YOU THINK THIS GUY EVEN *CARES?* IT'S BEEN YEARS, HE'S A WELL-ESTABLISHED PIECE OF SHIT--
HE'LL CARE.
HE'LL CARE.

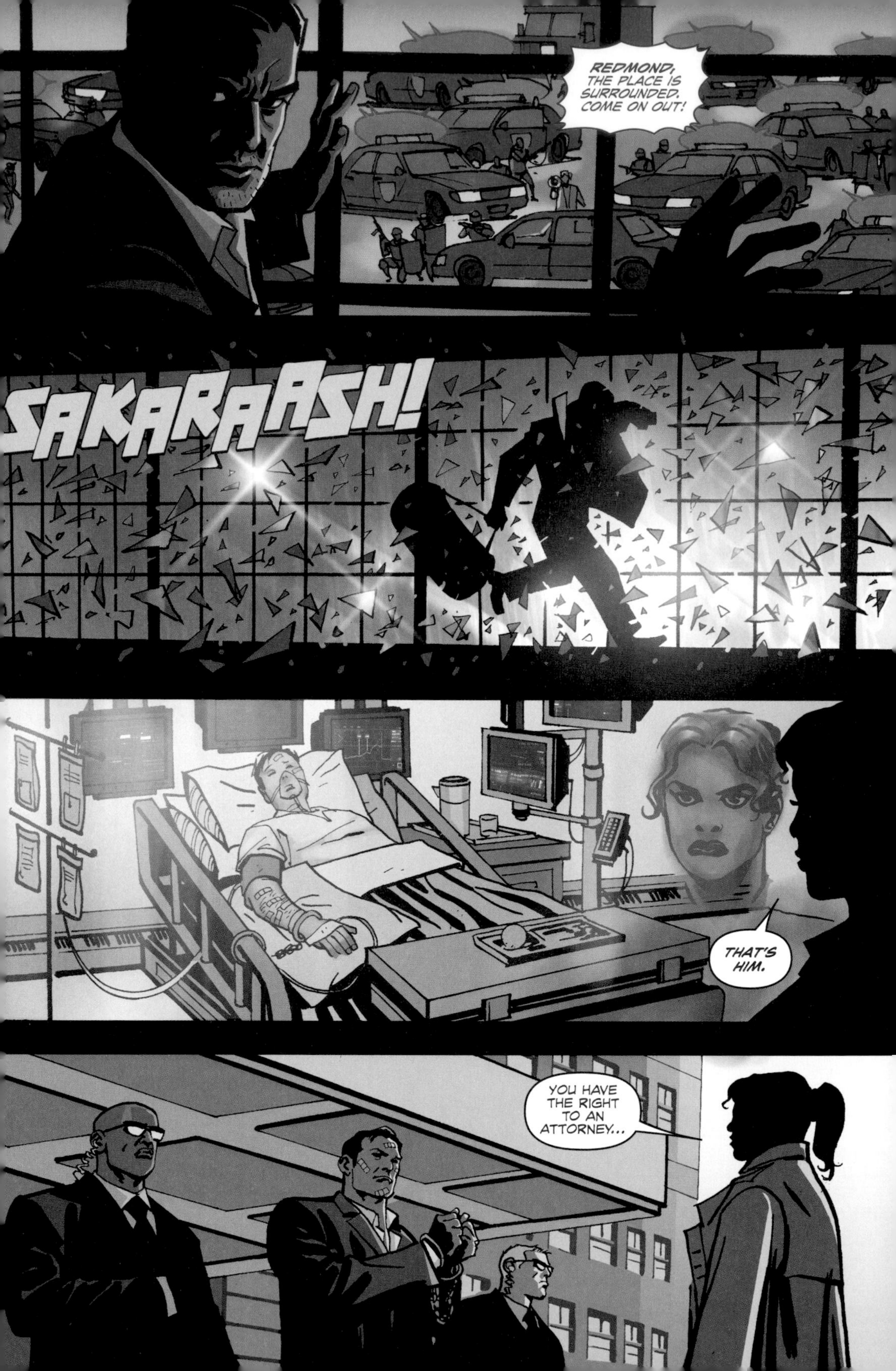
REDMOND, THE PLACE IS SURROUNDED. COME ON OUT!
SAKARAASH!
THAT'S HIM.
YOU HAVE THE RIGHT TO AN ATTORNEY...

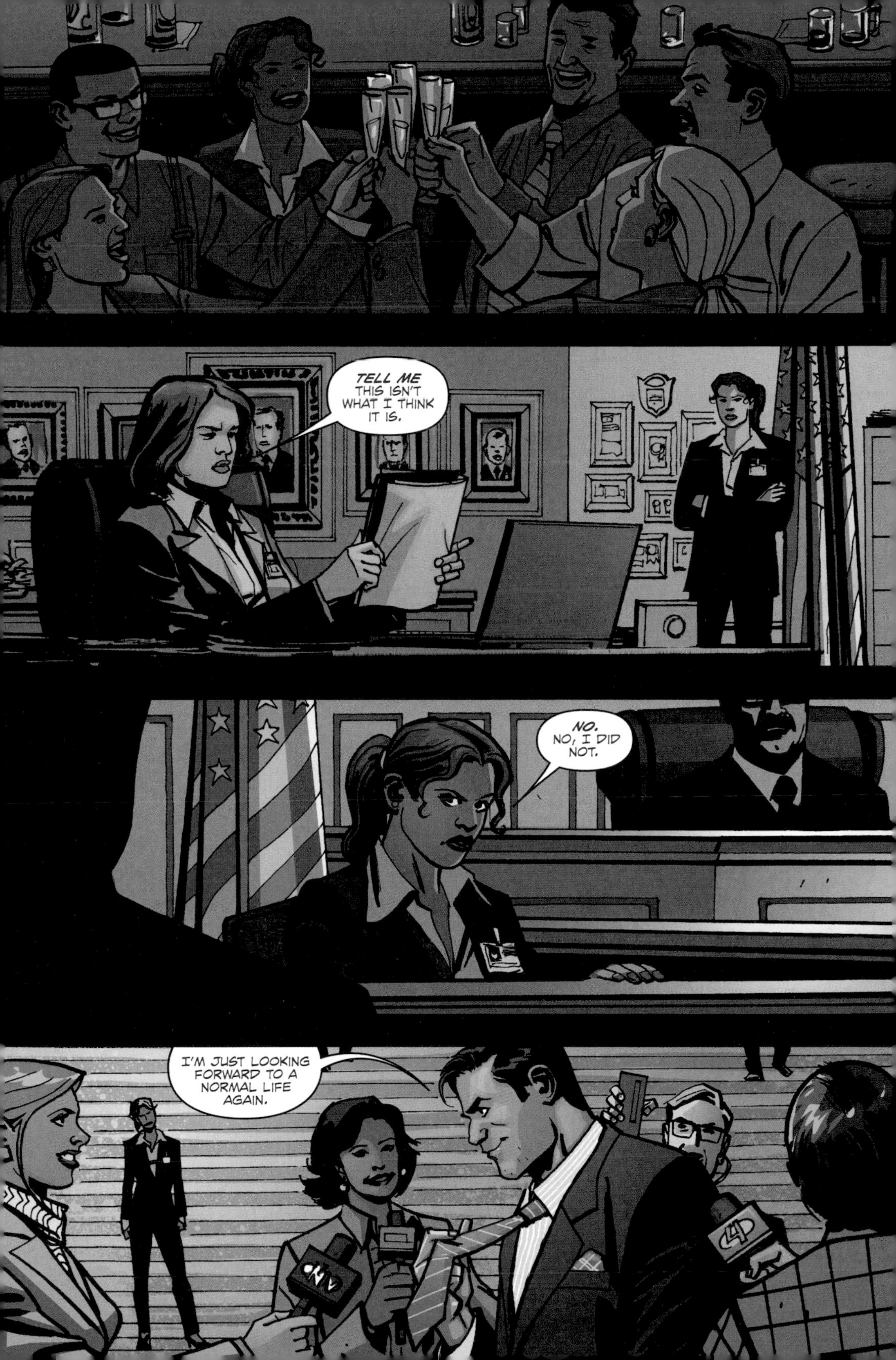
TELL ME THIS ISN'T WHAT I THINK IT IS.
NO. NO, I DID NOT.
I'M JUST LOOKING FORWARD TO A NORMAL LIFE AGAIN.

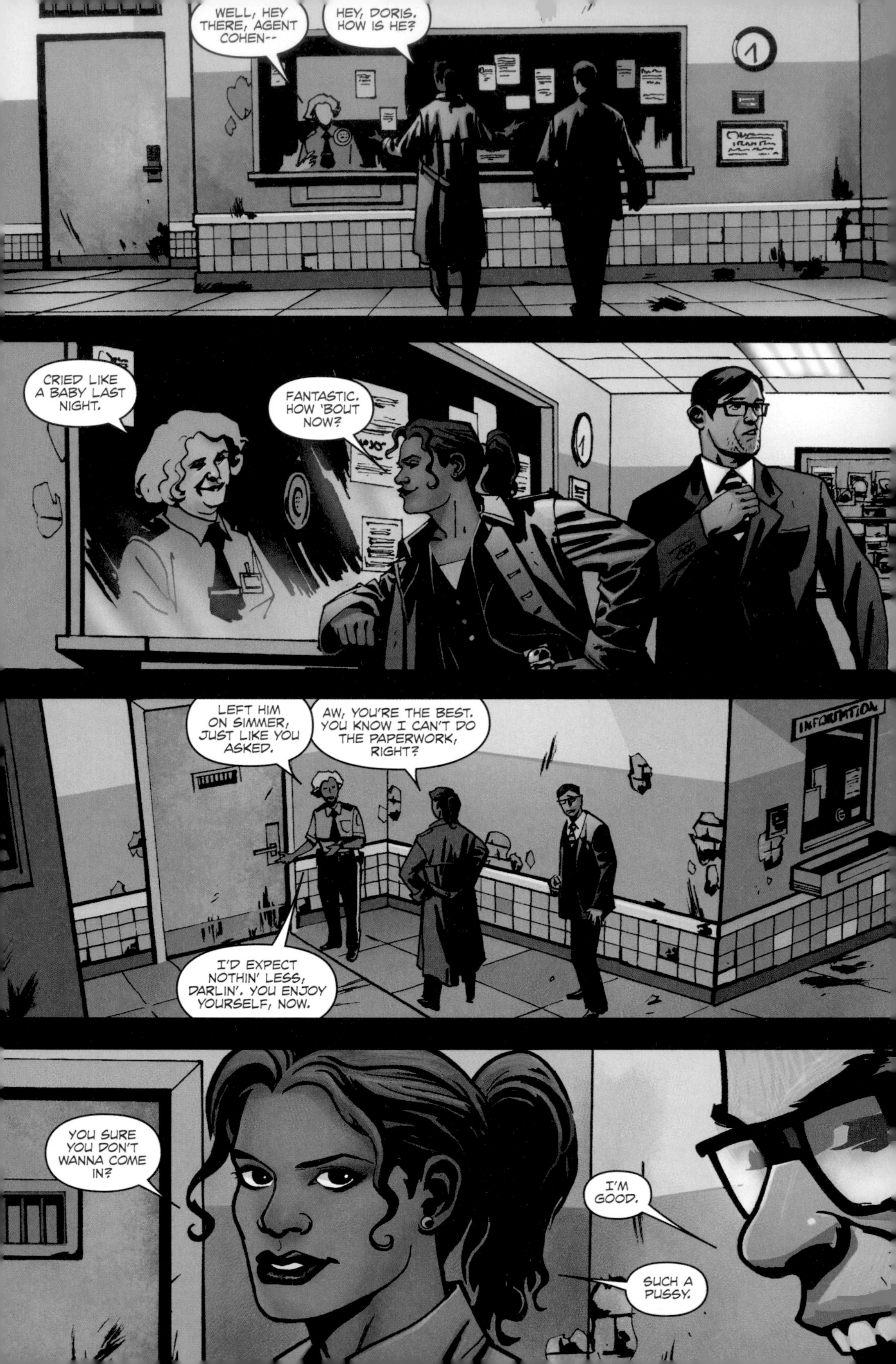
WELL, HEY THERE, AGENT COHEN--
HEY, DORIS. HOW IS HE?
CRIED LIKE A BABY LAST NIGHT.
FANTASTIC. HOW 'BOUT NOW?
LEFT HIM ON SIMMER, JUST LIKE YOU ASKED.
AW, YOU'RE THE BEST. YOU KNOW I CAN'T DO THE PAPERWORK, RIGHT?
INFORMATION
I'D EXPECT NOTHIN' LESS, DARLIN'. YOU ENJOY YOURSELF, NOW.
YOU SURE YOU DON'T WANNA COME IN?
I'M GOOD.
SUCH A PUSSY.

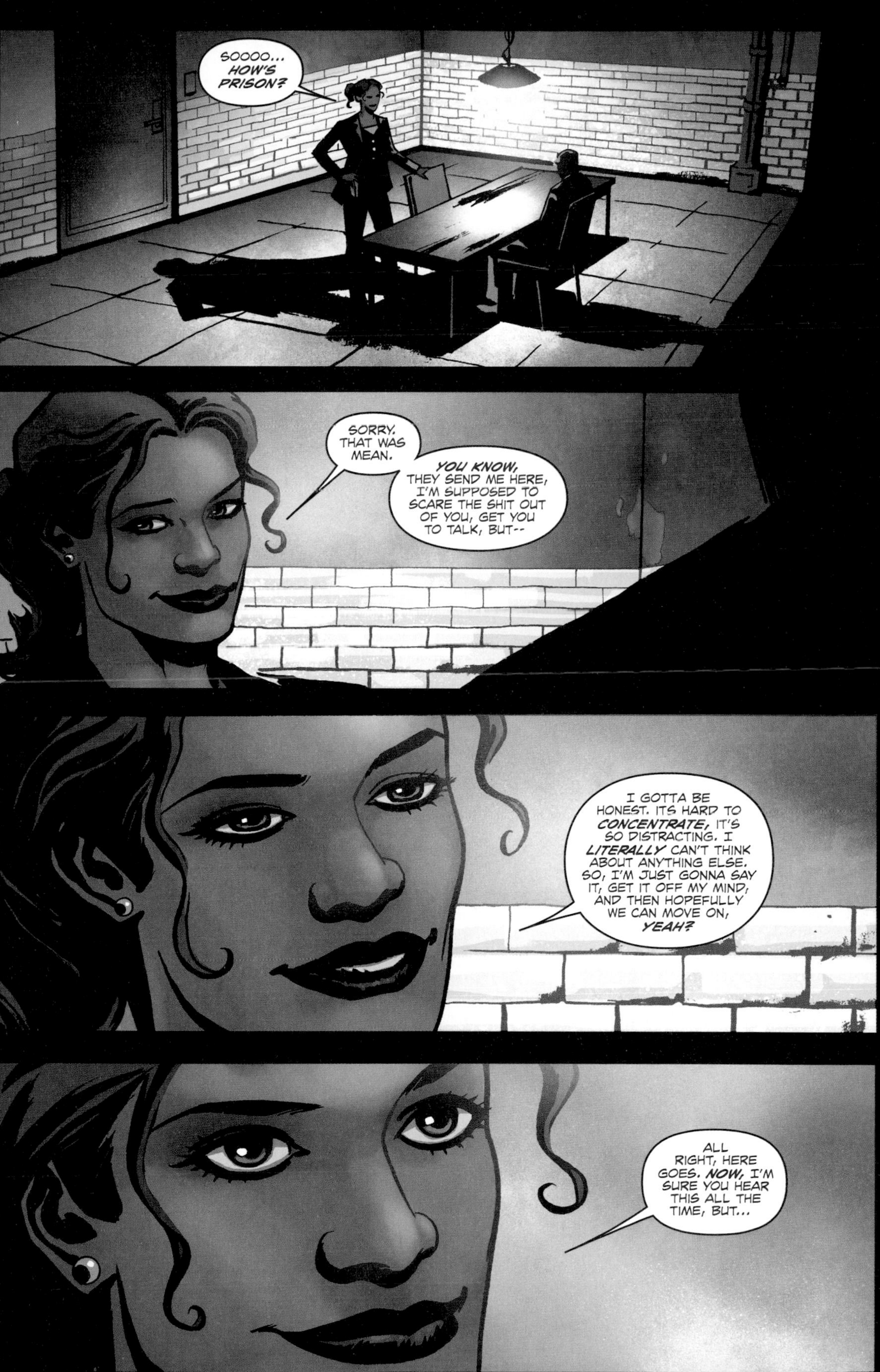
SOOOO... HOW'S PRISON?
SORRY. THAT WAS MEAN.
YOU KNOW, THEY SEND ME HERE, I'M SUPPOSED TO SCARE THE SHIT OUT OF YOU, GET YOU TO TALK, BUT--
I GOTTA BE HONEST. ITS HARD TO CONCENTRATE, IT'S SO DISTRACTING. I LITERALLY CAN'T THINK ABOUT ANYTHING ELSE. SO, I'M JUST GONNA SAY IT, GET IT OFF MY MIND, AND THEN HOPEFULLY WE CAN MOVE ON, YEAH?
ALL RIGHT, HERE GOES. NOW, I'M SURE YOU HEAR THIS ALL THE TIME, BUT...

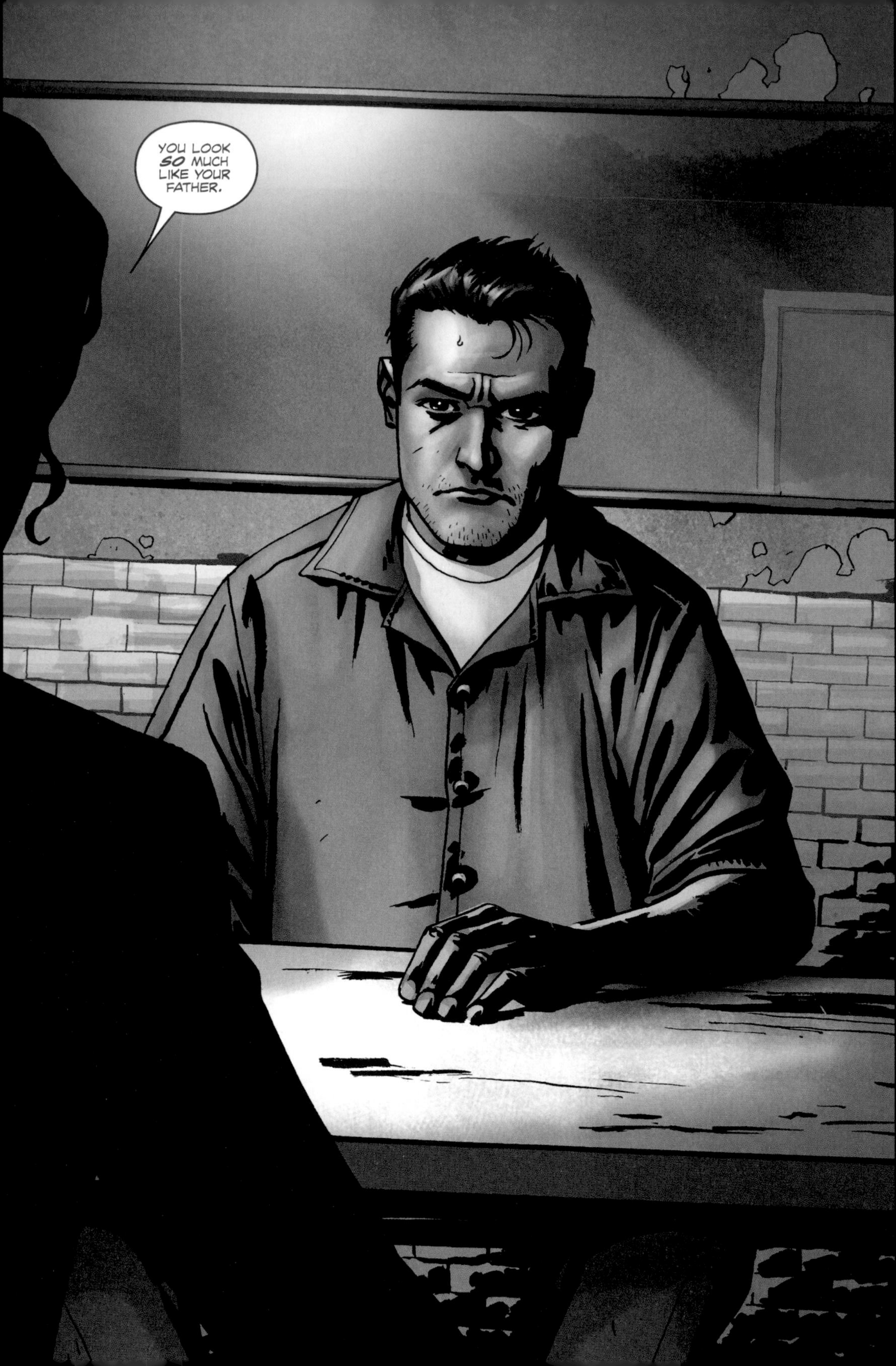
YOU LOOK SO MUCH LIKE YOUR FATHER.

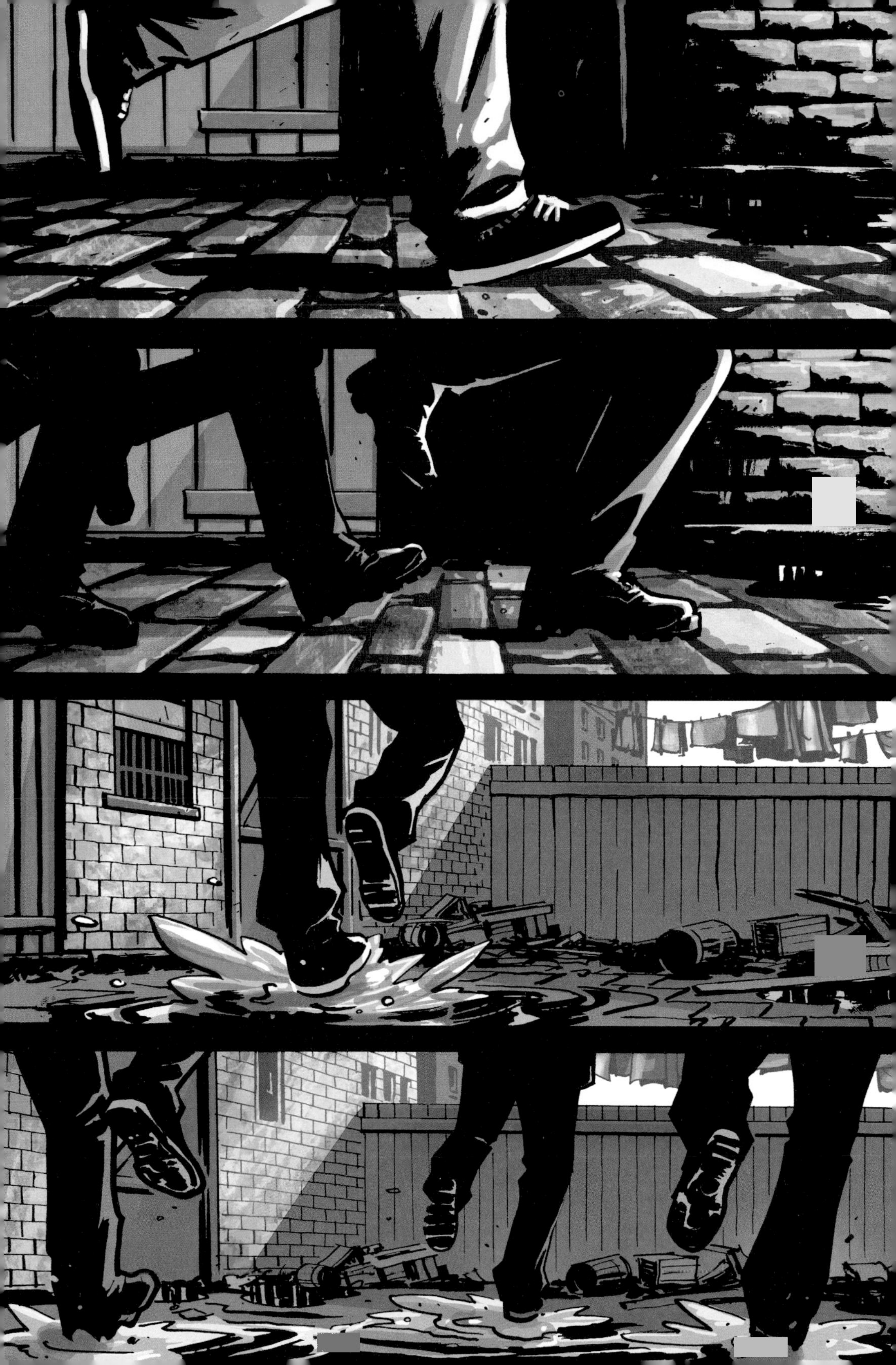

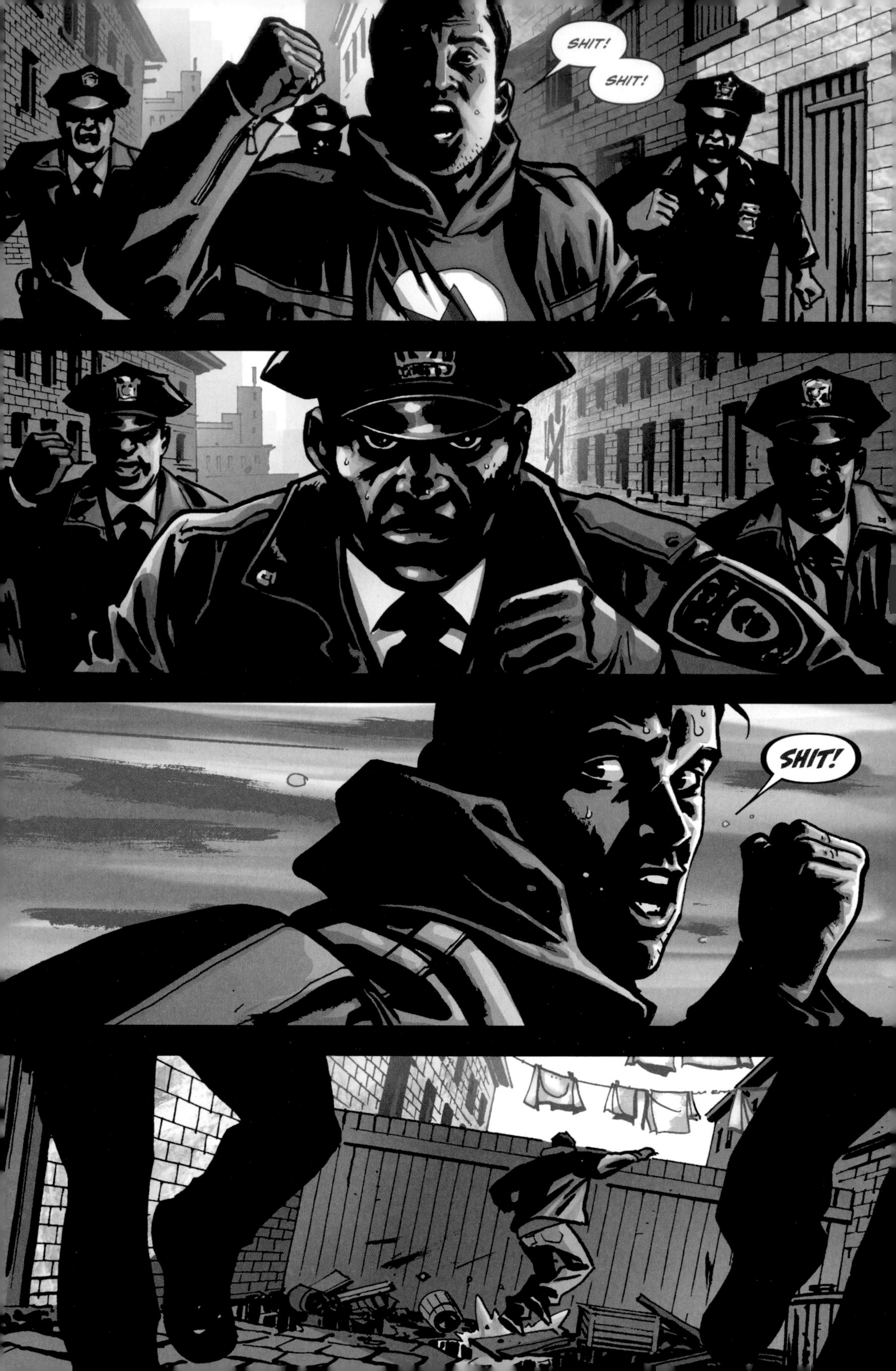
SHIT!
SHIT!
SHIT!

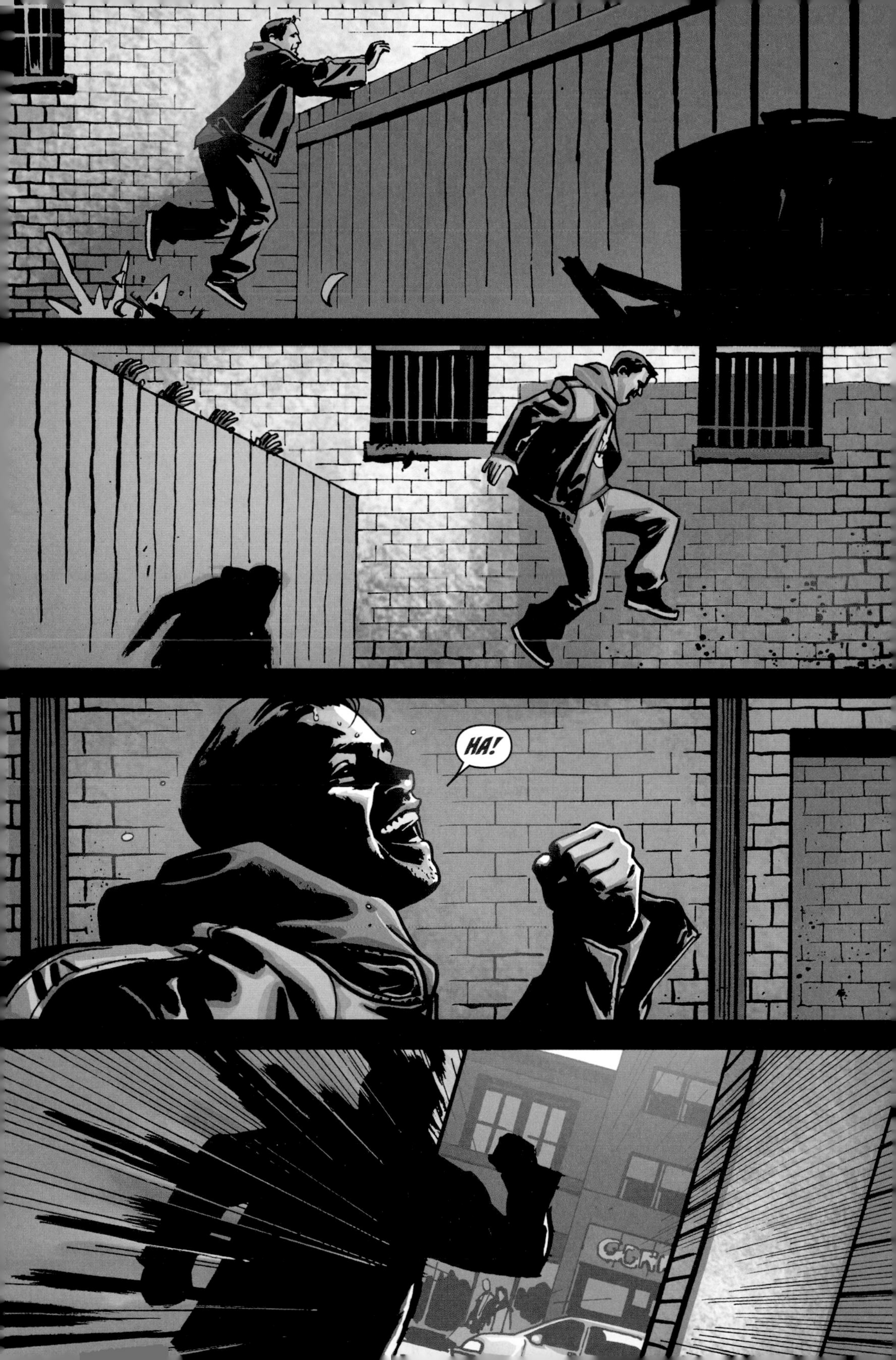
HA!

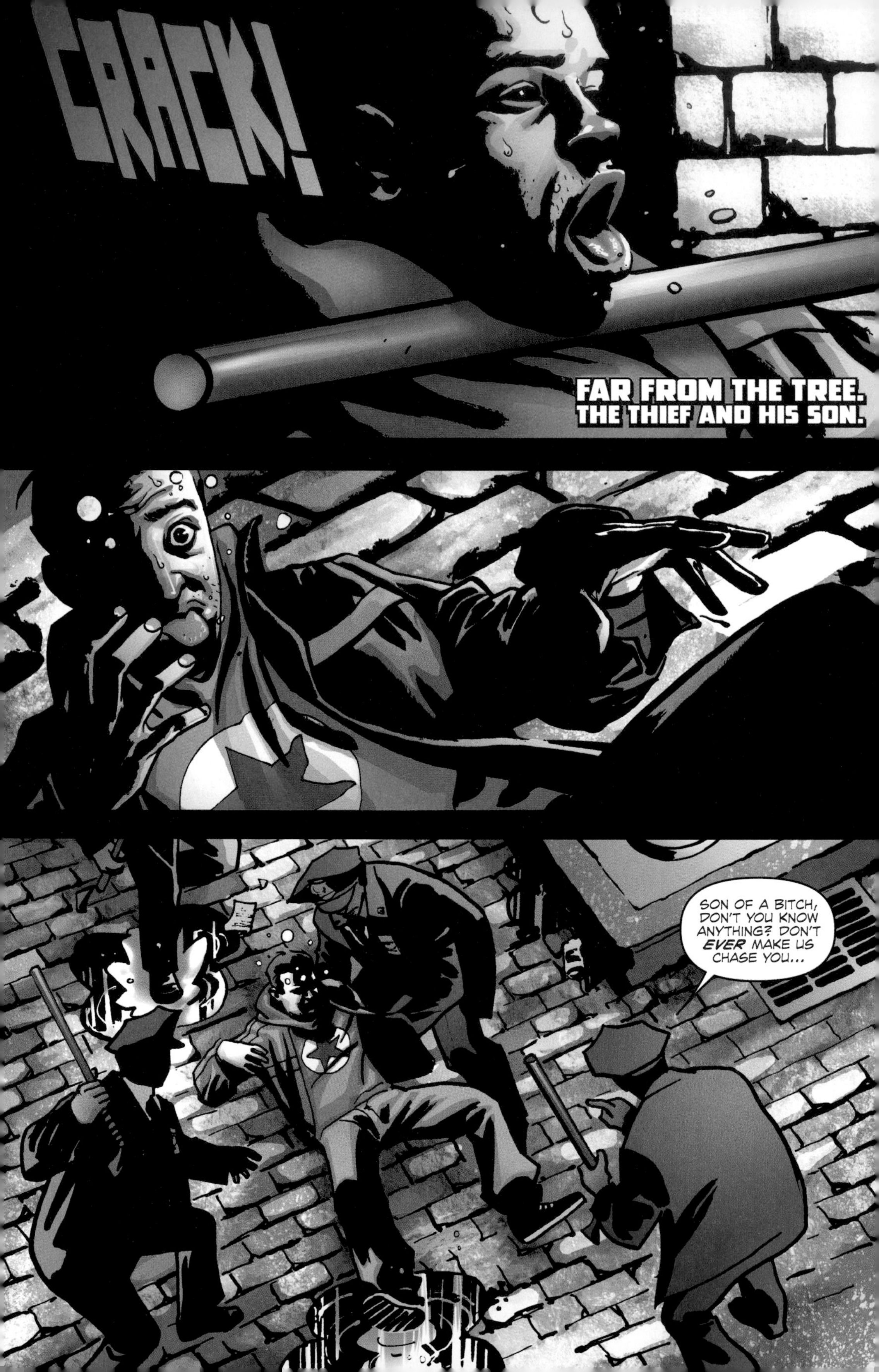
CRACK!
FAR FROM THE TREE.
THE THIEF AND HIS SON.
SON OF A BITCH, DON'T YOU KNOW ANYTHING? DON'T EVER MAKE US CHASE YOU...

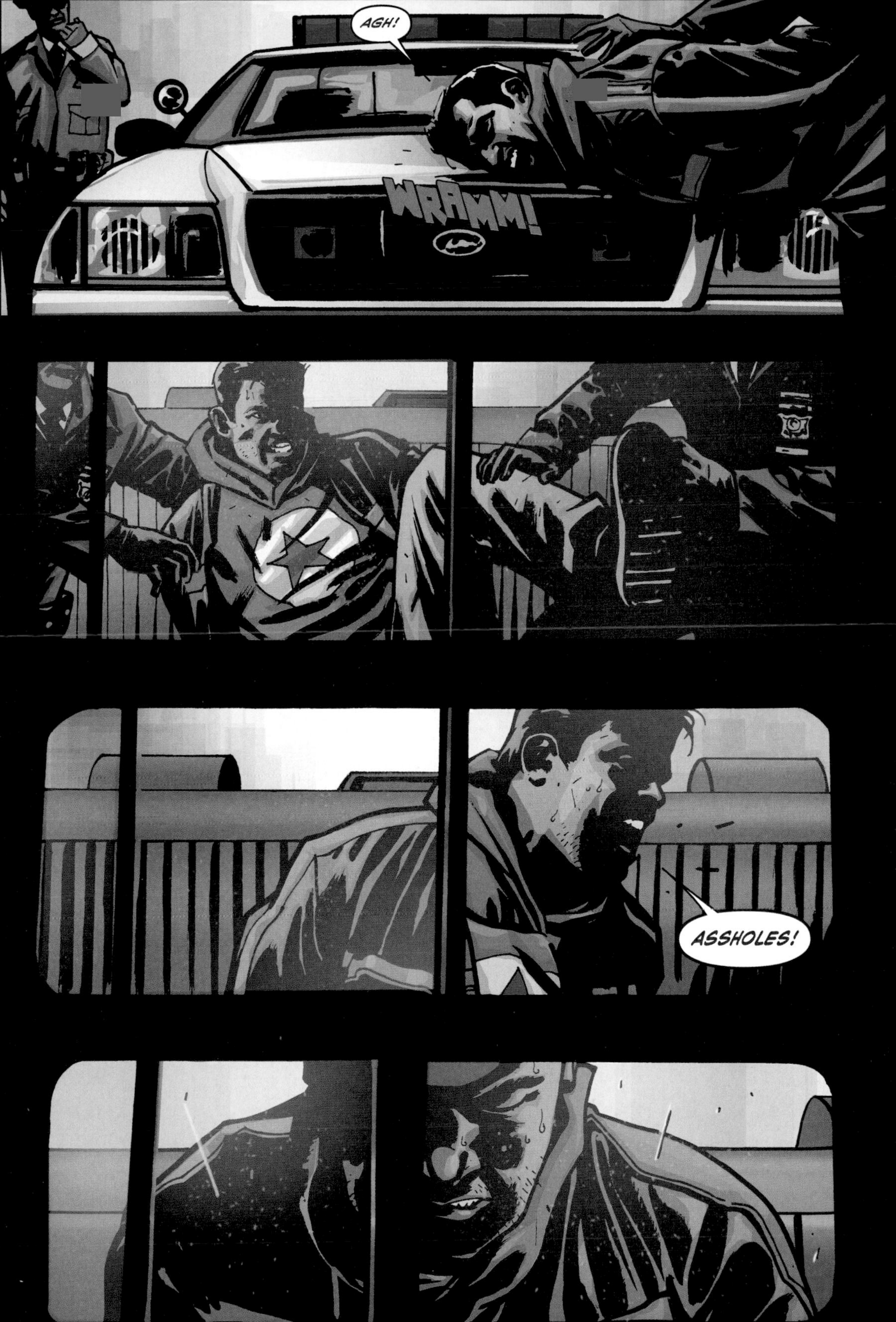
AGH!
WRAMM!
ASSHOLES!

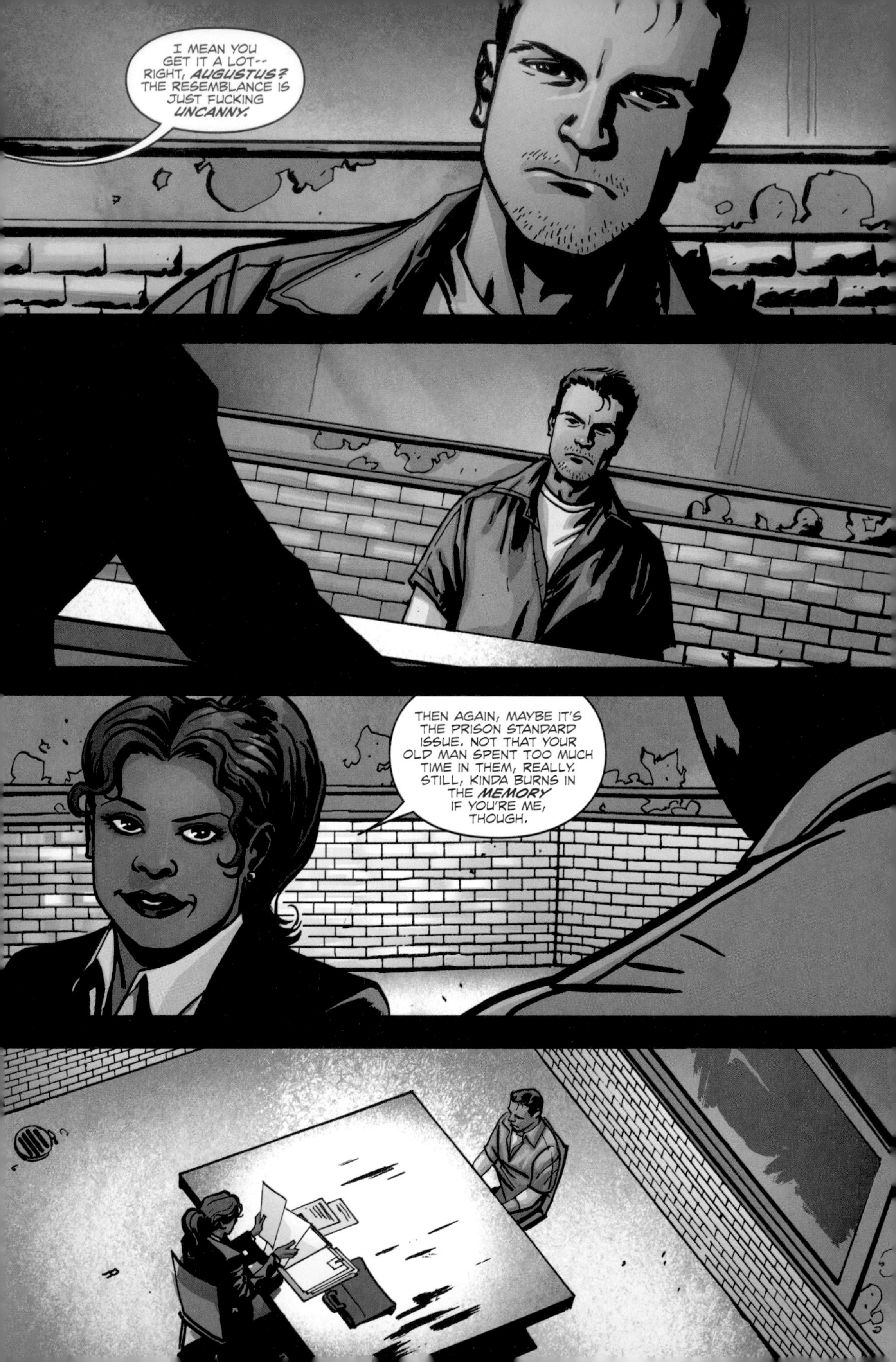
I MEAN YOU GET IT A LOT-- RIGHT, *AUGUSTUS?* THE RESEMBLANCE IS JUST FUCKING *UNCANNY.*
THEN AGAIN, MAYBE IT'S THE PRISON STANDARD ISSUE. NOT THAT YOUR OLD MAN SPENT TOO MUCH TIME IN THEM, REALLY. STILL, KINDA BURNS IN THE *MEMORY* IF YOU'RE ME, THOUGH.

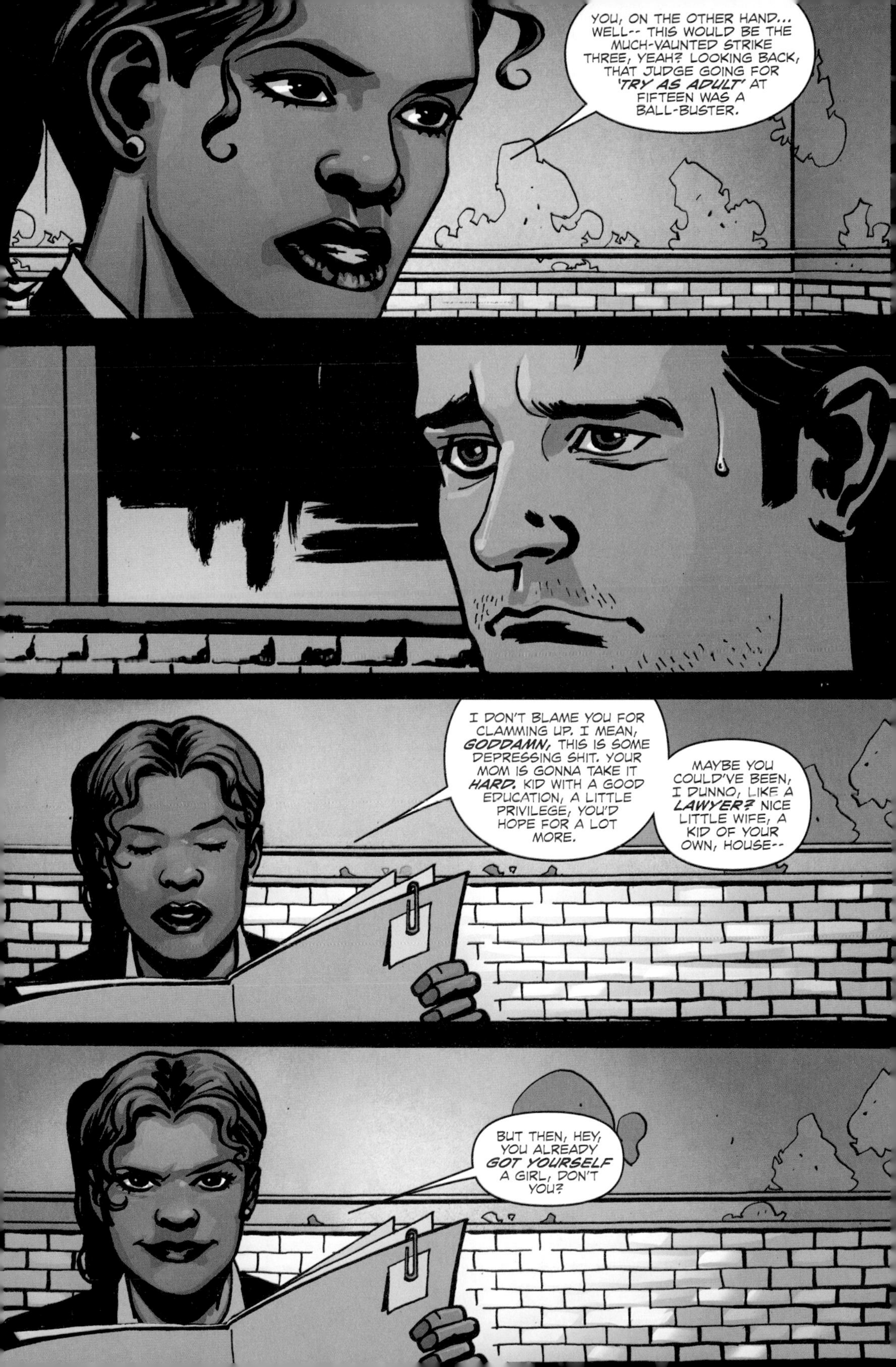
YOU, ON THE OTHER HAND... WELL-- THIS WOULD BE THE MUCH-VAUNTED STRIKE THREE, YEAH? LOOKING BACK, THAT JUDGE GOING FOR 'TRY AS ADULT' AT FIFTEEN WAS A BALL-BUSTER.
I DON'T BLAME YOU FOR CLAMMING UP. I MEAN, GODDAMN, THIS IS SOME DEPRESSING SHIT. YOUR MOM IS GONNA TAKE IT HARD. KID WITH A GOOD EDUCATION, A LITTLE PRIVILEGE, YOU'D HOPE FOR A LOT MORE.
MAYBE YOU COULD'VE BEEN, I DUNNO, LIKE A LAWYER? NICE LITTLE WIFE, A KID OF YOUR OWN, HOUSE--
BUT THEN, HEY, YOU ALREADY GOT YOURSELF A GIRL, DON'T YOU?

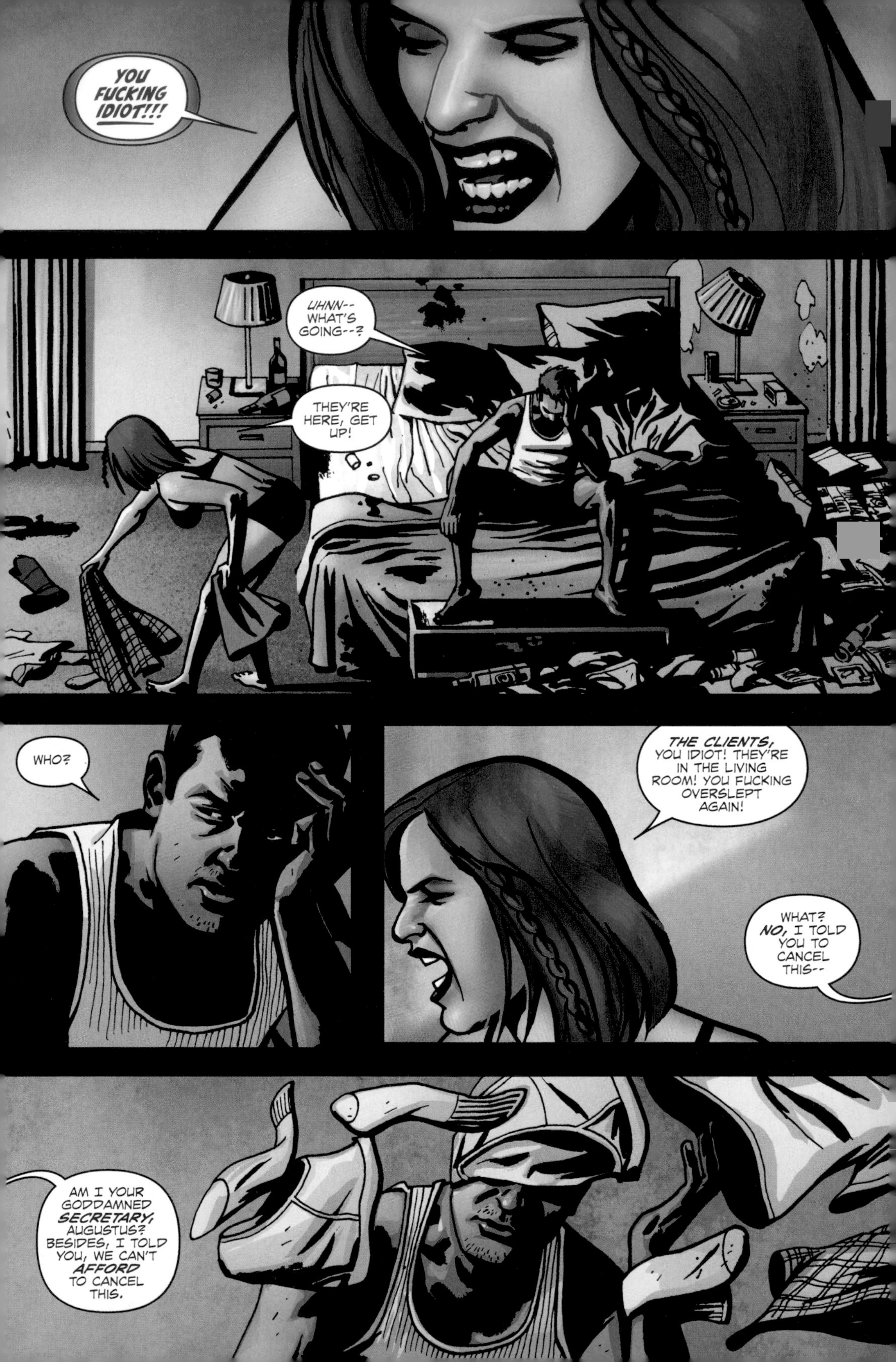
YOU FUCKING IDIOT!!!
UHNN-- WHAT'S GOING--?
THEY'RE HERE, GET UP!
WHO?
THE CLIENTS, YOU IDIOT! THEY'RE IN THE LIVING ROOM! YOU FUCKING OVERSLEPT AGAIN!
WHAT? NO, I TOLD YOU TO CANCEL THIS--
AM I YOUR GODDAMNED SECRETARY, AUGUSTUS? BESIDES, I TOLD YOU, WE CAN'T AFFORD TO CANCEL THIS.

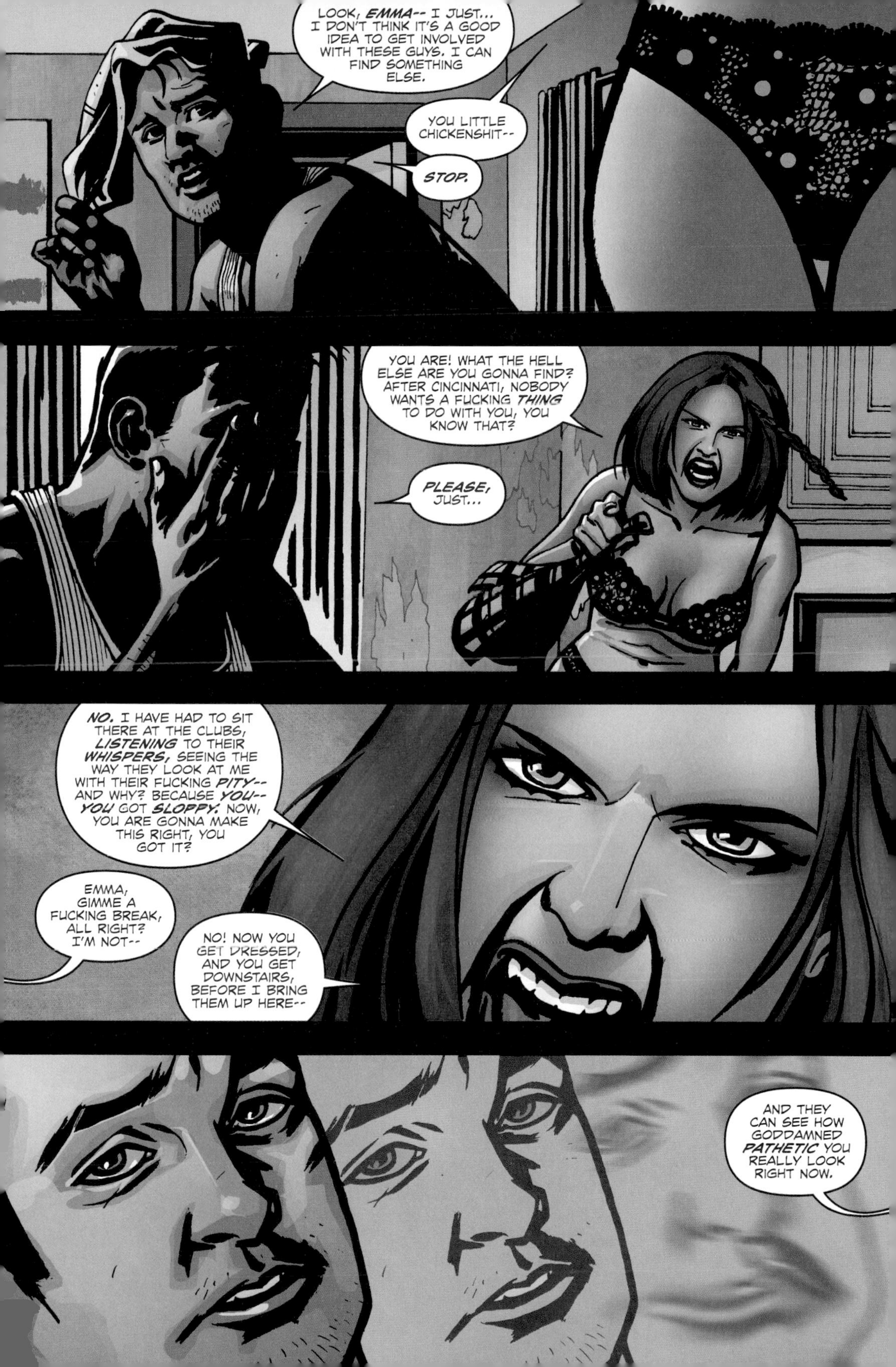
LOOK, EMMA-- I JUST... I DON'T THINK IT'S A GOOD IDEA TO GET INVOLVED WITH THESE GUYS. I CAN FIND SOMETHING ELSE.
YOU LITTLE CHICKENSHIT--
STOP.
YOU ARE! WHAT THE HELL ELSE ARE YOU GONNA FIND? AFTER CINCINNATI, NOBODY WANTS A FUCKING THING TO DO WITH YOU, YOU KNOW THAT?
PLEASE, JUST...
NO. I HAVE HAD TO SIT THERE AT THE CLUBS, LISTENING TO THEIR WHISPERS, SEEING THE WAY THEY LOOK AT ME WITH THEIR FUCKING PITY-- AND WHY? BECAUSE YOU-- YOU GOT SLOPPY. NOW, YOU ARE GONNA MAKE THIS RIGHT, YOU GOT IT?
EMMA, GIMME A FUCKING BREAK, ALL RIGHT? I'M NOT--
NO! NOW YOU GET DRESSED, AND YOU GET DOWNSTAIRS, BEFORE I BRING THEM UP HERE--
AND THEY CAN SEE HOW GODDAMNED PATHETIC YOU REALLY LOOK RIGHT NOW.

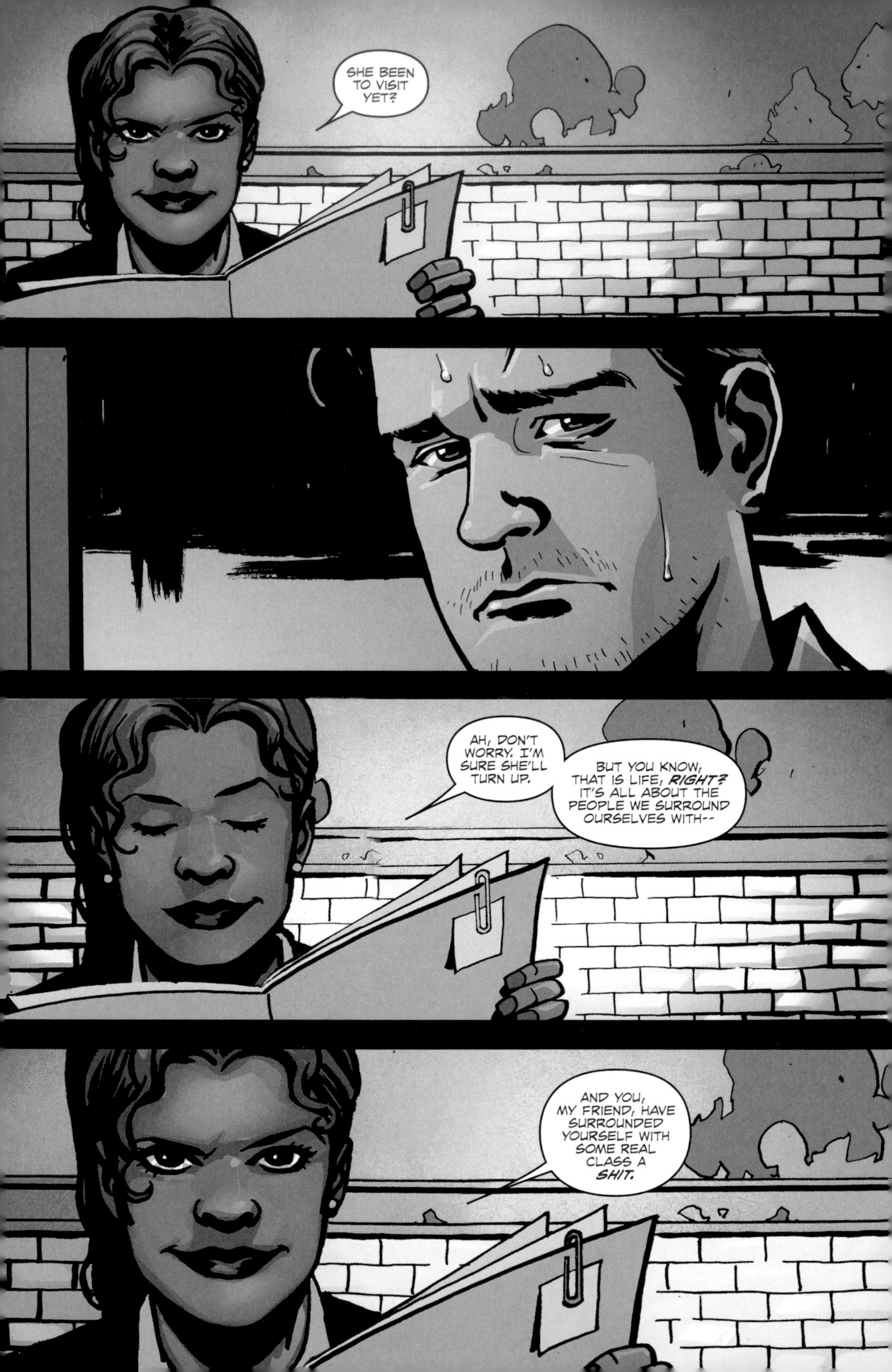
SHE BEEN TO VISIT YET?
AH, DON'T WORRY. I'M SURE SHE'LL TURN UP.
BUT YOU KNOW, THAT IS LIFE, RIGHT? IT'S ALL ABOUT THE PEOPLE WE SURROUND OURSELVES WITH--
AND YOU, MY FRIEND, HAVE SURROUNDED YOURSELF WITH SOME REAL CLASS A SHIT.

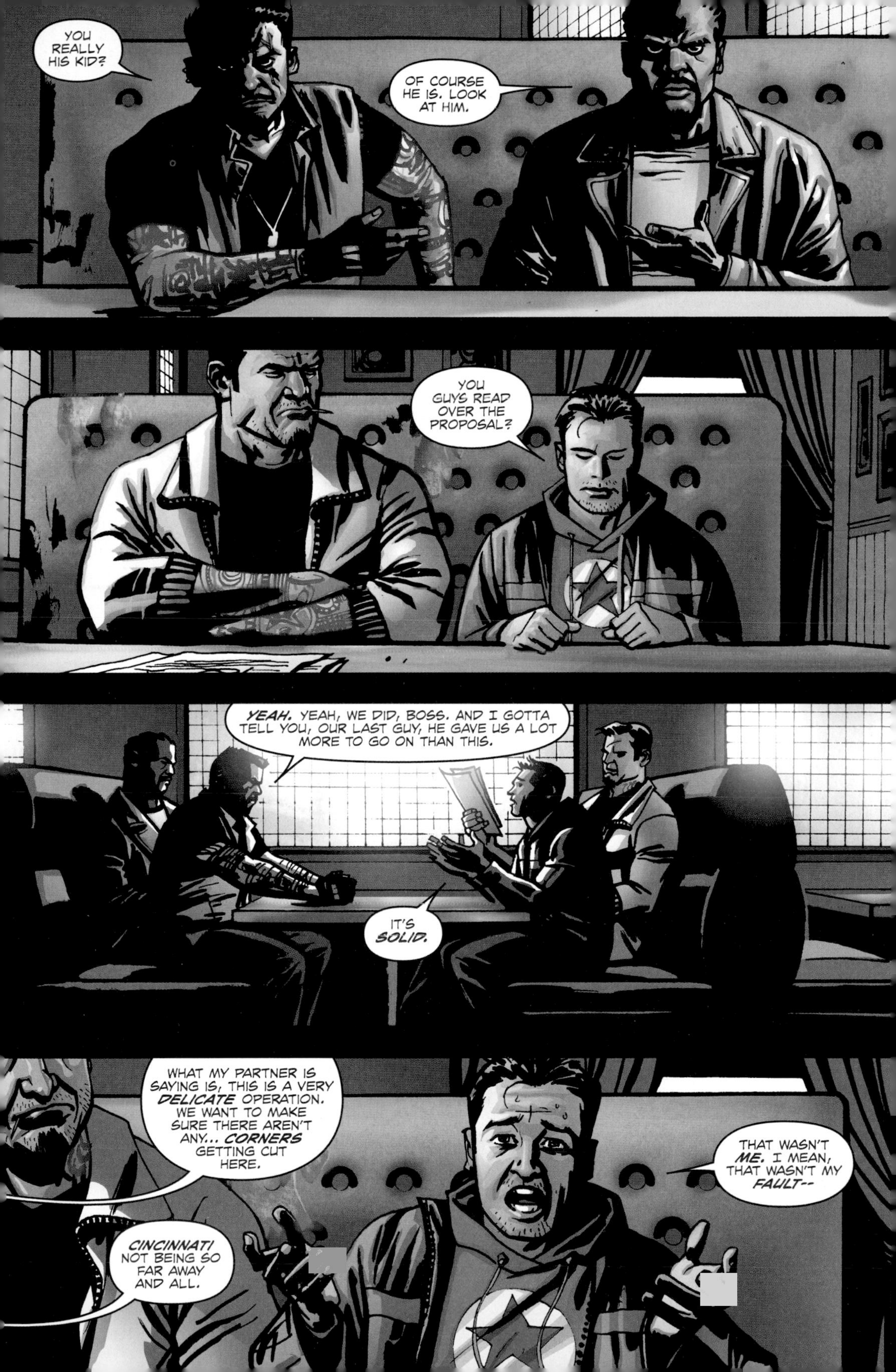
YOU REALLY HIS KID?
OF COURSE HE IS. LOOK AT HIM.
YOU GUYS READ OVER THE PROPOSAL?
YEAH. YEAH, WE DID, BOSS. AND I GOTTA TELL YOU, OUR LAST GUY, HE GAVE US A LOT MORE TO GO ON THAN THIS.
IT'S SOLID.
WHAT MY PARTNER IS SAYING IS, THIS IS A VERY DELICATE OPERATION. WE WANT TO MAKE SURE THERE AREN'T ANY... CORNERS GETTING CUT HERE.
CINCINNATI NOT BEING SO FAR AWAY AND ALL.
THAT WASN'T ME. I MEAN, THAT WASN'T MY FAULT--

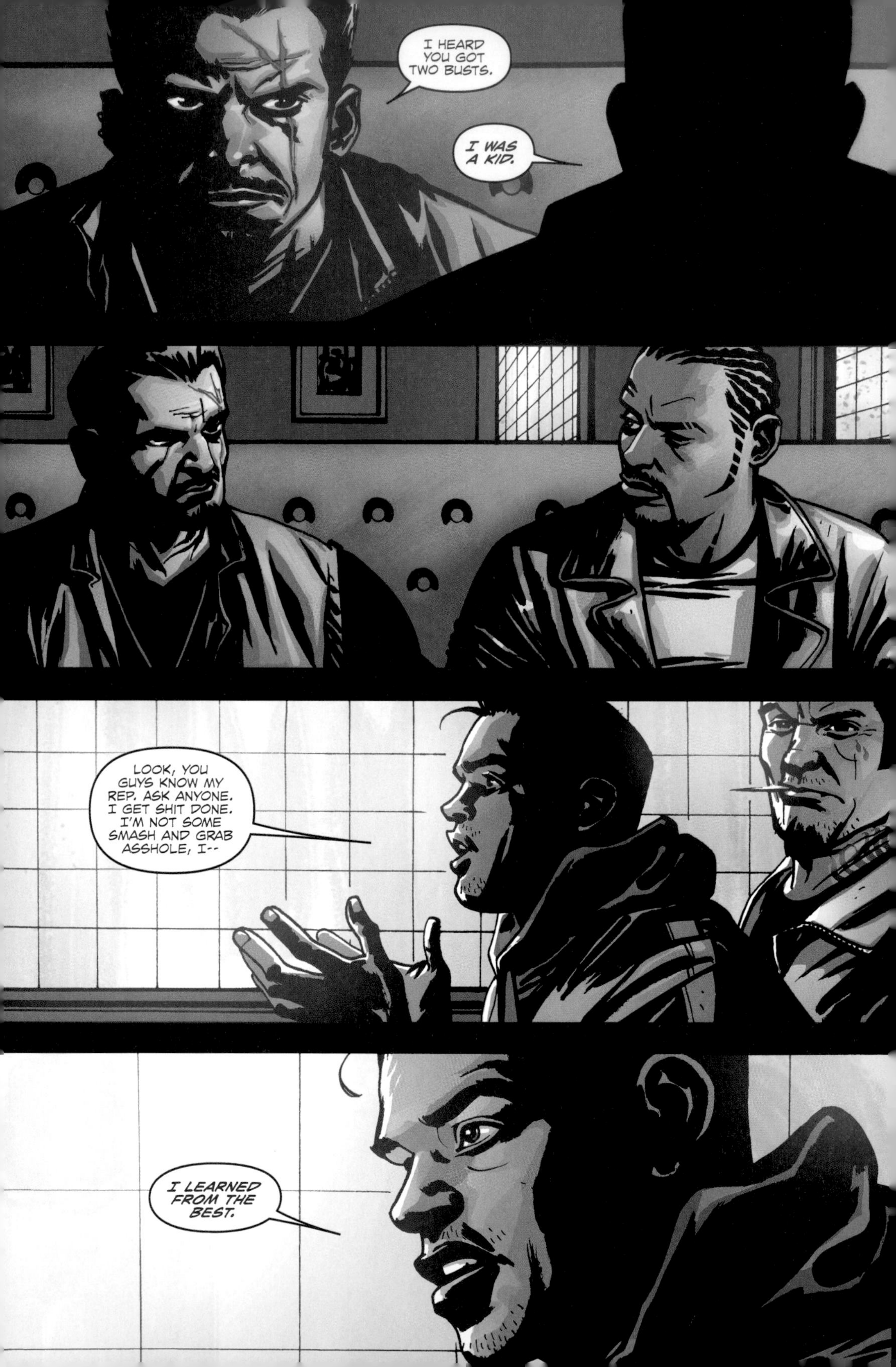
I HEARD YOU GOT TWO BUSTS.
I WAS A KID.
LOOK, YOU GUYS KNOW MY REP. ASK ANYONE. I GET SHIT DONE. I'M NOT SOME SMASH AND GRAB ASSHOLE, I--
I LEARNED FROM THE BEST.

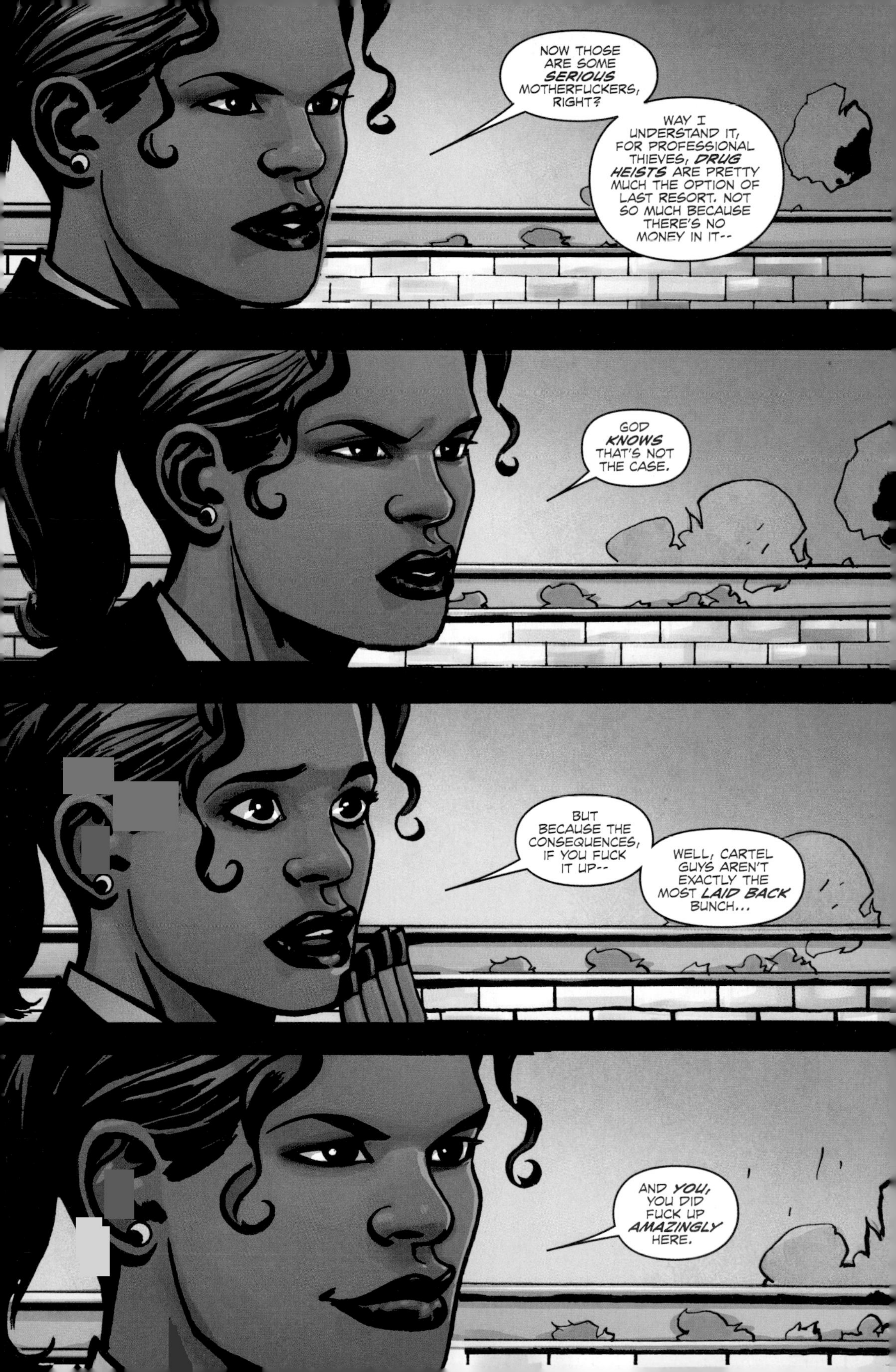
NOW THOSE ARE SOME SERIOUS MOTHERFUCKERS, RIGHT?
WAY I UNDERSTAND IT, FOR PROFESSIONAL THIEVES, DRUG HEISTS ARE PRETTY MUCH THE OPTION OF LAST RESORT. NOT SO MUCH BECAUSE THERE'S NO MONEY IN IT--
GOD KNOWS THAT'S NOT THE CASE.
BUT BECAUSE THE CONSEQUENCES, IF YOU FUCK IT UP--
WELL, CARTEL GUYS AREN'T EXACTLY THE MOST LAID BACK BUNCH...
AND YOU, YOU DID FUCK UP AMAZINGLY HERE.

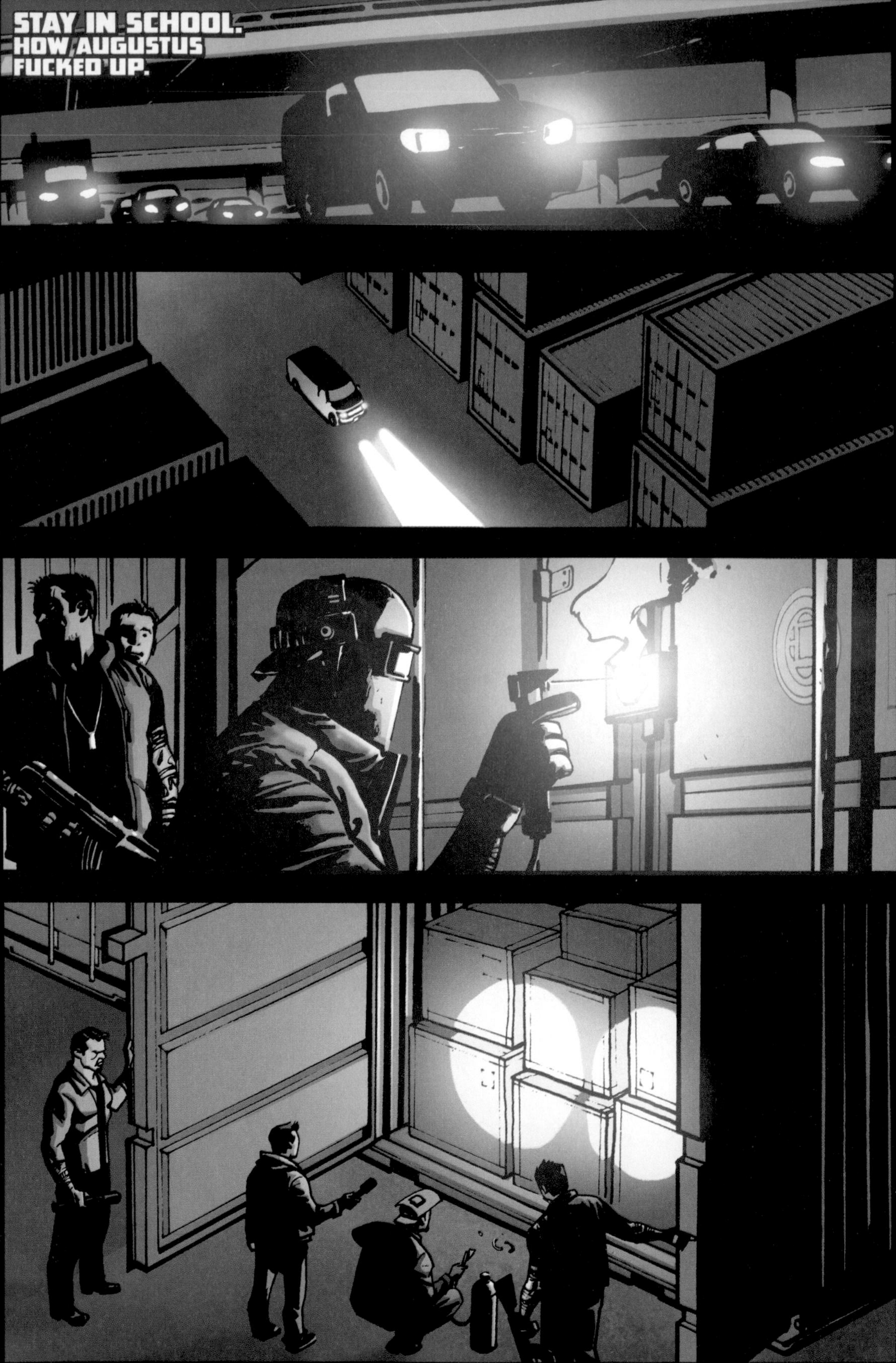
STAY IN SCHOOL.
HOW AUGUSTUS FUCKED UP.

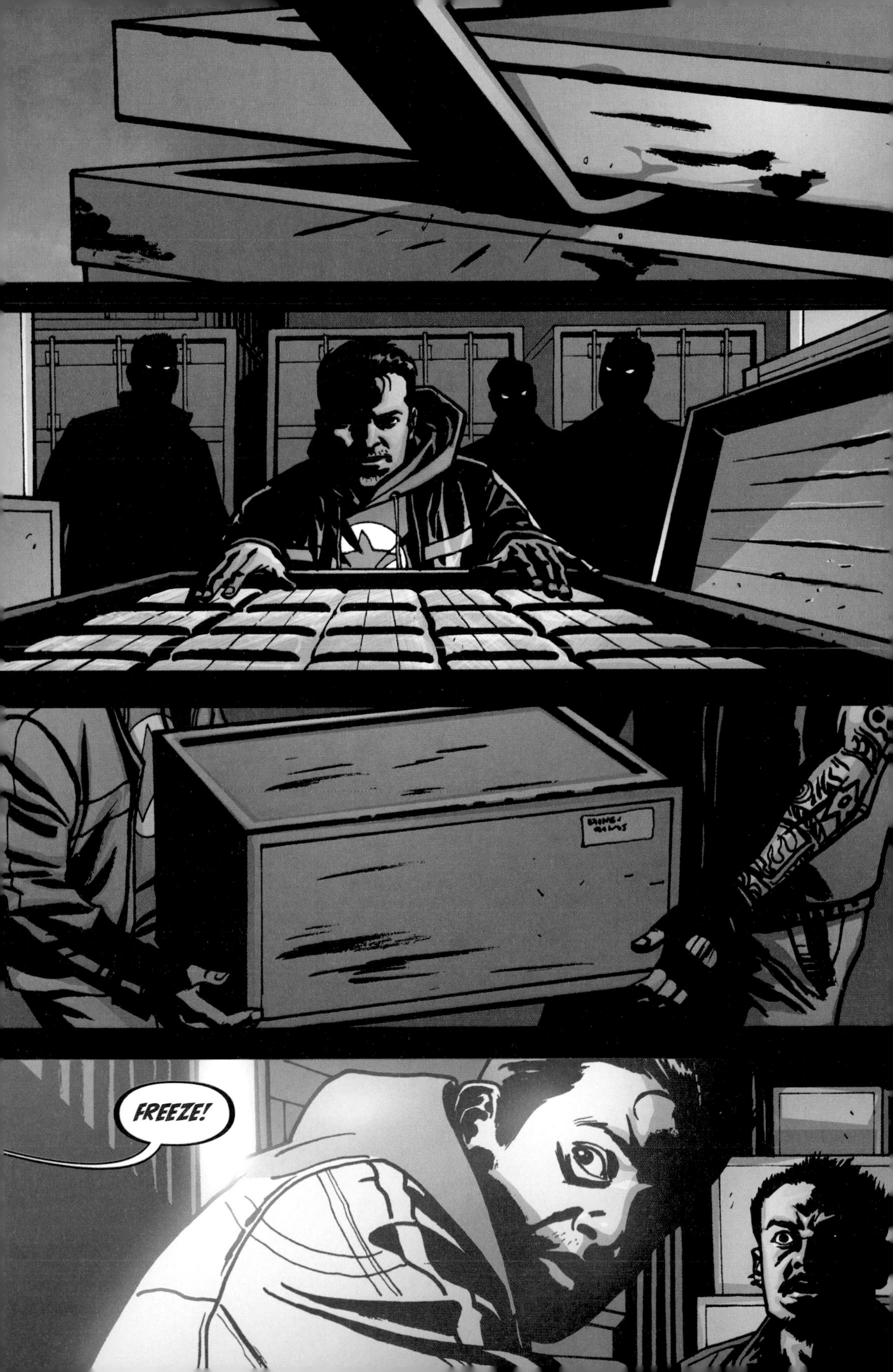
FREEZE!

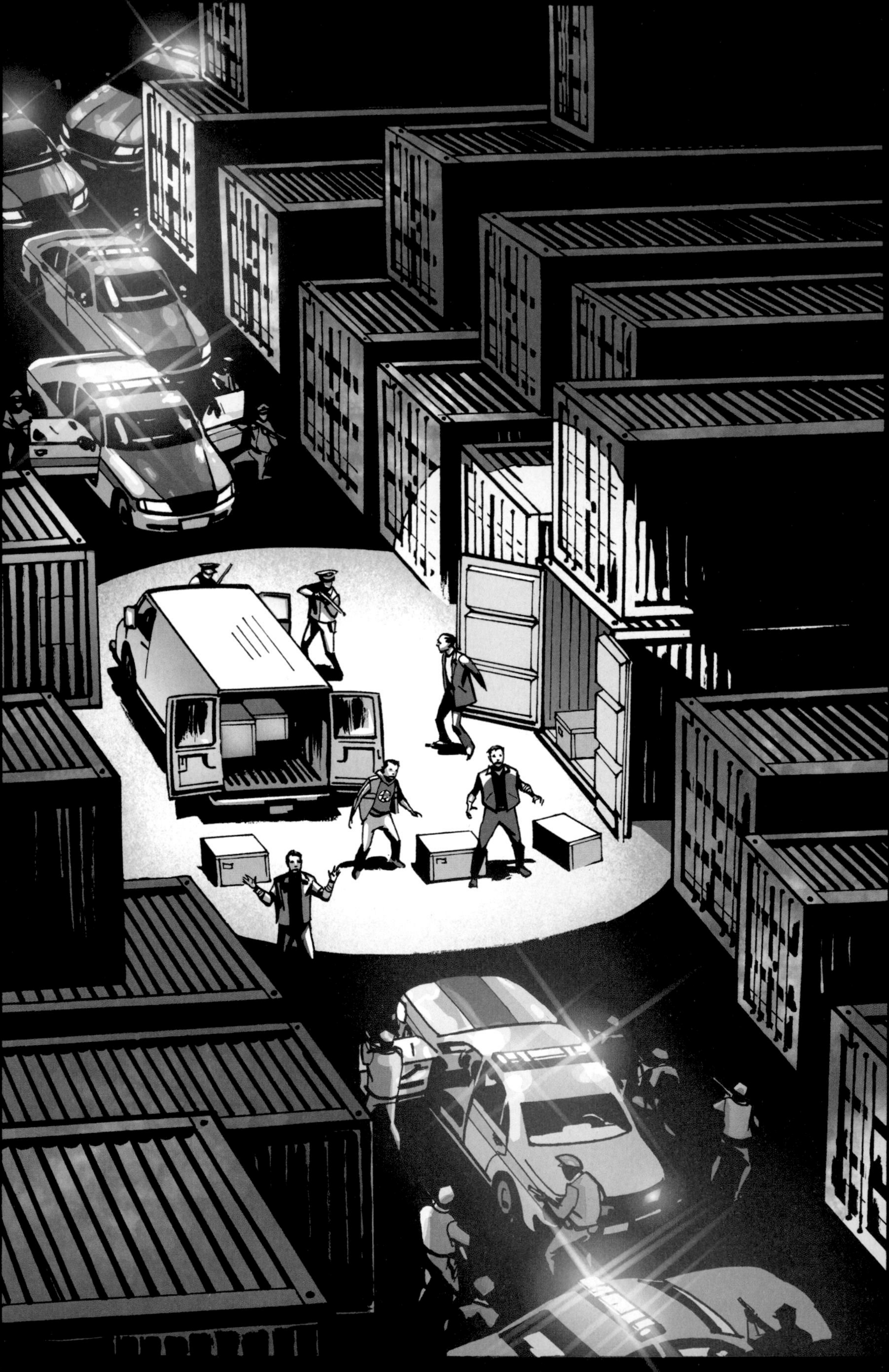

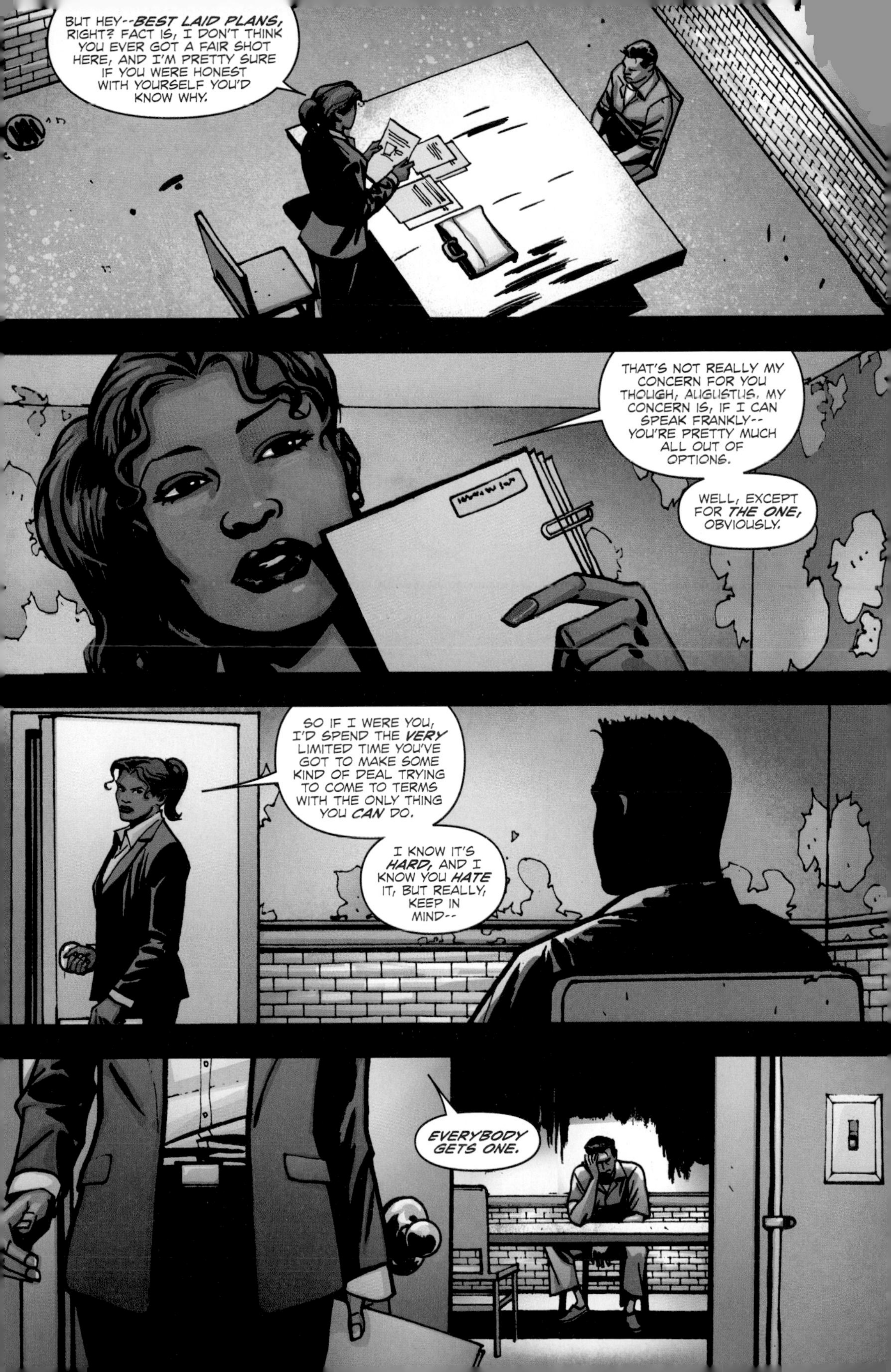
BUT HEY--BEST LAID PLANS, RIGHT? FACT IS, I DON'T THINK YOU EVER GOT A FAIR SHOT HERE, AND I'M PRETTY SURE IF YOU WERE HONEST WITH YOURSELF YOU'D KNOW WHY.
THAT'S NOT REALLY MY CONCERN FOR YOU THOUGH, AUGUSTUS. MY CONCERN IS, IF I CAN SPEAK FRANKLY-- YOU'RE PRETTY MUCH ALL OUT OF OPTIONS.
WELL, EXCEPT FOR THE ONE, OBVIOUSLY.
SO IF I WERE YOU, I'D SPEND THE VERY LIMITED TIME YOU'VE GOT TO MAKE SOME KIND OF DEAL TRYING TO COME TO TERMS WITH THE ONLY THING YOU CAN DO.
I KNOW IT'S HARD, AND I KNOW YOU HATE IT, BUT REALLY, KEEP IN MIND--
EVERYBODY GETS ONE.

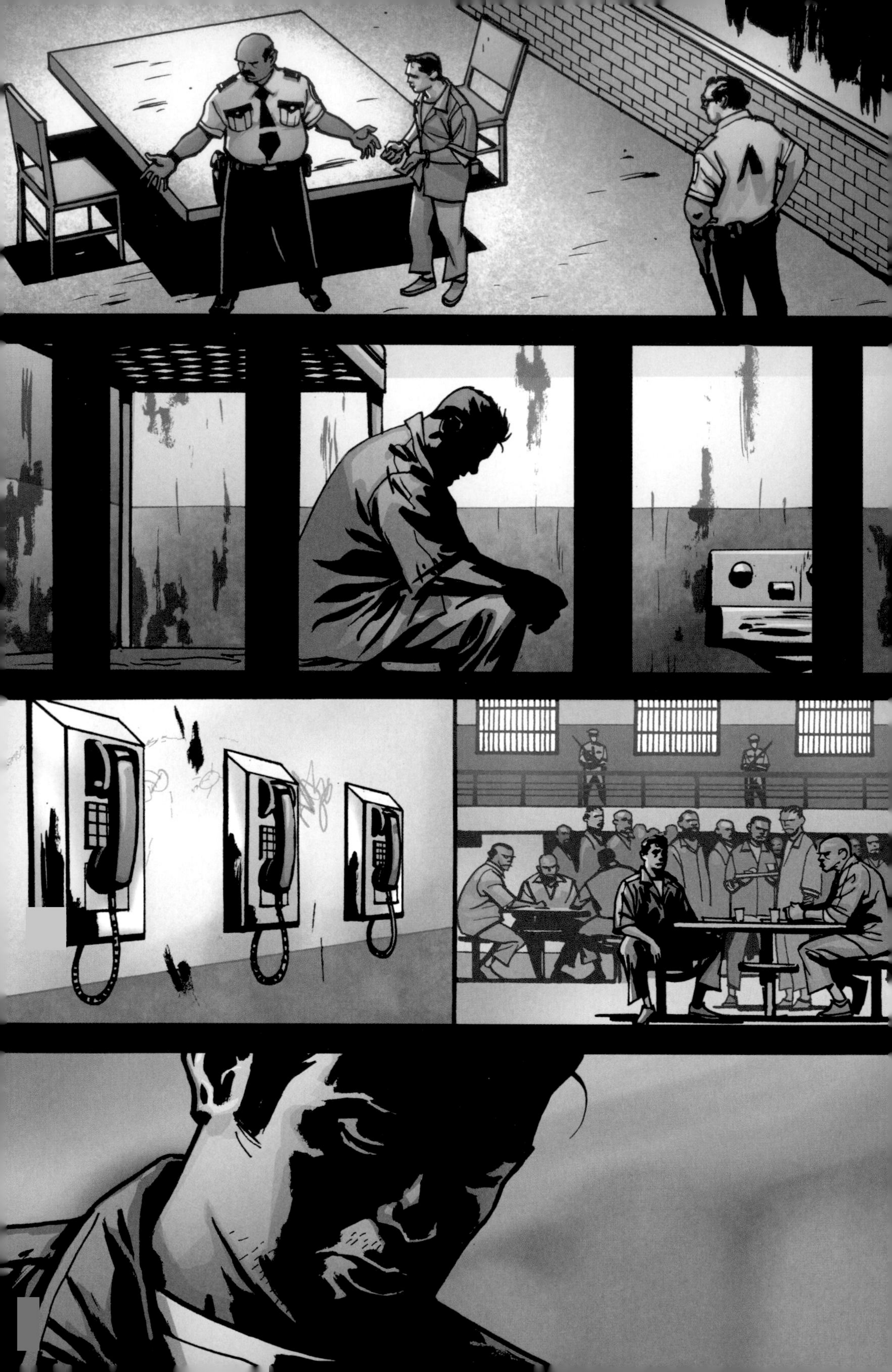

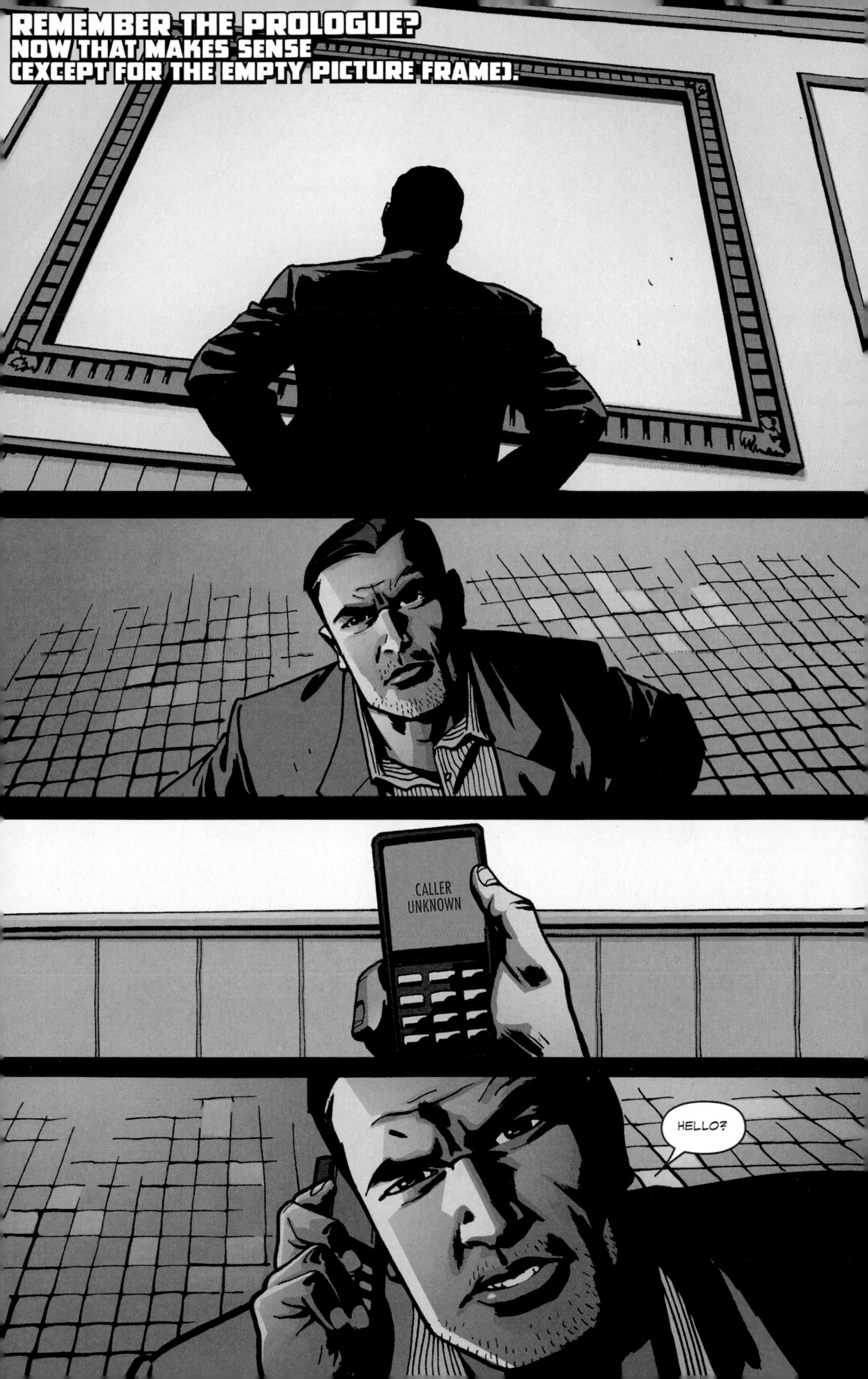
REMEMBER THE PROLOGUE?
NOW THAT MAKES SENSE
(EXCEPT FOR THE EMPTY PICTURE FRAME).
CALLER UNKNOWN
HELLO?

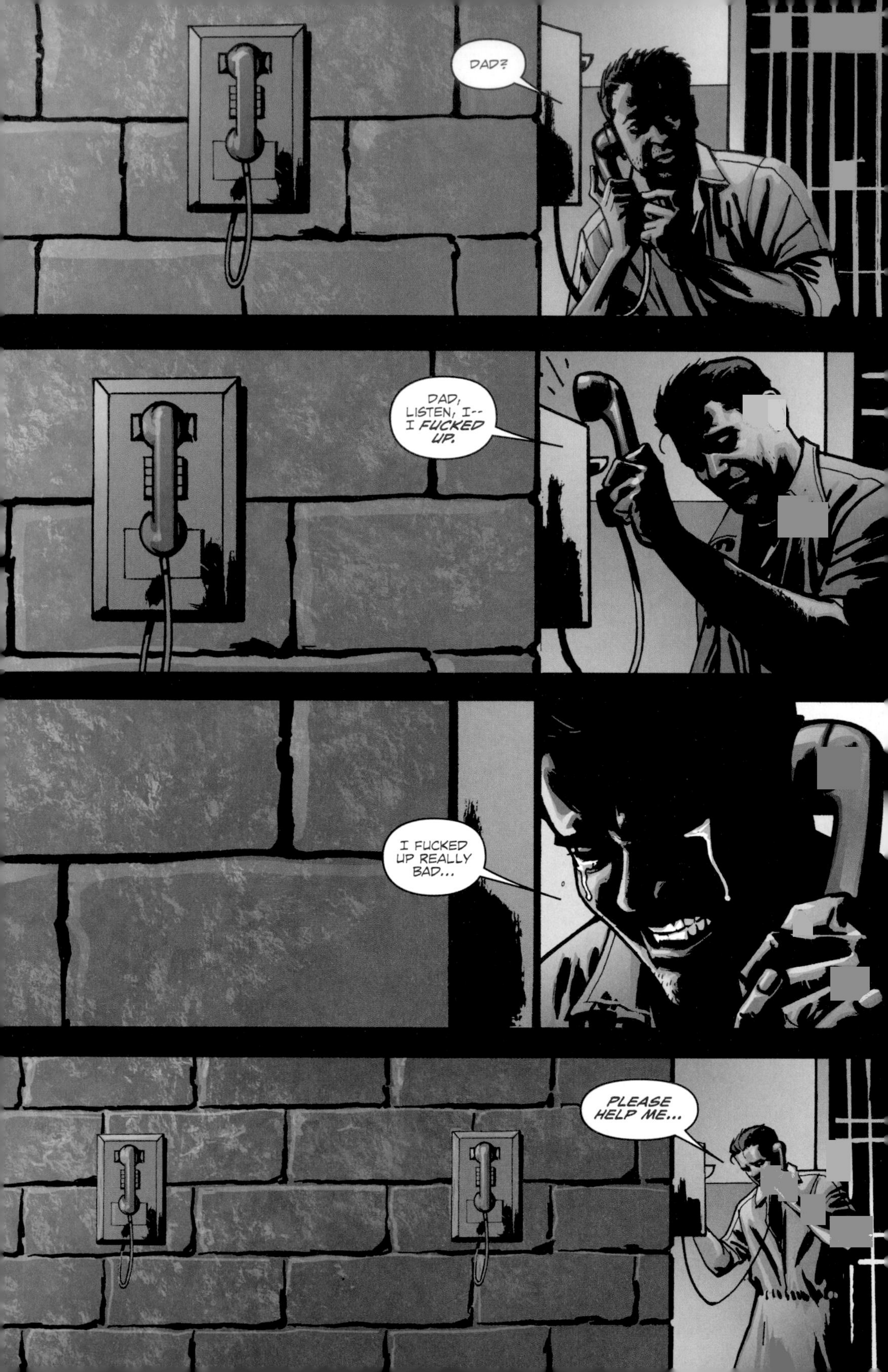
DAD?
DAD, LISTEN, I-- I *FUCKED UP.*
I FUCKED UP REALLY BAD...
PLEASE HELP ME...

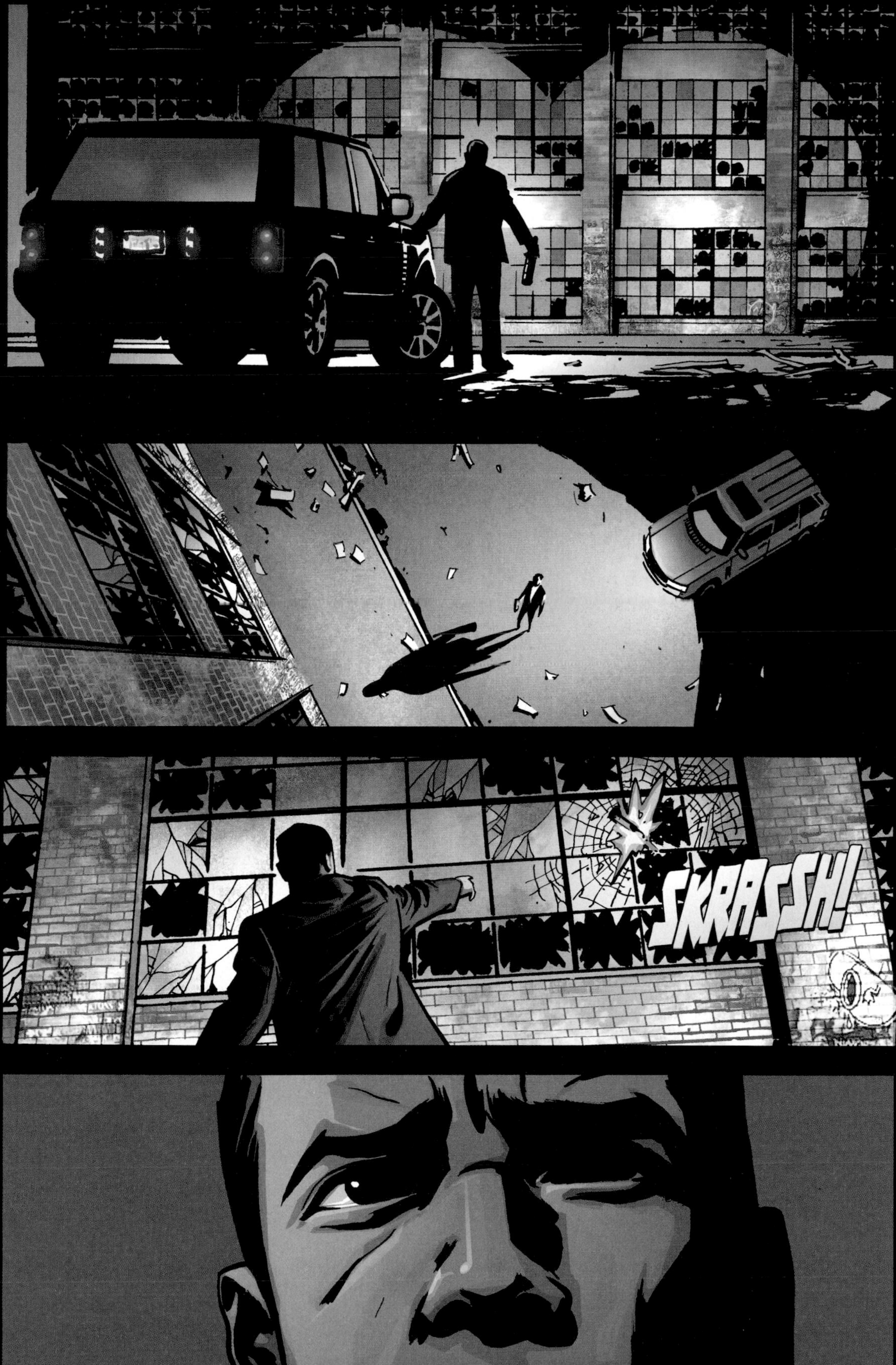
SKRASSH!

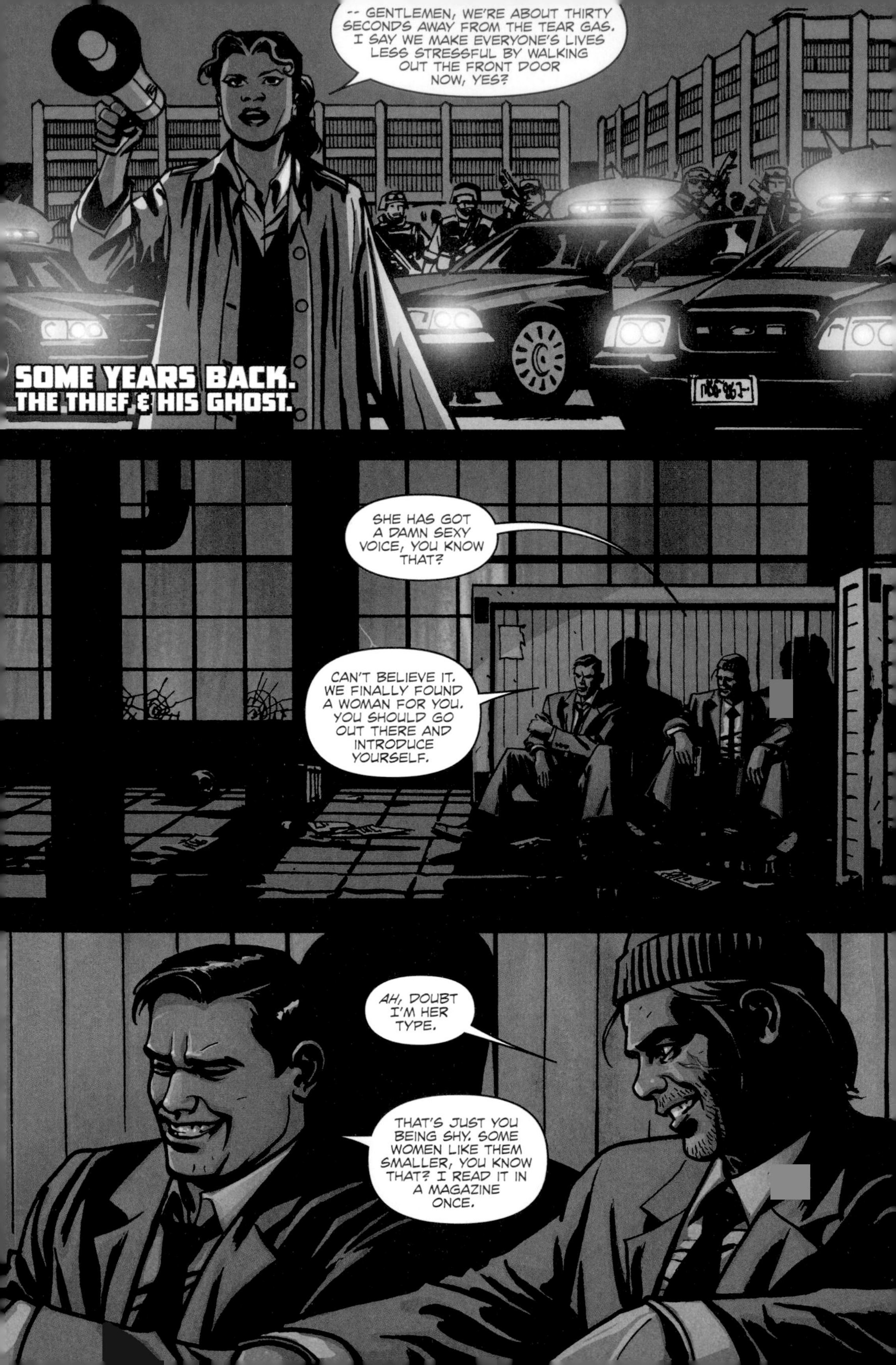
-- GENTLEMEN, WE'RE ABOUT THIRTY SECONDS AWAY FROM THE TEAR GAS. I SAY WE MAKE EVERYONE'S LIVES LESS STRESSFUL BY WALKING OUT THE FRONT DOOR NOW, YES?
SOME YEARS BACK. THE THIEF & HIS GHOST.
SHE HAS GOT A DAMN SEXY VOICE, YOU KNOW THAT?
CAN'T BELIEVE IT. WE FINALLY FOUND A WOMAN FOR YOU. YOU SHOULD GO OUT THERE AND INTRODUCE YOURSELF.
AH, DOUBT I'M HER TYPE.
THAT'S JUST YOU BEING SHY. SOME WOMEN LIKE THEM SMALLER, YOU KNOW THAT? I READ IT IN A MAGAZINE ONCE.

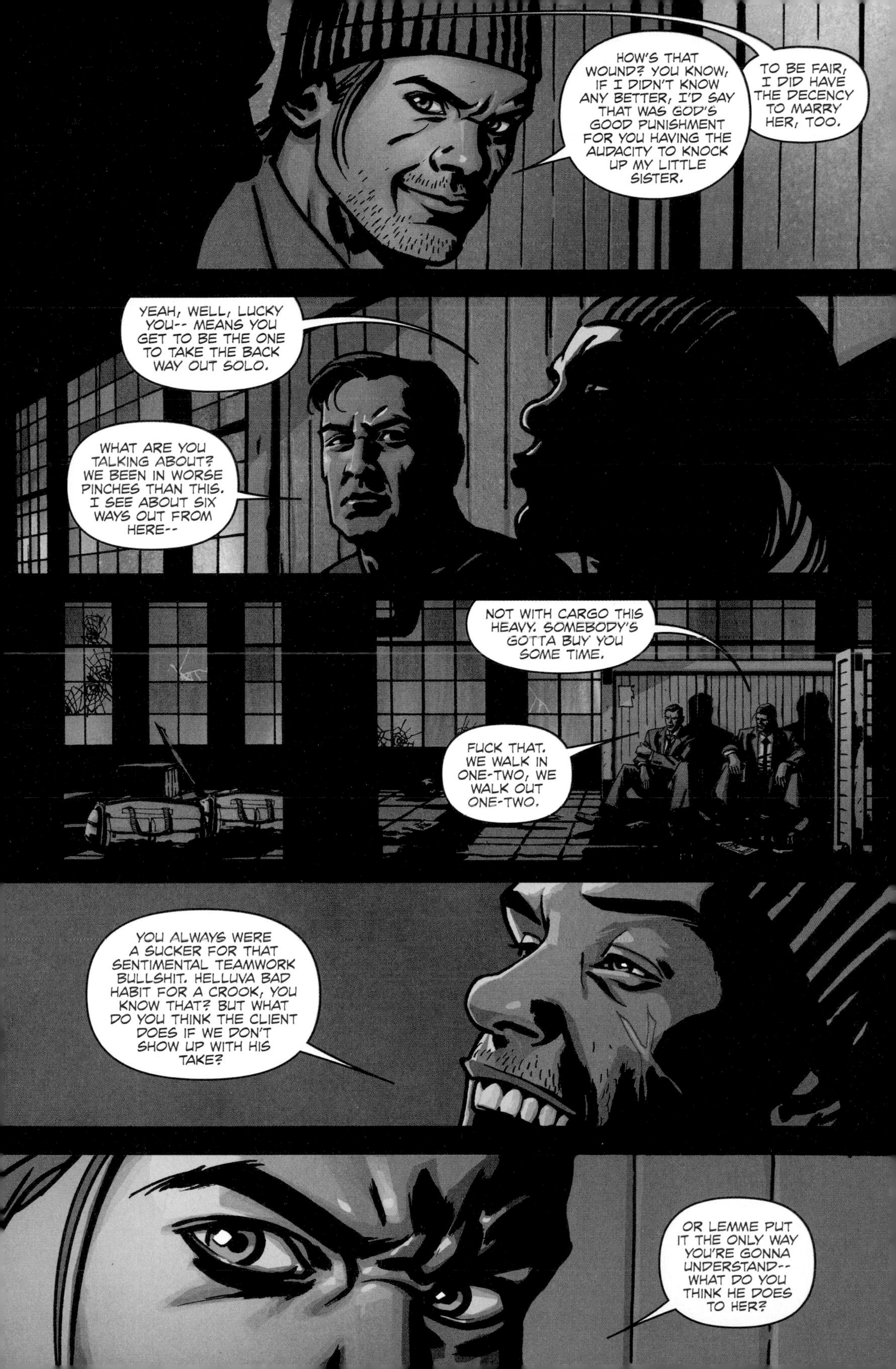
HOW'S THAT WOUND? YOU KNOW, IF I DIDN'T KNOW ANY BETTER, I'D SAY THAT WAS GOD'S GOOD PUNISHMENT FOR YOU HAVING THE AUDACITY TO KNOCK UP MY LITTLE SISTER.
TO BE FAIR, I DID HAVE THE DECENCY TO MARRY HER, TOO.
YEAH, WELL, LUCKY YOU-- MEANS YOU GET TO BE THE ONE TO TAKE THE BACK WAY OUT SOLO.
WHAT ARE YOU TALKING ABOUT? WE BEEN IN WORSE PINCHES THAN THIS. I SEE ABOUT SIX WAYS OUT FROM HERE--
NOT WITH CARGO THIS HEAVY. SOMEBODY'S GOTTA BUY YOU SOME TIME.
FUCK THAT. WE WALK IN ONE-TWO, WE WALK OUT ONE-TWO.
YOU ALWAYS WERE A SUCKER FOR THAT SENTIMENTAL TEAMWORK BULLSHIT. HELLUVA BAD HABIT FOR A CROOK, YOU KNOW THAT? BUT WHAT DO YOU THINK THE CLIENT DOES IF WE DON'T SHOW UP WITH HIS TAKE?
OR LEMME PUT IT THE ONLY WAY YOU'RE GONNA UNDERSTAND-- WHAT DO YOU THINK HE DOES TO HER?

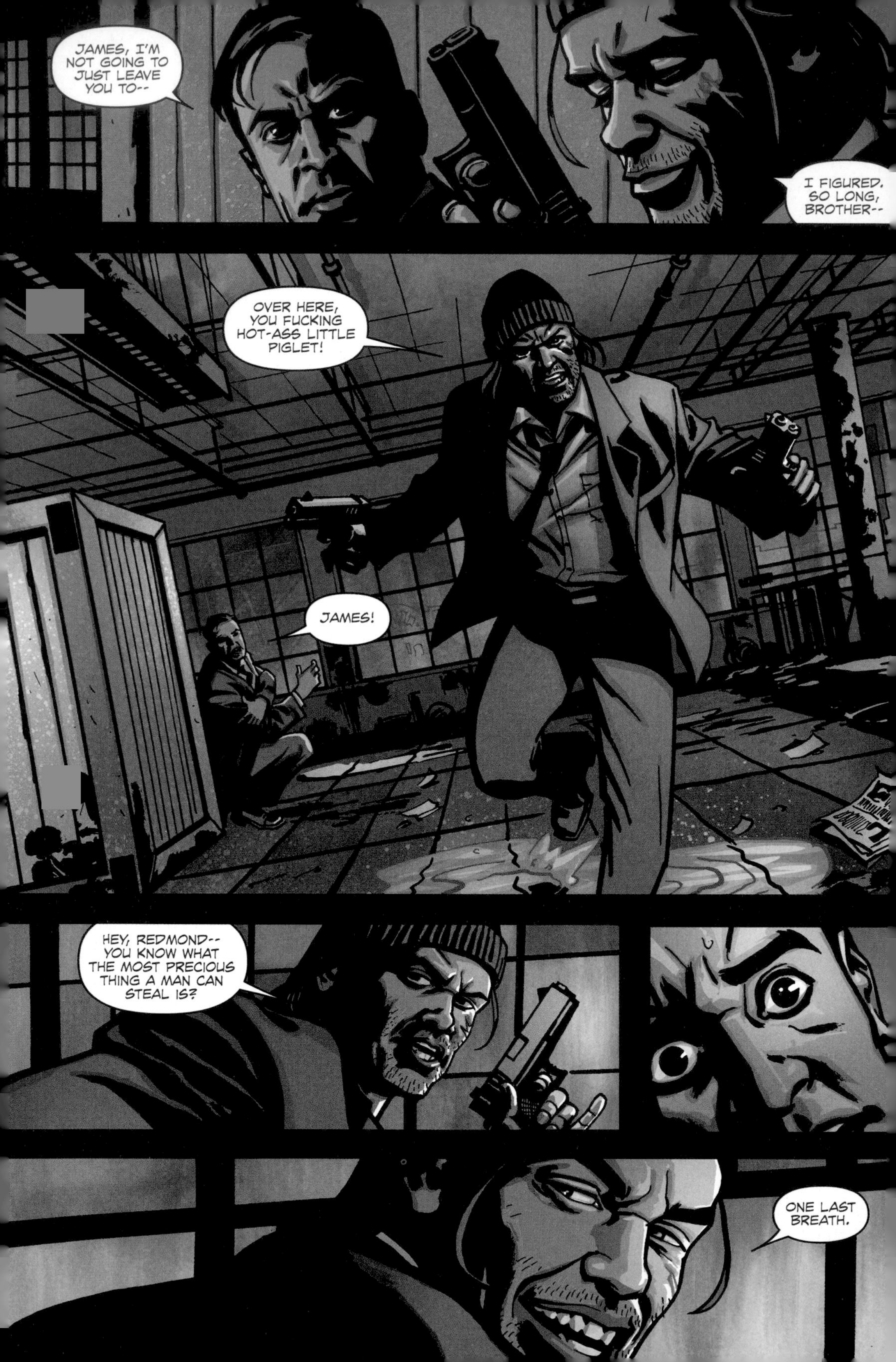
JAMES, I'M NOT GOING TO JUST LEAVE YOU TO--
I FIGURED. SO LONG, BROTHER--
OVER HERE, YOU FUCKING HOT-ASS LITTLE PIGLET!
JAMES!
HEY, REDMOND-- YOU KNOW WHAT THE MOST PRECIOUS THING A MAN CAN STEAL IS?
ONE LAST BREATH.

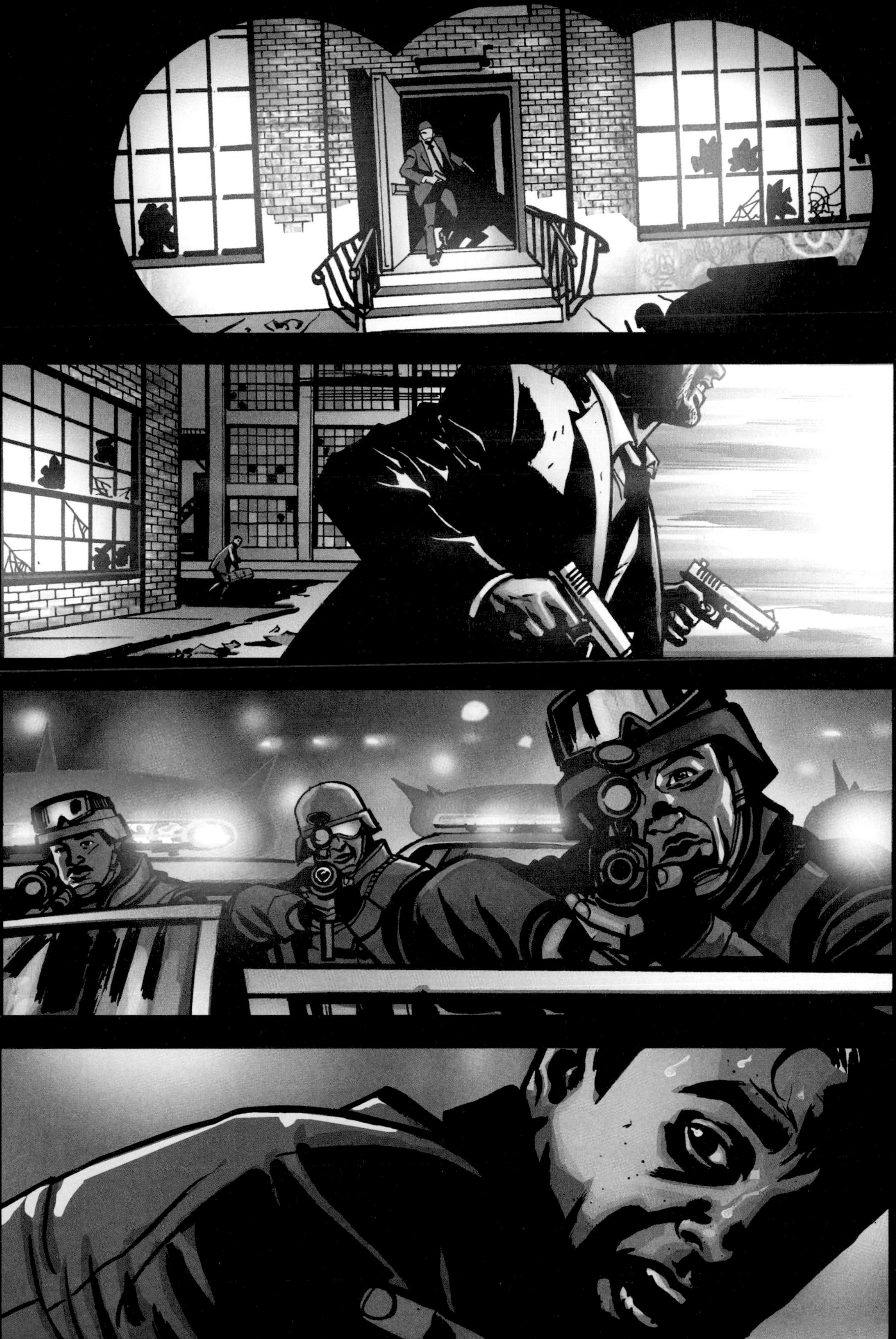

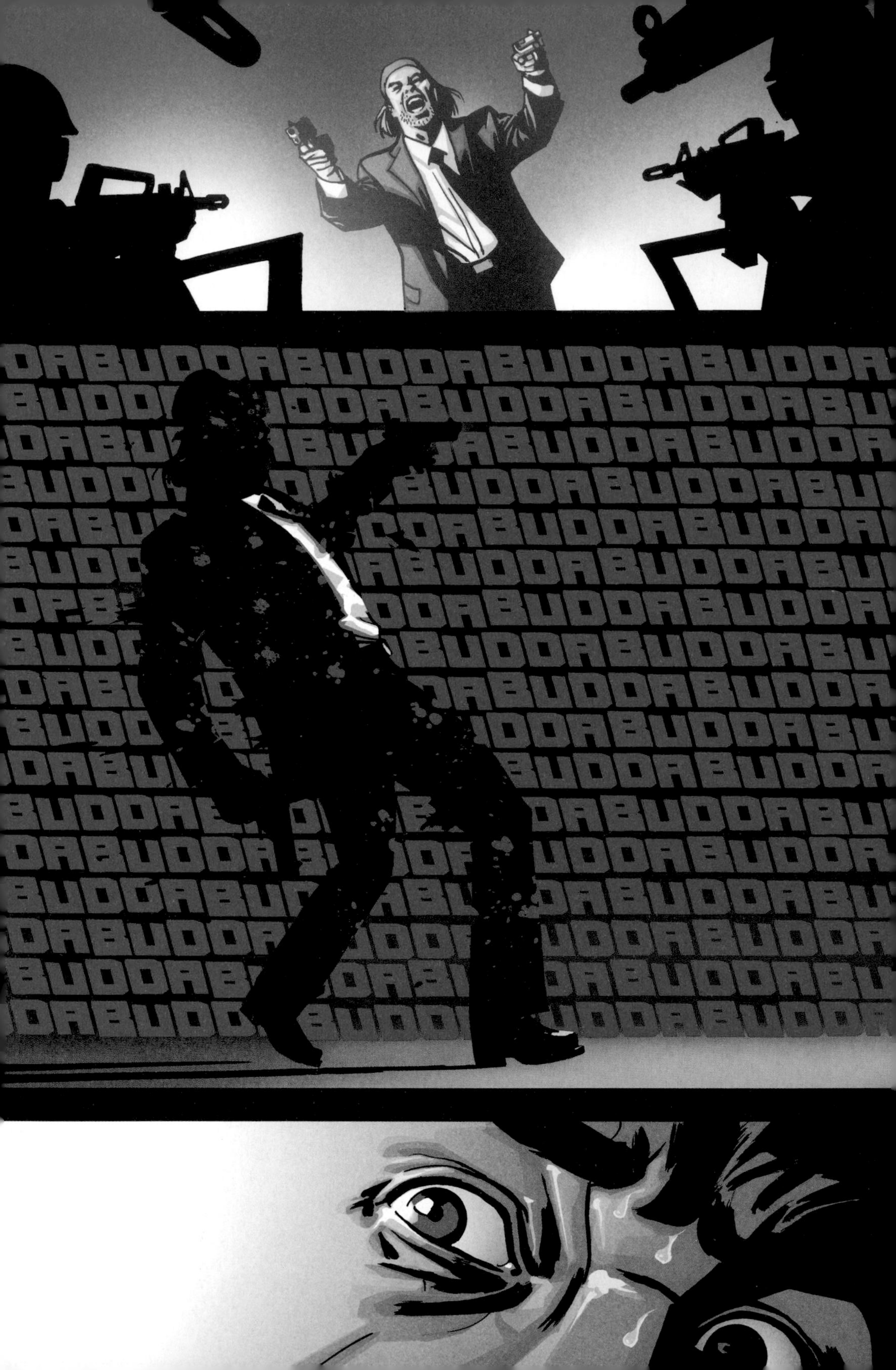
BUDDABUDDABUDDA

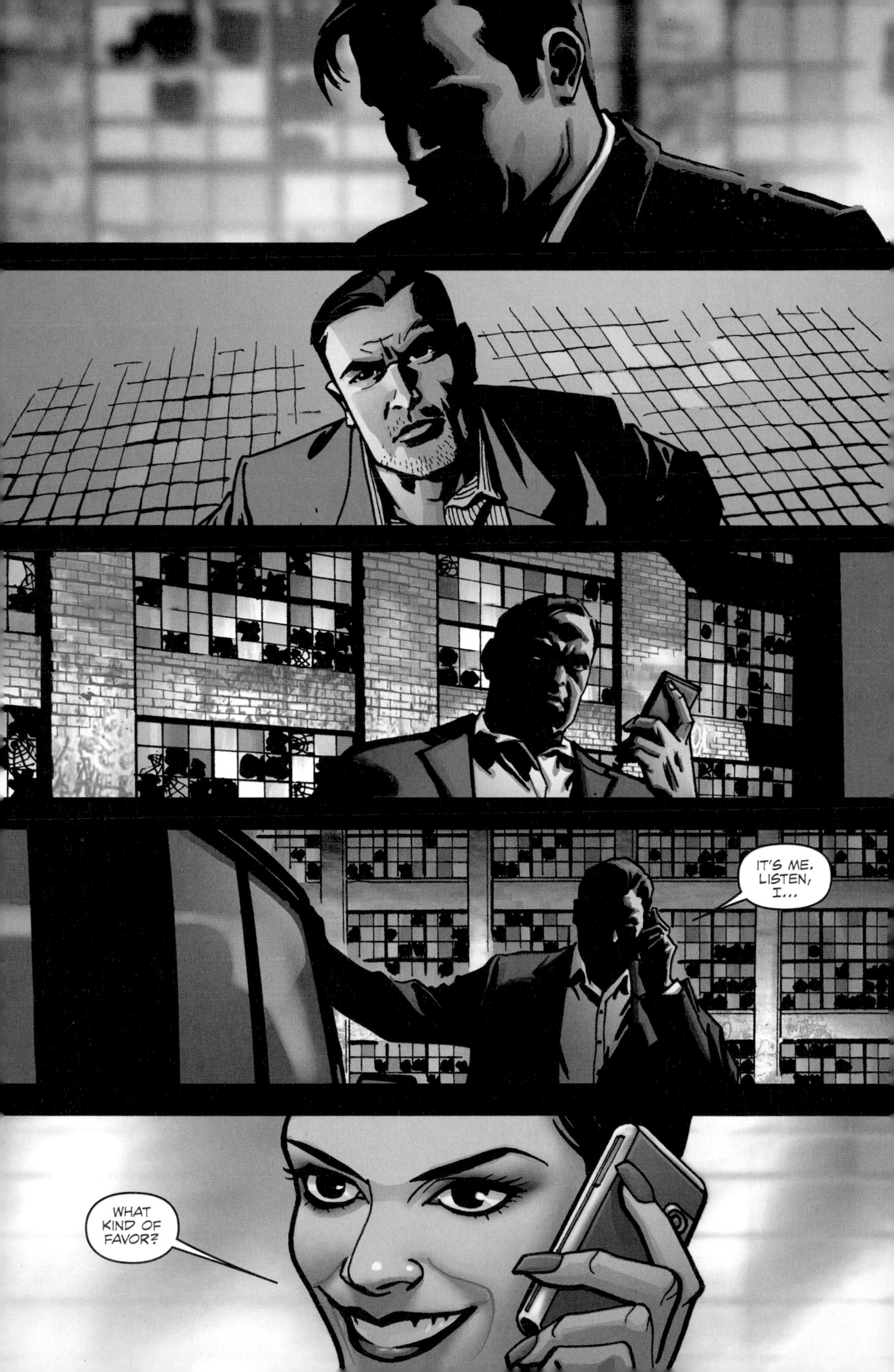
IT'S ME. LISTEN, I...
WHAT KIND OF FAVOR?

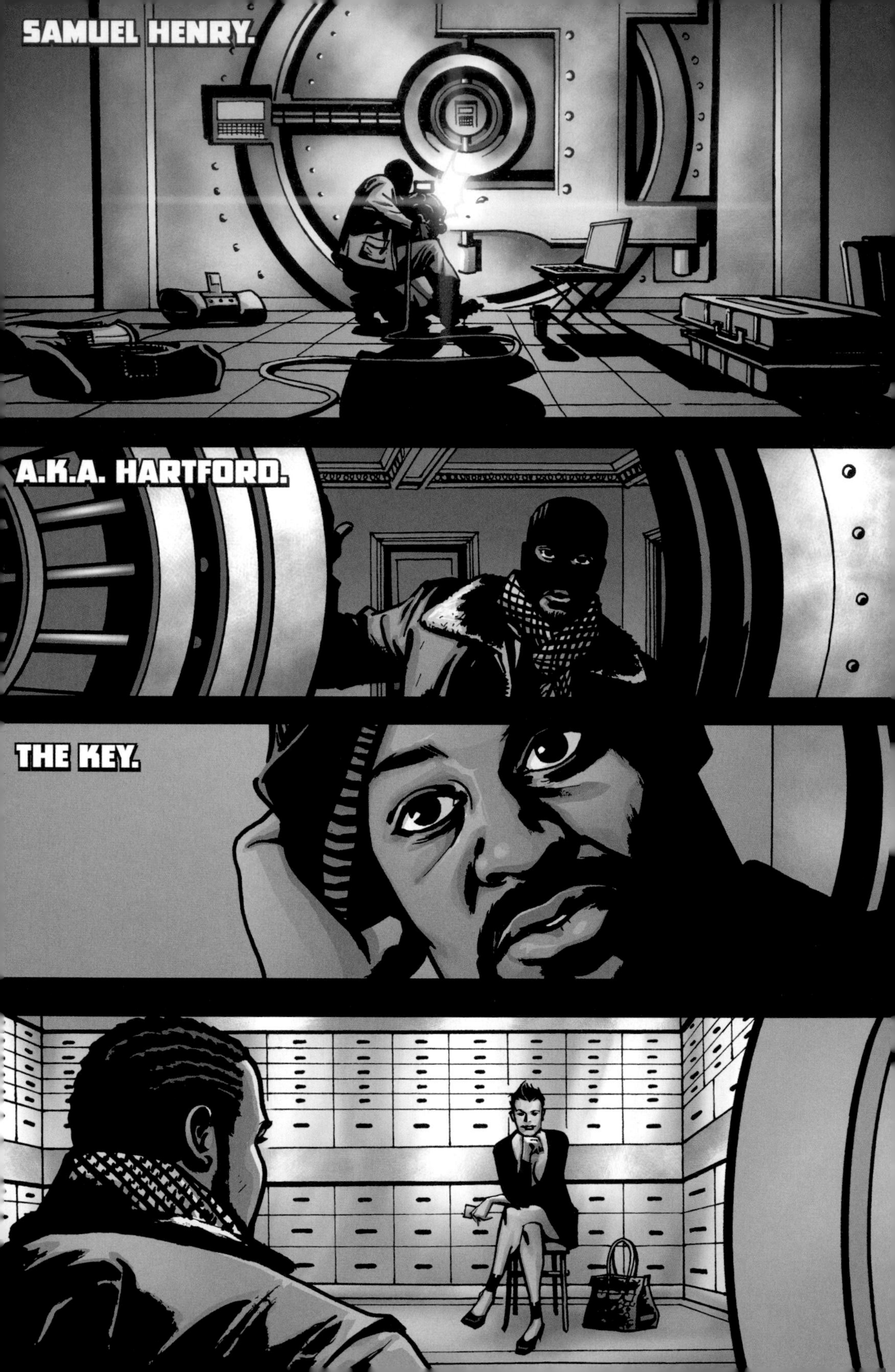
SAMUEL HENRY.
A.K.A. HARTFORD.
THE KEY.

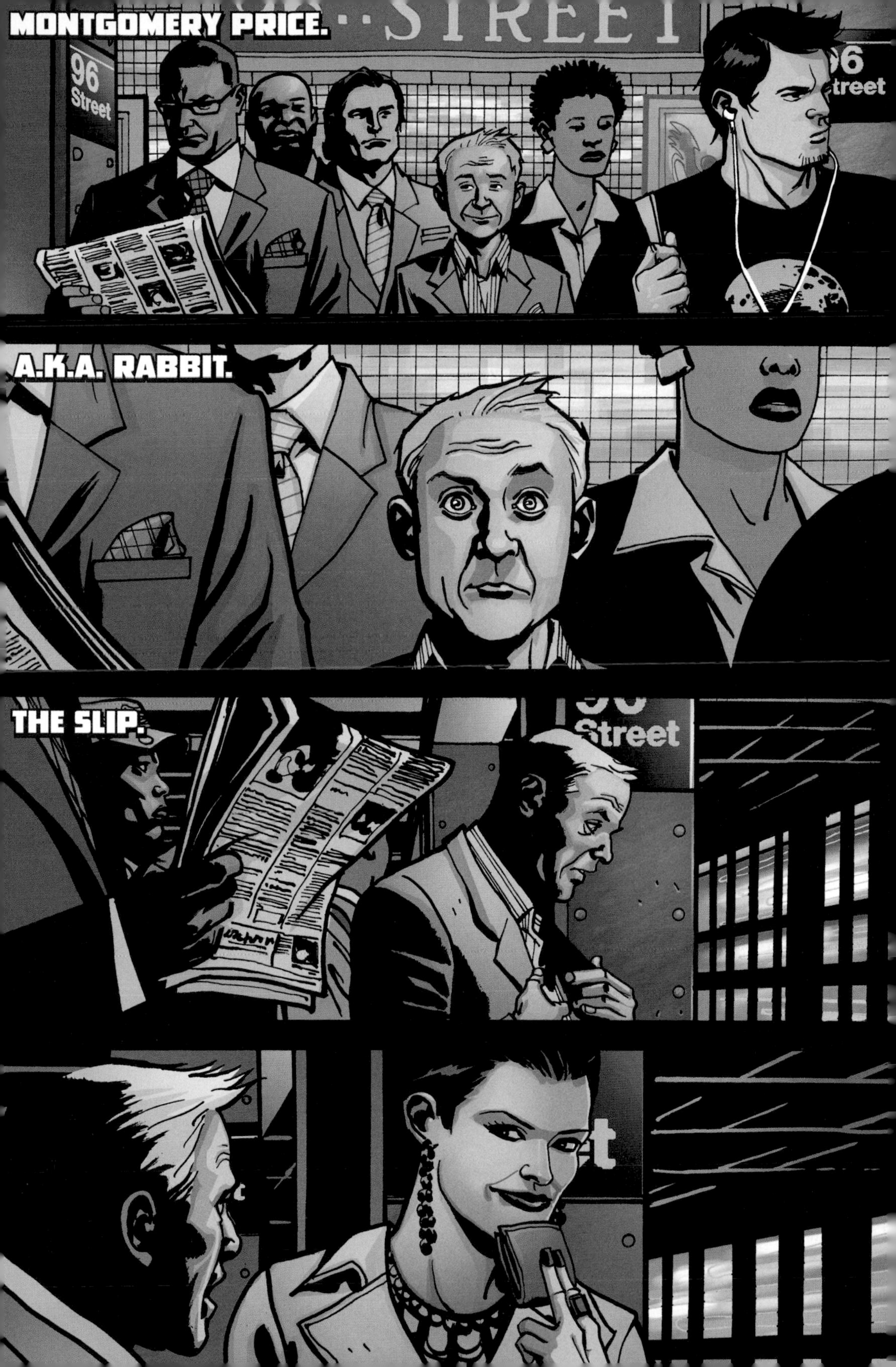

MONTGOMERY PRICE.
STREET
96 Street
96 Street
A.K.A. RABBIT.
THE SLIP.
Street

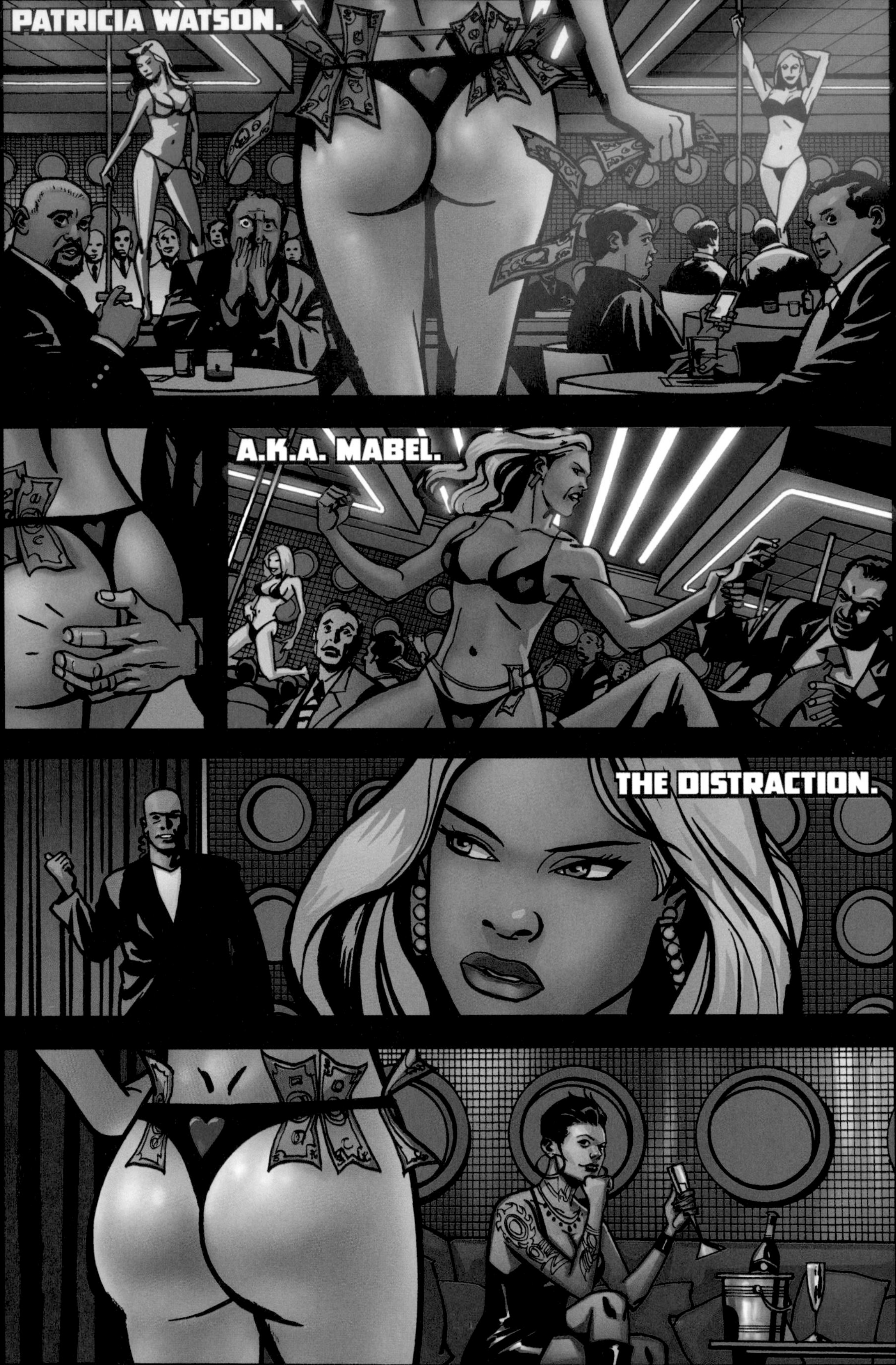
PATRICIA WATSON.
A.K.A. MABEL.
THE DISTRACTION.

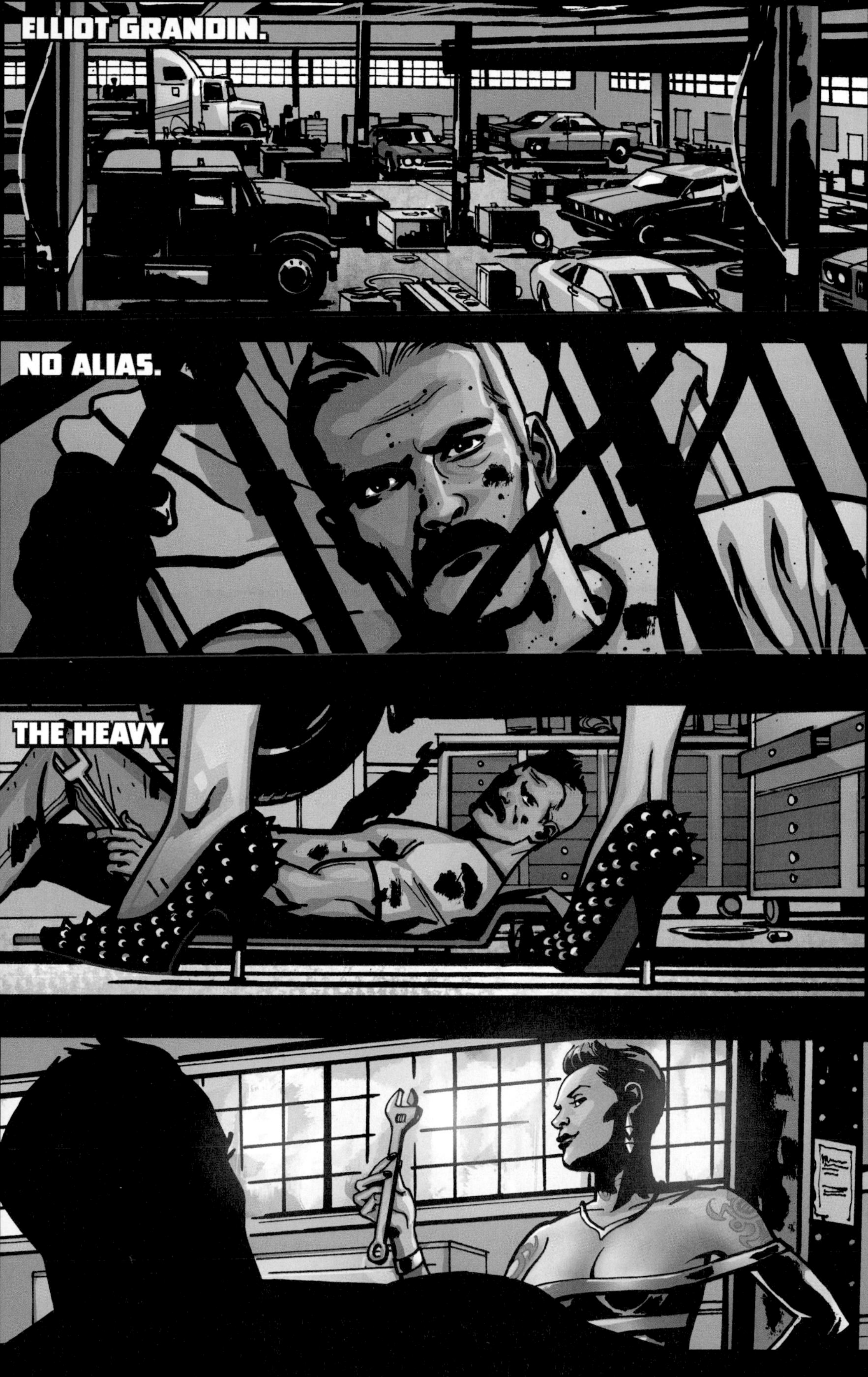
ELLIOT GRANDIN.
NO ALIAS.
THE HEAVY.

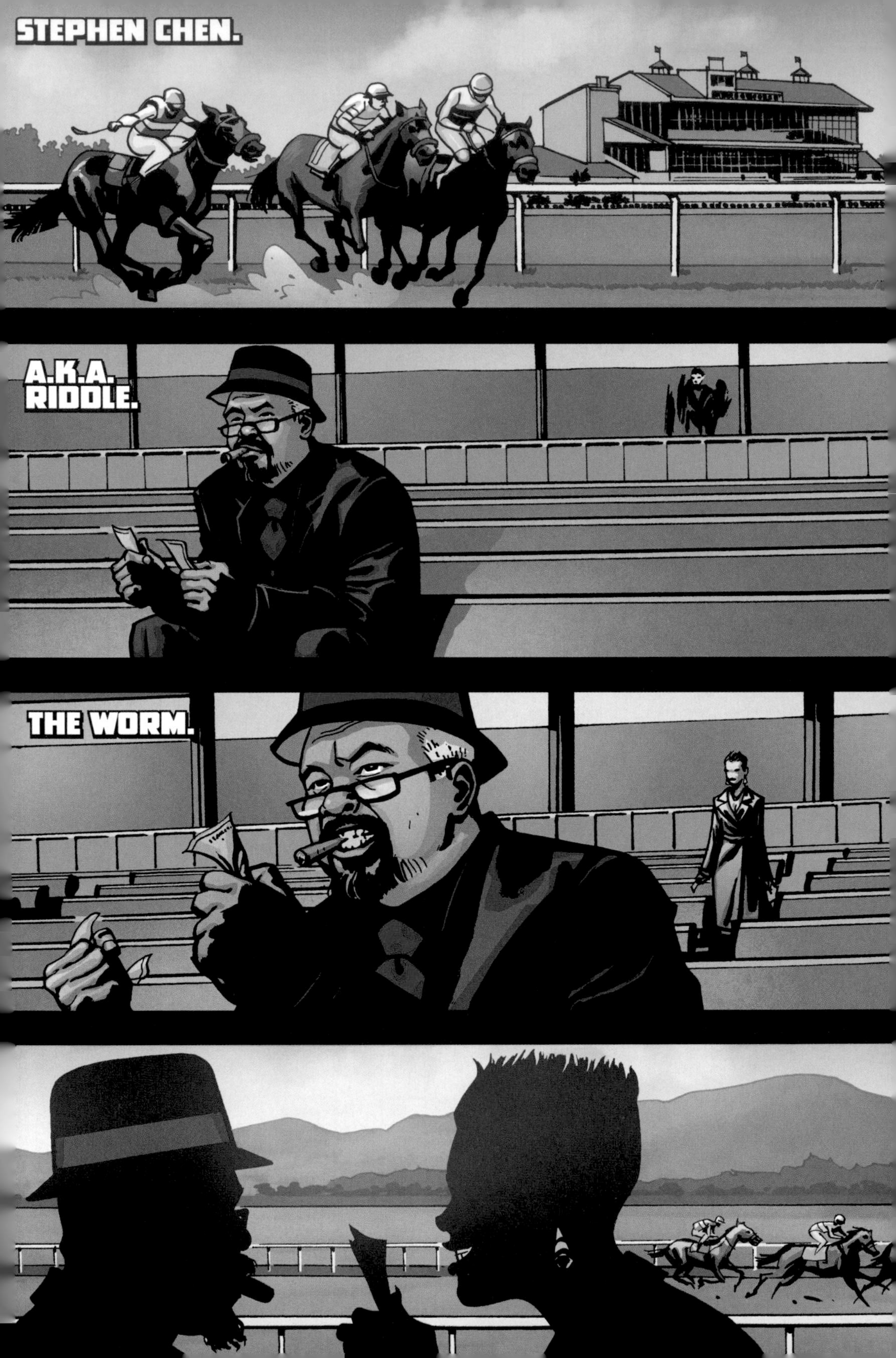
STEPHEN CHEN.
A.K.A. RIDDLE.
THE WORM.

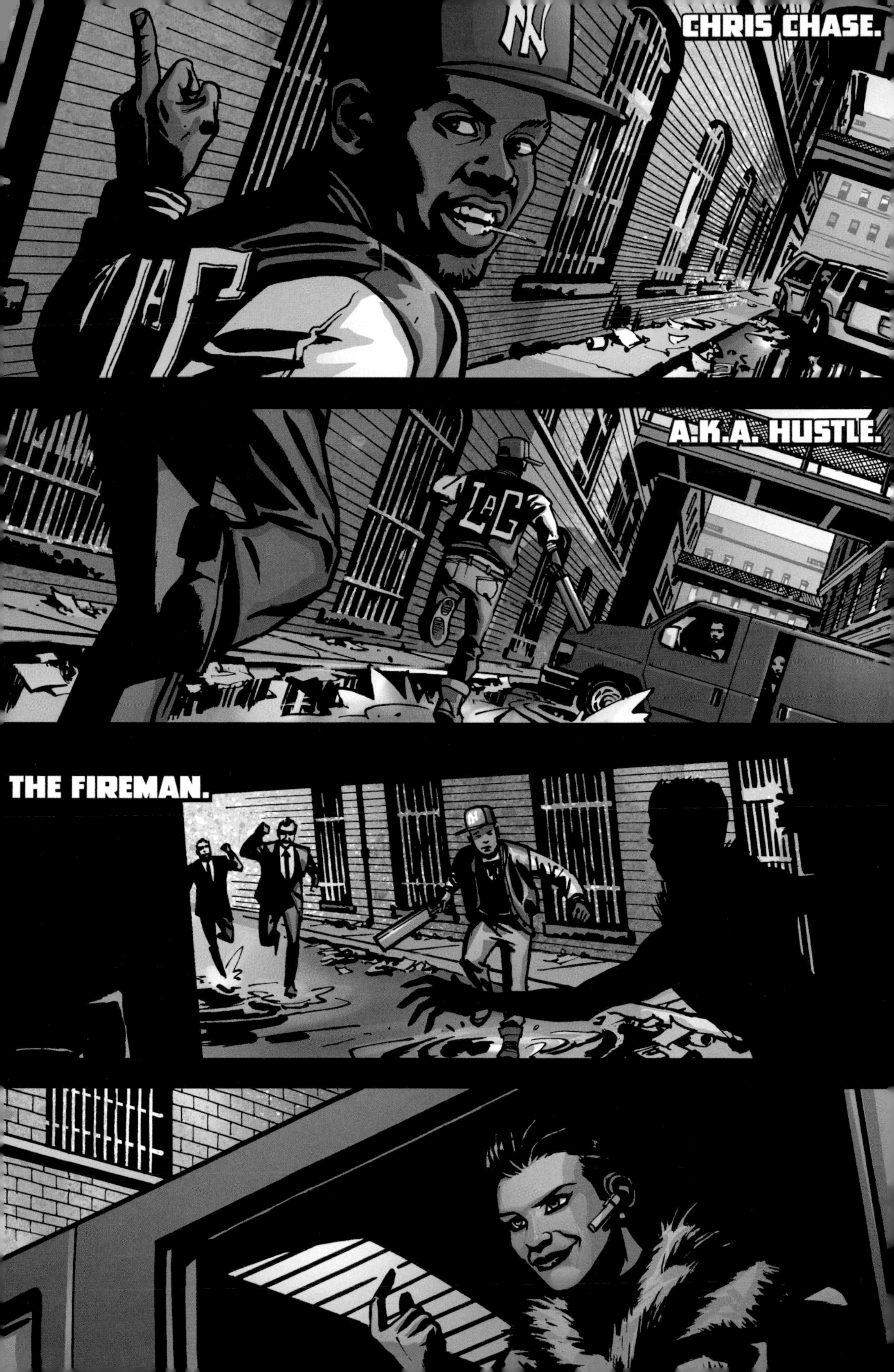
CHRIS CHASE.
A.K.A. HUSTLE.
THE FIREMAN.

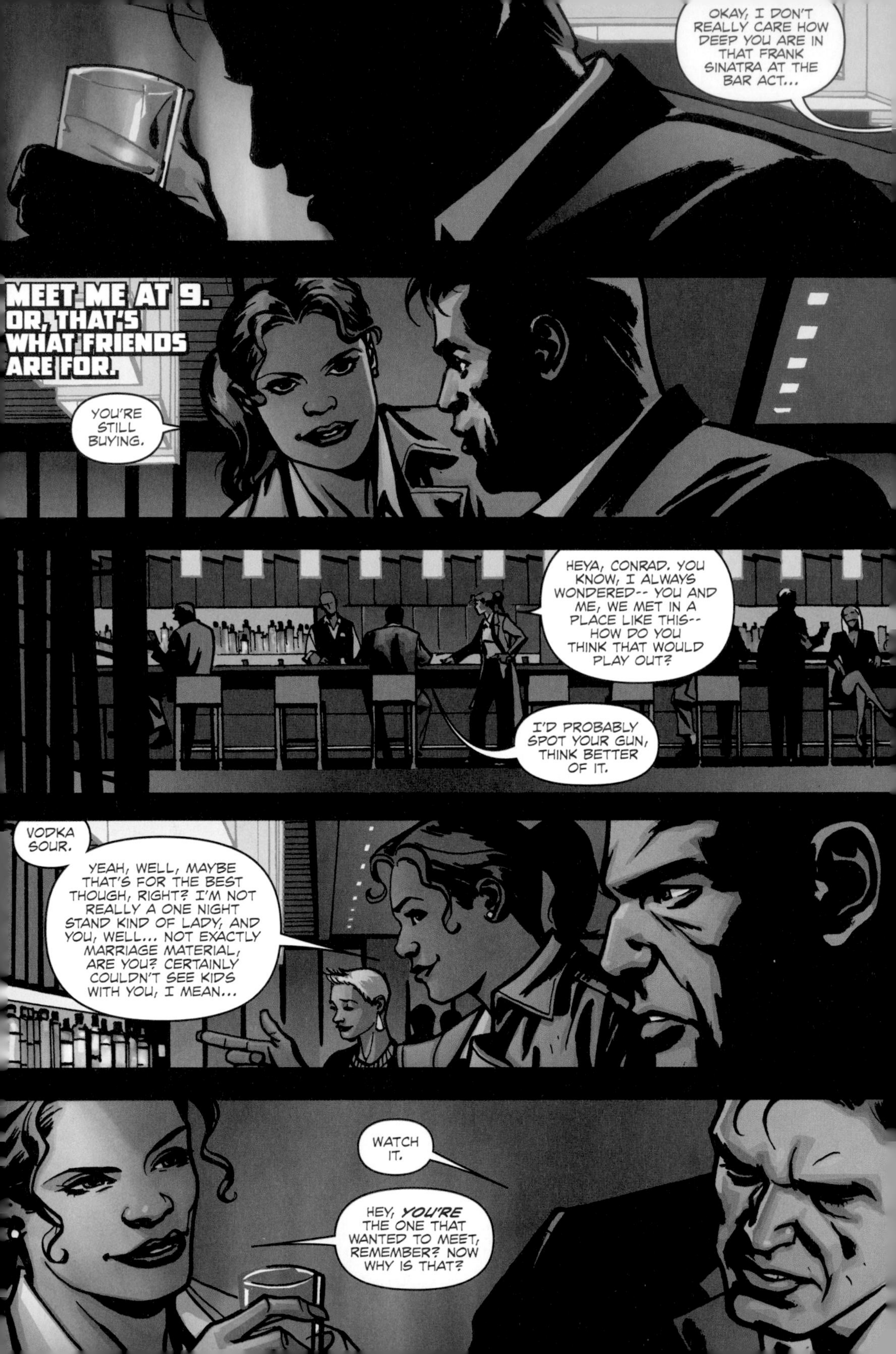
OKAY, I DON'T REALLY CARE HOW DEEP YOU ARE IN THAT FRANK SINATRA AT THE BAR ACT...
MEET ME AT 9. OR, THAT'S WHAT FRIENDS ARE FOR.
YOU'RE STILL BUYING.
HEYA, CONRAD. YOU KNOW, I ALWAYS WONDERED-- YOU AND ME, WE MET IN A PLACE LIKE THIS-- HOW DO YOU THINK THAT WOULD PLAY OUT?
I'D PROBABLY SPOT YOUR GUN, THINK BETTER OF IT.
VODKA SOUR.
YEAH, WELL, MAYBE THAT'S FOR THE BEST THOUGH, RIGHT? I'M NOT REALLY A ONE NIGHT STAND KIND OF LADY, AND YOU, WELL... NOT EXACTLY MARRIAGE MATERIAL, ARE YOU? CERTAINLY COULDN'T SEE KIDS WITH YOU, I MEAN...
WATCH IT.
HEY, *YOU'RE* THE ONE THAT WANTED TO MEET, REMEMBER? NOW WHY IS THAT?

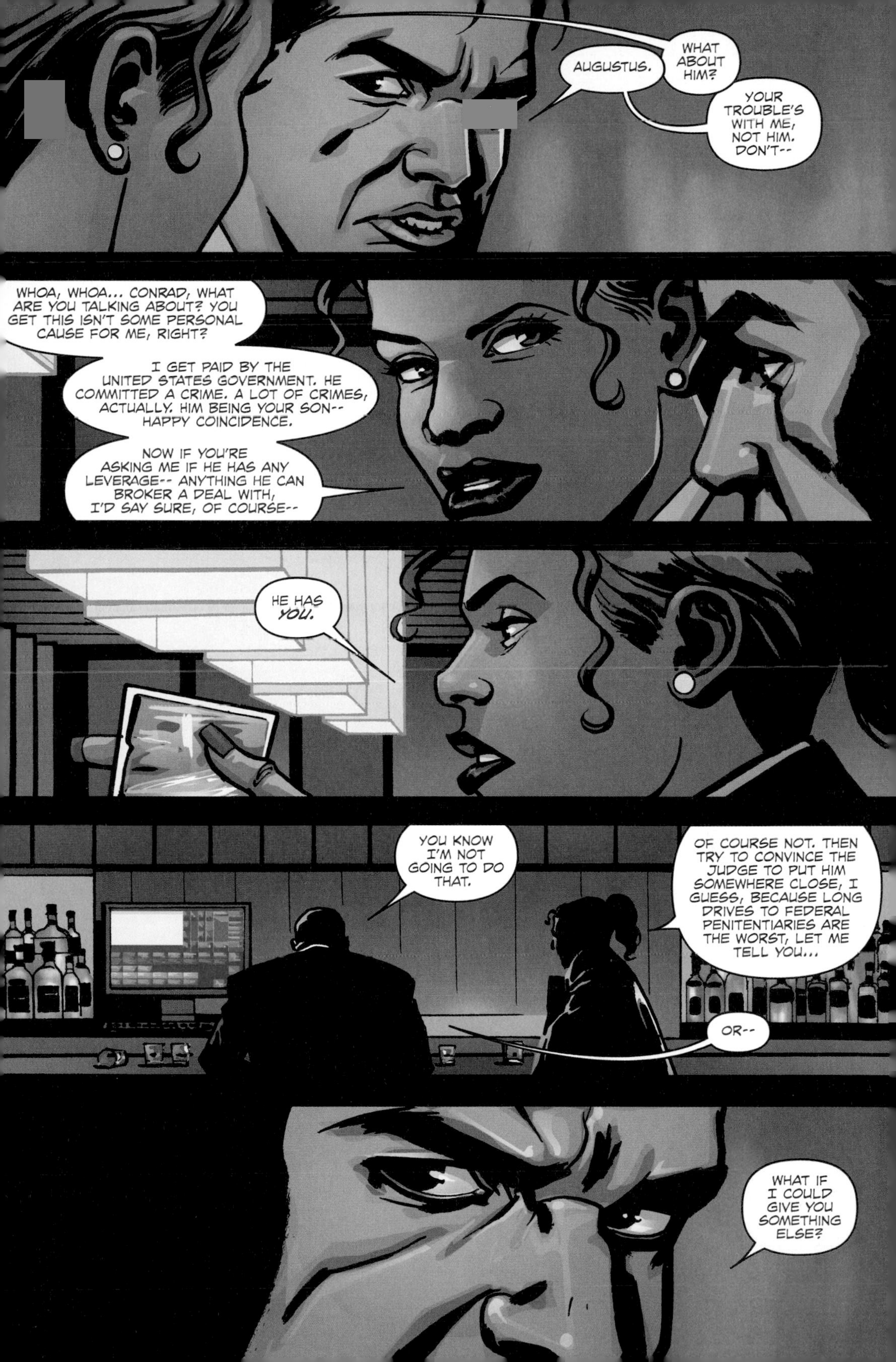
AUGUSTUS.
WHAT ABOUT HIM?
YOUR TROUBLE'S WITH ME, NOT HIM. DON'T--
WHOA, WHOA... CONRAD, WHAT ARE YOU TALKING ABOUT? YOU GET THIS ISN'T SOME PERSONAL CAUSE FOR ME, RIGHT?
I GET PAID BY THE UNITED STATES GOVERNMENT. HE COMMITTED A CRIME. A LOT OF CRIMES, ACTUALLY. HIM BEING YOUR SON-- HAPPY COINCIDENCE.
NOW IF YOU'RE ASKING ME IF HE HAS ANY LEVERAGE-- ANYTHING HE CAN BROKER A DEAL WITH, I'D SAY SURE, OF COURSE--
HE HAS *YOU.*
YOU KNOW I'M NOT GOING TO DO THAT.
OF COURSE NOT. THEN TRY TO CONVINCE THE JUDGE TO PUT HIM SOMEWHERE CLOSE, I GUESS, BECAUSE LONG DRIVES TO FEDERAL PENITENTIARIES ARE THE WORST, LET ME TELL YOU...
OR--
WHAT IF I COULD GIVE YOU SOMETHING ELSE?

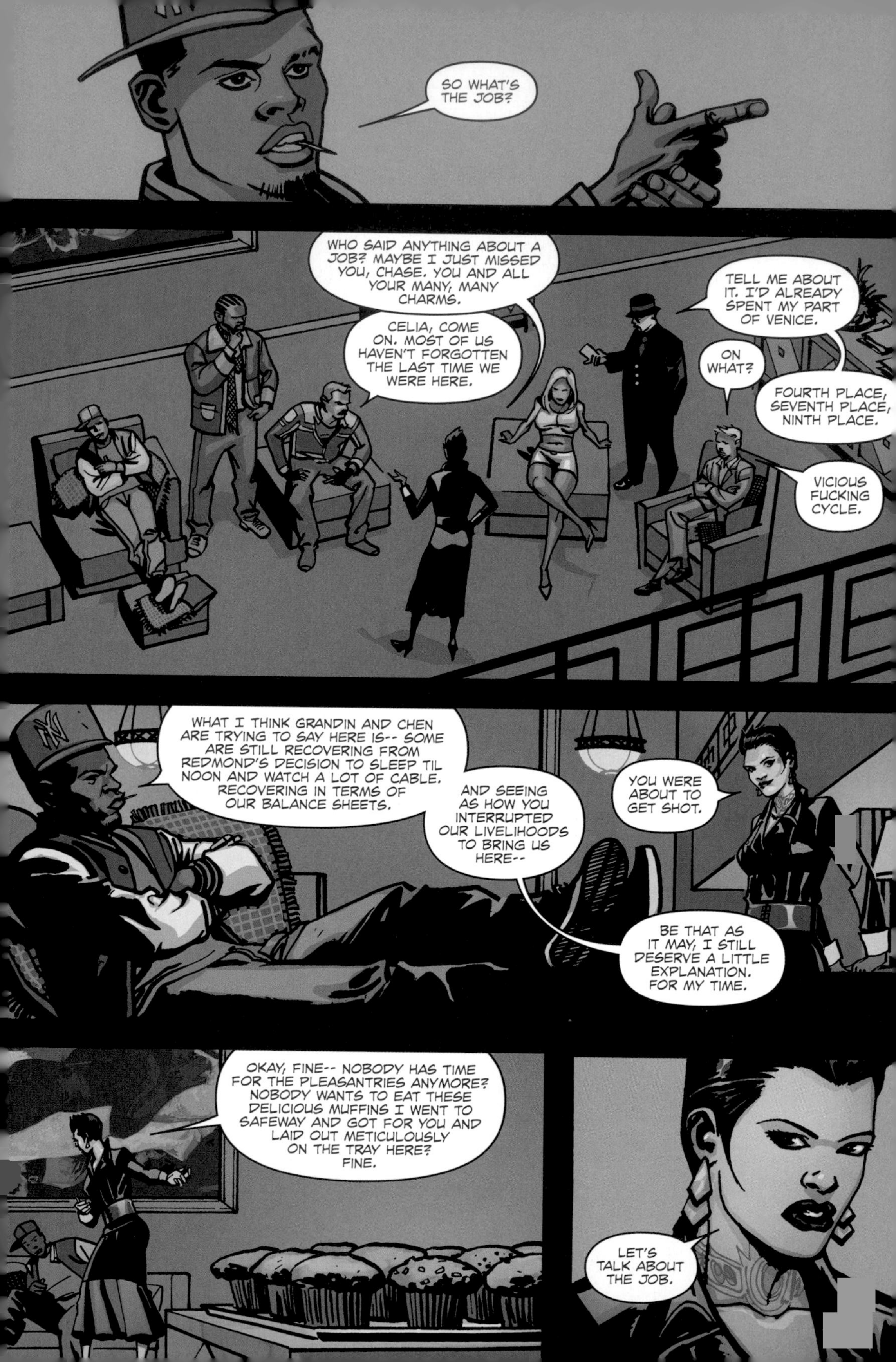
SO WHAT'S THE JOB?
WHO SAID ANYTHING ABOUT A JOB? MAYBE I JUST MISSED YOU, CHASE. YOU AND ALL YOUR MANY, MANY CHARMS.
CELIA, COME ON. MOST OF US HAVEN'T FORGOTTEN THE LAST TIME WE WERE HERE.
TELL ME ABOUT IT. I'D ALREADY SPENT MY PART OF VENICE.
ON WHAT?
FOURTH PLACE, SEVENTH PLACE, NINTH PLACE.
VICIOUS FUCKING CYCLE.
WHAT I THINK GRANDIN AND CHEN ARE TRYING TO SAY HERE IS-- SOME ARE STILL RECOVERING FROM REDMOND'S DECISION TO SLEEP TIL NOON AND WATCH A LOT OF CABLE. RECOVERING IN TERMS OF OUR BALANCE SHEETS.
AND SEEING AS HOW YOU INTERRUPTED OUR LIVELIHOODS TO BRING US HERE--
YOU WERE ABOUT TO GET SHOT.
BE THAT AS IT MAY, I STILL DESERVE A LITTLE EXPLANATION. FOR MY TIME.
OKAY, FINE-- NOBODY HAS TIME FOR THE PLEASANTRIES ANYMORE? NOBODY WANTS TO EAT THESE DELICIOUS MUFFINS I WENT TO SAFEWAY AND GOT FOR YOU AND LAID OUT METICULOUSLY ON THE TRAY HERE? FINE.
LET'S TALK ABOUT THE JOB.

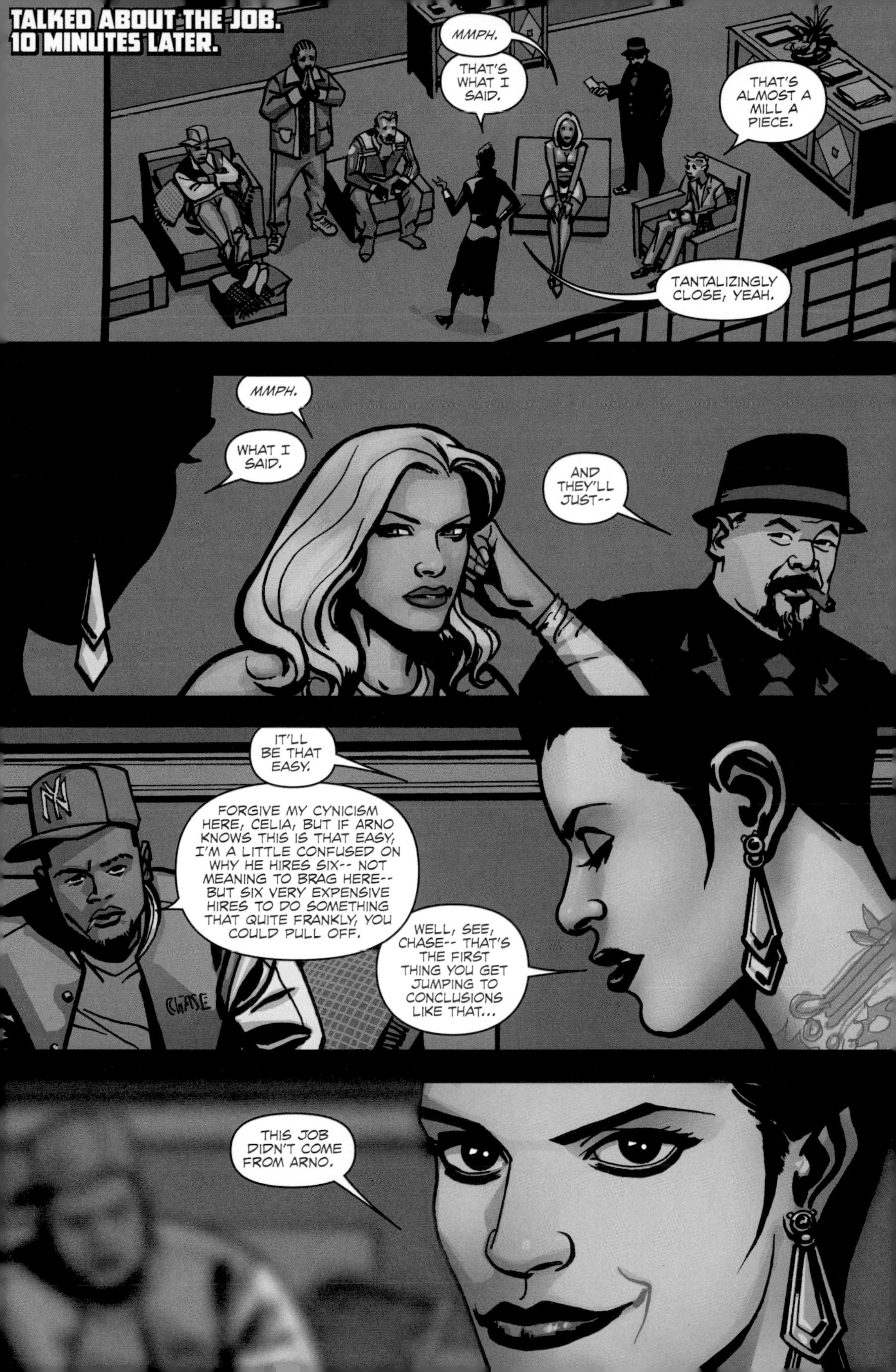
TALKED ABOUT THE JOB. 10 MINUTES LATER.
MMPH.
THAT'S WHAT I SAID.
THAT'S ALMOST A MILL A PIECE.
TANTALIZINGLY CLOSE, YEAH.
MMPH.
WHAT I SAID.
AND THEY'LL JUST--
IT'LL BE THAT EASY.
FORGIVE MY CYNICISM HERE, CELIA, BUT IF ARNO KNOWS THIS IS THAT EASY, I'M A LITTLE CONFUSED ON WHY HE HIRES SIX-- NOT MEANING TO BRAG HERE-- BUT SIX VERY EXPENSIVE HIRES TO DO SOMETHING THAT QUITE FRANKLY, YOU COULD PULL OFF.
CHASE
WELL, SEE, CHASE-- THAT'S THE FIRST THING YOU GET JUMPING TO CONCLUSIONS LIKE THAT...
THIS JOB DIDN'T COME FROM ARNO.

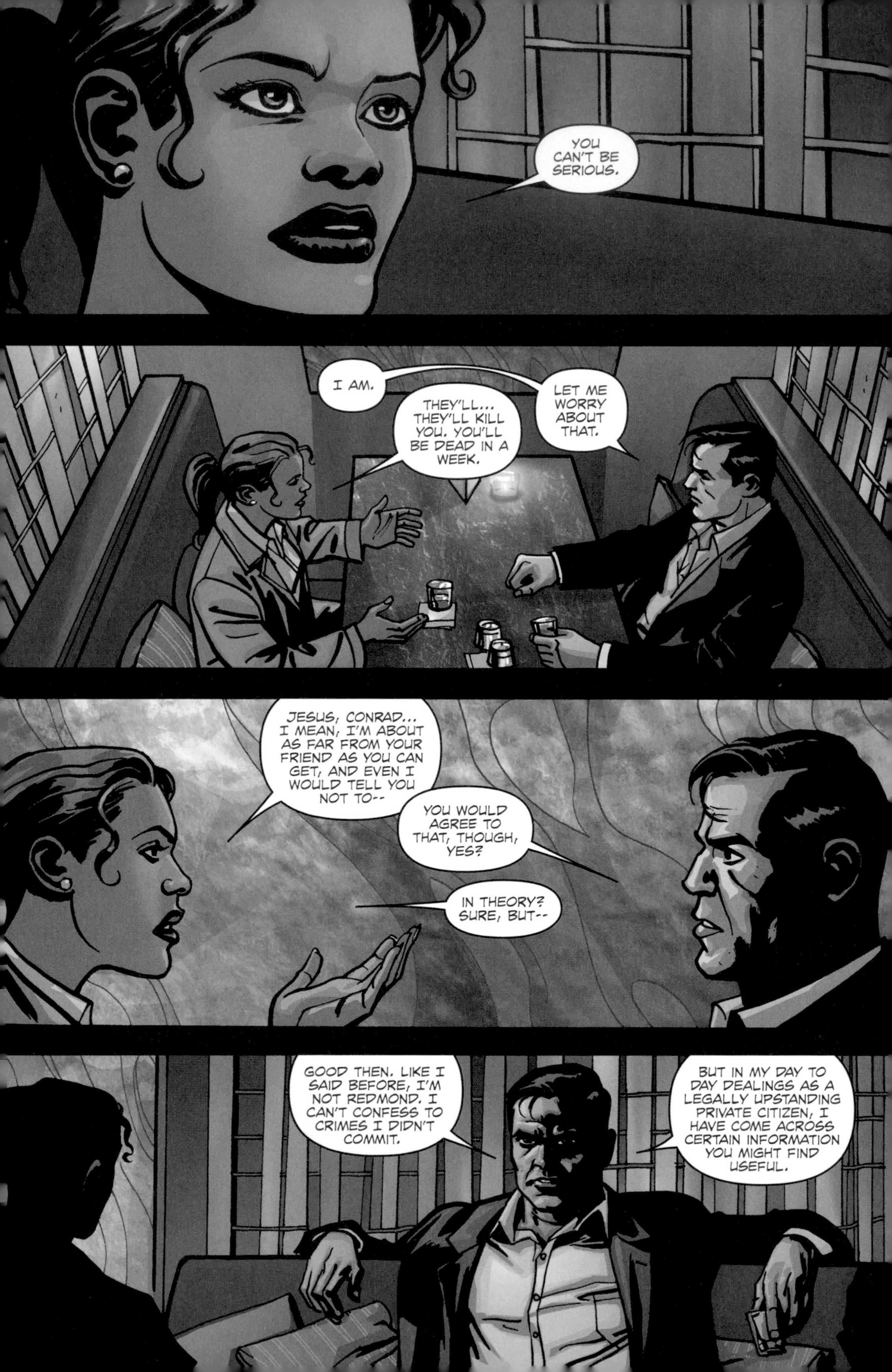
YOU CAN'T BE SERIOUS.
I AM.
LET ME WORRY ABOUT THAT.
THEY'LL... THEY'LL KILL YOU. YOU'LL BE DEAD IN A WEEK.
JESUS, CONRAD... I MEAN, I'M ABOUT AS FAR FROM YOUR FRIEND AS YOU CAN GET, AND EVEN I WOULD TELL YOU NOT TO--
YOU WOULD AGREE TO THAT, THOUGH, YES?
IN THEORY? SURE, BUT--
GOOD THEN. LIKE I SAID BEFORE, I'M NOT REDMOND. I CAN'T CONFESS TO CRIMES I DIDN'T COMMIT.
BUT IN MY DAY TO DAY DEALINGS AS A LEGALLY UPSTANDING PRIVATE CITIZEN, I HAVE COME ACROSS CERTAIN INFORMATION YOU MIGHT FIND USEFUL.

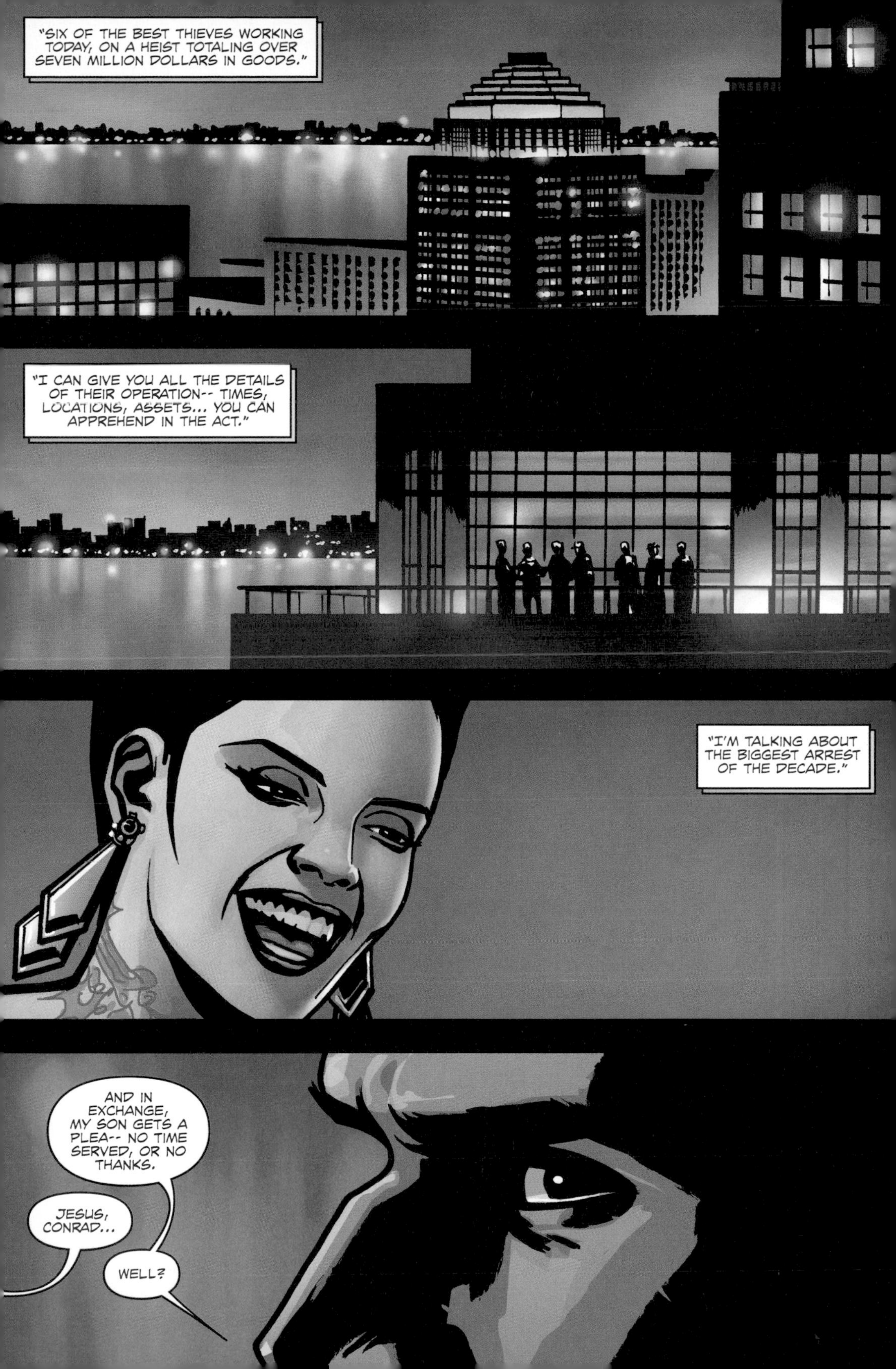
"SIX OF THE BEST THIEVES WORKING TODAY, ON A HEIST TOTALING OVER SEVEN MILLION DOLLARS IN GOODS."
"I CAN GIVE YOU ALL THE DETAILS OF THEIR OPERATION-- TIMES, LOCATIONS, ASSETS... YOU CAN APPREHEND IN THE ACT."
"I'M TALKING ABOUT THE BIGGEST ARREST OF THE DECADE."
AND IN EXCHANGE, MY SON GETS A PLEA-- NO TIME SERVED, OR NO THANKS.
JESUS, CONRAD...
WELL?

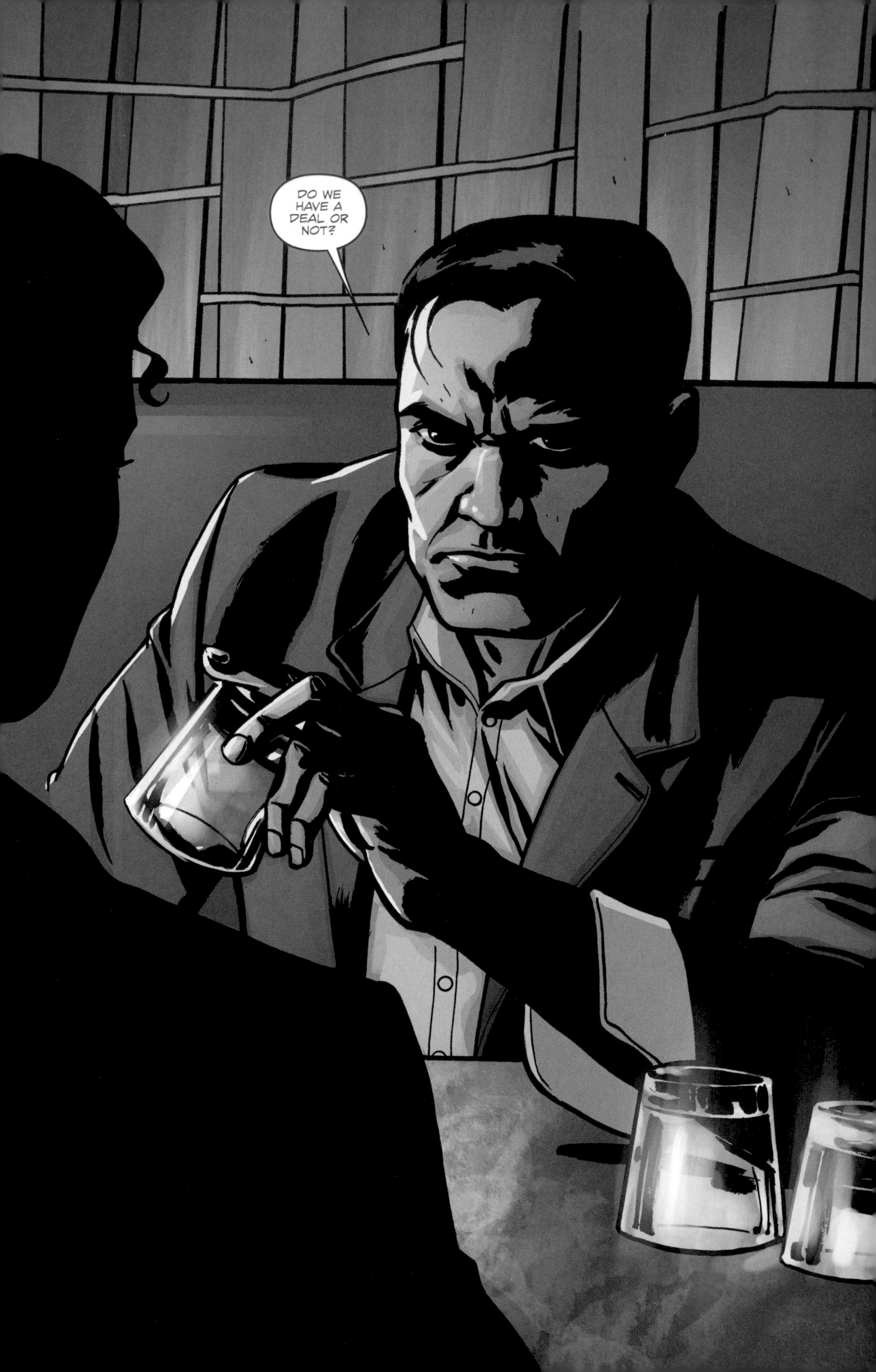
DO WE HAVE A DEAL OR NOT?

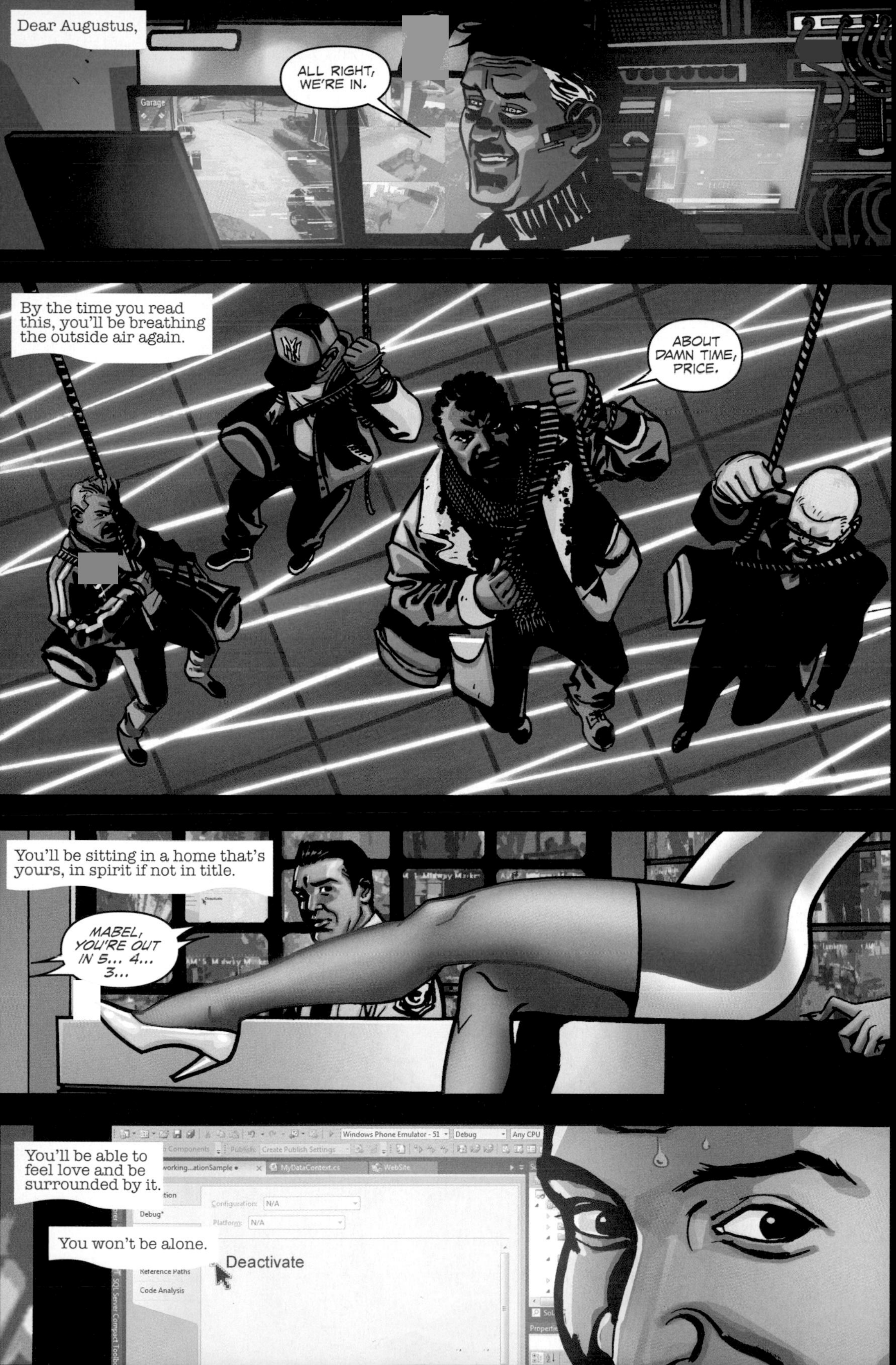
Dear Augustus,
Garage
ALL RIGHT, WE'RE IN.
By the time you read this, you'll be breathing the outside air again.
ABOUT DAMN TIME, PRICE.
You'll be sitting in a home that's yours, in spirit if not in title.
MABEL, YOU'RE OUT IN 5... 4... 3...
Windows Phone Emulator - 51
Debug
Any CPU
You'll be able to feel love and be surrounded by it.
You won't be alone.
Configuration: N/A
Platform: N/A
Deactivate
Reference Paths
Code Analysis

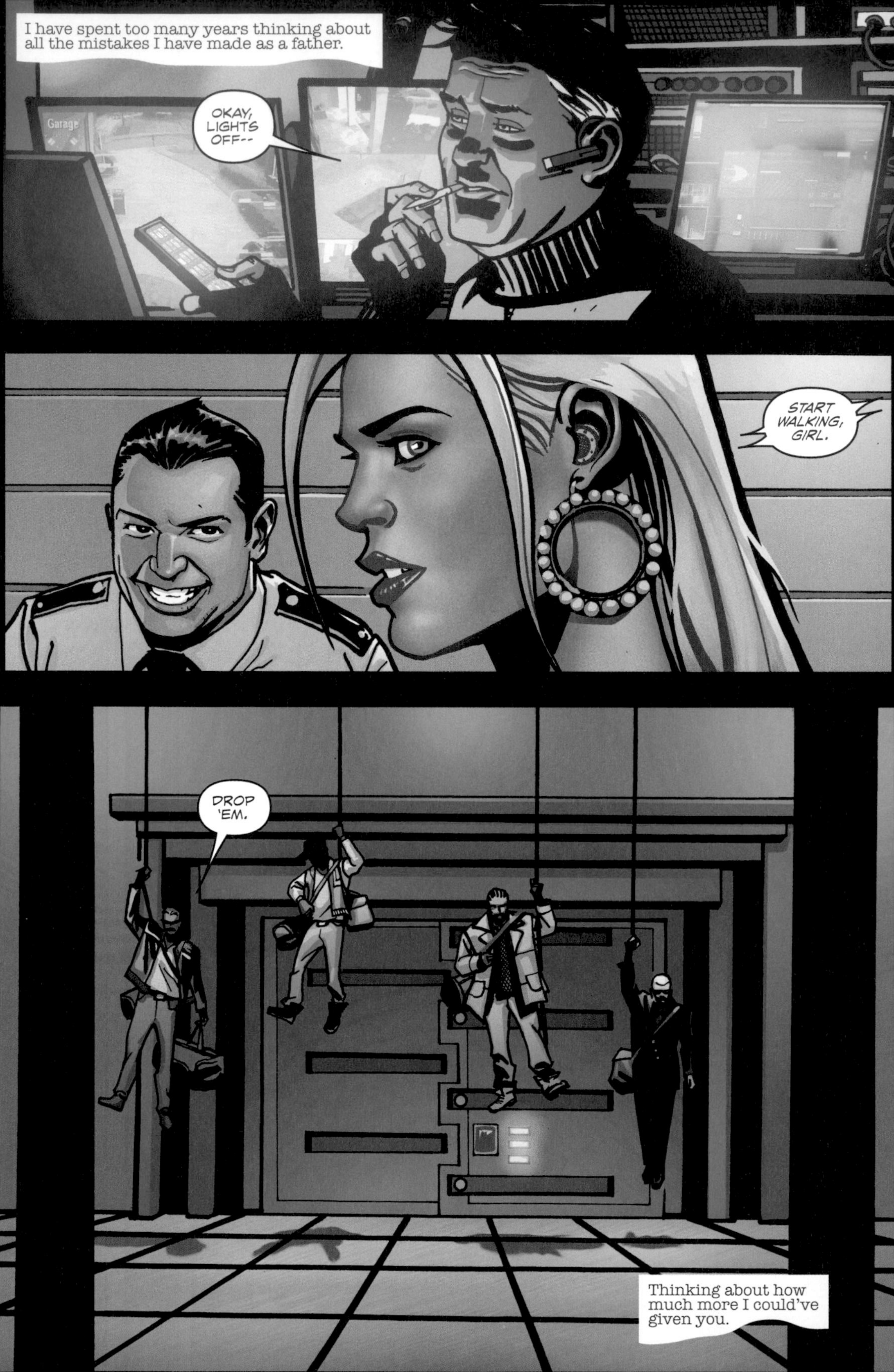

I have spent too many years thinking about all the mistakes I have made as a father.
Garage
OKAY, LIGHTS OFF--
START WALKING, GIRL.
DROP 'EM.
Thinking about how much more I could've given you.

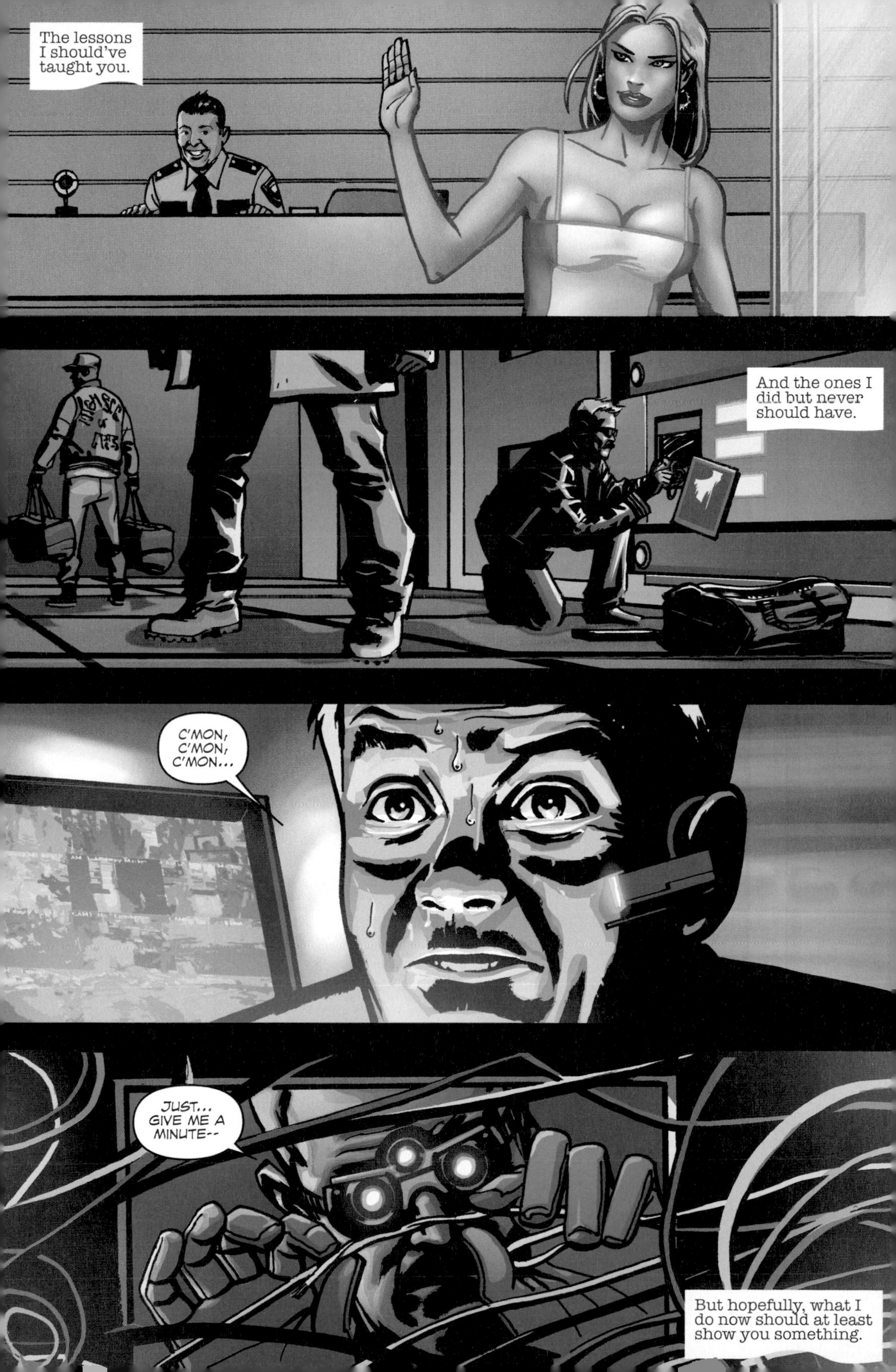

The lessons I should've taught you.
And the ones I did but never should have.
C'MON, C'MON, C'MON...
JUST... GIVE ME A MINUTE--
But hopefully, what I do now should at least show you something.

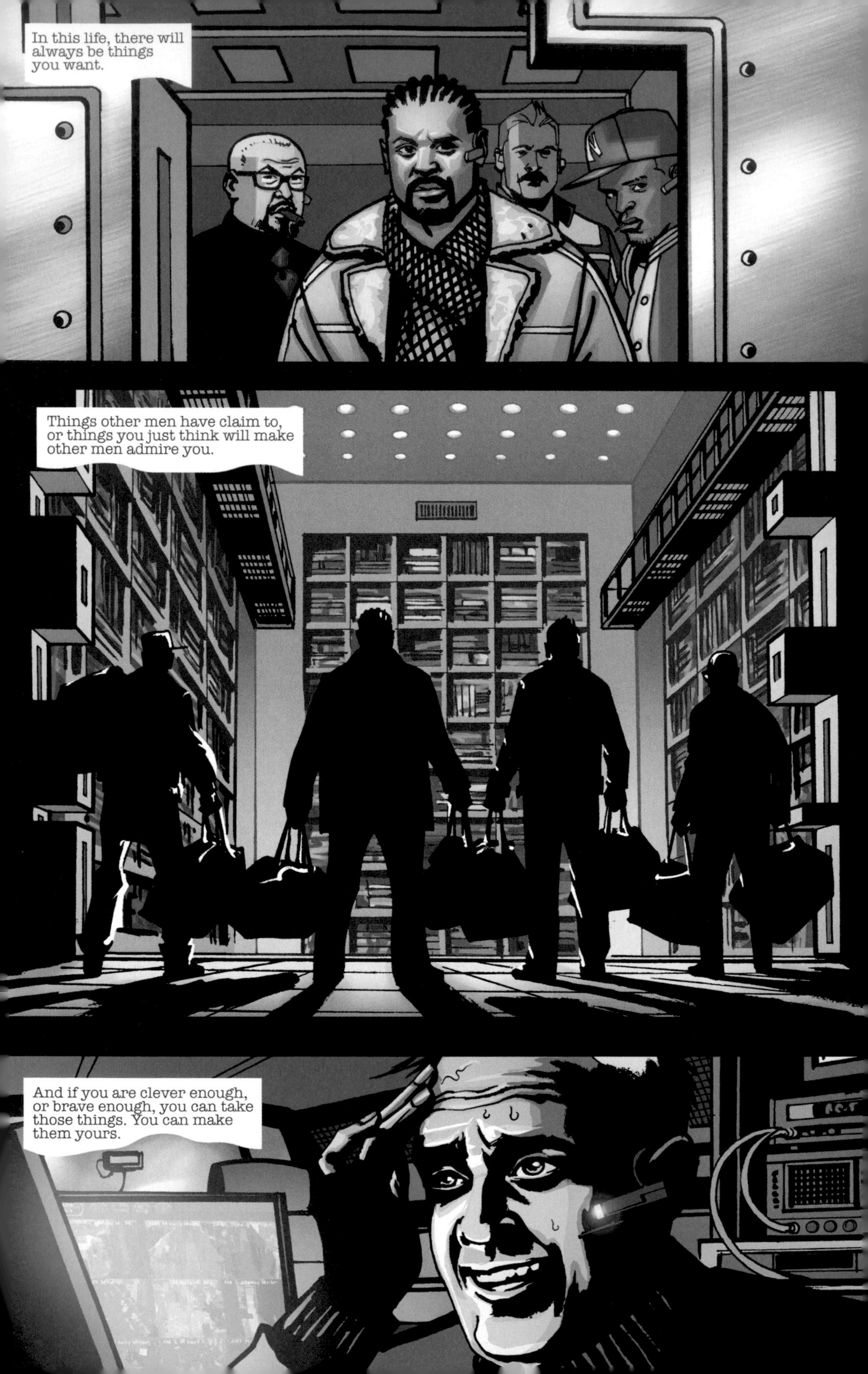
In this life, there will always be things you want.
Things other men have claim to, or things you just think will make other men admire you.
And if you are clever enough, or brave enough, you can take those things. You can make them yours.

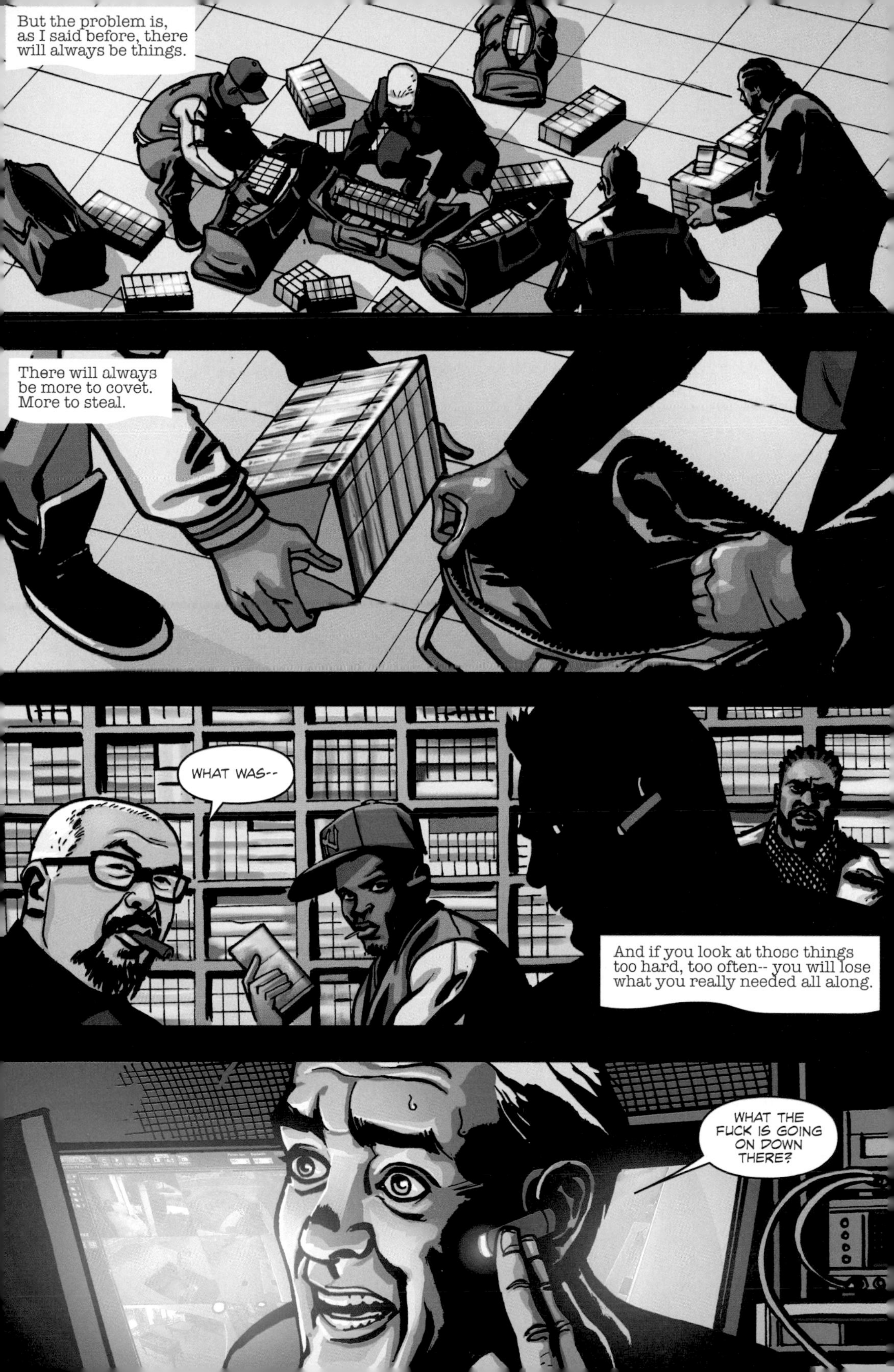
But the problem is, as I said before, there will always be things.
There will always be more to covet. More to steal.
WHAT WAS--
And if you look at those things too hard, too often-- you will lose what you really needed all along.
WHAT THE FUCK IS GOING ON DOWN THERE?

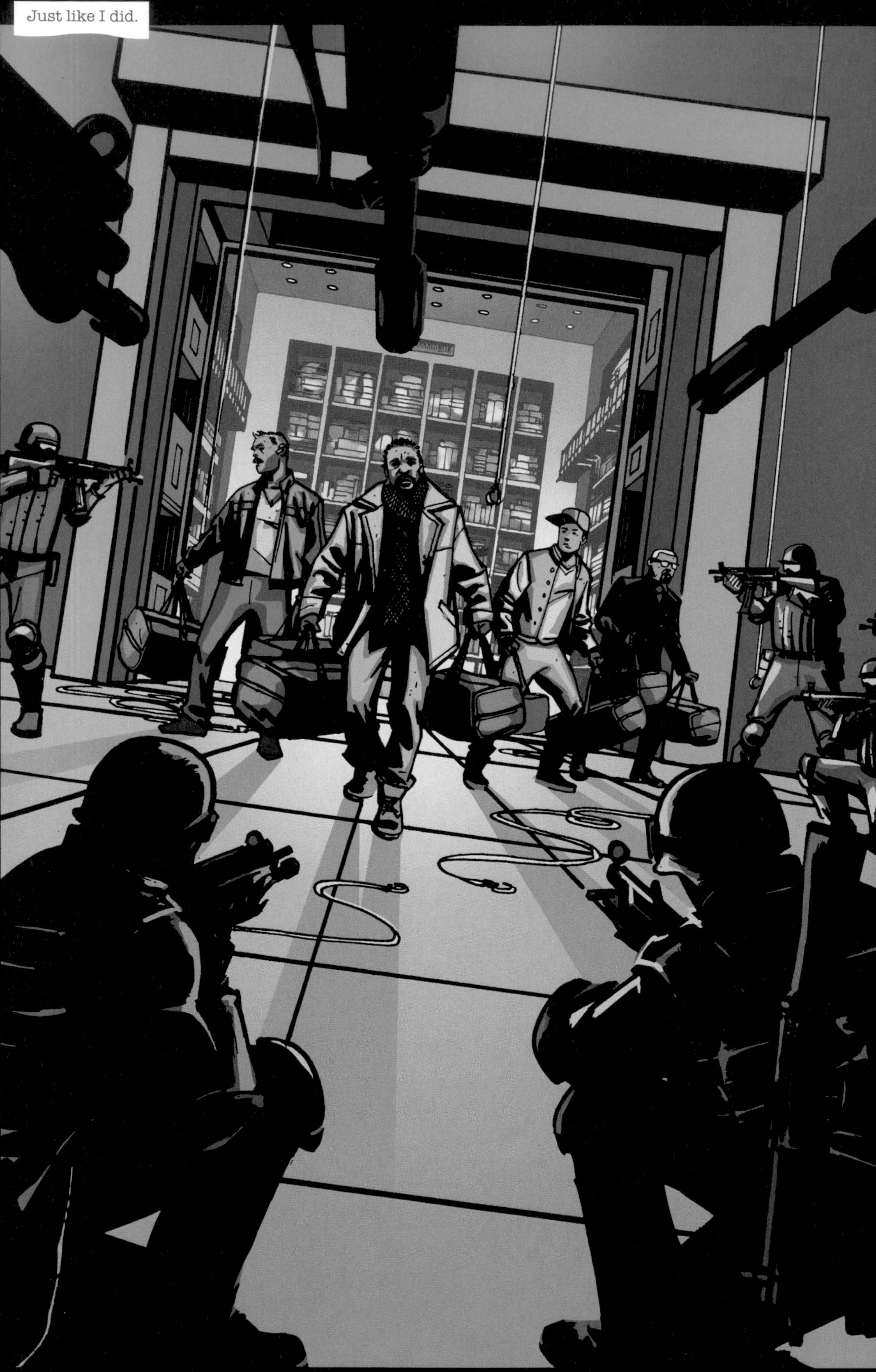
Just like I did.

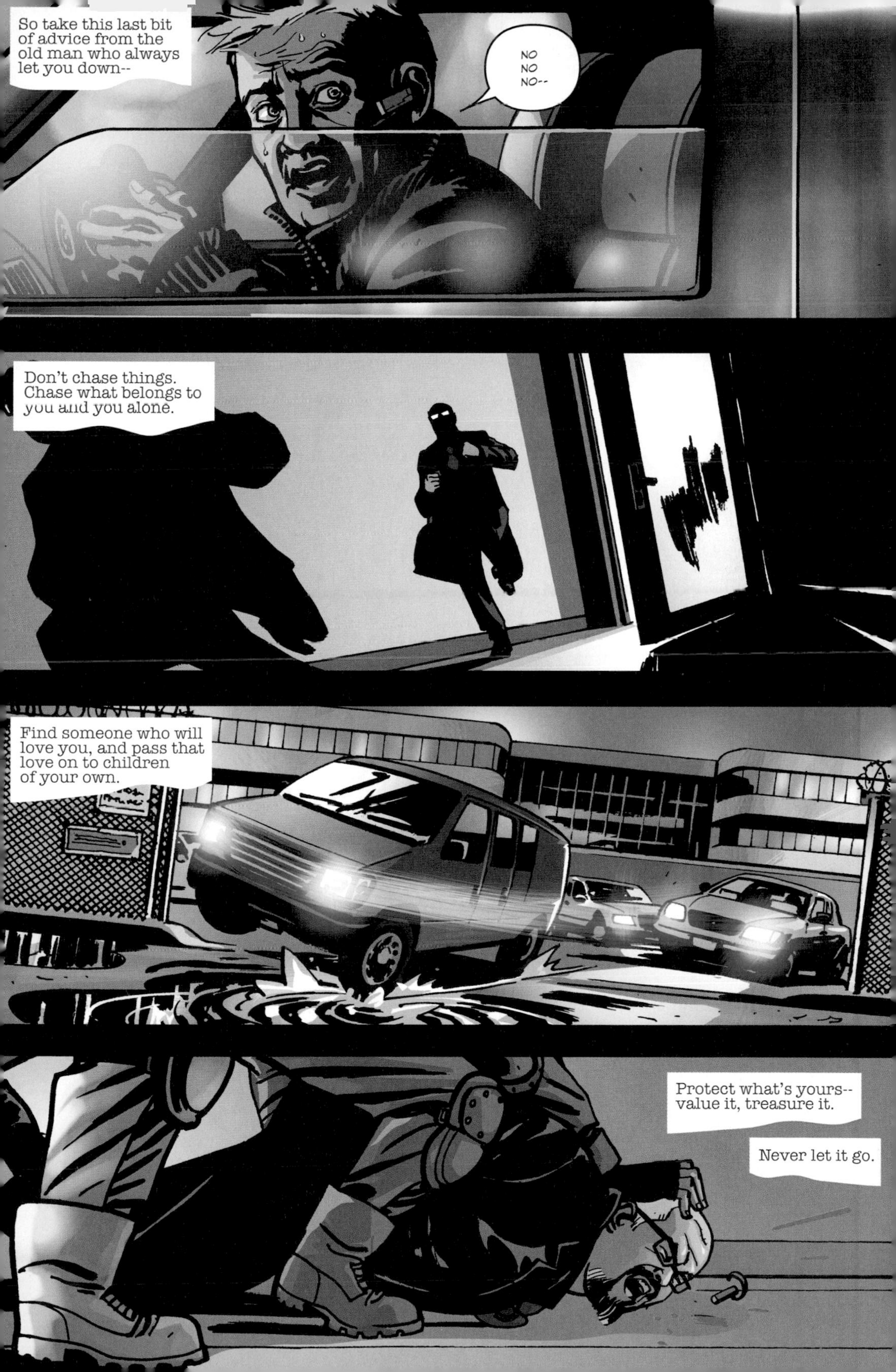
So take this last bit of advice from the old man who always let you down--
NO
NO
NO--
Don't chase things. Chase what belongs to you and you alone.
Find someone who will love you, and pass that love on to children of your own.
Protect what's yours-- value it, treasure it.
Never let it go.

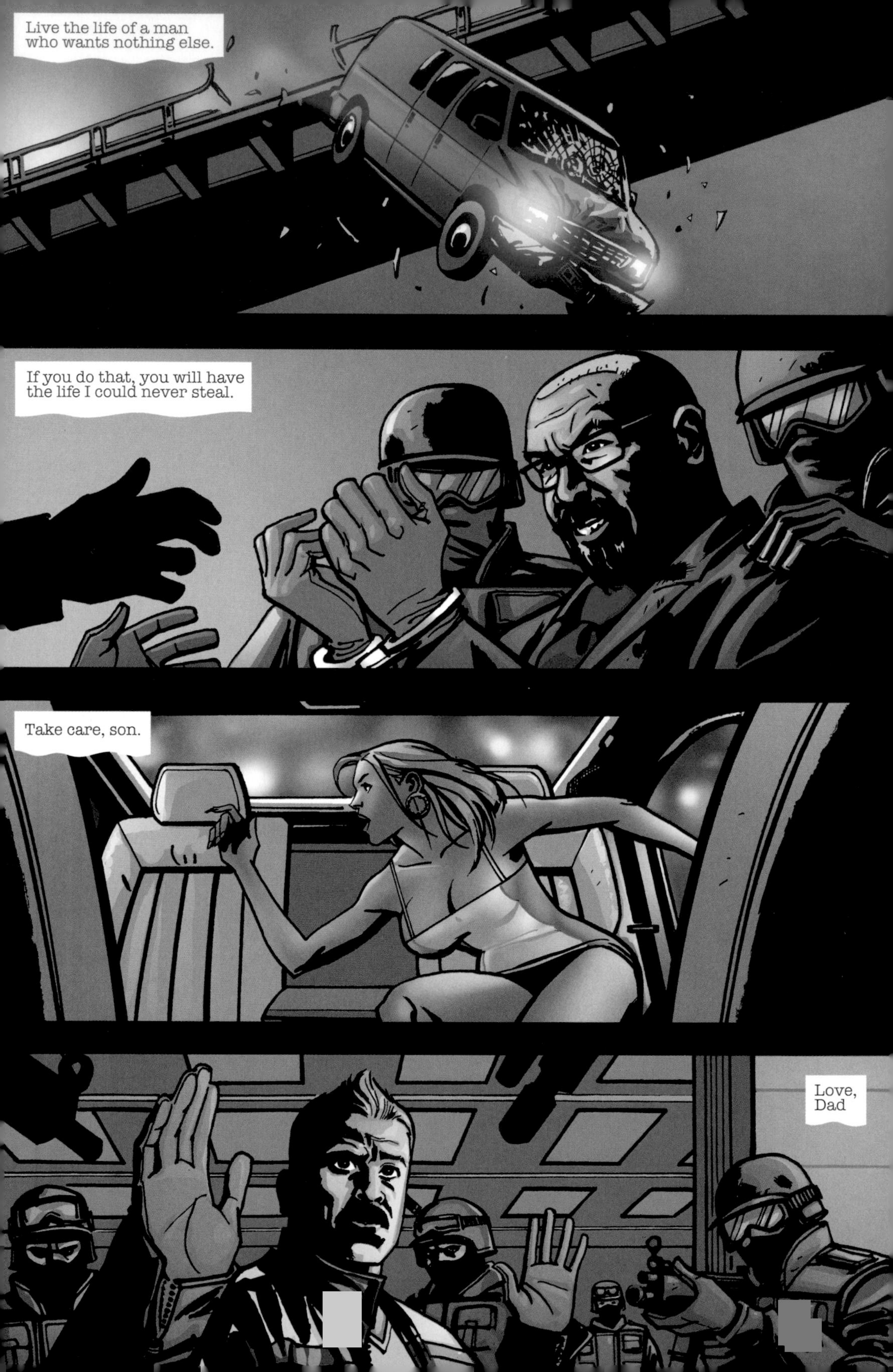
Live the life of a man who wants nothing else.
If you do that, you will have the life I could never steal.
Take care, son.
Love, Dad

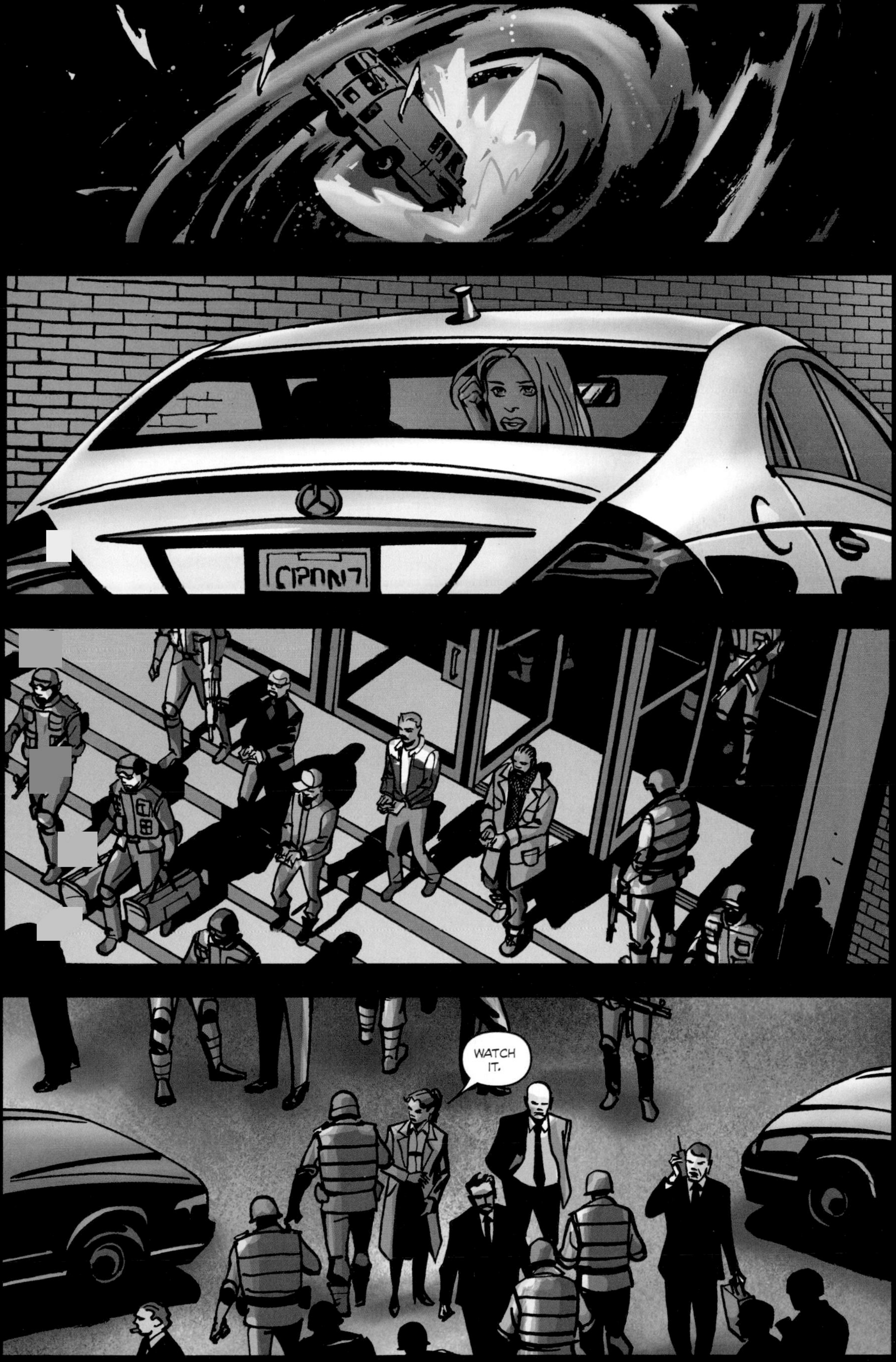
WATCH IT.

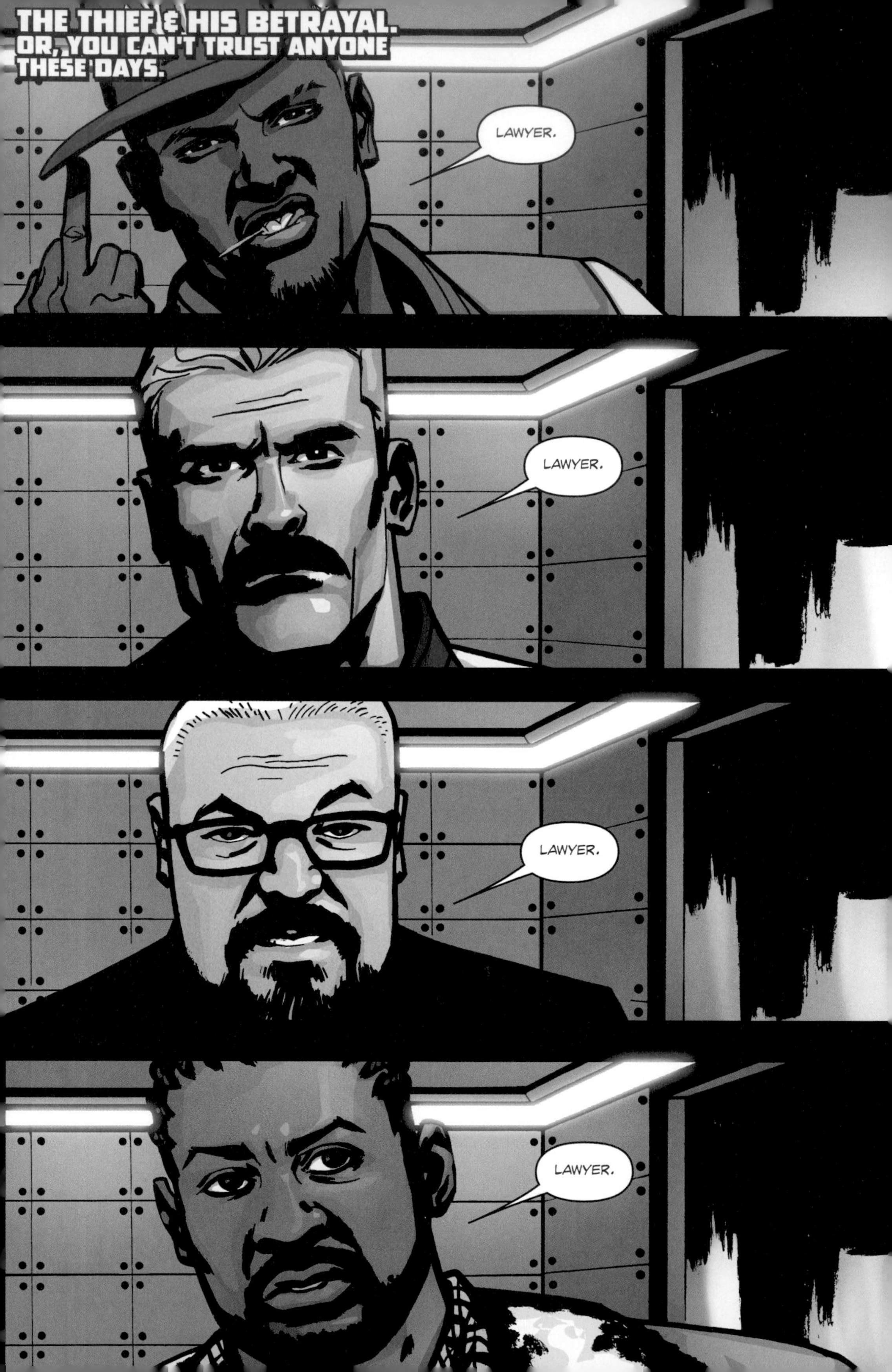
THE THIEF & HIS BETRAYAL.
OR, YOU CAN'T TRUST ANYONE THESE DAYS.
LAWYER.
LAWYER.
LAWYER.
LAWYER.

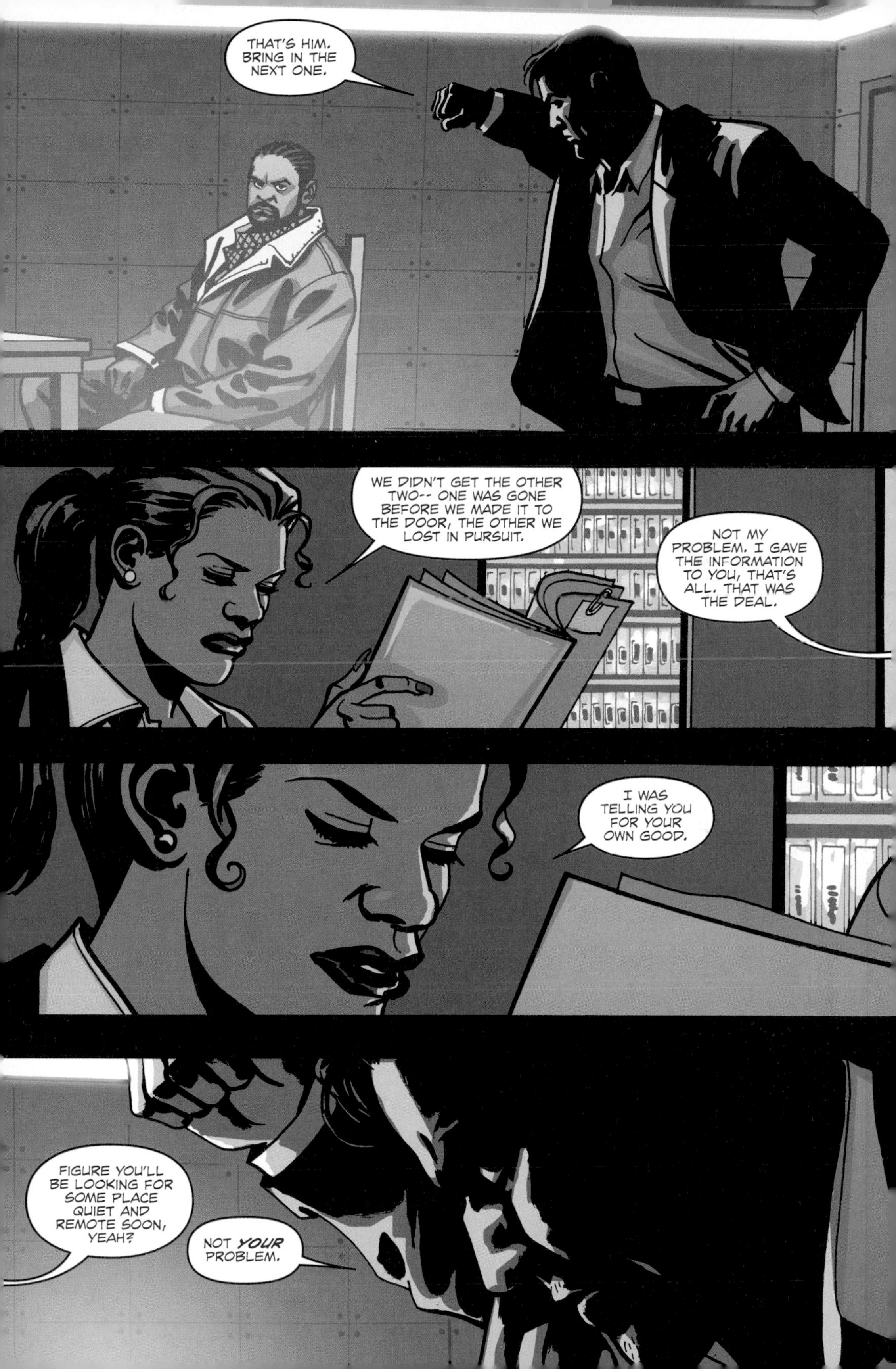
THAT'S HIM. BRING IN THE NEXT ONE.
WE DIDN'T GET THE OTHER TWO-- ONE WAS GONE BEFORE WE MADE IT TO THE DOOR, THE OTHER WE LOST IN PURSUIT.
NOT MY PROBLEM. I GAVE THE INFORMATION TO YOU, THAT'S ALL. THAT WAS THE DEAL.
I WAS TELLING YOU FOR YOUR OWN GOOD.
FIGURE YOU'LL BE LOOKING FOR SOME PLACE QUIET AND REMOTE SOON, YEAH?
NOT *YOUR* PROBLEM.

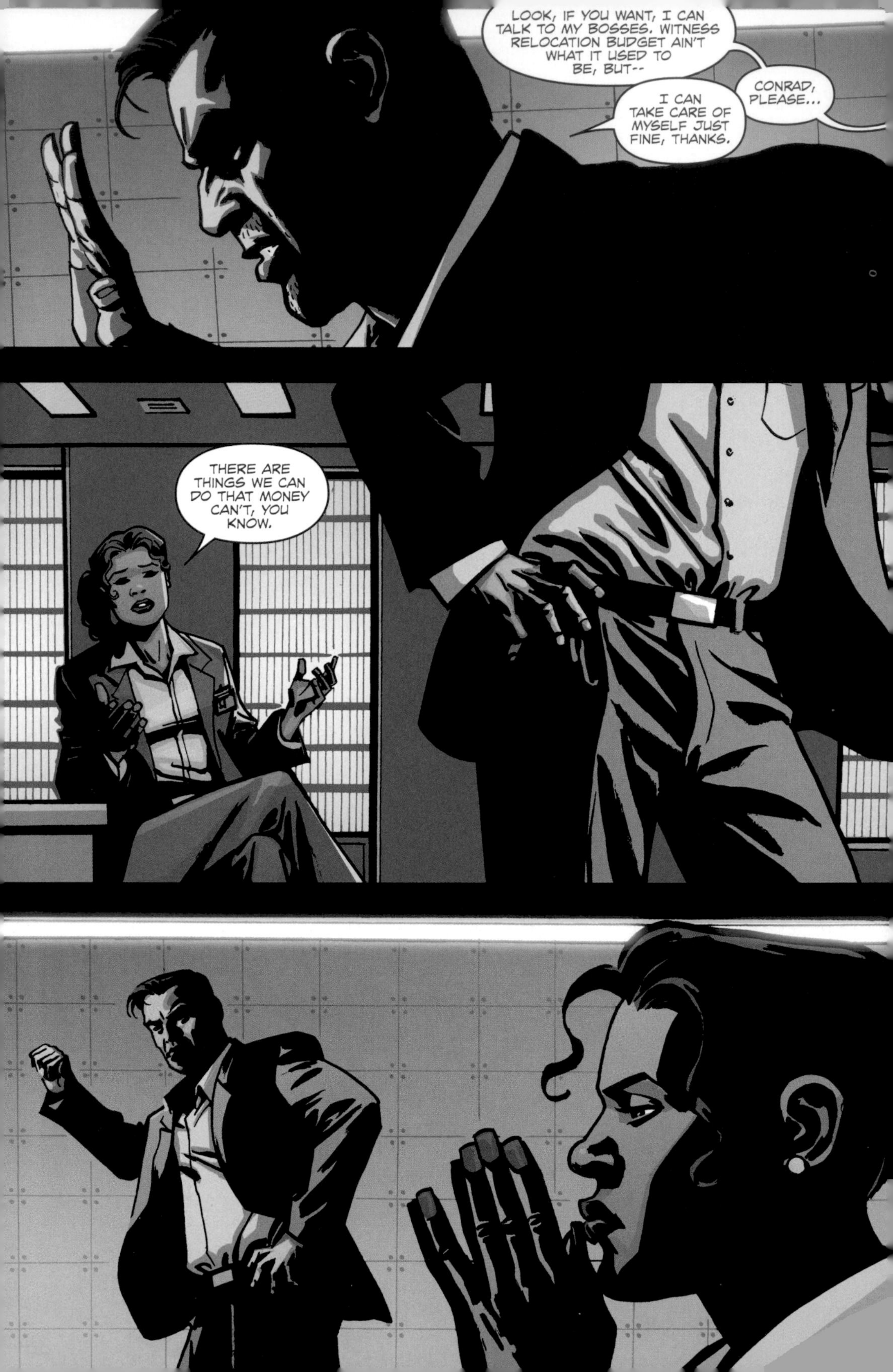
LOOK, IF YOU WANT, I CAN TALK TO MY BOSSES. WITNESS RELOCATION BUDGET AIN'T WHAT IT USED TO BE, BUT--
CONRAD, PLEASE...
I CAN TAKE CARE OF MYSELF JUST FINE, THANKS.
THERE ARE THINGS WE CAN DO THAT MONEY CAN'T, YOU KNOW.

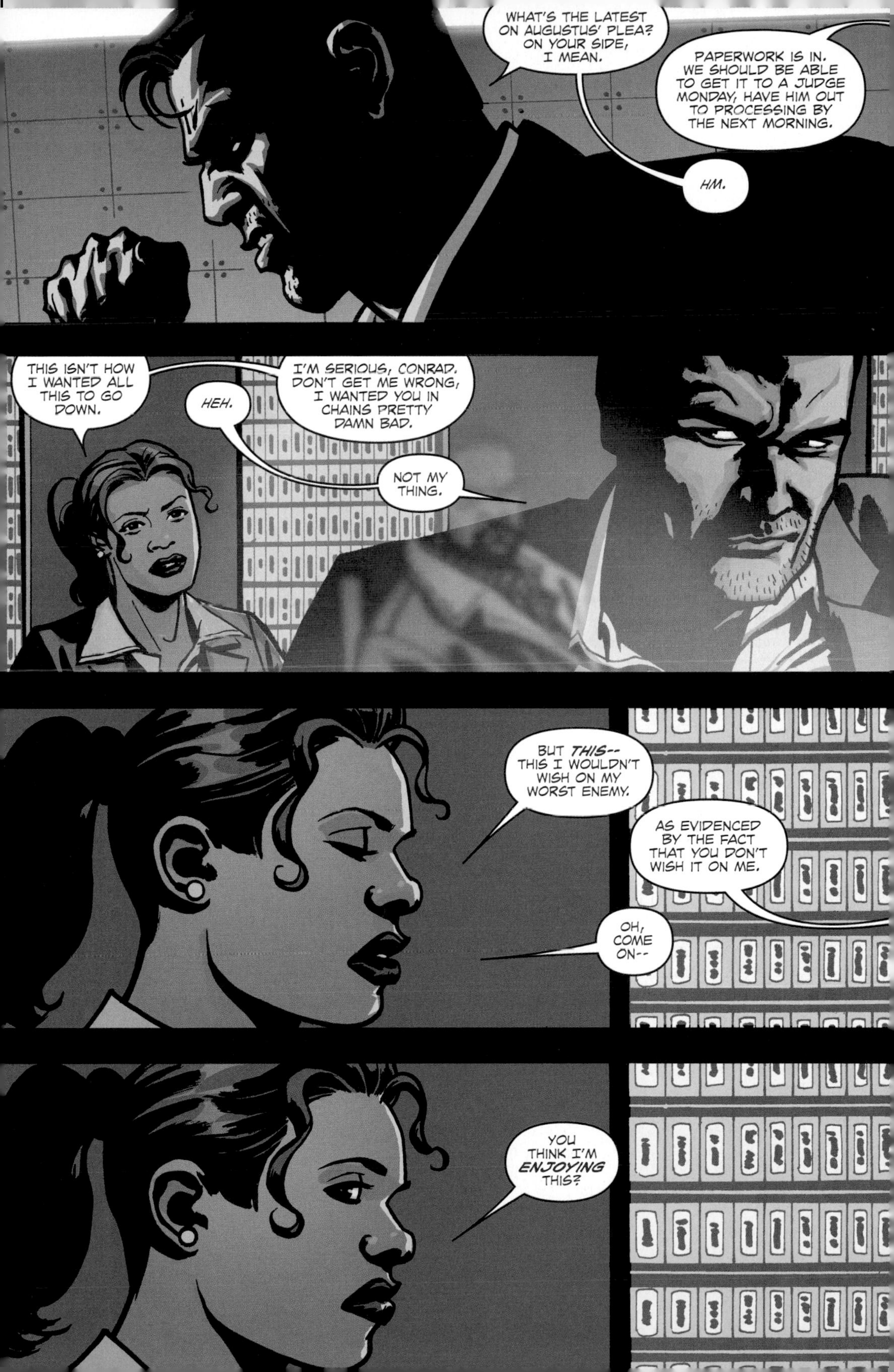
WHAT'S THE LATEST ON AUGUSTUS' PLEA? ON YOUR SIDE, I MEAN.
PAPERWORK IS IN. WE SHOULD BE ABLE TO GET IT TO A JUDGE MONDAY, HAVE HIM OUT TO PROCESSING BY THE NEXT MORNING.
HM.
THIS ISN'T HOW I WANTED ALL THIS TO GO DOWN.
HEH.
I'M SERIOUS, CONRAD. DON'T GET ME WRONG, I WANTED YOU IN CHAINS PRETTY DAMN BAD.
NOT MY THING.
BUT THIS-- THIS I WOULDN'T WISH ON MY WORST ENEMY.
AS EVIDENCED BY THE FACT THAT YOU DON'T WISH IT ON ME.
OH, COME ON--
YOU THINK I'M ENJOYING THIS?

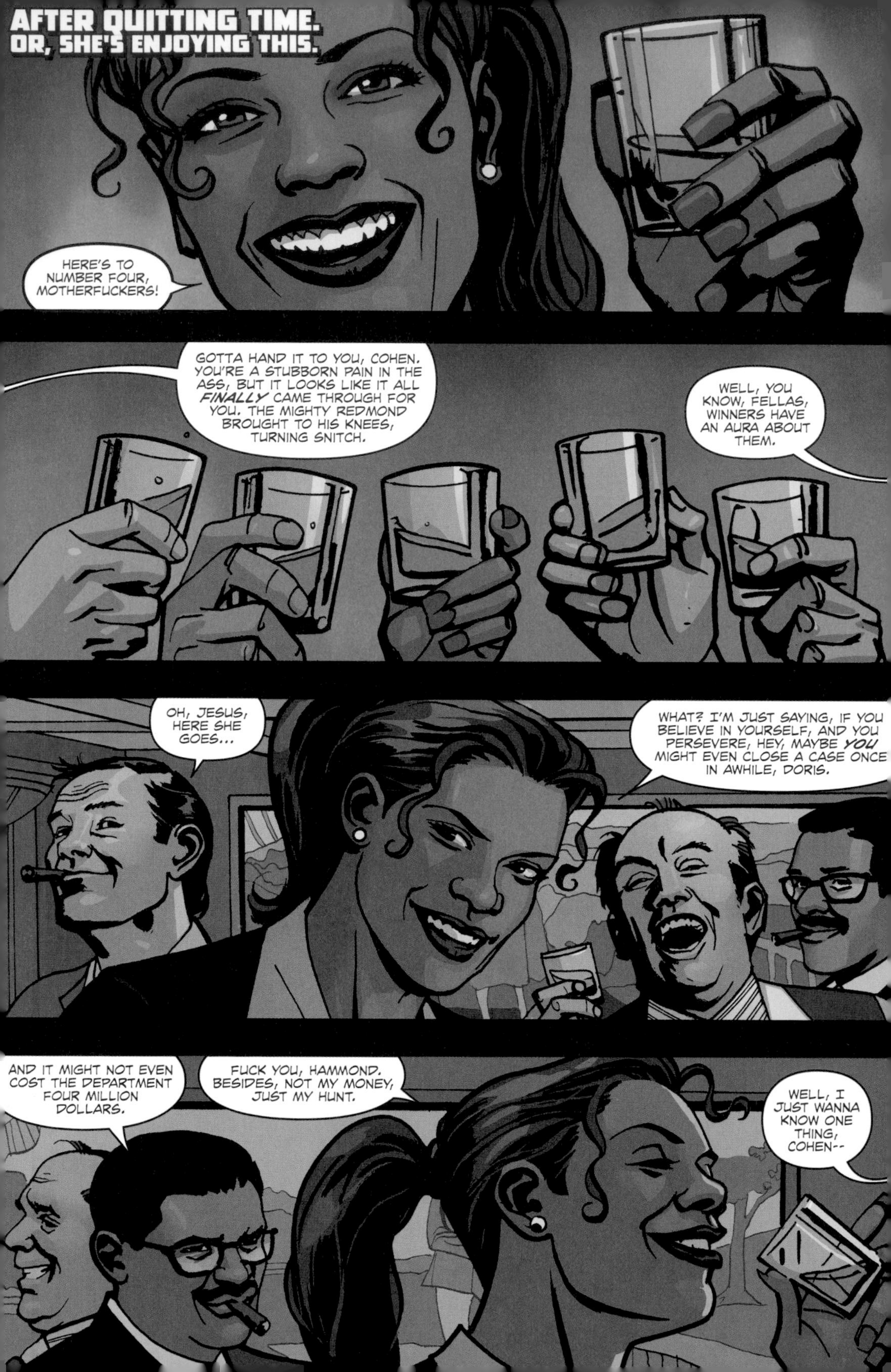
AFTER QUITTING TIME.
OR, SHE'S ENJOYING THIS.
HERE'S TO NUMBER FOUR, MOTHERFUCKERS!
GOTTA HAND IT TO YOU, COHEN. YOU'RE A STUBBORN PAIN IN THE ASS, BUT IT LOOKS LIKE IT ALL *FINALLY* CAME THROUGH FOR YOU. THE MIGHTY REDMOND BROUGHT TO HIS KNEES, TURNING SNITCH.
WELL, YOU KNOW, FELLAS, WINNERS HAVE AN AURA ABOUT THEM.
OH, JESUS, HERE SHE GOES...
WHAT? I'M JUST SAYING, IF YOU BELIEVE IN YOURSELF, AND YOU PERSEVERE, HEY, MAYBE *YOU* MIGHT EVEN CLOSE A CASE ONCE IN AWHILE, DORIS.
AND IT MIGHT NOT EVEN COST THE DEPARTMENT FOUR MILLION DOLLARS.
FUCK YOU, HAMMOND. BESIDES, NOT MY MONEY, JUST MY HUNT.
WELL, I JUST WANNA KNOW ONE THING, COHEN--

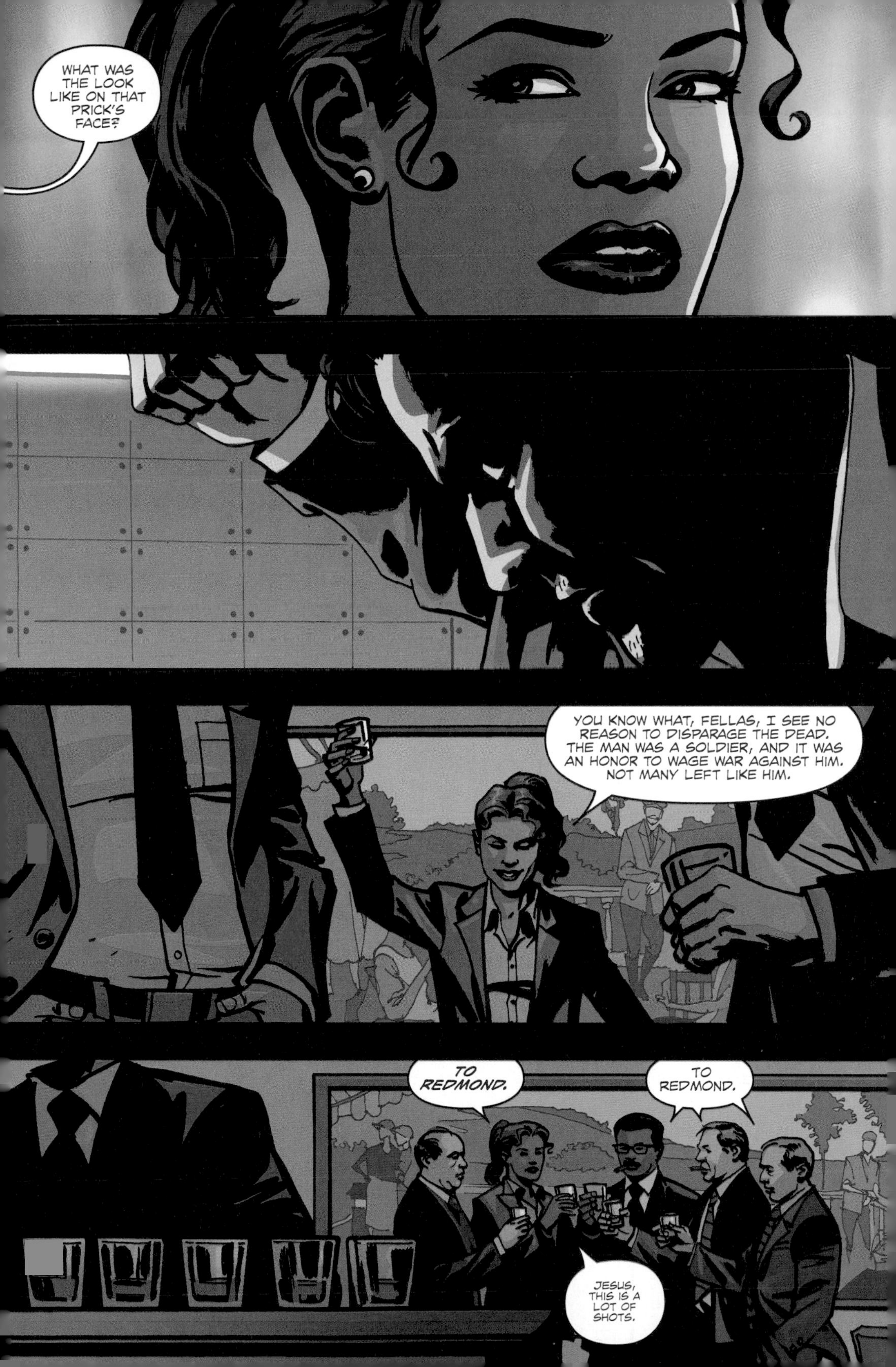
WHAT WAS THE LOOK LIKE ON THAT PRICK'S FACE?
YOU KNOW WHAT, FELLAS, I SEE NO REASON TO DISPARAGE THE DEAD. THE MAN WAS A SOLDIER, AND IT WAS AN HONOR TO WAGE WAR AGAINST HIM. NOT MANY LEFT LIKE HIM.
TO REDMOND.
TO REDMOND.
JESUS, THIS IS A LOT OF SHOTS.

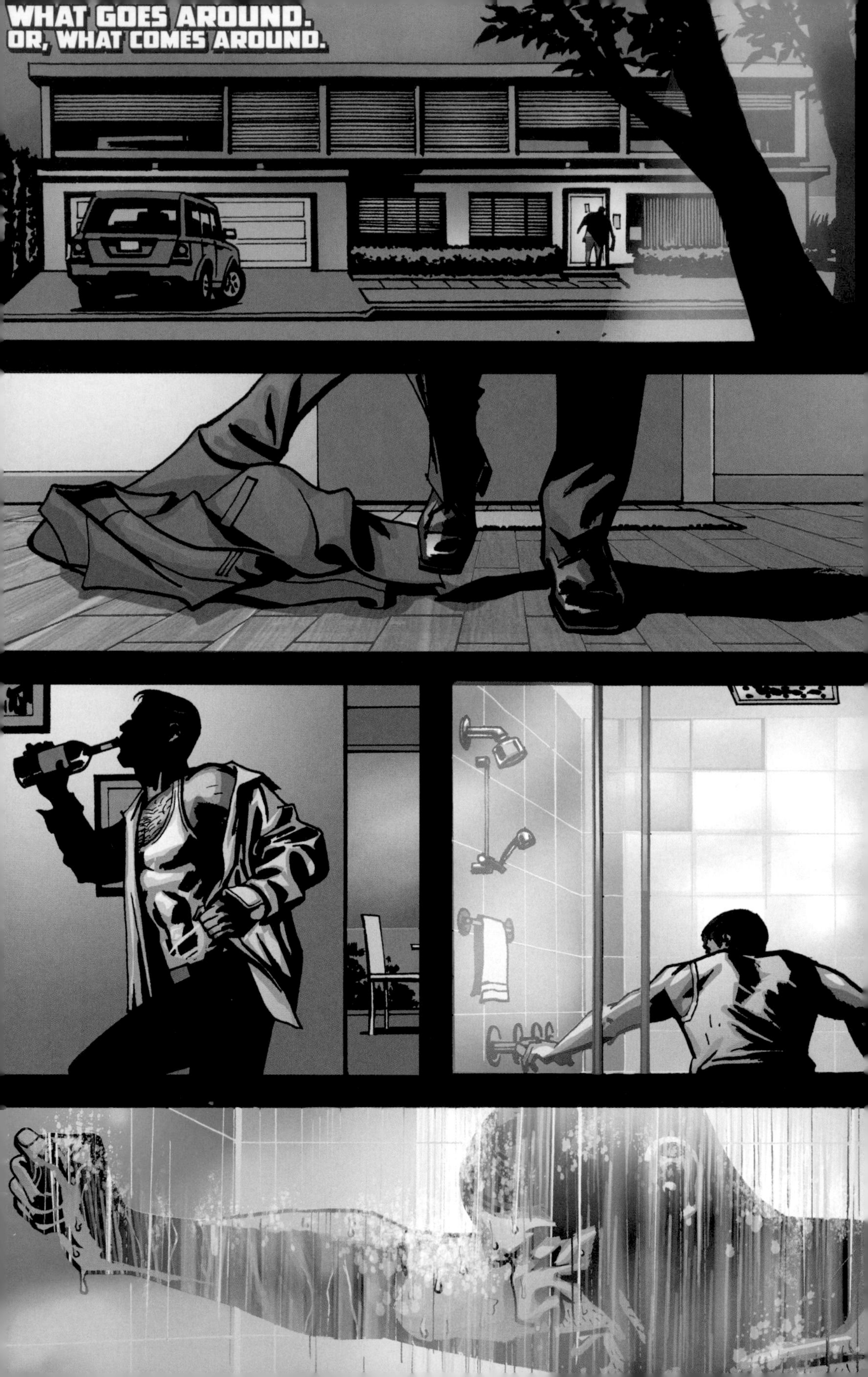
WHAT GOES AROUND.
OR, WHAT COMES AROUND.

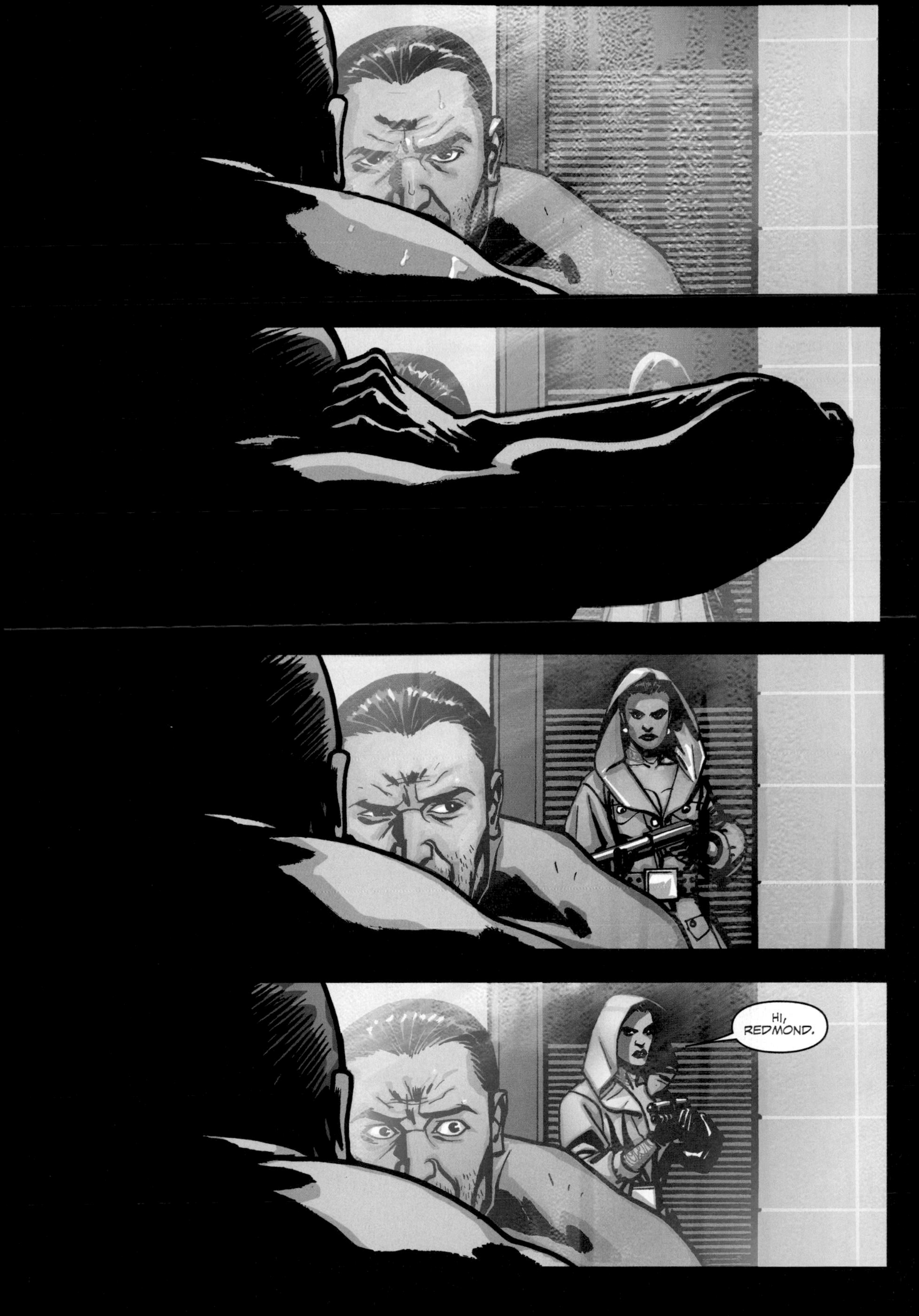
HI, REDMOND.

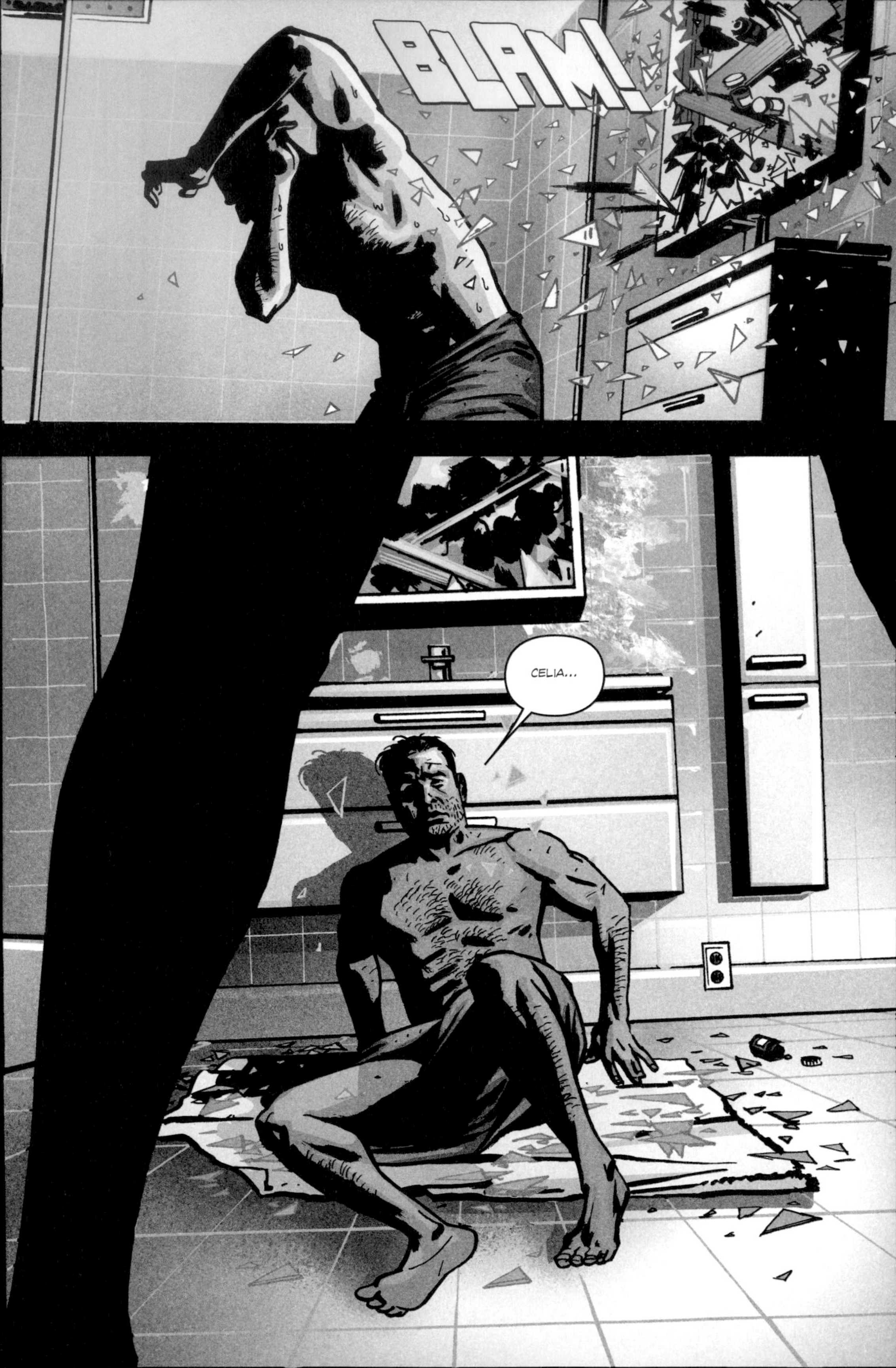
BLAM!
CELIA...

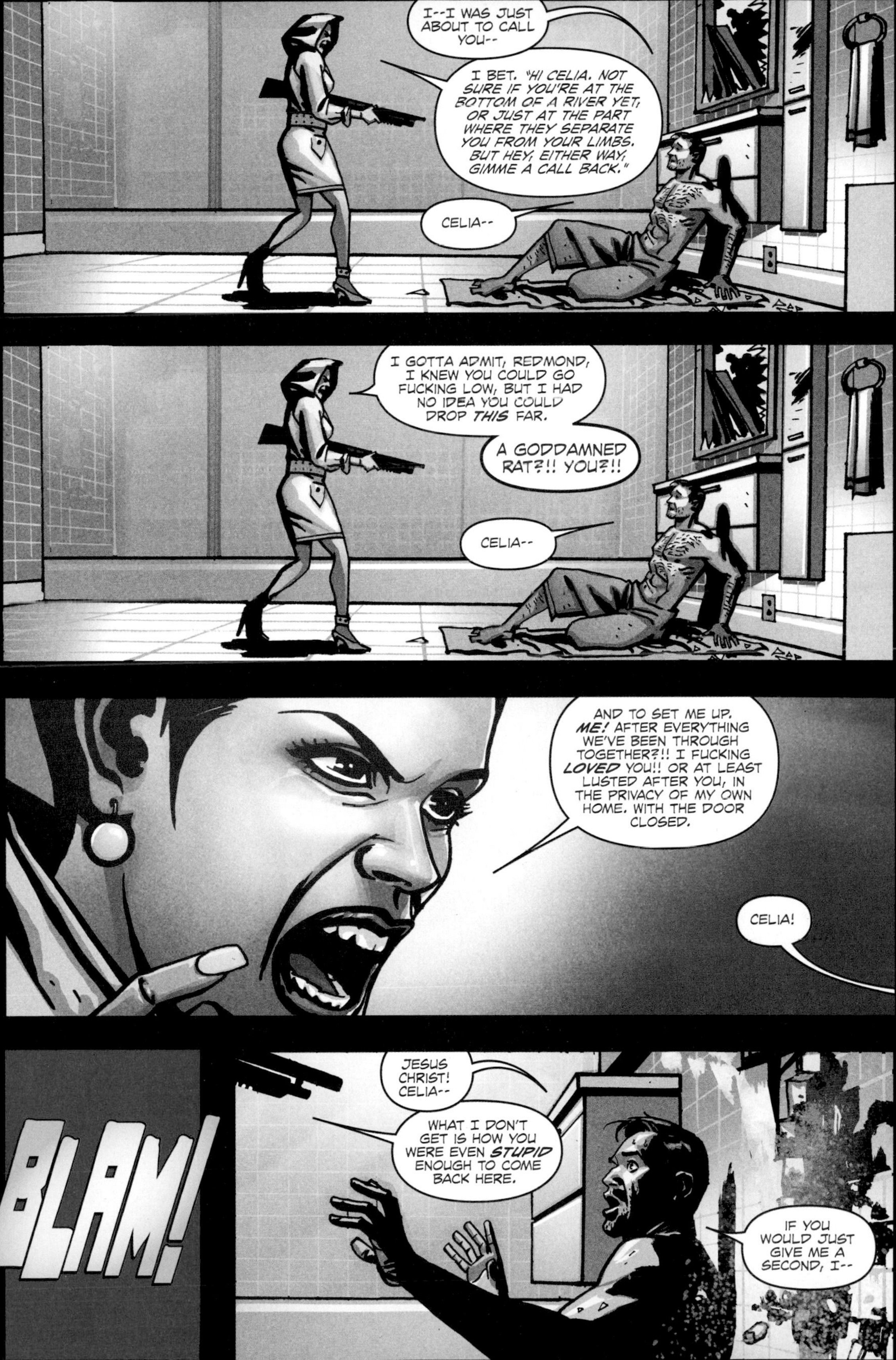
I--I WAS JUST ABOUT TO CALL YOU--
I BET. "HI CELIA. NOT SURE IF YOU'RE AT THE BOTTOM OF A RIVER YET, OR JUST AT THE PART WHERE THEY SEPARATE YOU FROM YOUR LIMBS. BUT HEY, EITHER WAY, GIMME A CALL BACK."
CELIA--
I GOTTA ADMIT, REDMOND, I KNEW YOU COULD GO FUCKING LOW, BUT I HAD NO IDEA YOU COULD DROP *THIS* FAR.
A GODDAMNED RAT?!! YOU?!!
CELIA--
AND TO SET ME UP. *ME!* AFTER EVERYTHING WE'VE BEEN THROUGH TOGETHER?!! I FUCKING *LOVED* YOU!! OR AT LEAST LUSTED AFTER YOU, IN THE PRIVACY OF MY OWN HOME. WITH THE DOOR CLOSED.
CELIA!
BLAM!
JESUS CHRIST! CELIA--
WHAT I DON'T GET IS HOW YOU WERE EVEN *STUPID* ENOUGH TO COME BACK HERE.
IF YOU WOULD JUST GIVE ME A SECOND, I--

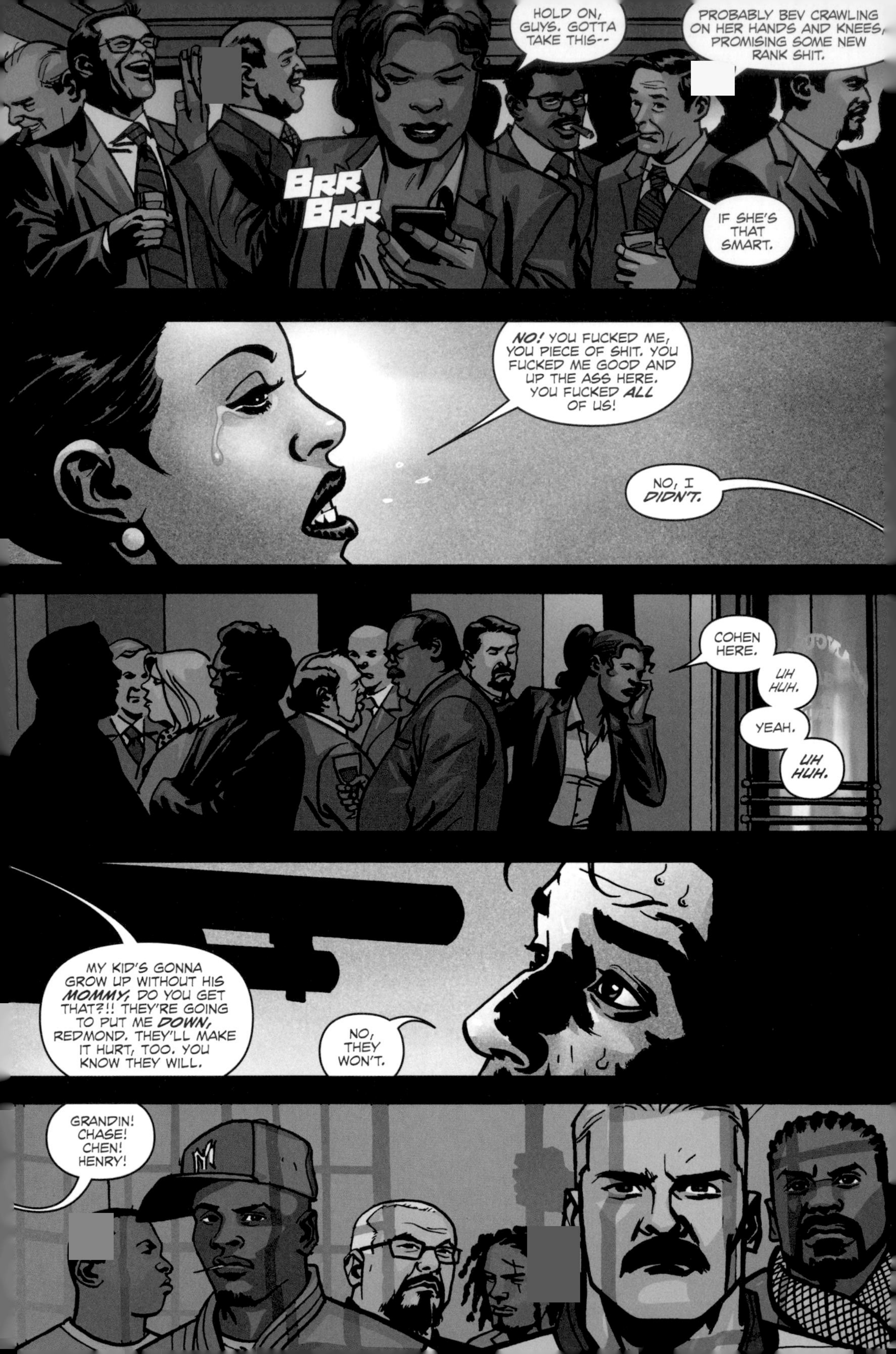
BRR BRR
HOLD ON, GUYS. GOTTA TAKE THIS--
PROBABLY BEV CRAWLING ON HER HANDS AND KNEES, PROMISING SOME NEW RANK SHIT.
IF SHE'S THAT SMART.
NO! YOU FUCKED ME, YOU PIECE OF SHIT. YOU FUCKED ME GOOD AND UP THE ASS HERE. YOU FUCKED ALL OF US!
NO, I DIDN'T.
COHEN HERE.
UH HUH.
YEAH.
UH HUH.
MY KID'S GONNA GROW UP WITHOUT HIS MOMMY, DO YOU GET THAT?!! THEY'RE GOING TO PUT ME DOWN, REDMOND. THEY'LL MAKE IT HURT, TOO. YOU KNOW THEY WILL.
NO, THEY WON'T.
GRANDIN! CHASE! CHEN! HENRY!

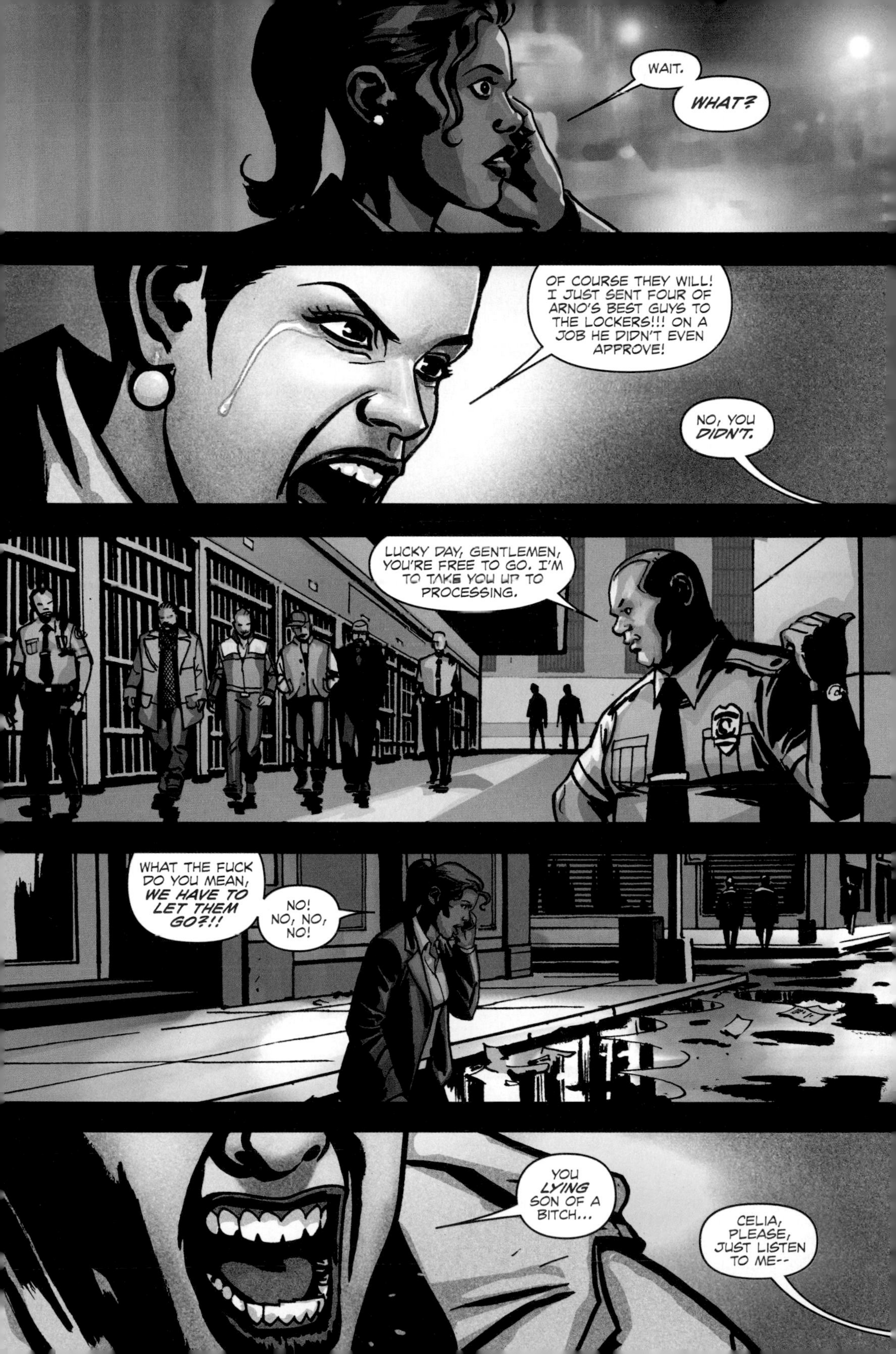

WAIT.
WHAT?
OF COURSE THEY WILL! I JUST SENT FOUR OF ARNO'S BEST GUYS TO THE LOCKERS!!! ON A JOB HE DIDN'T EVEN APPROVE!
NO, YOU DIDN'T.
LUCKY DAY, GENTLEMEN, YOU'RE FREE TO GO. I'M TO TAKE YOU UP TO PROCESSING.
WHAT THE FUCK DO YOU MEAN, WE HAVE TO LET THEM GO?!!
NO! NO, NO, NO!
YOU LYING SON OF A BITCH...
CELIA, PLEASE, JUST LISTEN TO ME--

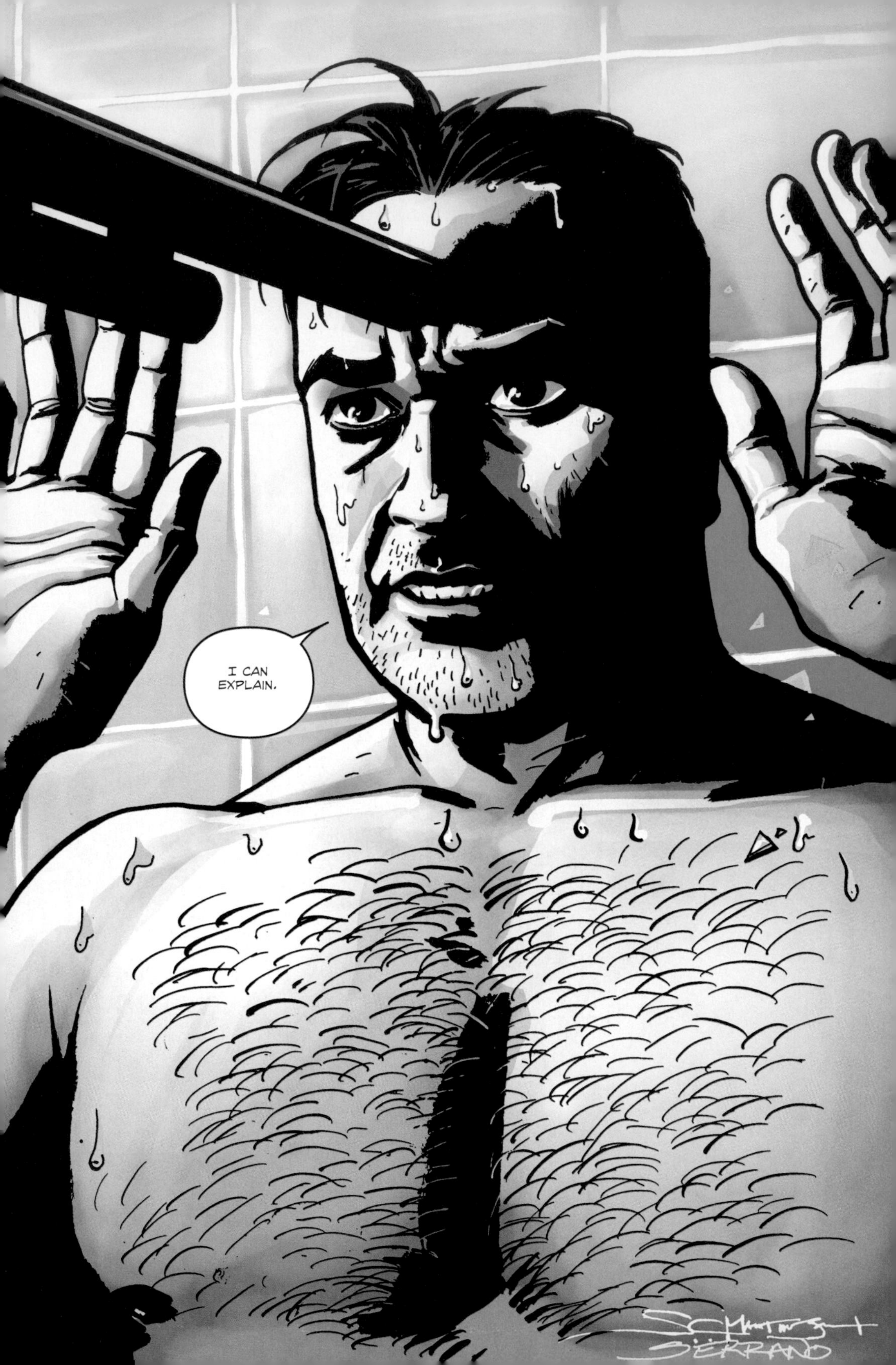
I CAN EXPLAIN.

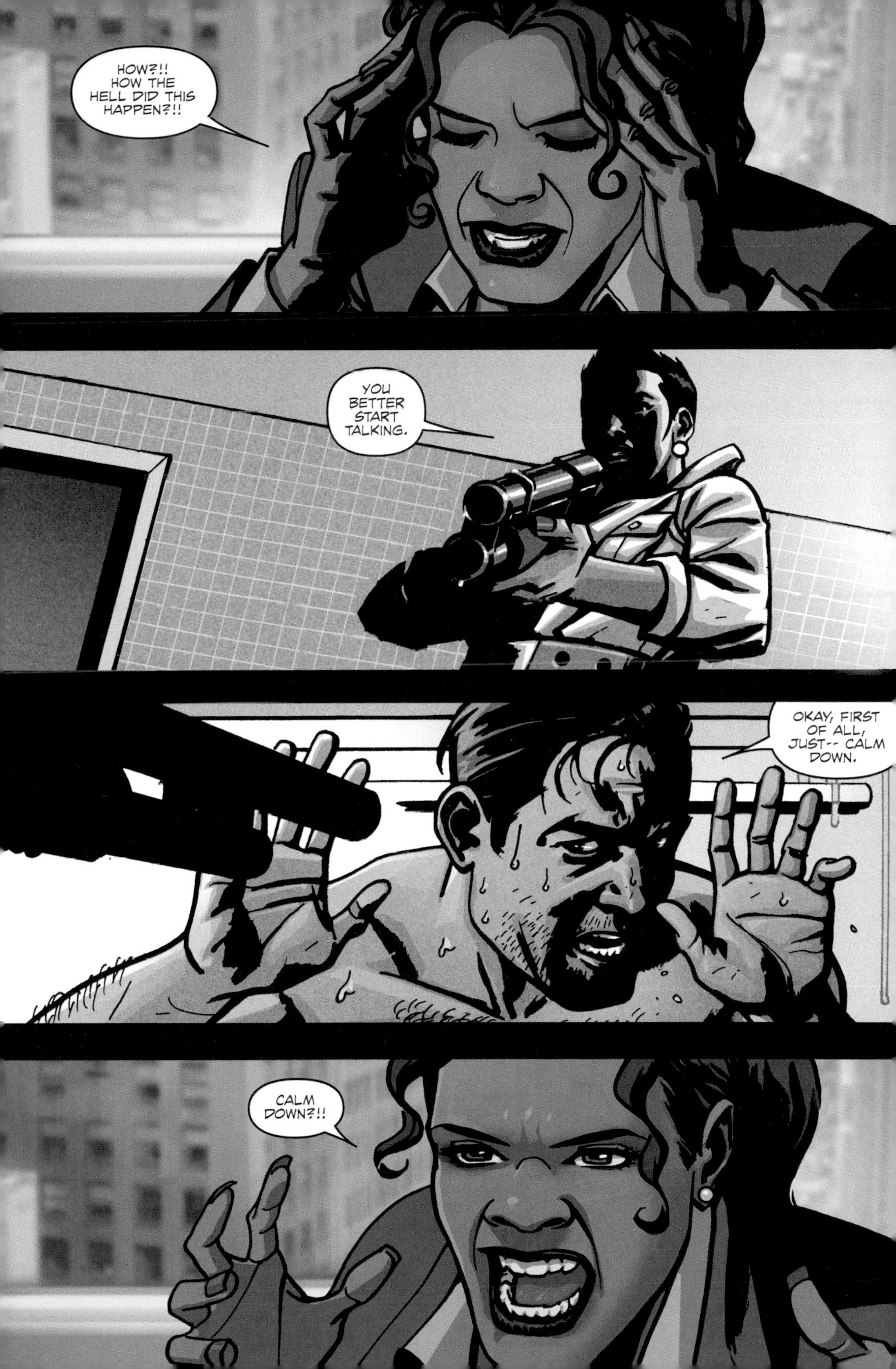
HOW?!! HOW THE HELL DID THIS HAPPEN?!!
YOU BETTER START TALKING.
OKAY, FIRST OF ALL, JUST-- CALM DOWN.
CALM DOWN?!!

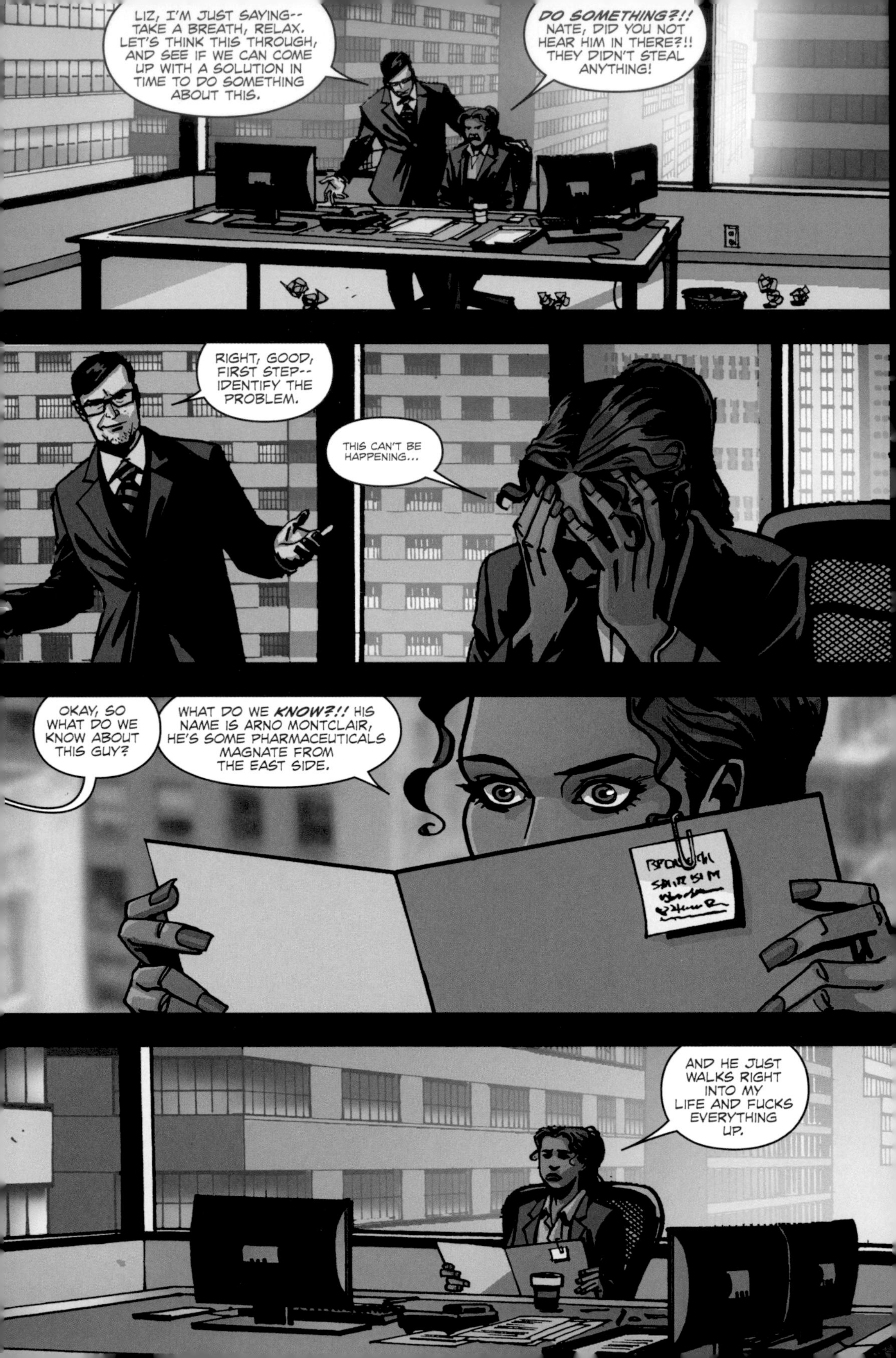
LIZ, I'M JUST SAYING-- TAKE A BREATH, RELAX. LET'S THINK THIS THROUGH, AND SEE IF WE CAN COME UP WITH A SOLUTION IN TIME TO DO SOMETHING ABOUT THIS.
DO SOMETHING?!! NATE, DID YOU NOT HEAR HIM IN THERE?!! THEY DIDN'T STEAL ANYTHING!
RIGHT, GOOD, FIRST STEP-- IDENTIFY THE PROBLEM.
THIS CAN'T BE HAPPENING...
OKAY, SO WHAT DO WE KNOW ABOUT THIS GUY?
WHAT DO WE KNOW?!! HIS NAME IS ARNO MONTCLAIR, HE'S SOME PHARMACEUTICALS MAGNATE FROM THE EAST SIDE.
AND HE JUST WALKS RIGHT INTO MY LIFE AND FUCKS EVERYTHING UP.

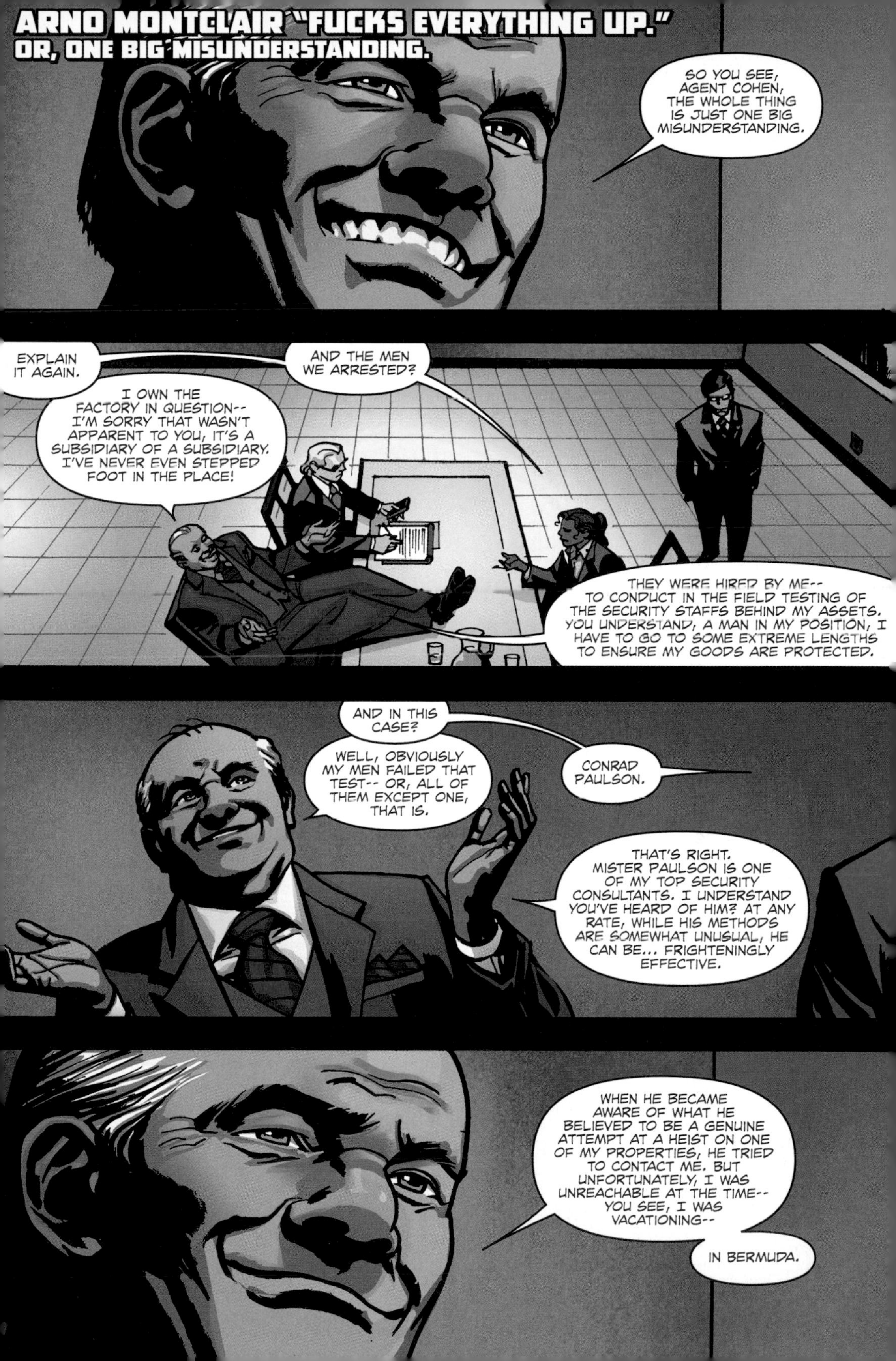
ARNO MONTCLAIR "FUCKS EVERYTHING UP."
OR, ONE BIG MISUNDERSTANDING.
SO YOU SEE, AGENT COHEN, THE WHOLE THING IS JUST ONE BIG MISUNDERSTANDING.
EXPLAIN IT AGAIN.
AND THE MEN WE ARRESTED?
I OWN THE FACTORY IN QUESTION-- I'M SORRY THAT WASN'T APPARENT TO YOU, IT'S A SUBSIDIARY OF A SUBSIDIARY. I'VE NEVER EVEN STEPPED FOOT IN THE PLACE!
THEY WERE HIRED BY ME-- TO CONDUCT IN THE FIELD TESTING OF THE SECURITY STAFFS BEHIND MY ASSETS. YOU UNDERSTAND, A MAN IN MY POSITION, I HAVE TO GO TO SOME EXTREME LENGTHS TO ENSURE MY GOODS ARE PROTECTED.
AND IN THIS CASE?
WELL, OBVIOUSLY MY MEN FAILED THAT TEST-- OR, ALL OF THEM EXCEPT ONE, THAT IS.
CONRAD PAULSON.
THAT'S RIGHT. MISTER PAULSON IS ONE OF MY TOP SECURITY CONSULTANTS. I UNDERSTAND YOU'VE HEARD OF HIM? AT ANY RATE, WHILE HIS METHODS ARE SOMEWHAT UNUSUAL, HE CAN BE... FRIGHTENINGLY EFFECTIVE.
WHEN HE BECAME AWARE OF WHAT HE BELIEVED TO BE A GENUINE ATTEMPT AT A HEIST ON ONE OF MY PROPERTIES, HE TRIED TO CONTACT ME. BUT UNFORTUNATELY, I WAS UNREACHABLE AT THE TIME-- YOU SEE, I WAS VACATIONING--
IN BERMUDA.

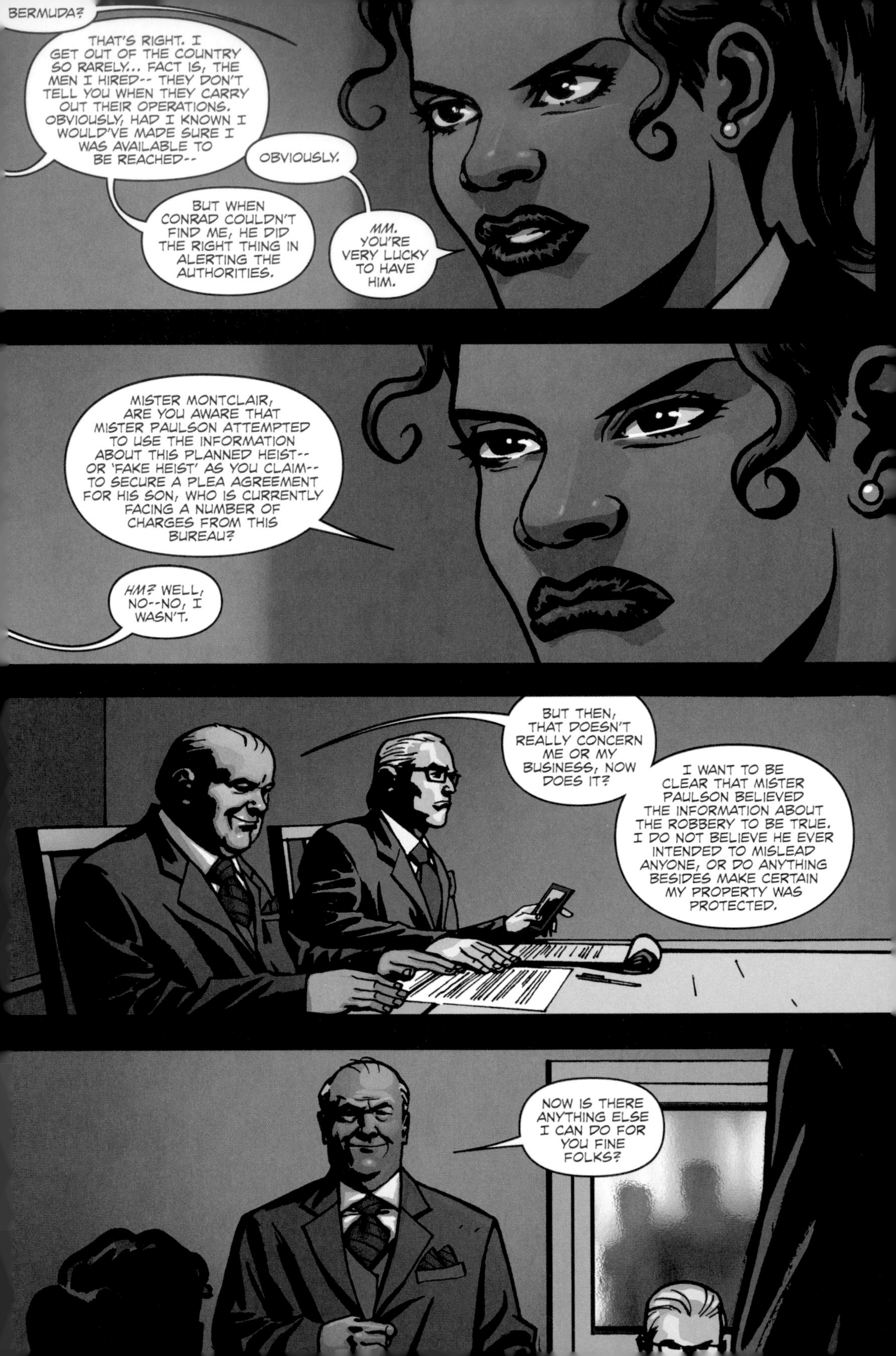
BERMUDA?
THAT'S RIGHT. I GET OUT OF THE COUNTRY SO RARELY... FACT IS, THE MEN I HIRED-- THEY DON'T TELL YOU WHEN THEY CARRY OUT THEIR OPERATIONS. OBVIOUSLY, HAD I KNOWN I WOULD'VE MADE SURE I WAS AVAILABLE TO BE REACHED--
OBVIOUSLY.
BUT WHEN CONRAD COULDN'T FIND ME, HE DID THE RIGHT THING IN ALERTING THE AUTHORITIES.
MM. YOU'RE VERY LUCKY TO HAVE HIM.
MISTER MONTCLAIR, ARE YOU AWARE THAT MISTER PAULSON ATTEMPTED TO USE THE INFORMATION ABOUT THIS PLANNED HEIST-- OR 'FAKE HEIST' AS YOU CLAIM-- TO SECURE A PLEA AGREEMENT FOR HIS SON, WHO IS CURRENTLY FACING A NUMBER OF CHARGES FROM THIS BUREAU?
HM? WELL, NO--NO, I WASN'T.
BUT THEN, THAT DOESN'T REALLY CONCERN ME OR MY BUSINESS, NOW DOES IT?
I WANT TO BE CLEAR THAT MISTER PAULSON BELIEVED THE INFORMATION ABOUT THE ROBBERY TO BE TRUE. I DO NOT BELIEVE HE EVER INTENDED TO MISLEAD ANYONE, OR DO ANYTHING BESIDES MAKE CERTAIN MY PROPERTY WAS PROTECTED.
NOW IS THERE ANYTHING ELSE I CAN DO FOR YOU FINE FOLKS?

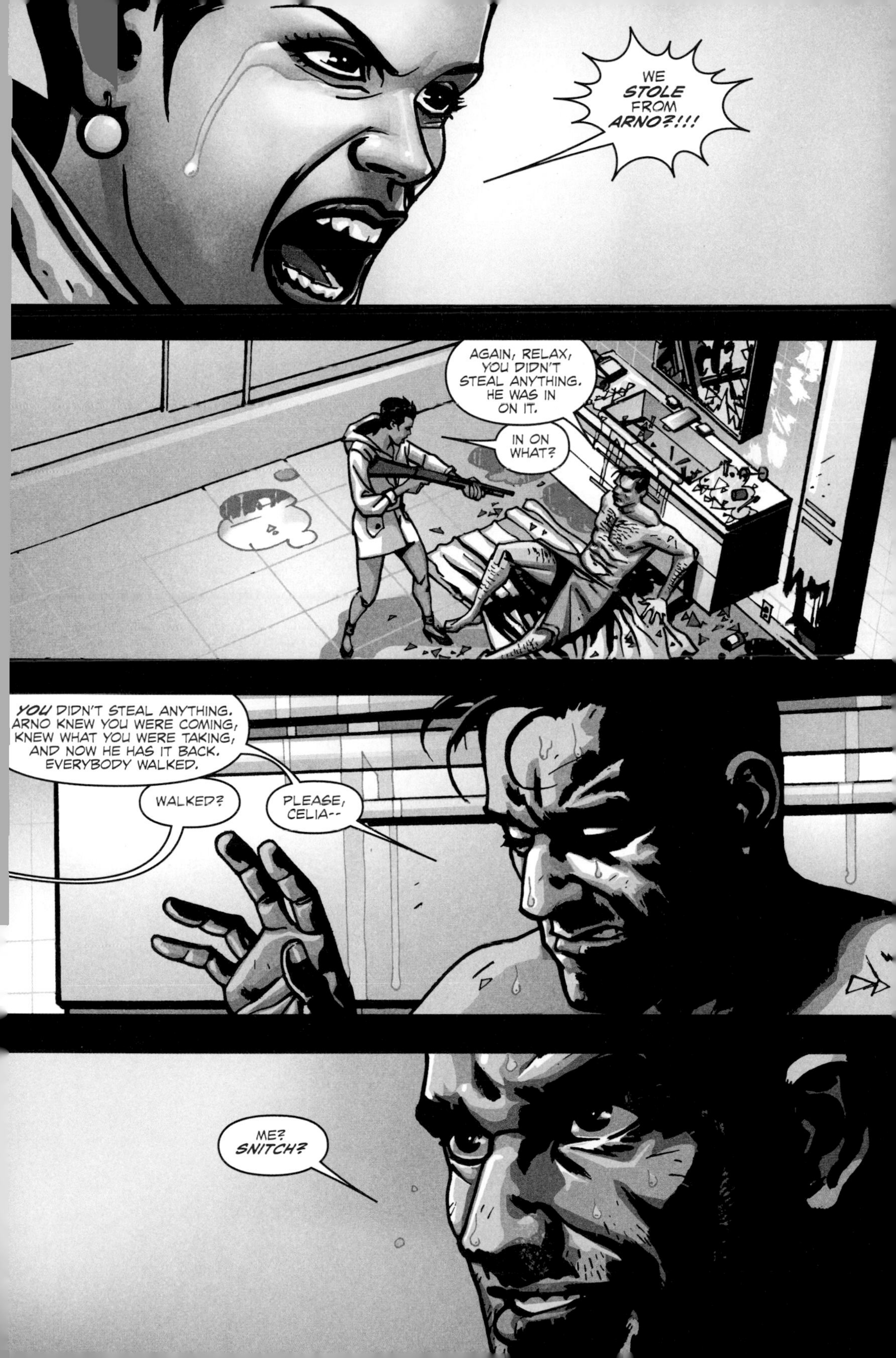
WE STOLE FROM ARNO?!!!
AGAIN, RELAX, YOU DIDN'T STEAL ANYTHING. HE WAS IN ON IT.
IN ON WHAT?
YOU DIDN'T STEAL ANYTHING. ARNO KNEW YOU WERE COMING, KNEW WHAT YOU WERE TAKING, AND NOW HE HAS IT BACK. EVERYBODY WALKED.
WALKED?
PLEASE, CELIA--
ME? SNITCH?

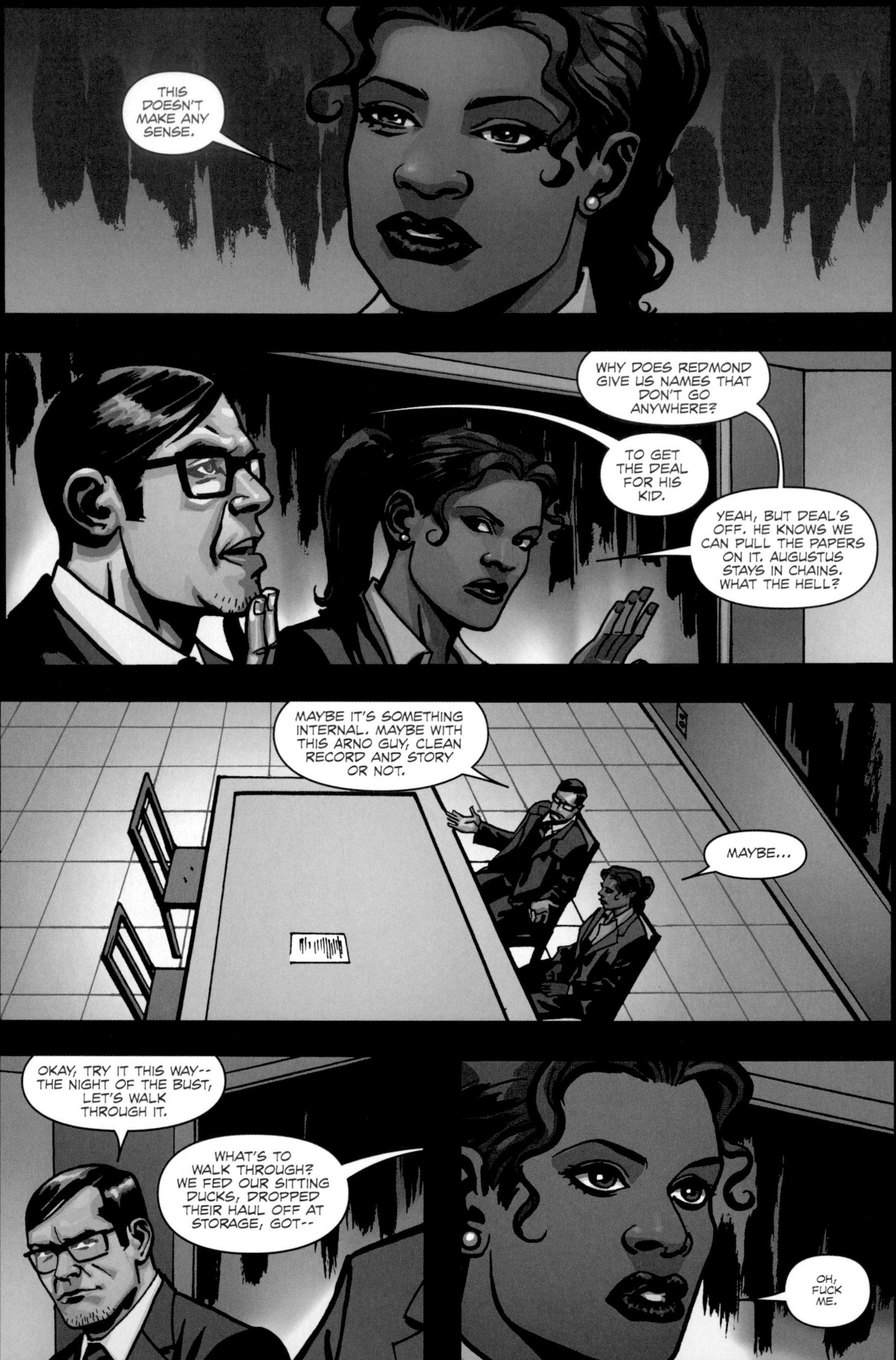
THIS DOESN'T MAKE ANY SENSE.
WHY DOES REDMOND GIVE US NAMES THAT DON'T GO ANYWHERE?
TO GET THE DEAL FOR HIS KID.
YEAH, BUT DEAL'S OFF. HE KNOWS WE CAN PULL THE PAPERS ON IT. AUGUSTUS STAYS IN CHAINS. WHAT THE HELL?
MAYBE IT'S SOMETHING INTERNAL. MAYBE WITH THIS ARNO GUY, CLEAN RECORD AND STORY OR NOT.
MAYBE...
OKAY, TRY IT THIS WAY-- THE NIGHT OF THE BUST, LET'S WALK THROUGH IT.
WHAT'S TO WALK THROUGH? WE FED OUR SITTING DUCKS, DROPPED THEIR HAUL OFF AT STORAGE, GOT--
OH, FUCK ME.

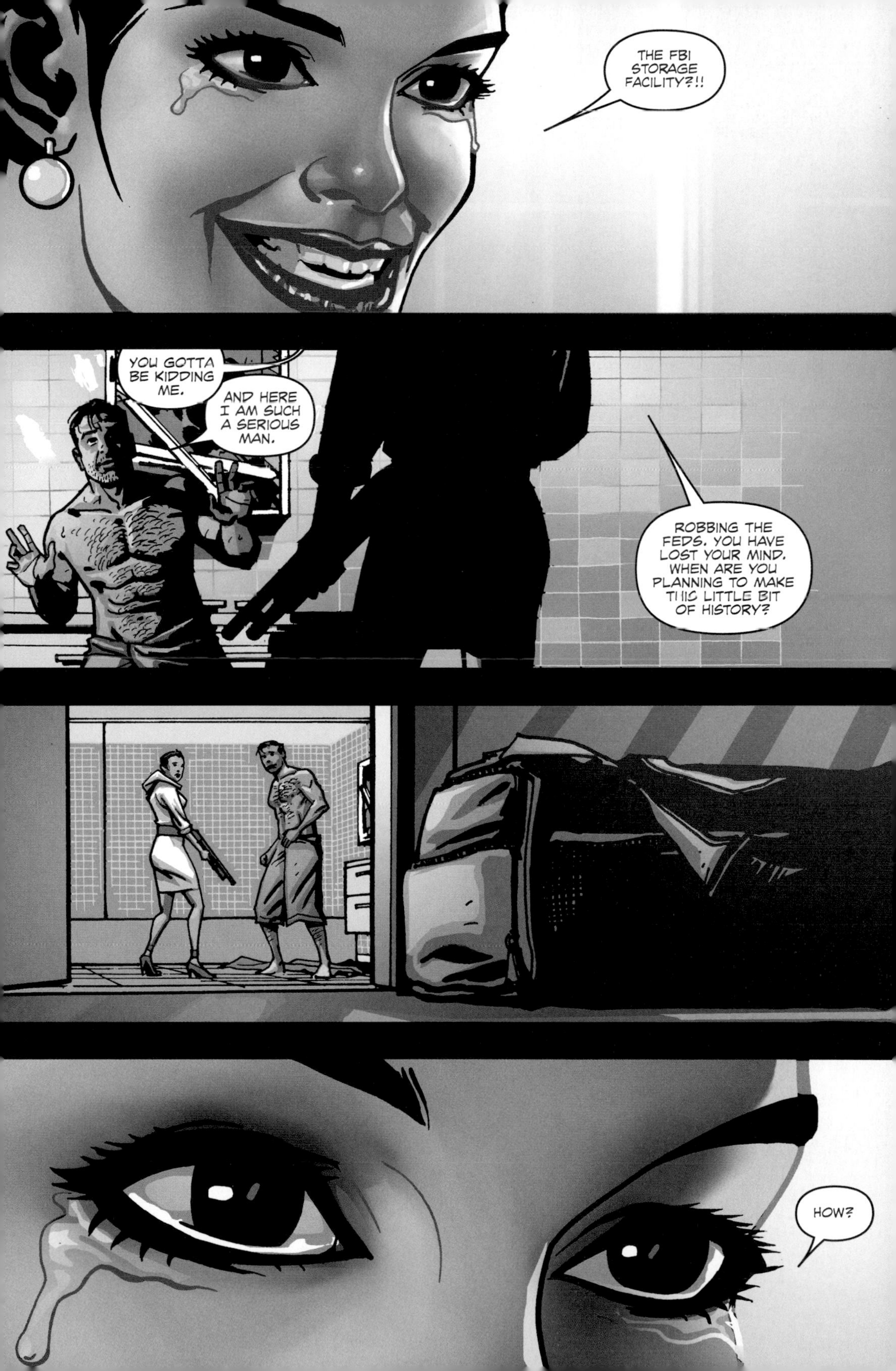
THE FBI STORAGE FACILITY?!!
YOU GOTTA BE KIDDING ME.
AND HERE I AM SUCH A SERIOUS MAN.
ROBBING THE FEDS. YOU HAVE LOST YOUR MIND. WHEN ARE YOU PLANNING TO MAKE THIS LITTLE BIT OF HISTORY?
HOW?

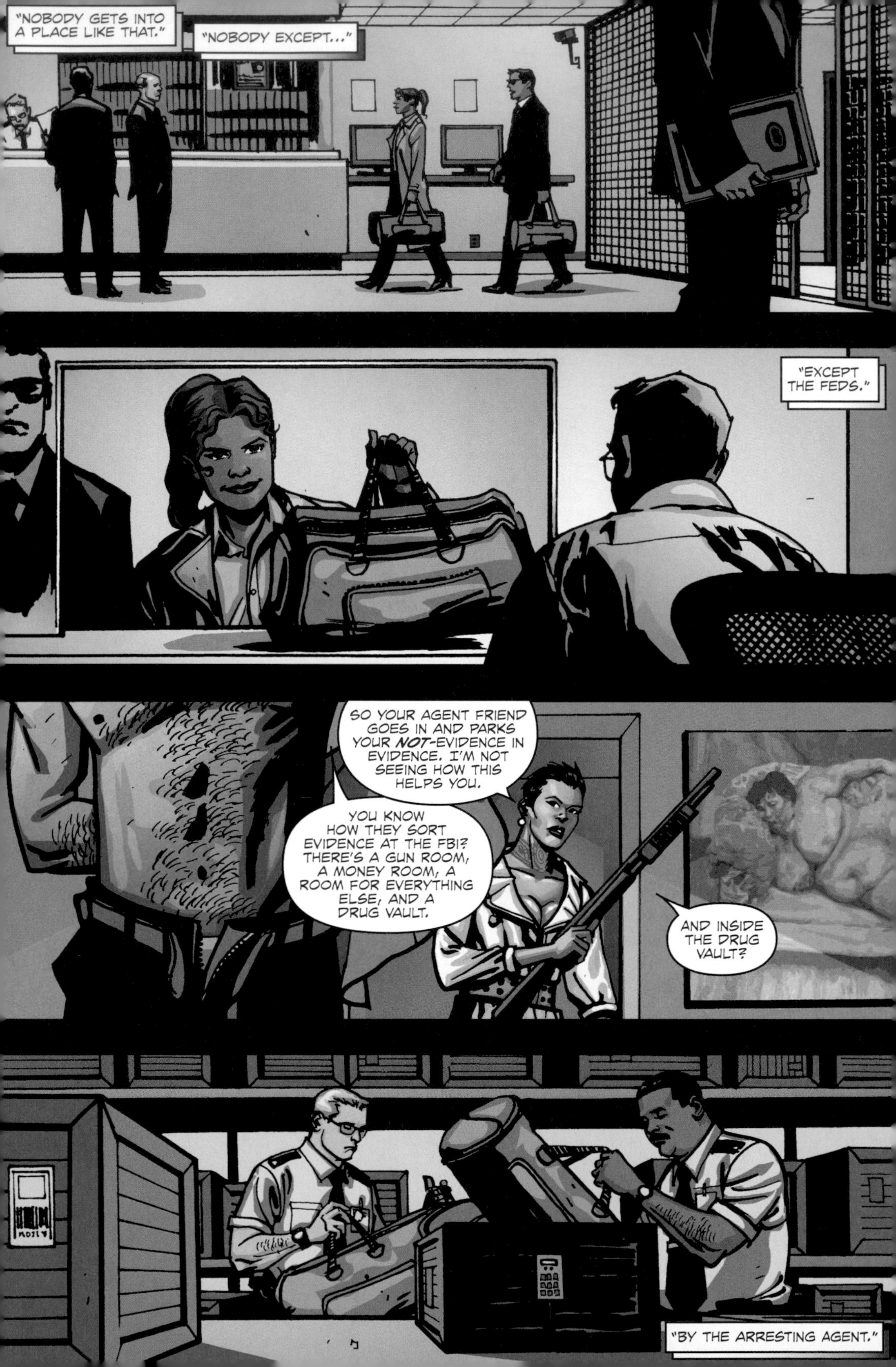
"NOBODY GETS INTO A PLACE LIKE THAT."
"NOBODY EXCEPT..."
"EXCEPT THE FEDS."
SO YOUR AGENT FRIEND GOES IN AND PARKS YOUR *NOT*-EVIDENCE IN EVIDENCE. I'M NOT SEEING HOW THIS HELPS YOU.
YOU KNOW HOW THEY SORT EVIDENCE AT THE FBI? THERE'S A GUN ROOM, A MONEY ROOM, A ROOM FOR EVERYTHING ELSE, AND A DRUG VAULT.
AND INSIDE THE DRUG VAULT?
"BY THE ARRESTING AGENT."

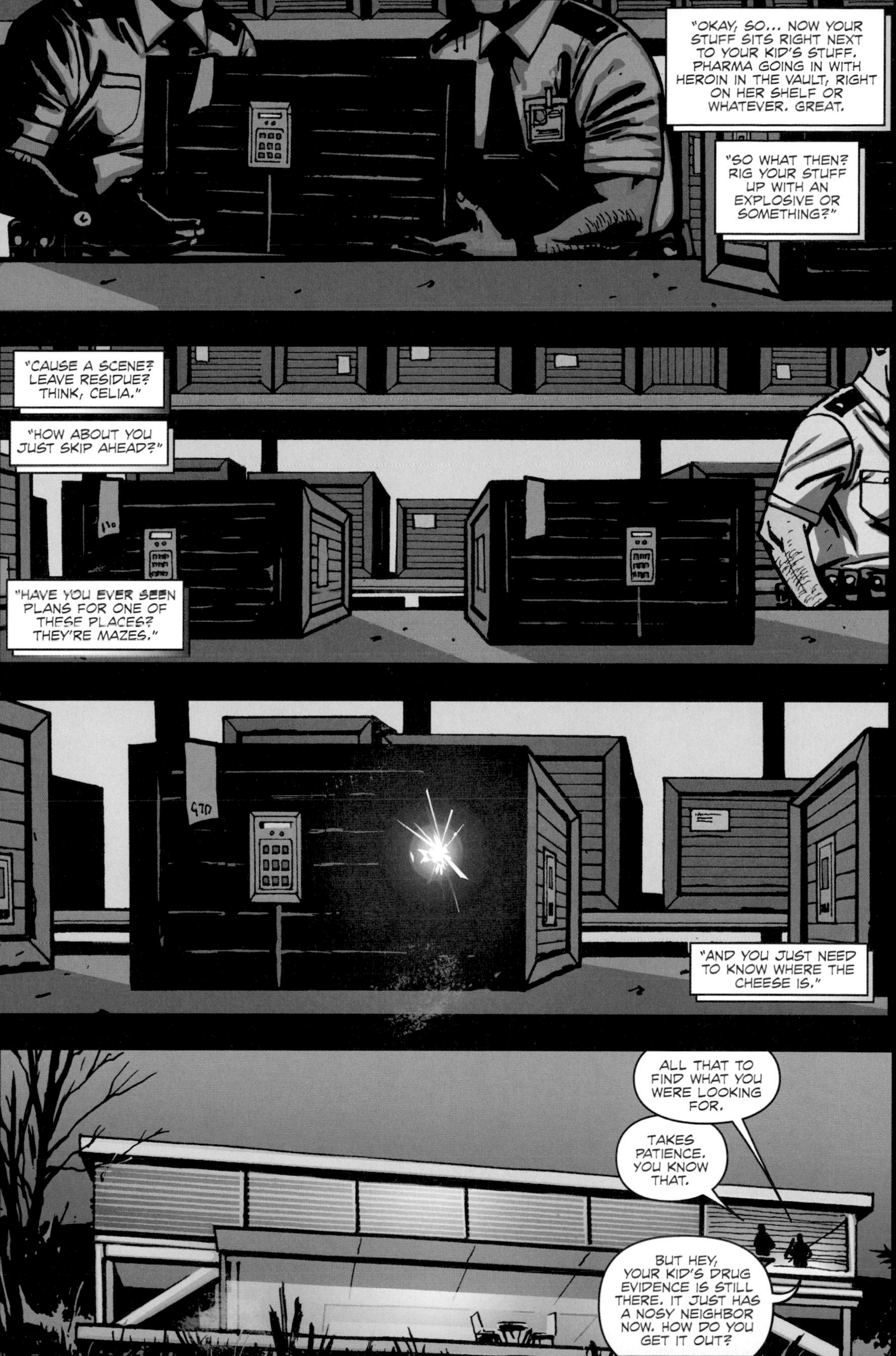
"OKAY, SO... NOW YOUR STUFF SITS RIGHT NEXT TO YOUR KID'S STUFF. PHARMA GOING IN WITH HEROIN IN THE VAULT, RIGHT ON HER SHELF OR WHATEVER. GREAT.
"SO WHAT THEN? RIG YOUR STUFF UP WITH AN EXPLOSIVE OR SOMETHING?"
"CAUSE A SCENE? LEAVE RESIDUE? THINK, CELIA."
"HOW ABOUT YOU JUST SKIP AHEAD?"
"HAVE YOU EVER SEEN PLANS FOR ONE OF THESE PLACES? THEY'RE MAZES."
"AND YOU JUST NEED TO KNOW WHERE THE CHEESE IS."
ALL THAT TO FIND WHAT YOU WERE LOOKING FOR.
TAKES PATIENCE. YOU KNOW THAT.
BUT HEY, YOUR KID'S DRUG EVIDENCE IS STILL THERE. IT JUST HAS A NOSY NEIGHBOR NOW. HOW DO YOU GET IT OUT?

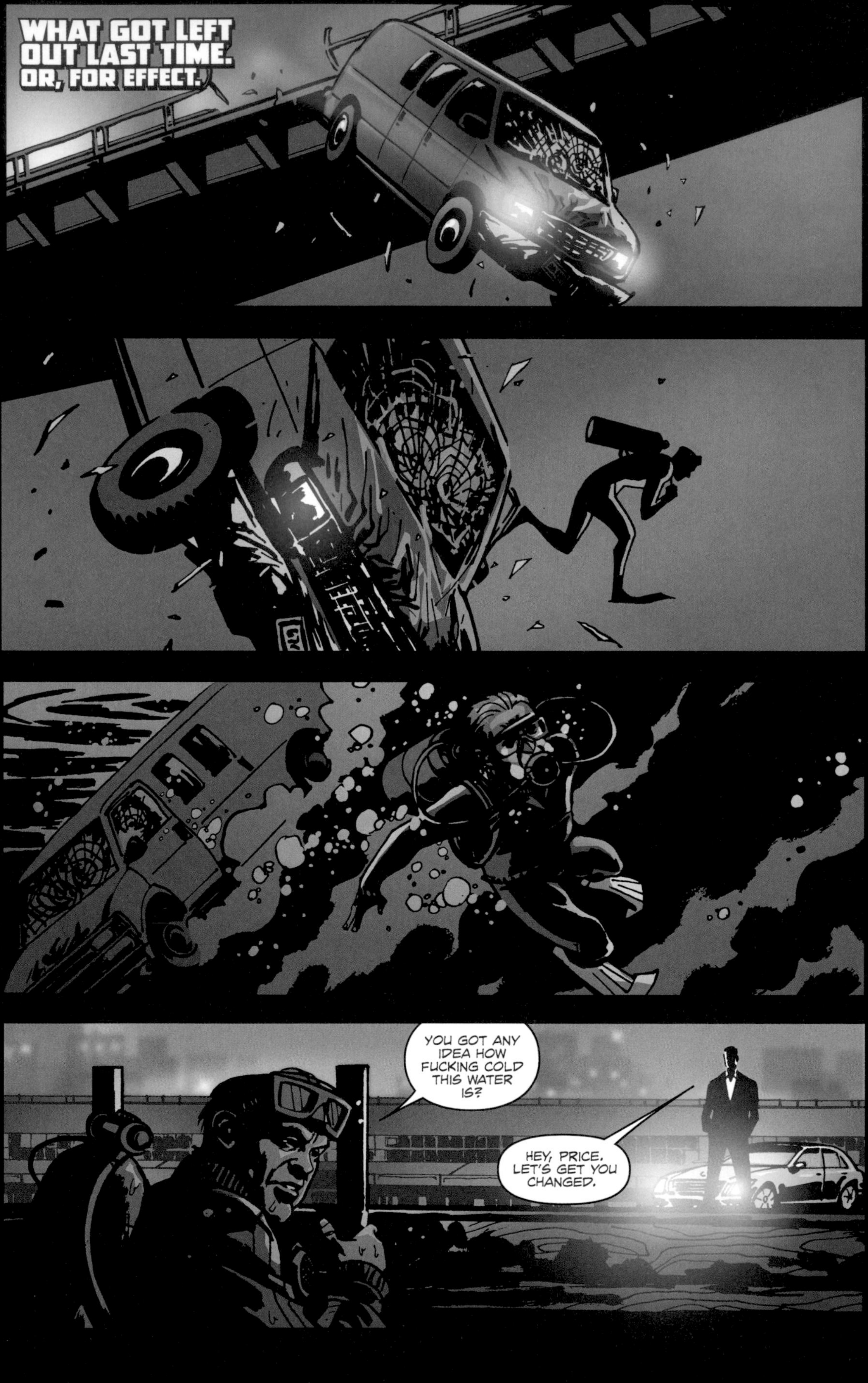
WHAT GOT LEFT OUT LAST TIME. OR, FOR EFFECT.
YOU GOT ANY IDEA HOW FUCKING COLD THIS WATER IS?
HEY, PRICE. LET'S GET YOU CHANGED.

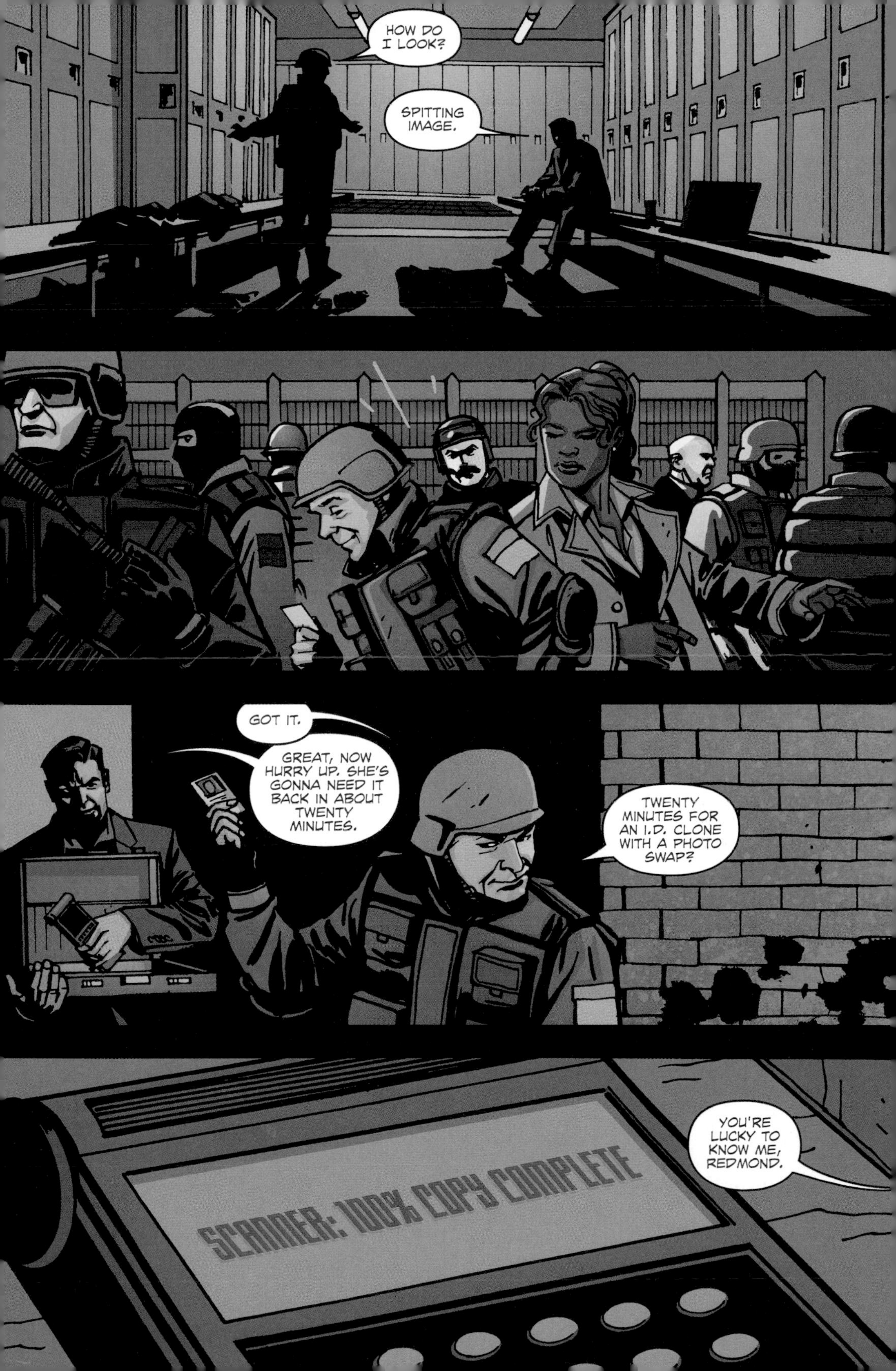
HOW DO I LOOK?
SPITTING IMAGE.
GOT IT.
GREAT, NOW HURRY UP. SHE'S GONNA NEED IT BACK IN ABOUT TWENTY MINUTES.
TWENTY MINUTES FOR AN I.D. CLONE WITH A PHOTO SWAP?
SCANNER: 100% COPY COMPLETE
YOU'RE LUCKY TO KNOW ME, REDMOND.

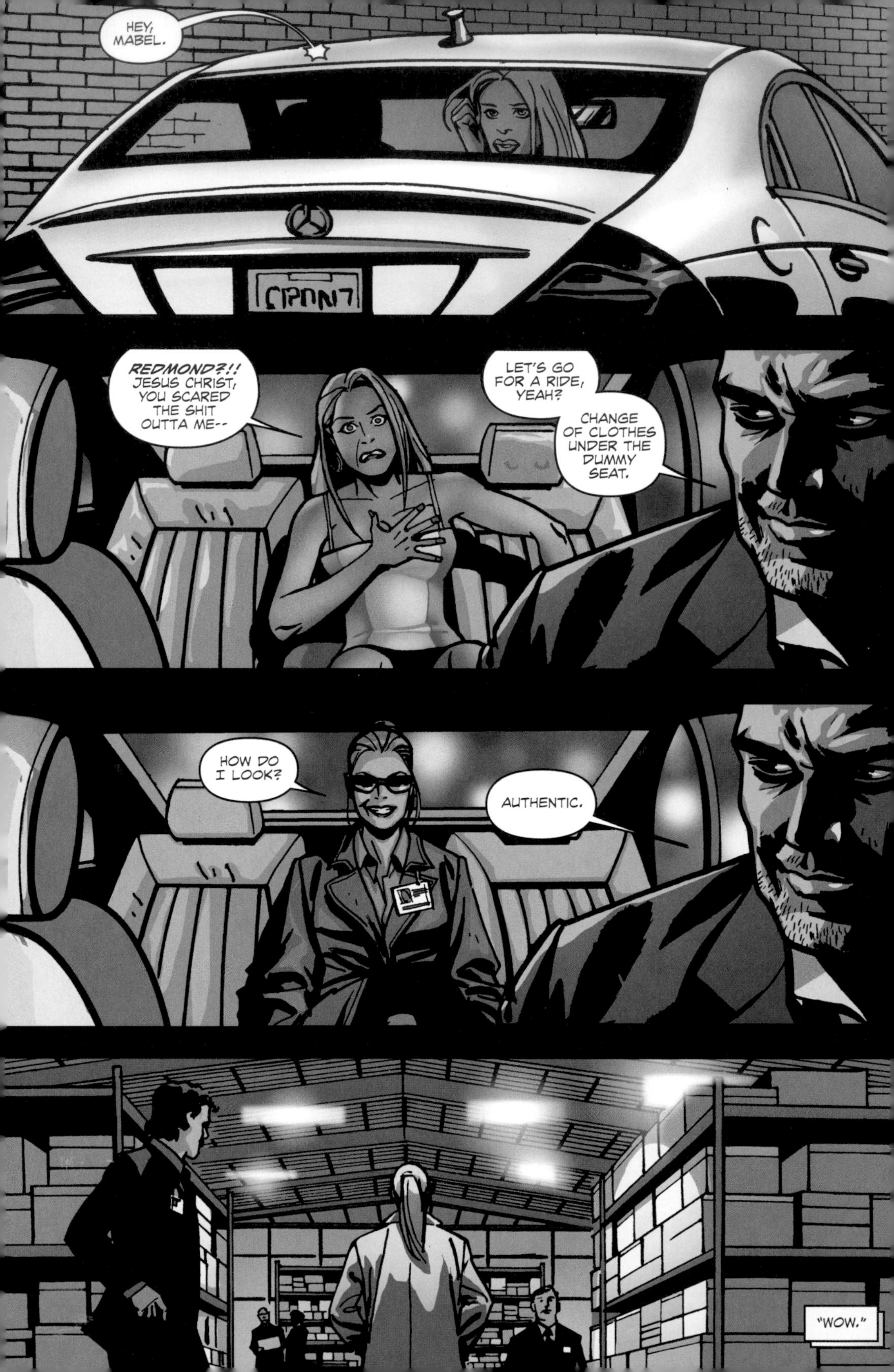
HEY, MABEL.
REDMOND?!! JESUS CHRIST, YOU SCARED THE SHIT OUTTA ME--
LET'S GO FOR A RIDE, YEAH?
CHANGE OF CLOTHES UNDER THE DUMMY SEAT.
HOW DO I LOOK?
AUTHENTIC.
"WOW."

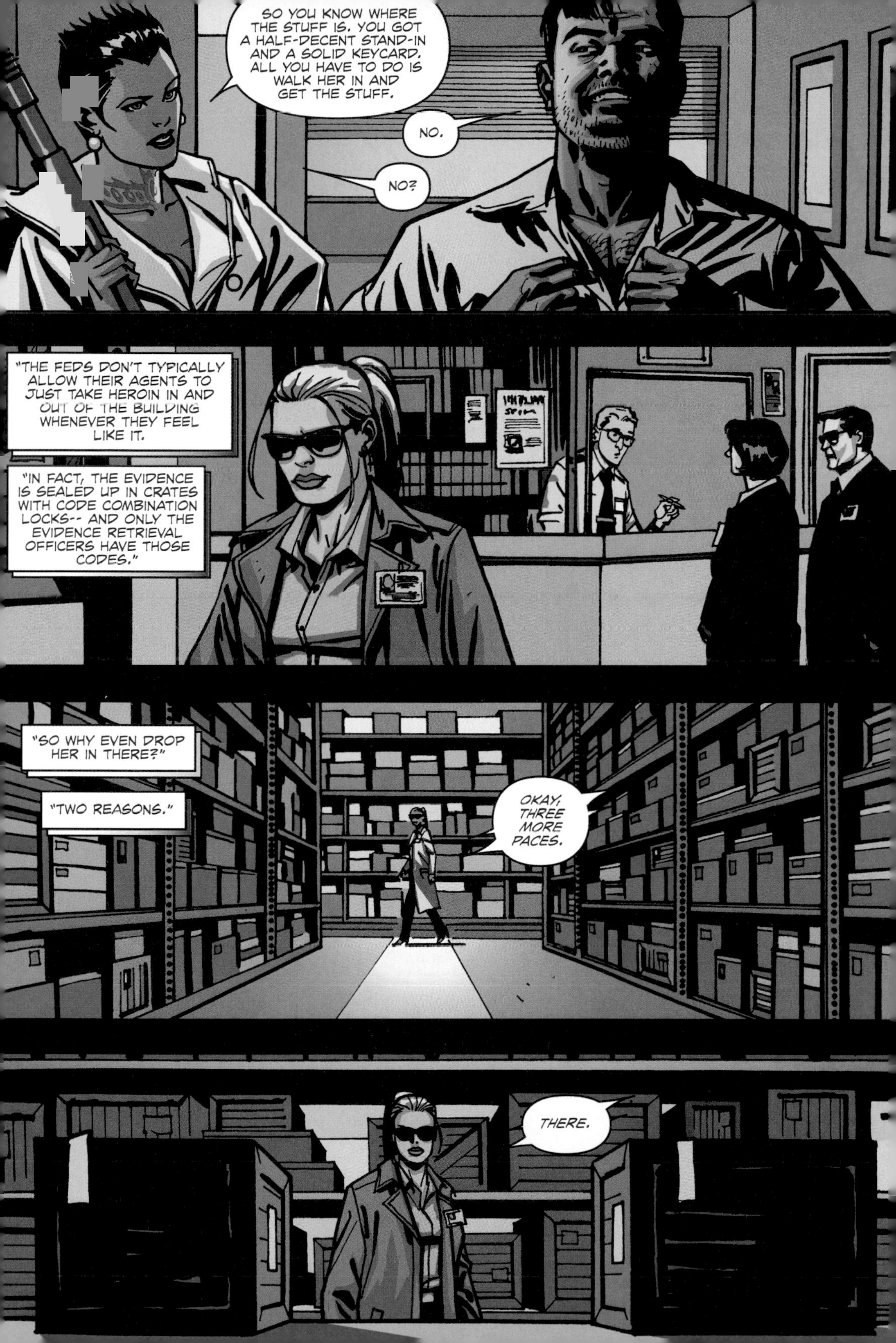
SO YOU KNOW WHERE THE STUFF IS. YOU GOT A HALF-DECENT STAND-IN AND A SOLID KEYCARD. ALL YOU HAVE TO DO IS WALK HER IN AND GET THE STUFF.
NO.
NO?
"THE FEDS DON'T TYPICALLY ALLOW THEIR AGENTS TO JUST TAKE HEROIN IN AND OUT OF THE BUILDING WHENEVER THEY FEEL LIKE IT.
"IN FACT, THE EVIDENCE IS SEALED UP IN CRATES WITH CODE COMBINATION LOCKS-- AND ONLY THE EVIDENCE RETRIEVAL OFFICERS HAVE THOSE CODES."
"SO WHY EVEN DROP HER IN THERE?"
"TWO REASONS."
OKAY, THREE MORE PACES.
THERE.

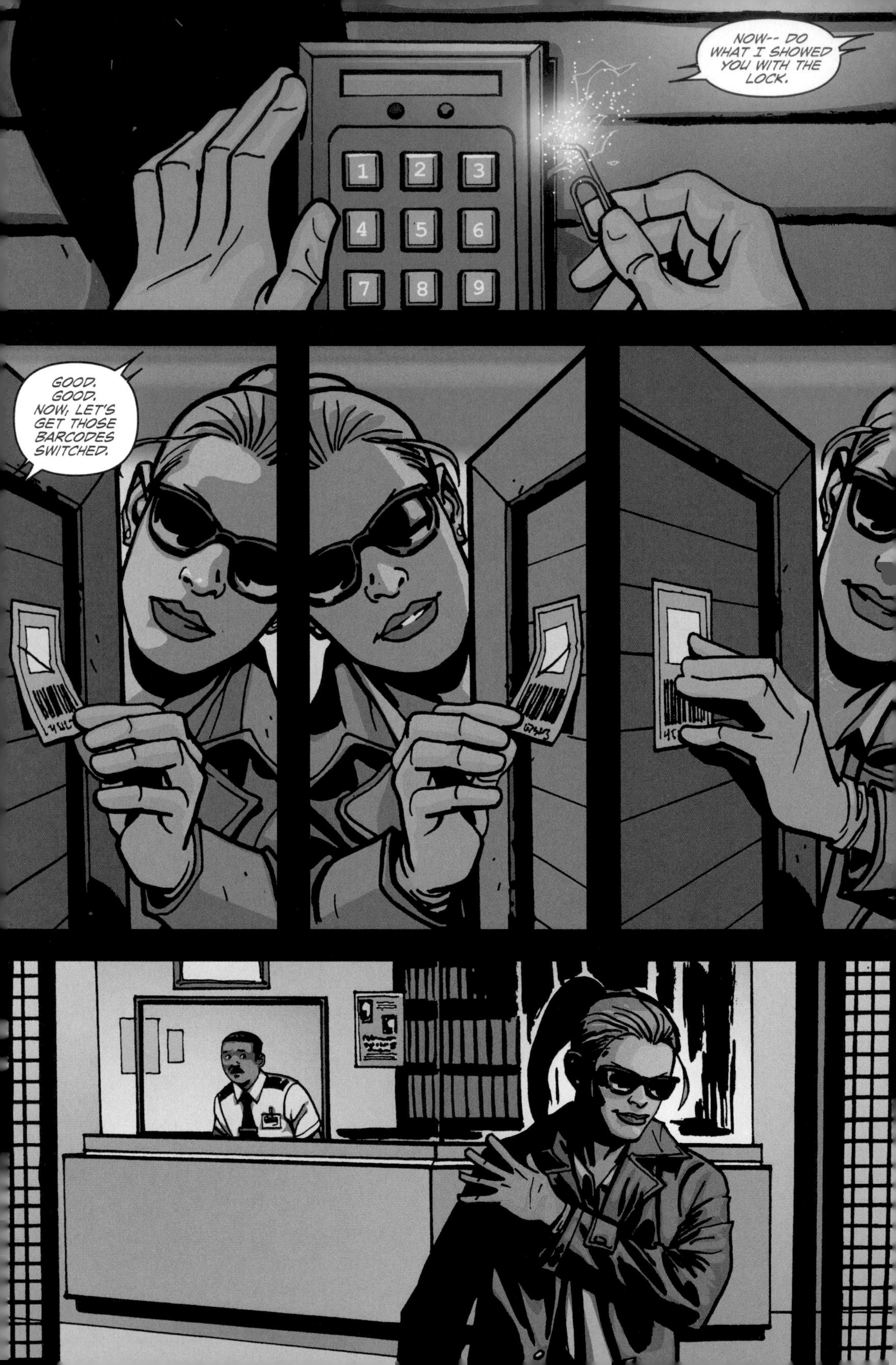
NOW-- DO WHAT I SHOWED YOU WITH THE LOCK.
GOOD. GOOD. NOW, LET'S GET THOSE BARCODES SWITCHED.

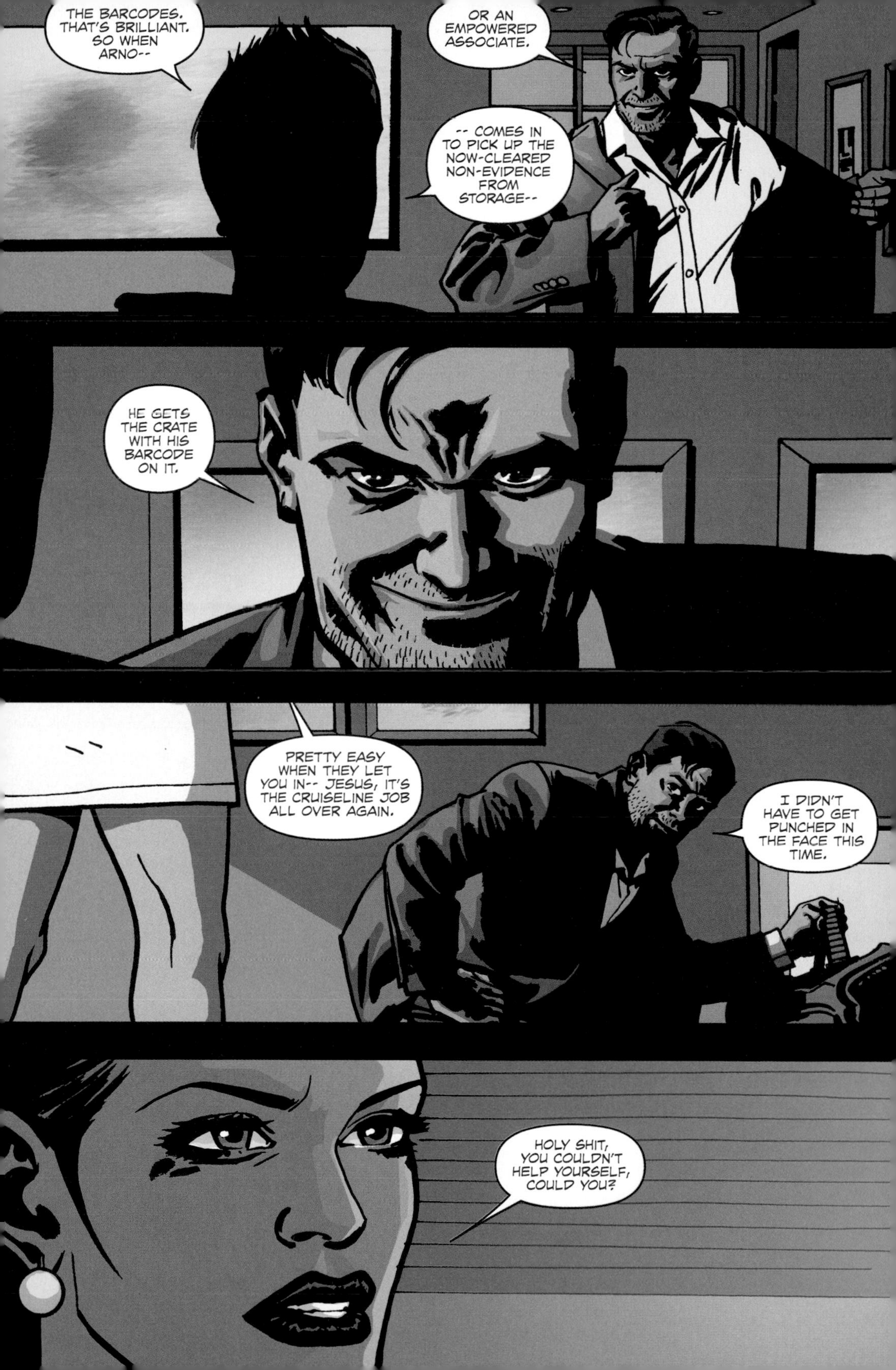
THE BARCODES. THAT'S BRILLIANT. SO WHEN ARNO--
OR AN EMPOWERED ASSOCIATE.
-- COMES IN TO PICK UP THE NOW-CLEARED NON-EVIDENCE FROM STORAGE--
HE GETS THE CRATE WITH HIS BARCODE ON IT.
PRETTY EASY WHEN THEY LET YOU IN-- JESUS, IT'S THE CRUISELINE JOB ALL OVER AGAIN.
I DIDN'T HAVE TO GET PUNCHED IN THE FACE THIS TIME.
HOLY SHIT, YOU COULDN'T HELP YOURSELF, COULD YOU?

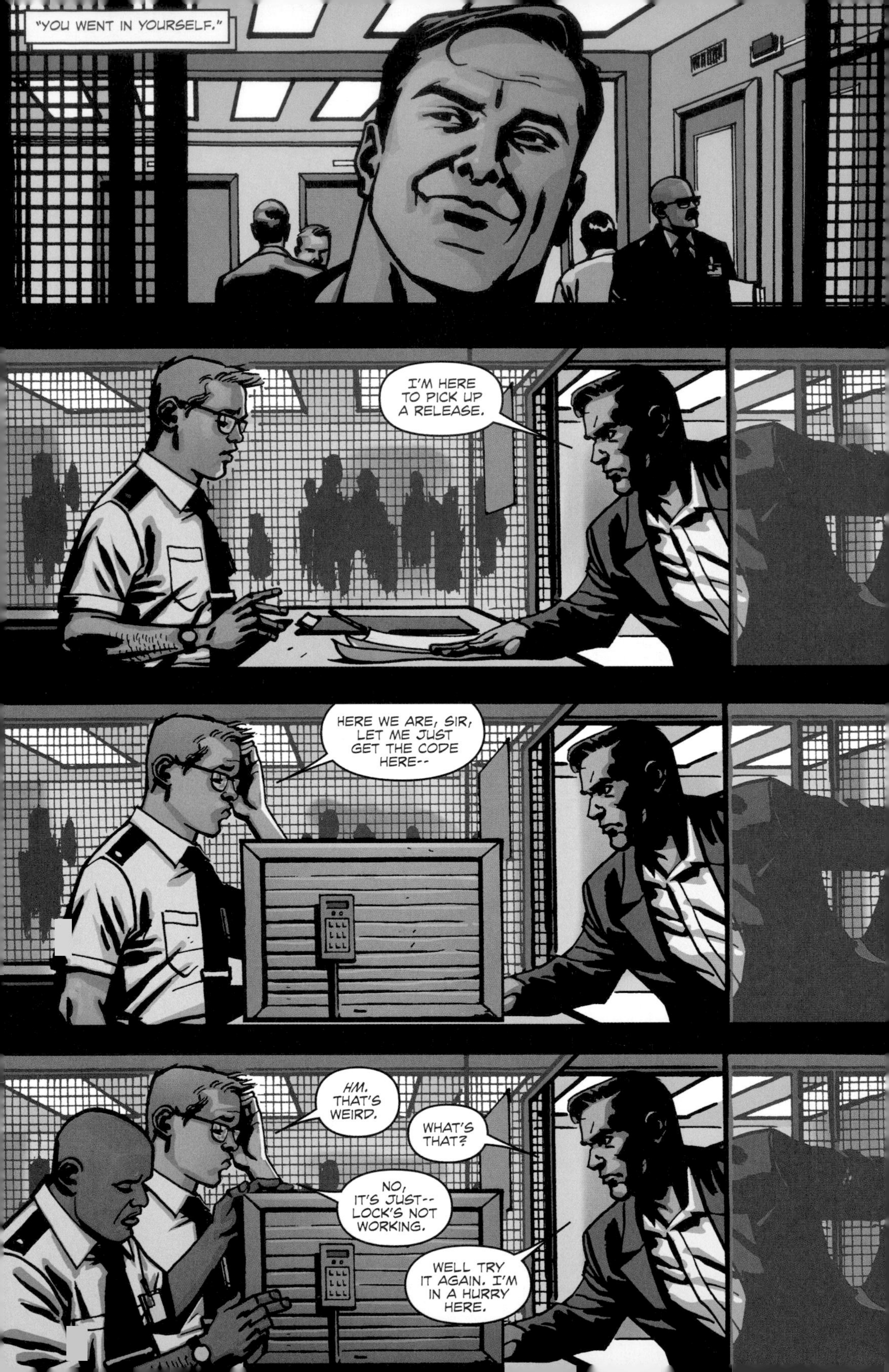
"YOU WENT IN YOURSELF."
I'M HERE TO PICK UP A RELEASE.
HERE WE ARE, SIR, LET ME JUST GET THE CODE HERE--
HM. THAT'S WEIRD.
WHAT'S THAT?
NO, IT'S JUST-- LOCK'S NOT WORKING.
WELL TRY IT AGAIN. I'M IN A HURRY HERE.

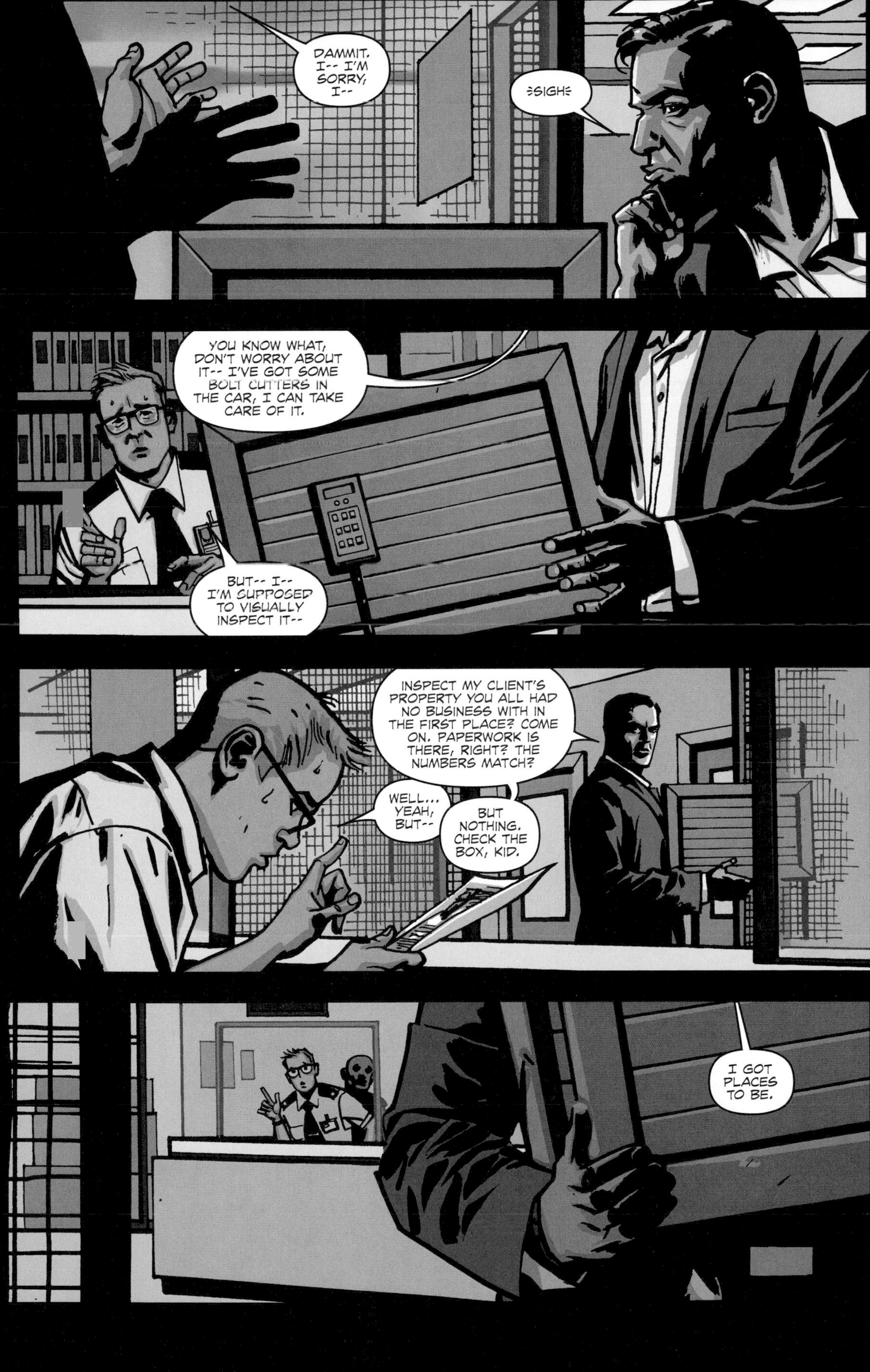
DAMMIT. I-- I'M SORRY, I--
=SIGH=
YOU KNOW WHAT, DON'T WORRY ABOUT IT-- I'VE GOT SOME BOLT CUTTERS IN THE CAR, I CAN TAKE CARE OF IT.
BUT-- I-- I'M SUPPOSED TO VISUALLY INSPECT IT--
INSPECT MY CLIENT'S PROPERTY YOU ALL HAD NO BUSINESS WITH IN THE FIRST PLACE? COME ON. PAPERWORK IS THERE, RIGHT? THE NUMBERS MATCH?
WELL... YEAH, BUT--
BUT NOTHING. CHECK THE BOX, KID.
I GOT PLACES TO BE.

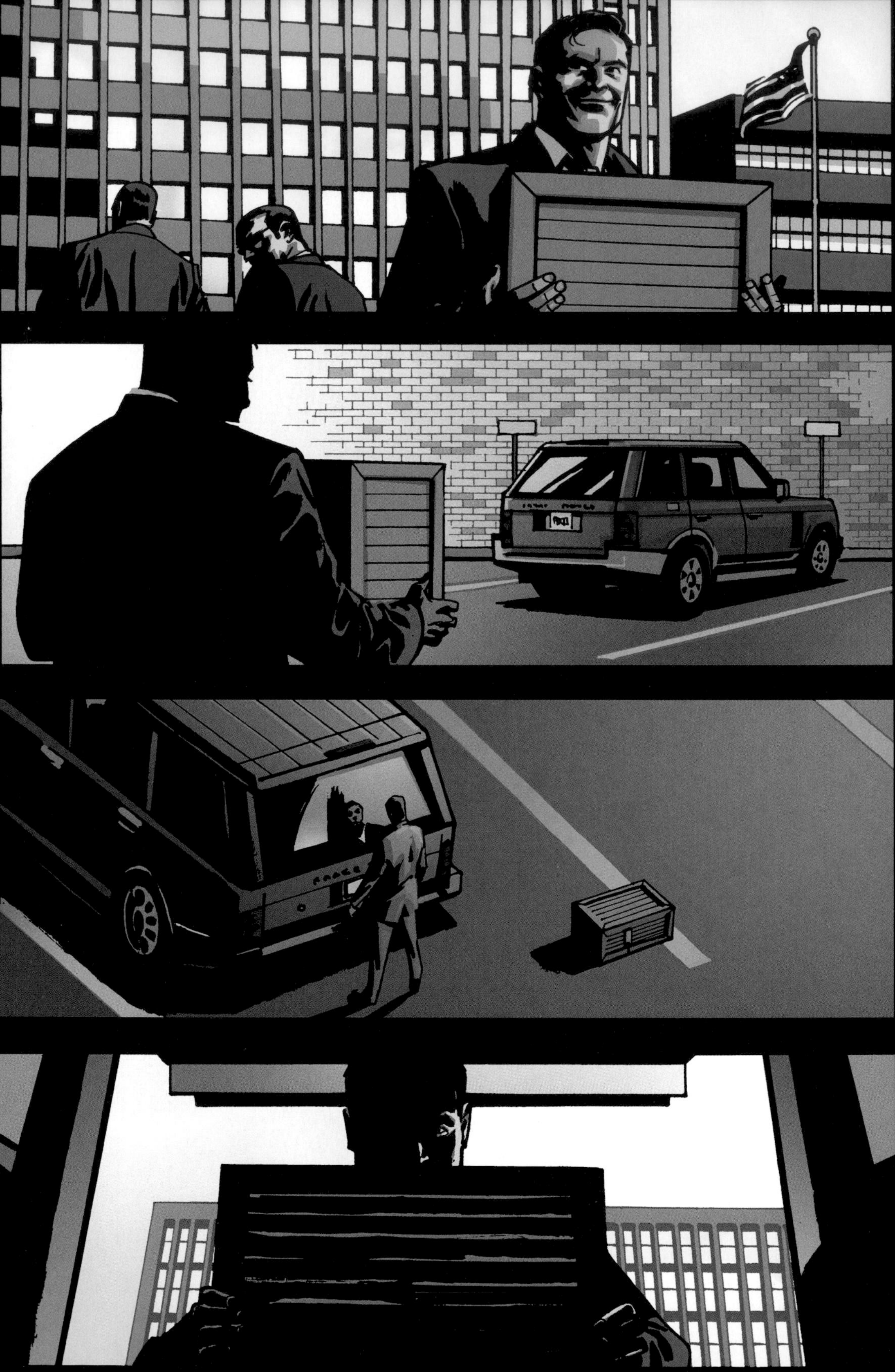

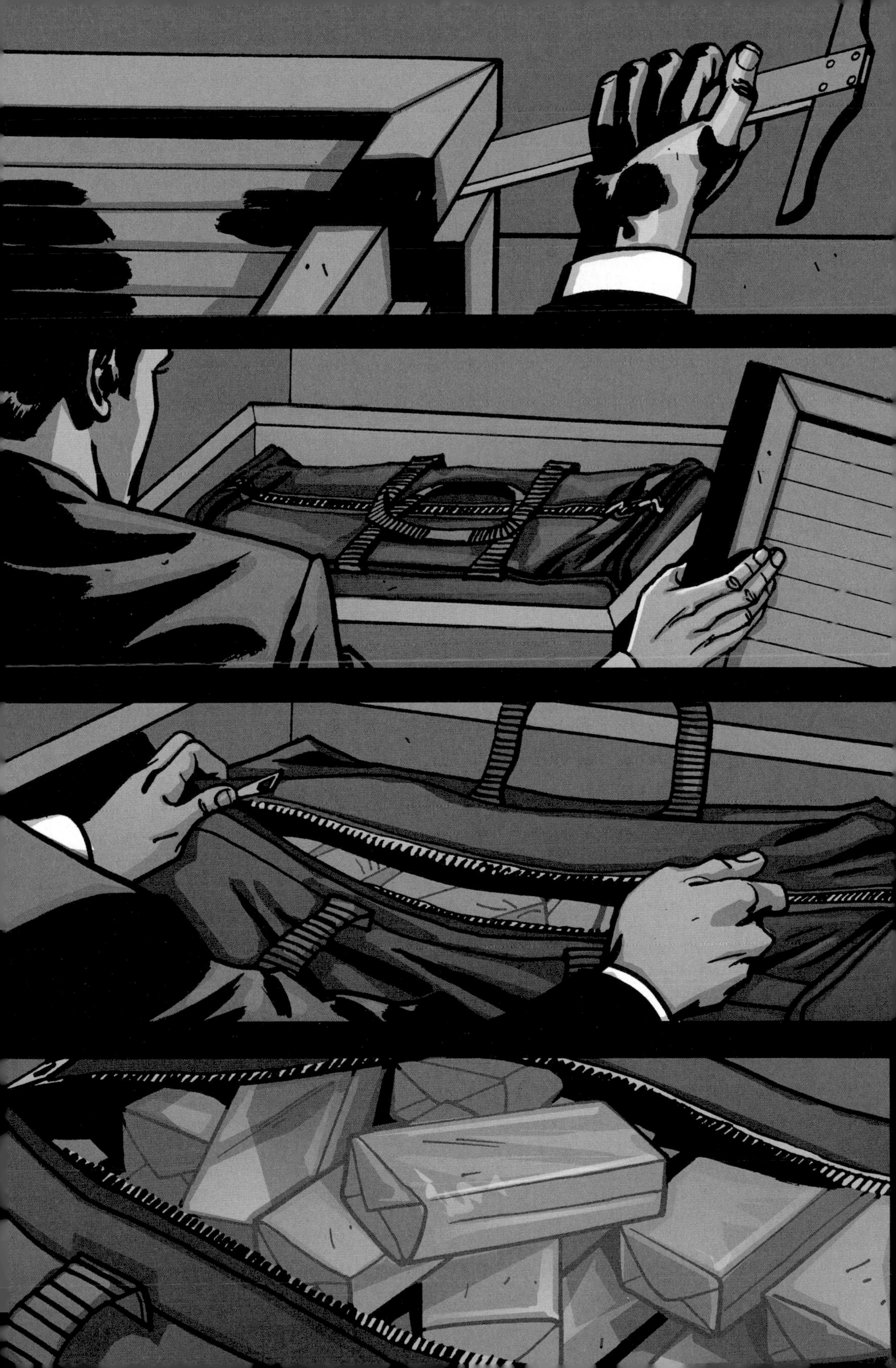

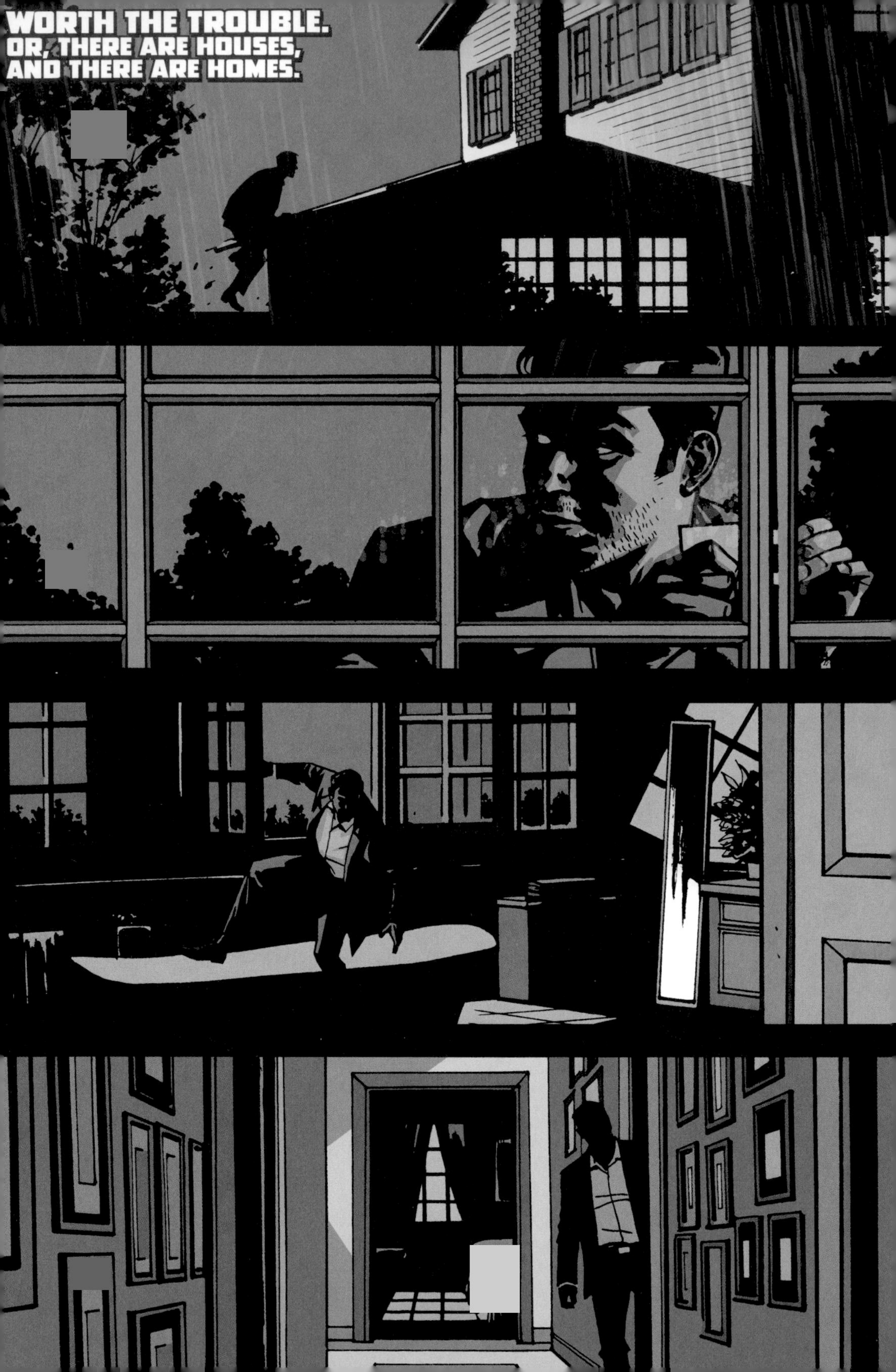
WORTH THE TROUBLE.
OR, THERE ARE HOUSES,
AND THERE ARE HOMES.

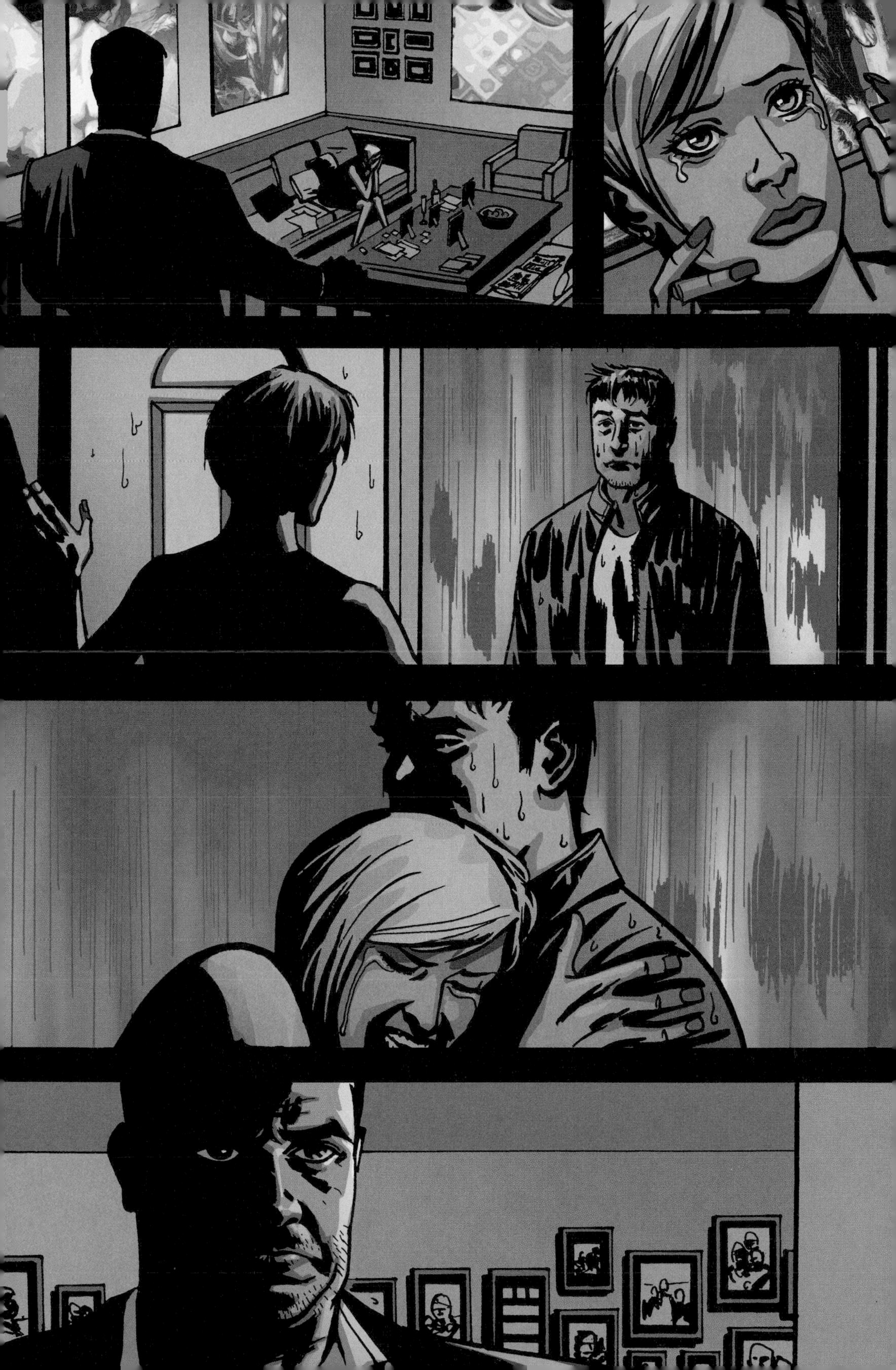

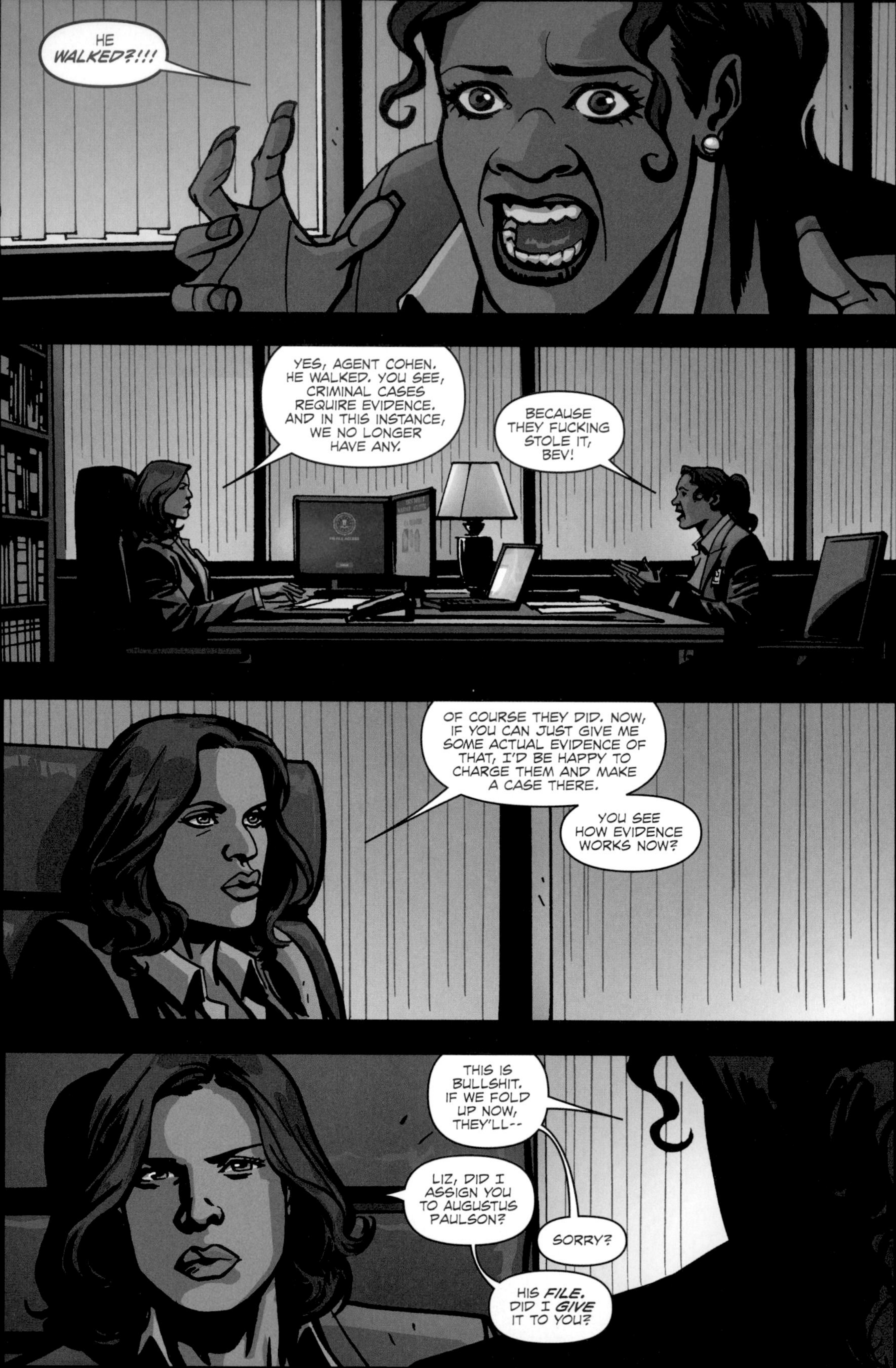
HE WALKED?!!!
YES, AGENT COHEN. HE WALKED. YOU SEE, CRIMINAL CASES REQUIRE EVIDENCE. AND IN THIS INSTANCE, WE NO LONGER HAVE ANY.
BECAUSE THEY FUCKING STOLE IT, BEV!
OF COURSE THEY DID. NOW, IF YOU CAN JUST GIVE ME SOME ACTUAL EVIDENCE OF THAT, I'D BE HAPPY TO CHARGE THEM AND MAKE A CASE THERE.
YOU SEE HOW EVIDENCE WORKS NOW?
THIS IS BULLSHIT. IF WE FOLD UP NOW, THEY'LL--
LIZ, DID I ASSIGN YOU TO AUGUSTUS PAULSON?
SORRY?
HIS FILE. DID I GIVE IT TO YOU?

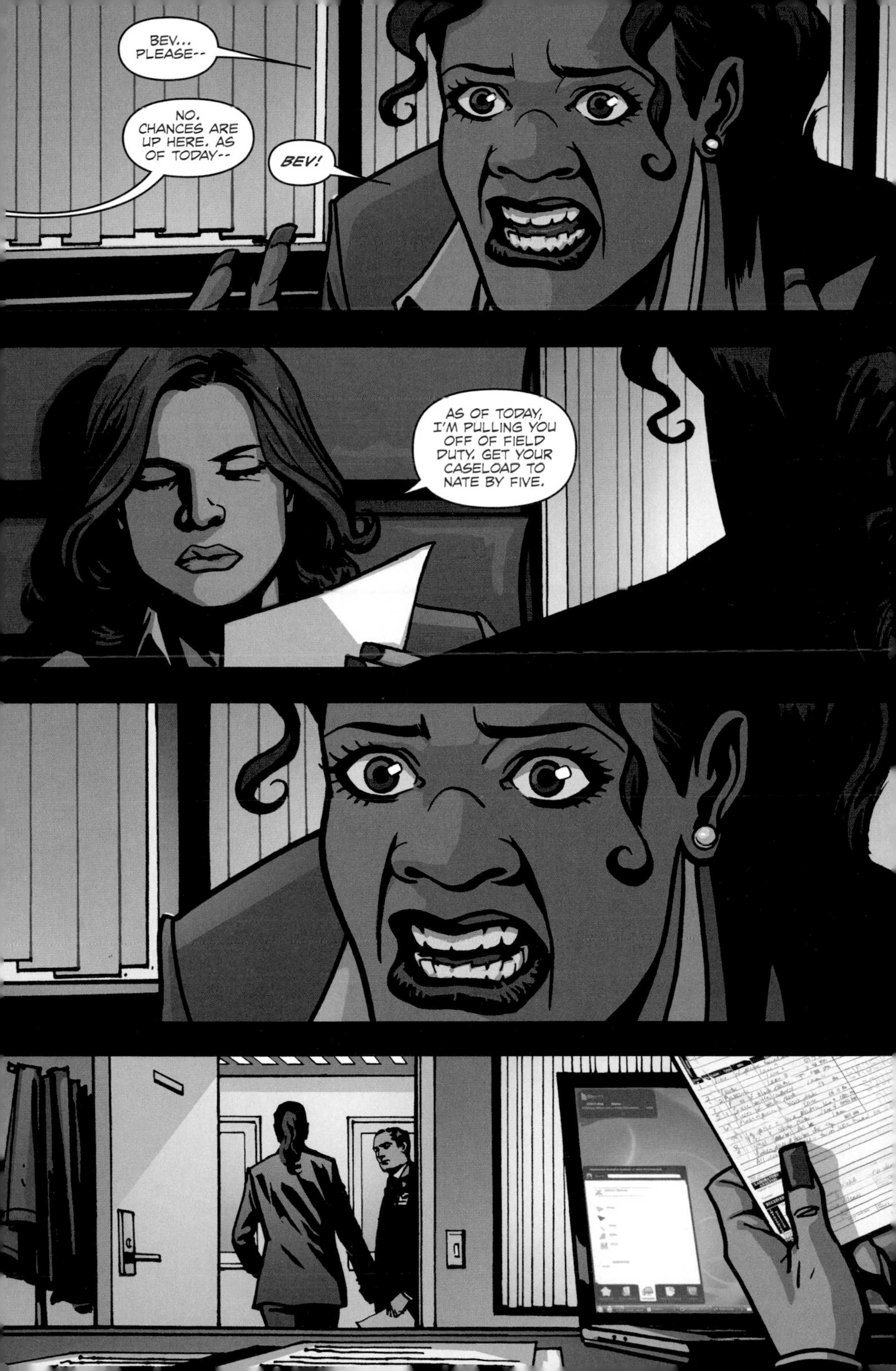
BEV... PLEASE--
NO. CHANCES ARE UP HERE. AS OF TODAY--
BEV!
AS OF TODAY, I'M PULLING YOU OFF OF FIELD DUTY. GET YOUR CASELOAD TO NATE BY FIVE.

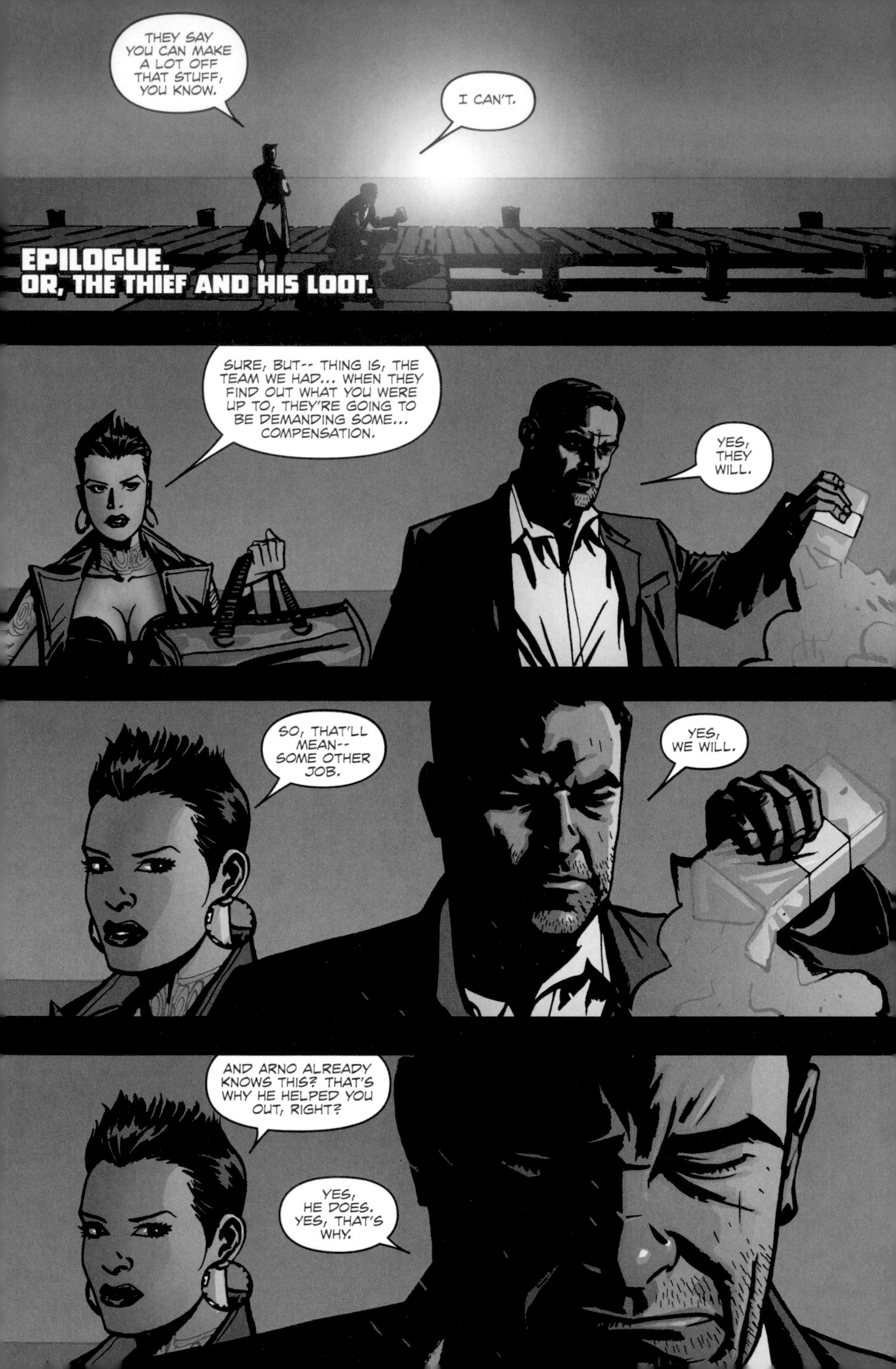
THEY SAY YOU CAN MAKE A LOT OFF THAT STUFF, YOU KNOW.
I CAN'T.
EPILOGUE.
OR, THE THIEF AND HIS LOOT.
SURE, BUT-- THING IS, THE TEAM WE HAD... WHEN THEY FIND OUT WHAT YOU WERE UP TO, THEY'RE GOING TO BE DEMANDING SOME... COMPENSATION.
YES, THEY WILL.
SO, THAT'LL MEAN-- SOME OTHER JOB.
YES, WE WILL.
AND ARNO ALREADY KNOWS THIS? THAT'S WHY HE HELPED YOU OUT, RIGHT?
YES, HE DOES. YES, THAT'S WHY.

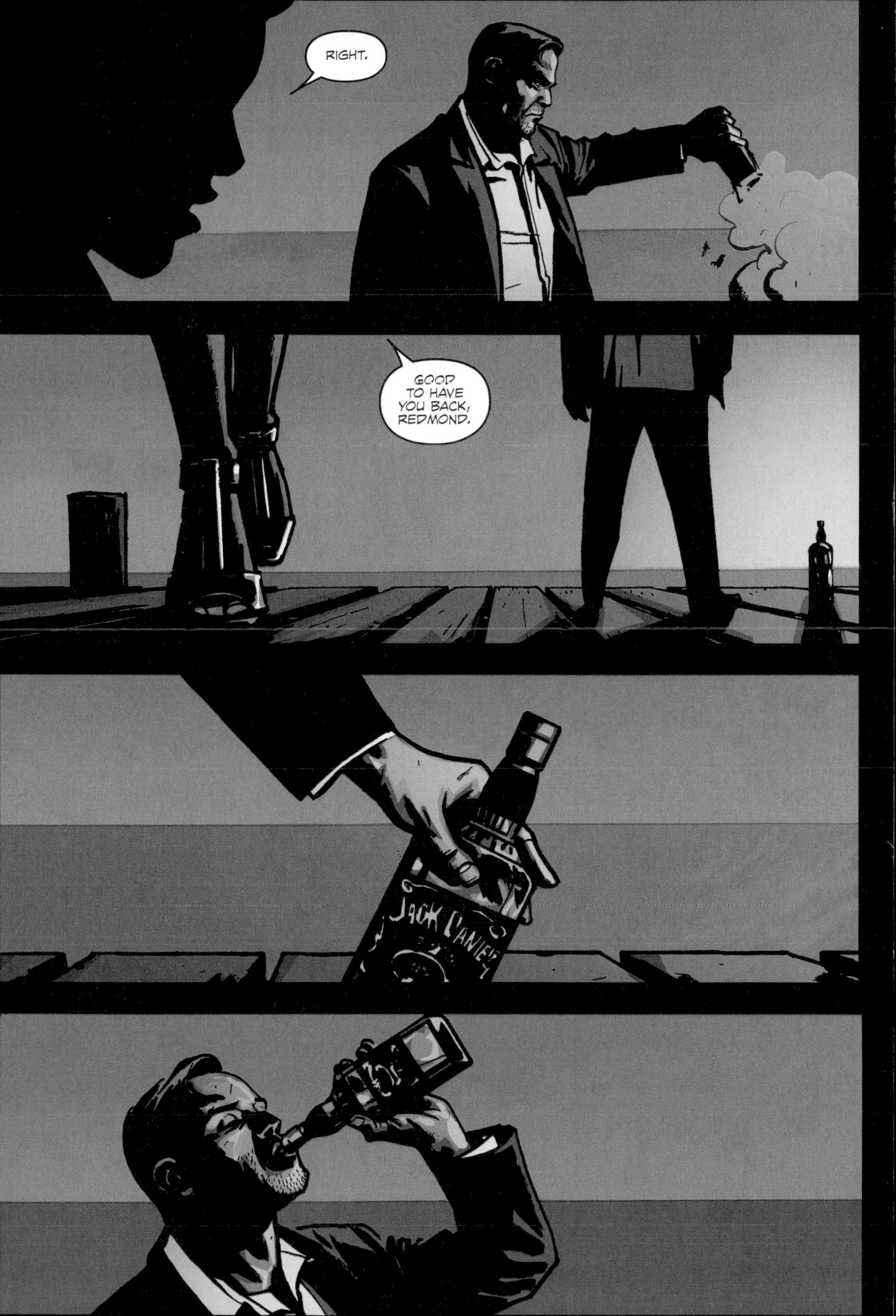

RIGHT.
GOOD TO HAVE YOU BACK, REDMOND.
JACK DANIEL'S

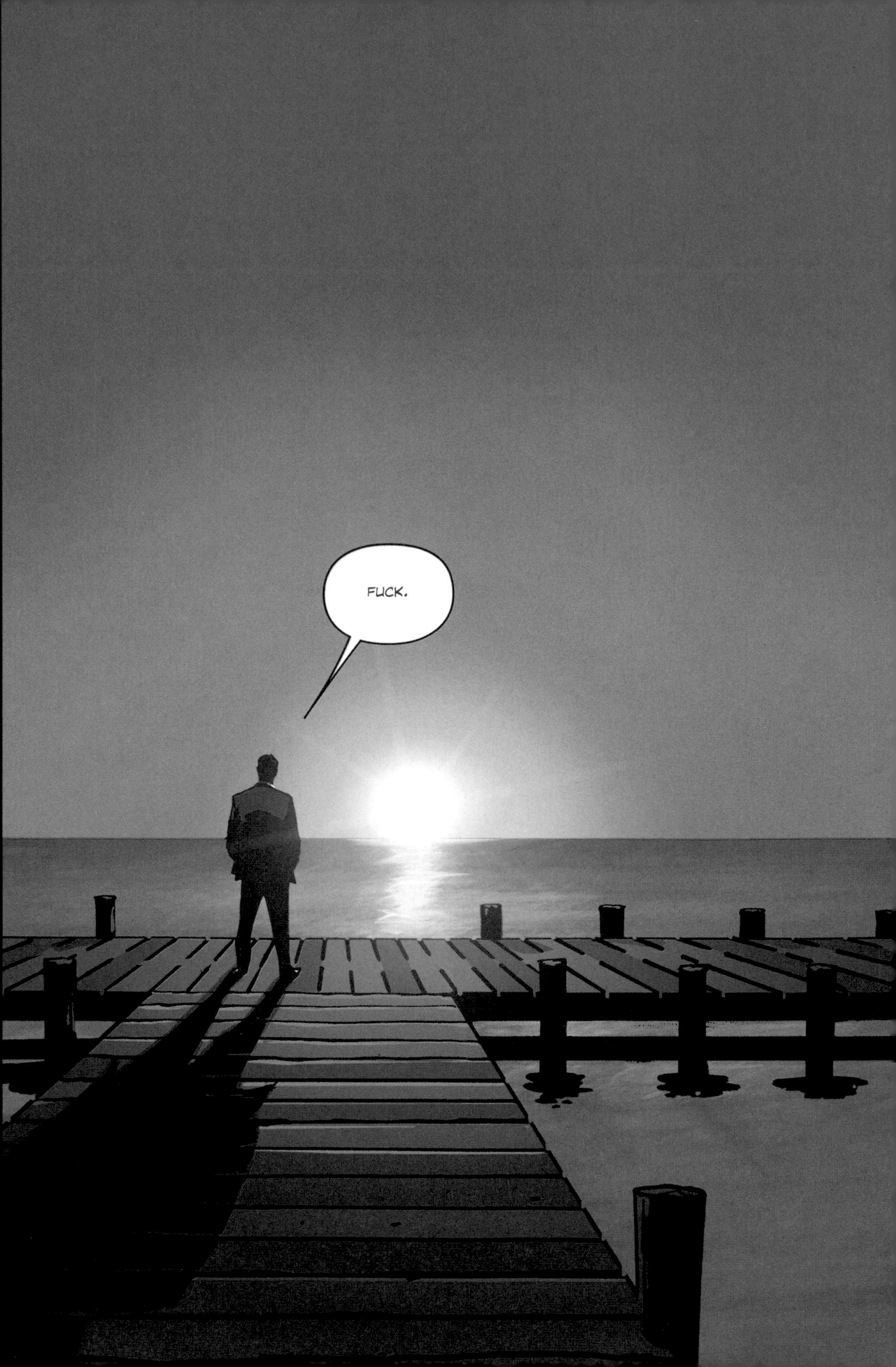
FUCK.

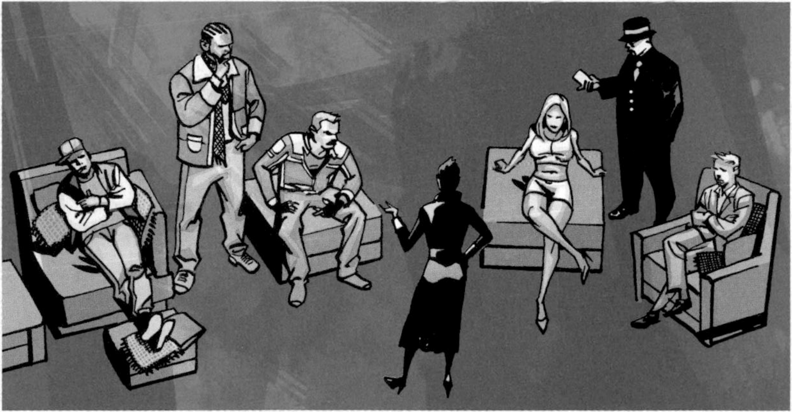

TO BE CONTINUED...

MORE GREAT BOOKS FROM ROBERT KIRKMAN & SKYBOUND!

THE ASTOUNDING WOLF-MAN

VOL. 1 TP
ISBN: 978-1-58240-862-0
$14.99
VOL. 2 TP
ISBN: 978-1-60706-007-9
$14.99
VOL. 3 TP
ISBN: 978-1-60706-111-3
$16.99
VOL. 4 TP
ISBN: 978-1-60706-249-3
$16.99

BATTLE POPE

VOL. 1: GENESIS TP
ISBN: 978-1-58240-572-8
$14.99
VOL. 2: MAYHEM TP
ISBN: 978-1-58240-529-2
$12.99
VOL. 3: PILLOW TALK TP
ISBN: 978-1-58240-677-0
$12.99
VOL. 4: WRATH OF GOD TP
ISBN: 978-1-58240-751-7
$9.99

BRIT

VOL. 1: OLD SOLDIER TP
ISBN: 978-1-58240-678-7
$14.99
VOL. 2: AWOL
ISBN: 978-1-58240-864-4
$14.99
VOL. 3: FUBAR
ISBN: 978-1-60706-061-1
$16.99

CAPES

VOL. 1: PUNCHING THE CLOCK TP
ISBN: 978-1-58240-756-2
$17.99

GUARDING THE GLOBE

VOL. 1: UNDER SIEGE TP
ISBN: 978-1-60706-356-8
$16.99

HAUNT

VOL. 1 TP
ISBN: 978-1-60706-154-0
$9.99
VOL. 2 TP
ISBN: 978-1-60706-229-5
$16.99
VOL. 3 TP
ISBN: 978-1-60706-552-4
$14.99
THE IMMORTAL EDITION, VOL. 1 HC
ISBN: 978-1-60706-241-7
$34.99

THE INFINITE

VOL. 1 TP
ISBN: 978-1-60706-475-6
$9.99

INVINCIBLE

VOL. 1: FAMILY MATTERS TP
ISBN: 978-1-58240-711-1
$12.99
VOL. 2: EIGHT IS ENOUGH TP
ISBN: 978-1-58240-347-2
$12.99
VOL. 3: PERFECT STRANGERS TP
ISBN: 978-1-58240-793-7
$12.99
VOL. 4: HEAD OF THE CLASS TP
ISBN: 978-1-58240-440-2
$14.95
VOL. 5: THE FACTS OF LIFE TP
ISBN: 978-1-58240-554-4
$14.99
VOL. 6: A DIFFERENT WORLD TP
ISBN: 978-1-58240-579-7
$14.99
VOL. 7: THREE'S COMPANY TP
ISBN: 978-1-58240-656-5
$14.99
VOL. 8: MY FAVORITE MARTIAN TP
ISBN: 978-1-58240-683-1
$14.99
VOL. 9: OUT OF THIS WORLD TP
ISBN: 978-1-58240-827-9
$14.99
VOL. 10: WHO'S THE BOSS TP
ISBN: 978-1-60706-013-0
$16.99
VOL. 11: HAPPY DAYS TP
ISBN: 978-1-60706-062-8
$16.99
VOL. 12: STILL STANDING TP
ISBN: 978-1-60706-166-3
$16.99
VOL. 13: GROWING PAINS TP
ISBN: 978-1-60706-251-6
$16.99
VOL. 14: THE VILTRUMITE WAR TP
ISBN: 978-1-60706-367-4
$19.99
VOL. 15: GET SMART TP
ISBN: 978-1-60706-498-5
$16.99
VOL. 16: FAMILY TIES TP
ISBN: 978-1-60706-579-1
$16.99
ULTIMATE COLLECTION, VOL. 1 HC
ISBN 978-1-58240-500-1
$34.95
ULTIMATE COLLECTION, VOL. 2 HC
ISBN: 978-1-58240-594-0
$34.99
ULTIMATE COLLECTION, VOL. 3 HC
ISBN: 978-1-58240-763-0
$34.99
ULTIMATE COLLECTION, VOL. 4 HC
ISBN: 978-1-58240-989-4
$34.99
ULTIMATE COLLECTION, VOL. 5 HC
ISBN: 978-1-60706-116-8
$34.99
ULTIMATE COLLECTION, VOL. 6 HC
ISBN: 978-1-60706-360-5
$34.99
ULTIMATE COLLECTION, VOL. 7 HC
ISBN: 978-1-60706-509-8
$39.99
COMPENDIUM VOL. 1
ISBN: 978-1-60706-411-4
$64.99
THE COMPLETE INVINCIBLE LIBRARY, VOL. 2 HC
ISBN: 978-1-60706-112-0
$125.00
THE COMPLETE INVINCIBLE LIBRARY, VOL. 3 HC
ISBN: 978-1-60706-421-3
$125.00
THE OFFICIAL HANDBOOK OF THE INVINCIBLE UNIVERSE TP
ISBN: 978-1-58240-831-6
$12.99
INVINCIBLE PRESENTS, VOL. 1: ATOM EVE & REX SPLODE TP
ISBN: 978-1-60706-255-4
$14.99

SUPER DINOSAUR

VOL. 1
ISBN: 978-1-60706-420-6
$9.99
VOL. 2
ISBN: 978-1-60706-568-5
$12.99
DELUXE COLORING BOOK
ISBN: 978-1-60706-481-7
$4.99

SUPERPATRIOT

AMERICA'S FIGHTING FORCE
ISBN: 978-1-58240-355-1
$14.99

TALES OF THE REALM

HARDCOVER
ISBN: 978-1-58240-426-0
$34.95
TRADE PAPERBACK
ISBN: 978-1-58240-394-6
$14.95

TECH JACKET

VOL. 1: THE BOY FROM EARTH TP
ISBN: 978-1-58240-771-5
$14.99

THIEF OF THIEVES

VOL. 1: "I QUIT."
ISBN: 978-1-60706-592-0
$14.99

THE WALKING DEAD

VOL. 1: DAYS GONE BYE TP
ISBN: 978-1-58240-672-5
$9.99
VOL. 2: MILES BEHIND US TP
ISBN: 978-1-58240-775-3
$14.99
VOL. 3: SAFETY BEHIND BARS TP
ISBN: 978-1-58240-805-7
$14.99
VOL. 4: THE HEART'S DESIRE TP
ISBN: 978-1-58240-530-8
$14.99
VOL. 5: THE BEST DEFENSE TP
ISBN: 978-1-58240-612-1
$14.99
VOL. 6: THIS SORROWFUL LIFE TP
ISBN: 978-1-58240-684-8
$14.99
VOL. 7: THE CALM BEFORE TP
ISBN: 978-1-58240-828-6
$14.99
VOL. 8: MADE TO SUFFER TP
ISBN: 978-1-58240-883-5
$14.99
VOL. 9: HERE WE REMAIN TP
ISBN: 978-1-60706-022-2
$14.99
VOL. 10: WHAT WE BECOME TP
ISBN: 978-1-60706-075-8
$14.99
VOL. 11: FEAR THE HUNTERS TP
ISBN: 978-1-60706-181-6
$14.99
VOL. 12: LIFE AMONG THEM TP
ISBN: 978-1-60706-254-7
$14.99
VOL. 13: TOO FAR GONE TP
ISBN: 978-1-60706-329-2
$14.99
VOL. 14: NO WAY OUT TP
ISBN: 978-1-60706-392-6
$14.99
VOL. 15: WE FIND OURSELVES TP
ISBN: 978-1-60706-392-6
$14.99
BOOK ONE HC
ISBN: 978-1-58240-619-0
$34.99
BOOK TWO HC
ISBN: 978-1-58240-698-5
$34.99
BOOK THREE HC
ISBN: 978-1-58240-825-5
$34.99
BOOK FOUR HC
ISBN: 978-1-60706-000-0
$34.99
BOOK FIVE HC
ISBN: 978-1-60706-171-7
$34.99
BOOK SIX HC
ISBN: 978-1-60706-327-8
$34.99
BOOK SEVEN HC
ISBN: 978-1-60706-439-8
$34.99
BOOK EIGHT HC
ISBN: 978-1-60706-593-7
$34.99
COMPENDIUM TP, VOL. 1
ISBN: 978-1-60706-076-5
$59.99
COMPENDIUM TP, VOL. 2
ISBN: 978-1-60706-596-8
$59.99
DELUXE HARDCOVER, VOL. 1
ISBN: 978-1-58240-619-0
$100.00
DELUXE HARDCOVER, VOL. 2
ISBN: 978-1-60706-029-7
$100.00
DELUXE HARDCOVER, VOL. 3
ISBN: 978-1-60706-330-8
$100.00
THE WALKING DEAD: THE COVERS, VOL. 1 HC
ISBN: 978-1-60706-002-4
$24.99
THE WALKING DEAD SURVIVORS' GUIDE
ISBN: 978-1-60706-458-9
$12.99

WITCH DOCTOR

VOL. 1: UNDER THE KNIFE TP
ISBN: 978-1-60706-441-1
$12.99

TO FIND YOUR NEAREST COMIC BOOK STORE, CALL:
1-888-COMIC-BOOK

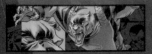

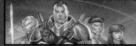

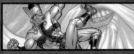

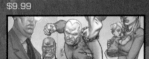

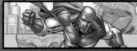

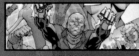

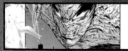

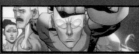

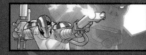

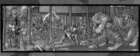

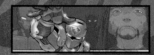

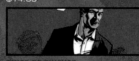

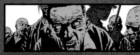

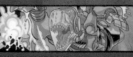

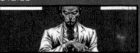